Oh Terrifying Mother

Oh Terrifying Mother

Sexuality, Violence and Worship of the Goddess Kali

SARAH CALDWELL

OXFORD
UNIVERSITY PRESS

OXFORD
UNIVERSITY PRESS

YMCA Library Building, Jai Singh Road, New Delhi 110 001

Oxford University Press is a department of the University of Oxford. It furthers the University's objective of excellence in research, scholarship, and education by publishing worldwide in

Oxford New York

Athens Auckland Bangkok Bogota Buenos Aires Cape Town Chennai Dar es Salaam Delhi Florence Hong Kong Istanbul Karachi Kolkata Kuala Lumpur Madrid Melbourne Mexico City Mumbai Nairobi Paris Sao Paulo Shanghai Singapore Taipei Tokyo Toronto Warsaw

with associated companies in Berlin Ibadan

Published in India
By Oxford University Press, New Delhi

First published in 1999
Oxford India Paperbacks 2001

ISBN 019 565 7969

Typeset in Times
by Excellent Laser Typesetters, Delhi 110 034
Printed by Saurabh Print-O-Pack, Noida
Published by Manzar Khan, Oxford University Press
YMCA Library Building, Jai Singh Road, New Delhi 110 001

To She

Who sprouts in the tender green paddy seedling
Who drinks the cup of blood
Who shivers through trembling coconut fronds
Whose blessing is hard to bear

And to L. and R., who also suffered and learned

CONTENTS

Preface ix

Acknowledgements xiii

Note on Transliteration xv

List of Figures xvii

Prelude: A Way in 1

1. The Goddess and Her People 10
   - Bhagavati's Living History 10
   - Kāḷi in the Kaḷari: the Śākta Tradition in Kerala 27
   - Performers and Patrons 33
   - Fieldwork, Backstage 51

2. Dēvikōpam: The Wrath of the Goddess 64
   - Dusk 69
   - Enlivenment 72
   - Setting Forth 82
   - Comic Relief 93
   - Kūḷi 95
   - War 98
   - Blessings 100
   - Blood for Spirits 100
   - Dawn 101

3. Landscapes of Feminine Power 104
   - Marutam: Trees and Food 105
   - Bleeding Stones and Red Earth 114
   - From Virgin to Mother: Three Kerala Temples 122
   - Seasons, Time, Space 131
   - Snakes and the Underworld 142
   - The Three Landscapes: Transformations of Kāḷi in Kerala 150

4. Male Experiences 155
Ball of Fire: The Angry Mother 156
Yakṣis: Dangerous Virgins 162
Fellatio and the Self-feeding Breast 170
Kūḷi: The Voice of Protest 184
Kinds of Power 188

5. Female Frustrations, Women's Worlds 195
So Much for Matriarchy 195
'The Place of Delivery and Ąll' 202
Hysteria and Bādhā 213
Seductive Virgins: Whose Lust? 218
The Theme of Vengeance Revisited 236

6. Transformation Through Theatre 252

7. An Open End 274

Glossary 286

Works Cited 289

Index 307

PREFACE

About ten years ago I began to think about ways of doing ethnography that would recapture the goal of empathy that I perceived to be anthropology's greatest inheritance. While I admired the post-modern concerns of the 1980s and 90s for breaking colonial, orientalist, racist, sexist, and bourgeois traditions of ethnography, I could not accept the somewhat nihilistic assertion that we are all pawns of transnational forces beyond our control, or the psychologistic dictum that we are locked into mental prisons of our own and society's making. Furthermore, the opaque, alienating language in which much of this discussion was couched seemed to propel us ever farther from an idea of empathy that haunted me. Perhaps my blind faith in the possibility of empathy had roots in my personal experience. I had travelled to north India in 1981, living in a Hindu ashram. My entire worldview had been restructured then by adherence to strict disciplines and immersion in elaborate philosophies totally alien to my own upbringing. In many ways those experiences of my youth had already shown me the flexibility of culture and human behaviour. More importantly, they had confirmed my belief in 'truth'—some kind of ultimate reality, beyond the vicissitudes of culture.

Later, as a student of anthropology, I gained greater respect for the forces of culture and history at work in personal lives, and a greater knowledge of the vicissitudes I had hoped to transcend; yet an interest in 'ultimate' realities still informed these studies. When I chose to work on an obscure ritual drama I had never seen, in a place I had never been, it was because I believed this art form would shed light on such questions. *Mutiyēttu* is a form of theatre with complex music, art, and staging that also claims, through spirit possession, to be a true spiritual experience of the supernatural.

Muṭiyēṯṯu also raises interesting questions of gender, as the enactment of a fierce mother goddess can only be performed by a male actor. I wondered what the inner experience of this possession was like for the male actors, and what the understanding of female spectators might be.

The consequent study must be understood to be primarily an ethnography of muṭiyēṯṯu, an entirely male-dominated art form. It is not an ethnography of women or the female point of view. I conducted about thirty in-depth interviews with women of diverse ages and backgrounds, including audience members, mothers, wives and daughters of the male artists, friends, scholars, and professionals.[1] By spending time with women in the houses I visited and lived in, adopting local dress, diet, and standards of modesty, I experienced both the society and the performances in many ways as a Malayali woman would. The feminine point of view thus enters my study in a very significant way. But unlike any Malayali woman I met, most of my time was spent observing, studying, interviewing, and relating to men. This ethnography is first and foremost about their experience. My remarks about women, then, serve mainly to throw light on aspects of the male ideology and performance tradition related to muṭiyēṯṯu and should not be taken as a definitive account of the inner lives of women in Kerala.

My research required me to probe certain areas that were not ordinarily discussed in daily conversation in Kerala. Such topics as sexuality and personal experience were probed only after establishing relations of friendship and trust. Any descriptions, anecdotes, or quotes based on discussion of such sensitive matters employ pseudonyms to protect the identity of the individuals who shared these confidences. My family members and personal friends are all referred to pseudonymously; but the names of the artists (except where identified otherwise in footnotes) and of my field assistant have not been changed.

Although not everything in this book is flattering or pleasant, my profound love, respect, and gratitude towards the people of Kerala and appreciation for their culture informs every word. Responses to this book are bound to be varied. More than a few people will no doubt be disturbed at some of what it contains. But like the goddess who inspired it, this ethnography is not content to skim the pleasant, orderly surfaces of things. The writing of this book, like the gruelling performance tradition it chronicles, has taken more than a little courage and dedication. I invite you, reader, whoever and wherever you are, to enter these pages with an open mind and a generous heart.

Notes

[1] Interviews in Malayalam were conducted through translators, taped, transcribed, and retranslated back into English.

ACKNOWLEDGEMENTS

The field research on which this account is based was supported by a Junior Fellowship from the American Institute of Indian Studies in 1991–2; and a Fulbright Doctoral Dissertation Research Award in 1992. Writing and revisions were supported by the Townsend Center for the Humanities at the University of California, Berkeley and the Michigan Society of Fellows at the University of Michigan, Ann Arbor. My heartfelt thanks are due to the following institutions and individuals in India: the late Dr Chummar Choondal of Trichur, Kerala; Dr V. V. Pillai and Dr A. K. Nambiar of The University of Calicut School of Drama; Payipra Radhakrishnan, Secretary of the Kerala Sahitya Akademi in Trichur; Mr V. S. Paul of Trichur; Mr G. Venu of Irinjalakkuda; Trichur Public Library; Kerala Sangeet Natak Akademy; Hill Palace Museum at Tripunithura; C. S. N. Menon of Chavakkad Kalarisangham; K. Jos of Anaswara Studios, Trichur; L. S. Rajagopalan, C. G. Prince, Bijith Induchoodan, the Induchoodan family of Tripunithura, and the Kattungal family of Chazhur. Many temple authorities in Kerala generously allowed me to observe their rituals and festivities, and in some cases to make audio and video recordings. Without their cooperation this study could not have been completed.

The troupe leaders of the seven muṭiyēṯṯu troupes in Kerala all received me with warmth, sincerity, and kindness. They fed and accommodated my family and co-workers, travelled long distances at their own expense, and helped and befriended us in times of difficulty; they also interceded with temple authorities on our behalf and endured countless hours of observations, questions, and probing into all the details of their art form and family lives. For their hospitality, generosity, and human kindness I am deeply grateful.

Laji P. Kattungal's skill, dedication, loyalty, persistence, and perceptive grasp of every aspect of the research project were only outmatched by his love for the work, which he took on as his very own. Countless hours of gruelling travel, tedious transcription, and painful personal challenges never deterred him from seeing this project through. In a very real sense he is the co-researcher and co-author of this work. Although I take full responsibility for the statements and conclusions reached herein, it is in large part his effort that produced the rich data on which those conclusions are based.

J. Richardson Freeman suggested the research topic of muṭiyēṯṯu, and encouraged me to pursue fieldwork in Kerala. Thanks are due to the following readers for commenting on drafts or portions of this manuscript: J. Bernard Bate, Lawrence Cohen, Alan Dundes, Laurie Eisler, Phoebe Ellsworth, Tanya Luhrmann, Herbert Phillips, and Lee Schlesinger. Special thanks are due to Patricia Caldwell. Linda Hess, and Jeffrey Kripal, for their detailed critical readings, which greatly improved the manuscript. This work also benefited from discussions in the 1993–4 Townsend Seminar at the University of California, Berkeley; colloquia of the Michigan Society of Fellows; the 1995 'Negotiating Feminist Anthropology' Conference at the University of Michigan, Ann Arbor; and my graduate seminar on Psychoanalysis in South Asia at the University of Michigan in fall 1996. A single conversation with David Shulman caused me to completely rethink portions of chapters 1 and 2. While acknowledging the impact of comments from all these sources on the present work, I take full responsibility for any and all errors and misrepresentations herein.

Sections of chapters 2, 3, 4, and 5 have appeared in different form in my 'Bhagavati: Ball of Fire', in J. S. Hawley and D. Wulff (eds), *Devi: Goddesses of India* (University of California Press, 1996), and 'The Bloodthirsty Tongue and the Self-Feeding Breast: Homosexual Fellatio Fantasy in a South Indian Ritual Tradition', in T. G. Vaidyanathan and J. Kripal (eds), *Vishnu on Freud's Desk: A Reader in Psychoanalysis and Hinduism* (Oxford University Press, 1998). I thank Kattamanita Ramakrishnan for permission to retranslate and publish his poem 'Shanta'.

Ann Arbor, Michigan — Sarah Caldwell
December 1997

Note on Transliteration

All Malayalam, Tamil, and Sanskrit words are transliterated using standard Library of Congress transliterations, excepting south Asian terms that have entered the English lexicon (e.g. 'puranic', 'karma', names of south Asian languages) and proper names. Many terms derived from Sanskrit, including proper names such as Kāḷi [Skt. Kālī], undergo phonetic and orthographic changes in Malayalam. Spellings in this essay conform to standard Malayalam usage. The Glossary defines all foreign words that appear more than once.

FIGURES

1. Map of Kerala xviii
2. Popular poster of Kāḷi 22
3. Female *veḷiccappāṭu* at Kodungallur Bharaṇi (Photograph courtesy K. Gopalakrishnan) 26
4. Bhagavati *kaḷam* 74
5. 64-hand *kaḷam* of Bhagavati 120
6. Tirumāndāmkunnu Bhagavati 127
7. Mūkāmbika Bhagavati 149

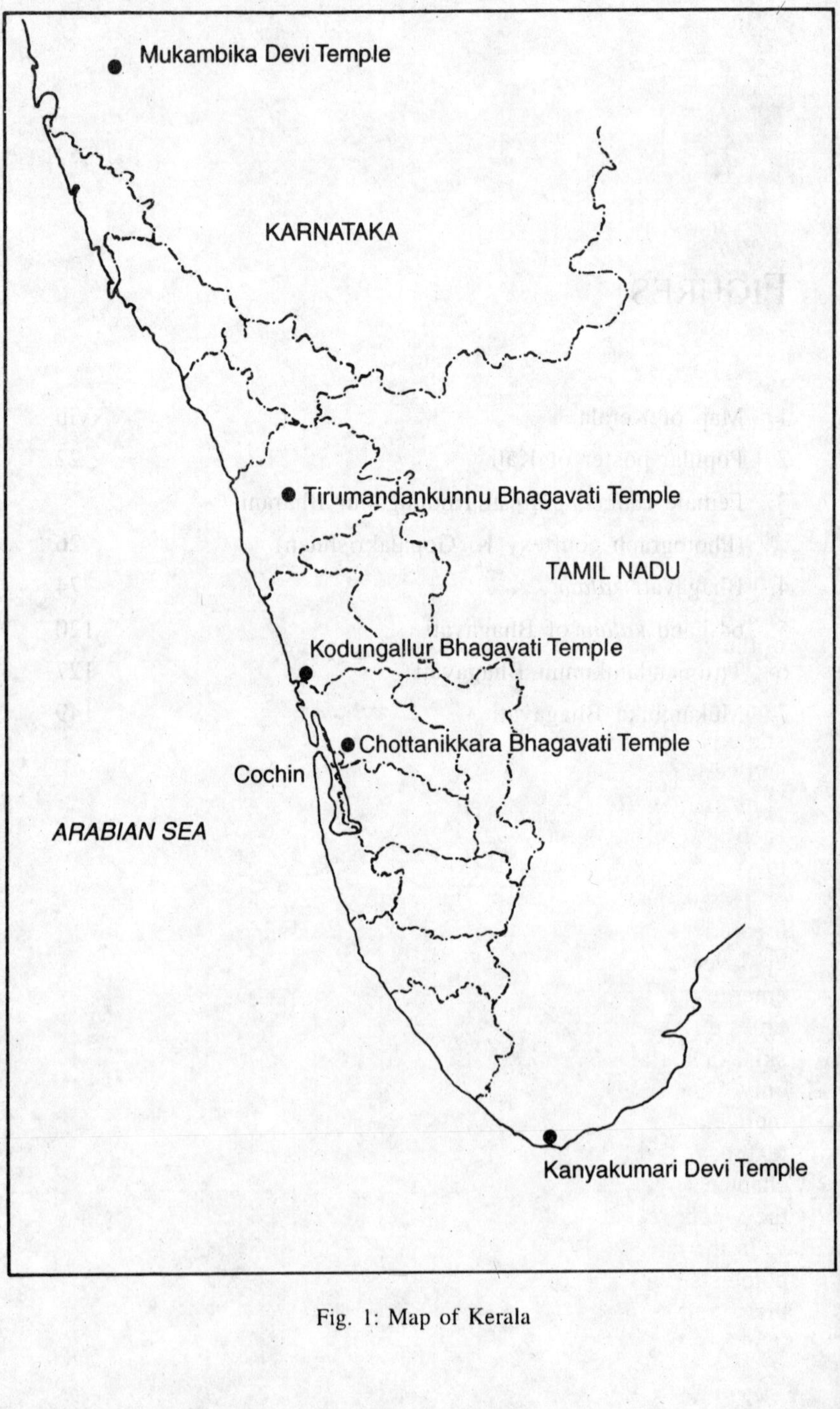

Fig. 1: Map of Kerala

PRELUDE
A WAY IN

Hours before the performance of muṭiyēṯṯu begins, a multicoloured drawing of the goddess is drawn on the floor of the temple's inner rooms. The very first step in the construction of the image, which takes many hours to complete, is the outlining of a simple circle in black. This *yantra*, or geometric ritual diagram, represents the whole universe in miniature. At its centre is a tiny point, out of which will explode in a profusion of colours the enormous form of the goddess Bhagavati, patron deity of the performance to come. The *Nātya Śāstra*, an ancient Sanskrit text, describes the preparation of this ritual space before drawing commences: 'Entrances should be made for the four sides. In the centre two lines, horizontal and vertical, should be made' (*Nātya Śāstra* [1987] 3.21–2). There is no single doorway to enter the diagram. Four different entrances each lead to the centre. Where you choose to begin is entirely up to you.

This ethnography uses a similar strategy, adopting a variety of theoretical and rhetorical stances in interpreting its subject. Built up layer by layer, in variegated colours, the form of Bhagavati emerges. It takes a long time for the final product to appear. At times during the drawing process one can see only the green of her skin, or the black of her hair. The spirit of the goddess can enter only when the drawing is complete. Similarly, the full meaning of muṭiyēṯṯu can only be appreciated once the various layers of this text have been read and the whole reflected upon. Any given chapter, any particular statement, is by necessity incomplete. Only the whole reveals the picture in its entirety.

In the movement known as 'post-modern ethnography', anthropologists over the last fifteen years have begun to question how their craft is practised and how the results disseminated. Before

1980, ethnographic method was more or less straightforward. As a social science, anthropology favoured method and discourse emphasizing objectivity, univocality, and linearity. With an increasing awareness of the inequalities of wealth, power, and gender that informed the discipline, anthropologists began to challenge this stance of objectivity. 'Native' anthropologists with allegiances to both the studying and the studied cultures, have been particularly sensitive analysts of ethnographic positionality and modes of representation (Kondo 1986; Narayan 1993; Rosaldo 1984; Visweswaran 1994). The majority of these debates centred on textual strategies of ethnographic representation, exploring semiotic, linguistic, and philosophical theory, and making use of new ways of organizing their own theoretical remarks (see e.g., Daniel 1996; P. Stoller 1986; Tyler 1986). Various approaches have been tried, with varying degrees of success. These include personal impressionistic narratives, dialogic collaborations in which native and anthropological voices alternate, direct presentation of native statements with annotations by the ethnographer, interviews and life histories focusing on the reality of individual lives, and novelistic treatments that attempt to evoke more than denote. In all these new techniques there is the recognition of the inadequacy of the linear, discursive argument which characterized most earlier ethnographies.

Linearity and univocality are rhetorical strategies which emphasize both the writer's control over the material and his penetration to its simplest formal essence, both highly valued qualities in the Euro-American epistemological tradition. But there exist other cultural epistemologies that have a high tolerance for paradox, ambiguity, and multiply coexisting perspectives. This complexity and context-sensitivity may be responsible for our insistence on exclusively qualitative modes of analysing cultures. The 'interpretative anthropology' pioneered by Geertz (1973) likened cultures to texts, artefacts which require some kind of divination special to the literary critic or humanist (the shaman of western culture). As Berreman and others have suggested, this split between the 'rational' and the 'intuitive' is an artificial division of the West, which in reality may be a difference of degree, not of kind (Berreman 1966).

Another important element of the ethnographic enterprise is anthropology's unique methodological insistence on firsthand experience in gathering data. Participant observation is investigation 'from within, taking an inside view of another culture...' (Saliba 1974: 146). But inner experience has often been swept under the rug of pristine, coherent ethnographic presentations (Clifford 1988). This core of inner experience became the focus of the reflexive movement in anthropology in the late 1970s and early '80s (Crapanzano 1980; Rabinow 1977; Ruby 1982), precipitated in part by the publication of Malinowski's Trobriand diaries (Malinowski 1967). Yet, even these reflexive treatments do not deal with the fundamental epistemological issues involved in the use of the analyst's personal experience as method and data in the study of other human beings.

In this study I have tried to face these issues head on. I have exposed the entire process, including data collection, personal experiences, hypothesis formation, and analysis, to view, using an experimental, multi-layered style. Two separate fonts signal the distinct voices of a 'text' and a 'subtext'. Often, but not always, the subtext consists of direct entries from my field journals and actual letters home. It is always an intimately personal voice, written either for myself (the journal entries), or for my close friends (the letters). At the time these were written, I had no idea that I would use them extensively in this book. Some were ordinary field notes, some deeply personal diary entries, and some attempts to communicate my findings to others. By juxtaposing this 'subtext' directly to the analytic text constructed out of it, the reader is able to see the vast difference between these two levels of understanding.

It is as if Malinowski's diary had appeared side by side on the page with *The Sexual Life of Savages* (Malinowski 1967, 1987). In one voice, the ethnographer objectively analyses the deeply personal and highly emotional experiences of others; in another voice, his own tortured fantasies emerge. The text and subtext of this work are woven around the particular themes addressed in each chapter. A chronological development, from the beginning to the end of my fieldwork, unfolds throughout the book. The use of a different font for the subtext clearly identifies it as a separate voice, but is not meant to imply a secondary epistemological status. The 'sub' portion of the text represents the fluid, secret, inner experience that informs, enlivens, and subverts the dominant textual exposition. Both the text and subtext portions must stand as equally valid views of the final whole. As the reader moves through the pages, (s)he can identify which voice (s)he is in but not that either is dispensable.

The personal story told in the subtext is not presented merely as a sensational diversion. The experiences chronicled there and their intense emotional tenor were inseparable from the phenomenological reality of muṭiyēṯṯu. It is simply impossible to enter fully into the analysis of disturbing emotions of violence, sexuality, and spirit possession without a more intimate sense of how it feels to undergo such experiences. Yet, the ethnographer's life story in the field is presented cryptically, in bits and pieces as the book proceeds.

The subtext shows the development of my understanding of events around me from the beginning of my stay in Kerala in October 1991 until its conclusion at the end of December 1992. At first I didn't understand anything. The best strategy in such a situation (at least the one I had been trained to fall back on) is phenomenological description. I compulsively described everything I saw and felt. A second component of the 'participant observation' strategy was the adoption of external postures in conformity with the culture. The various reactions of my host culture and the misunderstandings which resulted are documented in 'Fieldwork, Backstage'. Over time, the immersion in this unfamiliar environment started to restructure my consciousness (subtext portions, chapter 2). After the intensive period of attending performances during the festival season (which fell during the first six months of my fieldwork), a severe personal crisis forced me to completely reorient myself (portions of chapters 4 and 5).

Only after nearly a year of fieldwork did some of the deeper meanings of muṭiyēṯṯu and its cultural context begin to come together for me. I often came up with profound insights in the most unlikely places when my mind was drifting off. For example, much of the analysis in chapter 3 on the meaning of the Malayalam year emerged into my mind in a flash while I was standing on a rickety bus staring at a glittery plaque of Śiva and Viṣṇu mounted above the driver's head. After that, ideas just seemed to bubble up and melt together into non-verbal flashes of meaning. Pearce (1982) has described this process of intuition, which has received insufficient attention in cognitive psychology. Towards the very end of my field stay I was asked to put my first public paper together for a talk in Madras. Only then did I sit down to write discursive, analytic prose.

It took three more years to flesh out these ideas into their present form.

Many ethnographies present only the 'cream'—the final product of all these years of turmoil, confusion, pain, elation, mistakes, and cogitation. Consumers of ethnographies get pristine, carefully constructed accounts of very messy cultures and experiences. That is not the case in this book. The usual pristine analytic explanations are presented, but the sudden interpolation of relevant journal entries prevents the reader from getting too detached. Suddenly we are not talking about 'those weird people over there' but about someone very familiar: a western ethnographer. Most readers will identify with that character, if not with the subjects of the ethnography. Between the two, some kind of emotional resonance is bound to take place.

In addition, I have tried to avoid using alienating jargon. I want the people who shared their hearts and lives with me to be able to understand what I am saying, to the extent possible. Some will call this romantic. So be it. We cannot break the imbalance of power inherent in the ethnographic enterprise if we continue to frame our conclusions in elitist, inaccessible language from which all hints of a human being have been excised (K. Brown 1985).

This ethnography is consciously 'theatrical'. As its subject matter is a dynamic form of ritual theatre, the text attempts to recreate at least some of the dimensions of that experience in its presentation. The juxtaposition of conventional, linear prose with experiential, first- and second-person narrative in a non-linear structure breaks the frame of the performance situation in a manner similar to that exploited in some forms of experimental theatre; and, in fact, in muṭiyēṯṯu itself.[1] This Prelude, like the *kēḷi* or overture to muṭiyēṯṯu, calls the audience to the performance arena in meandering but insistent tones, giving glimpses of things to come. Like the seven scenes of muṭiyēṯṯu, the text proceeds in seven chapters. Chapter 1 introduces the plot, characters, and historical background, while chapter 2 describes the structure and experience of the ritual itself. The four chapters that follow, like the four entrances to the goddess's sacred diagram, offer different theoretical perspectives from which to understand the events described in chapters 1 and 2. Chapter 3 uses a combination of indigenous theory and symbolic anthropology to explore the hidden meanings of time and space in the Bhagavati rituals. Chapter 4 makes use of psychoanalytic object relations theory, following Klein, Horney, and Chodorow, but introducing new themes in the psychodynamics of male transvestite performance. Chapter 5 re-evaluates the psychological picture painted by the previous chapter using a feminist lens. By taking the perspective of women into account, a very different picture of female power emerges. Child abuse and dissociation theory are considered as possible tools for understanding women's possession and the fundamental message of the muṭiyēṯṯu drama. Chapter 6 moves away from these reductionist explanations, combining elements of performance theory (following Schechner and Turner) with Obeyesekere's concept of progressive symbols. By examining my own personal experience frankly, I attempt to show the interconnection of these themes at work in an individual's life. How my inner experience resonates with that of members of the culture I was studying is addressed at the end of chapter 7. Journal entries from late in my fieldwork stay present culminating insights through a deeply personal story.

The emotional tenor of the subtext at the end of chapter 5 recalls the mood towards the end of the muṭiyēṯṯu performance after Bhagavati's intense fight with the demon, when the actor's possessed rage has become dangerous. Violent energies have been released, and some calm must be restored, distance established, before the drama can resume. Chapter 7 is both an offering and a closure. Like the goddess's waving of sleeping babies before the sacred flame, it provides a quieting, a centering, a release, a lightening of the energy, as dawn breaks. The violence of the play has been released and contained; a transformation has occurred, but now life must continue on. It is time to depart. The subtext portions of chapters 5 and 6 are perhaps the most overtly 'theatrical', or may seem so in the context of ethnography. Tragic, almost operatic, the story they tell mirrors closely the themes enacted in muṭiyēṯṯu. Many people have spoken personally in ethnographic writing but perhaps not to the degree I have done here. Yet, I feel such self-revelation is essential in this particular case for several reasons: first, because it truthfully exposes how I arrived at the hypotheses argued in the previous chapters; and second, because I wish to explore the possibility that such an account of inner experience authentically replicates something true about the meaning of the muṭiyēṯṯu drama for Keralites. Finally, such a posture of vulnerability meaningfully reverses the power differential between myself and my subject, and between myself and the reader. This posture is controversial, and I don't know if I have been successful. But I am encouraged by recent calls to stop 'cutting the life out' of ethnographies; a process that can only be reversed by opening the human process of ethnography as fully as possible to view (Herdt and Stoller 1990: ix).

Obeyesekere has objected to the anthropological use of a theatrical model to account for 'the painful yet creative activities of modern-day ecstatic priests and shamans' on the very grounds that such models cut the life out:

> There is a sufferer or patient, not an actor; there is a priest, not a director; there is a congregation, not an audience.... Pain and human suffering are easy enough to eliminate from the model, but not from life.

Attention to human suffering, says Obeyesekere, has been the hallmark of all great social theorists.

> Current anthropology, however, is like the modern funeral parlor or, better still, like a bourgeois bathroom: everything is tidy, everything smells clean, and the shit is flushed in the dark, rat-infested sewers that line the belly of the city.... What is hidden is dung and death. And like dung and death, pain and human suffering are also confined to sanitized environments (1990: 288).

The work of Scheper-Hughes (1992) and Taussig (1987) are outstanding exceptions that boldly embrace those dark sides of human experience. Here I have tried to follow the lead of these authors but also to go even further by exposing the interaction of the cultural symbols of the Bhagavati cult with my own personal psychological process. This final taboo—the admission of weakness, vulnerability, confusion, and desire by the ethnographer—must be broken for the truth both of the fieldwork interaction and of the resultant conclusions to come fully to light.

In a psychological analysis like the present work, it is traditional for the analyst to remain invisible as an omniscient being. Psychoanalysis requires the analyst to keep constant tabs on his or her own counter-transference, and so provides an interesting model for current post-modern debates on reflexivity (Ewing 1992). But one flaw in this analogy is the extreme power differential between the analyst and the patient. One is constructed as omniscient and the other as ill. An asymmetrical financial transaction takes place. Furthermore, until very recently, it was considered utterly unprofessional for psychiatrists to share their personal histories and reactions with their patients. Many aspects of the traditional psychiatric session's structure therefore emphasize the power and unavailability of the therapist, while insisting upon the vulnerability and openness of the patient, who has no human reason to trust a total stranger. Some psychiatrists have realized in recent years that this asymmetrical structure can be terrifying, especially to individuals with histories of childhood abuse. For such individuals, the compulsory self-exposure and forced vulnerability of the psychiatric encounter are experienced as victimization. New forms of therapy developed for use in these contexts encourage revelation of the therapist's own personal history and feelings, in a shared, supportive therapeutic exchange (Gill 1994). The therapist's greater knowledge and experience are thereby perceived as a help, not a threat, and much of the alienation caused by traditional psychoanalytic mirroring technique is alleviated.

These issues are extremely relevant to the ethnographic enterprise. A similar asymmetry of power, wealth, and knowledge usually obtains between the ethnographer and the people studied. The maintenance of an objective, omniscient stance without self-revelation only perpetuates the inheritance of the colonial gaze that has victimized so many of these societies. In this work, I have attempted to reverse these inequalities, or rather to show how the very situation of fieldwork reversed them for me, by exposing both my own counter-transference, my own fantasies and fears, and their relation to the development of my analytical understanding of what I was studying.[2]

Kamala Visweswaran notes that 'first-person narratives have been consigned to the margins of anthropological discourse. In traditional ethnographic practice, if the first-person narrative is allowed to creep into the ethnographic text, it is confined to the introduction or postscript; if a book is devoted to the firsthand experiences of the novice ethnographer, it is after a monograph written in the proper objective manner has been produced.' Such personal narratives, labelled 'confessional', or 'popular', were often written by the wives of professional male anthropologists, whose work was the dominant text to which the feminine, personal account formed a separate and dispensable subtext (Visweswaran 1994: 21). There is no fundamental epistemological justification for such splitting aside from an ideology of objectivity and control.

Excision of the highly personal from ethnographies seems to be a strategy of pseudo-objectivity motivated more by concerns for career and academic acceptance than an authentic search for meaning. In fact some readers of this manuscript warned me to 'cut the autobiographical stuff' precisely because it would create a bad impression or endanger my chances of tenure. Such a move would be cowardly, a failure to face squarely the challenges posed by feminist and post-modern critiques of ethnography. Some recent ethnographies, all authored by women, have however begun to push these boundaries (Behar 1993, 1996; K. Brown 1991; Tsing 1993). These authors have combined their own and their 'subjects', voices, personal and objective rhetorical strategies, fiction and ethnography, in an effort to explore the complexities of cross-cultural encounter.

By combining all of these, we can go beyond a dialogue or a pastiche, and construct a cultural crystal. The metaphor of a crystal is apt because it is organic, multifaceted, and informed by a principle of growth whose rationale is none the less cryptic. Each facet refracts the others in different degrees. The multivocality of this text tries to approximate the many points of view present in both Kerala society and the ethnographer herself. This multivocality is not reducible to a single linear, propositional argument. My own voice, though still dominant, is augmented by the voices of other people—artists, scholars, researchers, devotees and friends. In the resultant crystal not every facet is of the same size, clarity, or quality. Some are dim and discoloured, some are wide and transparent, providing a clear view to the interior. On one side, many little facets cluster together. What is the crystal itself? At least you, holding it in your hand at this moment, must reflect upon this.

Notes

[1] See Schechner (1985, chapter 7).

[2] cf. Kakar (1996: 3–4; Behar 1996).

1

THE GODDESS AND HER PEOPLE

Bhagavati's Living History

Bhagavati ('The Goddess') is the predominant Hindu deity of Kerala. Encompassing a variety of divine personalities ranging from the benign to the ferocious, Bhagavati is associated with both the Sanskritic goddesses of the greater pan-Indian Hindu tradition, and local village goddesses associated with fever diseases.[1] As Bhagavati, the goddess is conceived of as primarily benevolent and powerful, simultaneously a chaste virgin and a caring mother. She is seldom portrayed either in mythology or iconography as being the consort of any male deity, but stands on her own. Every community in Kerala worships her in a distinctive way, ranging from simple costumed possession dances to elite Sanskrit operatic theatre. The many ritual traditions associated with the worship of Bhagavati reflect Kerala's eclectic historical and social development.

Bhagavati is important to Malayalis not only as a legendary protectress, but as a deity of the land. Thousands of temples dedicated to Bhagavati grace the landscape of Kerala, forming the core of daily worship for most Hindu Malayalis.[2] For communities dwelling in the hills, she is the spirit of the mountains; for lowland agriculturists, she is the paddy and the earth from which it grows; for toddy-tappers, the graceful coconut palm is her form. The idea of human embodiment is not opposed to the concept of Bhagavati as permeating all living things through the energies of the soil. She is essentially life itself, and as integral participants in the natural world, human beings can easily invoke, contain, and experience her presence through the myriad ritual arts offered as devotions during annual temple festivals.

The idea of the deity entering a human body is an essential part of all worship of the goddess. Temples dedicated to Bhagavati require the permanent presence of an oracle (*veḷiccappāṭu*), who embodies the goddess before her devotees in daily worship. The unique Kerala institution of the veḷiccappāṭu reflects the shamanic heritage of ancient south Indian religion, in which enacted and felt bodily presence of the deity is the essential form of contact with the divine.[3] The veḷiccappāṭu is in a special relationship to the goddess, sharing her substance when possessed by her, and functioning as her vehicle and oracle. He can both understand and control her. While only Brahmin priests may conduct *pūjā* or worship of the goddess's enlivened image within the shrine, the oracle is always a male of non-Brahmin (ordinarily Nāyar) caste. Chosen by the temple authorities, the veḷiccappāṭu draws the goddess's power into his own body, and through this mediumship, enables devotees to interact intimately with the goddess outside the protected inner sanctum of the traditional Kerala Hindu temple. The temple is constructed to allow an unbroken line of sight between the eyes of the deity, enshrined in the inner sanctum, and those of non-Brahmin devotees, considered too impure to enter the shrine, and relegated to standing outside its walls.[4] The oracle mediates between these two areas. The oracle, who is not allowed to enter the inner sanctum, stands directly in front of the shrine while the priest hands him the goddess's sacred sword from inside. With the sword the spirit of the goddess enters the oracle. Moaning and shaking his body, he runs out of the inner sanctum and through the temple courtyard, blessing people, answering questions, and giving advice.

The many dance-drama and possession rituals performed as offerings in Bhagavati temples build on this principle of embodied deity.[5] A plethora of ritual arts, encompassing music, dance, theatre, visual art, possession, curing, magic, comedy, and exorcism, form the core of worship in Kerala. Amongst these performative styles of worship is muṭiyēṯṯu, 'the carrying of the head-dress (*muṭi*)'. The origin of muṭiyēṯṯu is unknown, but it appears to have ancient roots, and to have developed into its modern form since the introduction of Kathakaḷi drama in the seventeenth century. It has some features in common with both Kathakaḷi and another dramatic art of Kerala, Kūṭiyāṭṭam, a form of Sanskrit theatre which some consider the oldest surviving dramatic art in the world.[6] But unlike these classical forms, which conform closely to the standards and techniques described in Bharata's *Nātya Śāstra*, muṭiyē<u>tt</u>u is for the most part a folk dramatic form. It provides a striking combination of the ritual immediacy of possession performance and structural features of classical Sanskrit drama.[7]

Muṭiyē<u>tt</u>u is a complex multimedia event. Combining elaborate rituals, art, music, dance, and theatre, the performance lasts from noon until dawn of the following day. The play tells a traditional story of the vanquishing of the male demon Dārika by the violent goddess Bhadrakāḷi. Only men of the high-ranking Mārār and Ku<u>r</u>up castes, who have purified themselves with strict penances and fasts, may perform the role of the goddess and the accompanying rituals. Performed exclusively in Ernakulam district and its environs in central Kerala (the former princely states of Cochin and northern Travancore), muṭiyē<u>tt</u>u is a high-caste temple art rooted deeply in folk religious tradition.

The goddess who dominates both the landscape and consciousness of the people of Kerala is a complex figure who embodies diverse streams of geography, culture, history, and religious expression. Over the many centuries of her development, she has incorporated all of these myriad dimensions into herself. Muṭiyē<u>tt</u>u, among her many ritual arts, clearly reveals Kerala's remarkable, syncretic religious history. Its artistic complexity and beauty, worthy of study in their own right, express key themes of heat and coolness, power and fertility, essential to the understanding of traditional concepts of gender that still inform daily social relations. These themes will be explored throughout this book. But first let us set the stage of Bhagavati's remarkable living history, and see the many cultural streams that have merged into the goddess's drama.

Kerala has a unique place within Indian history and culture. The modern-day state, whose boundaries were drawn on linguistic grounds in 1956, is slightly smaller than the domain covered by this distinct cultural area over more than two thousand years of recorded history.[8] Although until the tenth century it was part of the greater Tamil tradition of south India, sharing language and many traditions with neighbouring areas, Kerala's geography has always demarcated it as a separate region. A narrow strip of fertile land about 350 miles long, Kerala is bounded on the east by an inland mountain range (the Western Ghats) reaching heights of around 5,000 feet, and on the west by alluvial plains, swamps, and the Arabian Sea. Due to its topography, Kerala was both physically isolated from the rest of India throughout much of its history, and open to extensive trade contacts with other countries, ranging from Europe to China, through its busy sea trade.

The Tamilian culture of south India formed the substrate of Kerala's early history, but this was also modified by continual contact with China, Greece, Rome, Egypt, the ancient Near East and Europe.

> History tells us that Babylonians had contacts with Kerala as early as 3000 BC People of the Middle East and Phoenicians came to the shores of Kerala for trade around 10th c. BC. Arabs, Greeks, Syrians and Jews came in large numbers and Europe had large scale trade connections with Kerala from 400 BC. Crangannore [Kodungallur] had contacts with Egypt before the Christian era. Contacts with the Middle East led to Christianity coming to Kerala early in the Christian era. Buddhism and Jainism were once popular in Kerala. Though there were brahmin settlements in Kerala even before Christ, brahmins came in large numbers and assumed power only by about 7th century AD, after the decline of Buddhism and Jainism. Islam came to Kerala during the 7th century and the first mosque in India was built at Crangannore in the 8th century. The Portuguese started coming to Kerala from the 13th century onwards. Soon they were displaced by the Dutch, who were followed by the English. (V. G. Mathew 1984: 224–5)

This extraordinary mixture of influences resulted in a unique culture that was not at all homogeneous. Separate traditions were followed by groups of people living side by side. The Nambūtiri Brahmins followed patriarchal and patrilineal social organization, whereas the martial Nāyar and temple-serving castes followed the matrilineal system.[9] Communities of Christians, Jews, Muslims, and Hindus have coexisted more or less peacefully for centuries, each following their own customs and traditions. Social life tended to be localized, oriented around the residential complex or *ta̱ravāḍu*, which in the upper castes traditionally housed huge family groups of up to several hundred members. This relative closure typified social life in Kerala until quite recently:

> People traditionally gathered only for formal occasions connected with worship, festivals or ceremonies associated with marriage and death. Children are not encouraged to make friends with others outside the

> family. They are not encouraged to develop social skills and traditionally there were prohibitions against forming friendships disregarding the [previously very] rigid hierarchy of castes and subcastes (V. G. Mathew 1984: 225)

The narrow belt of fertile land running from north to south through Kerala's centre has always been fairly heavily populated, with villages shading gradually into one another. As Freeman points out, this 'continuous settlement pattern [is] quite unlike the nucleated villages of the Tamil country' (Freeman 1991: 4). Greater political organization was also distinctive, characterized by 'relatively de-centered congeries of political systems and cultural nodes quite unlike most other regions of south India' (ibid.: 5). Throughout the medieval period and into the nineteenth century, small traditional kingdoms (or chiefdoms) were centred in the foothills and inland areas where paddy production was most intensive. A feudal social organization bonded agricultural workers to landowners, who were mostly of the martial Nāyar caste. Temples supported by the wealth of the land were also dispersed throughout these political centres. Each royal house was allied by marriage to Brahmin families, whose male members also served as priests in their temples. Bhagavati became the predominant deity of the martial temple-owners, such that each king had his own local installation of the goddess, who was considered to be a tutelary matrilineal ancestor and protectress of his family's personal political interests. Kinship relationships were often imputed to the different Bhagavatis, perhaps reflecting actual networks of political alliance through marriage. Propitiation of one's own local Bhagavati ensured the power and success of the kingdom and its dependants.

In order to export their agricultural resources, kings made use of Kerala's extensive network of rivers, flowing down from the mountains in the east to the Arabian Sea on the western coast. These rivers integrated Kerala from the mountainous regions to the shore, but divided it from north to south, into fragmentary regions 'defined by these transverse segments' (ibid.: 5). From the mountain forests, kings obtained important wild natural resources, such as wood, medicines, gum, animals, and minerals. Low-caste groups in the foothills and lowlands specialized in the manufacture of palm-leaf umbrellas, coconut cultivation, and leather work. Some lower-caste groups (such as the Pulluvans) became ritual experts in the propitiation of the dangerous serpent deities revered throughout Kerala; others specialized in sorcery (*mantravādam*). Service castes, including washermen and barbers, tailors, sweepers, elephant trainers, tree-cutters, and carpenters, developed special skills which they exchanged with other castes as a livelihood.

This variegated physical and social landscape was characterized not only by rich cultural diversity and cooperation, but also by conflict. The conflictual model is the essential drama of ancient Indian culture, as reflected in the stories enacted in muṭiyēṯṯu and related arts. The mythic battle between the demonic king Dārika and the warrior goddess Bhadrakāḷi has thus been seen by many as an allegory of historical conflict between real political rivals. However, interpretations of this allegorical history are widely varied. All agree that Kāḷi represents the good and Dārika the evil; but exactly how these are defined depends largely on one's point of view. Some identify Kāḷi with the high-caste rulers of the lowlands; others claim her to be a deity of the mountain tribes. The mythology of the Bhagavati cult is thus an allegory of living history, reflecting the development of Kerala's unique culture through numerous layers of external contact and conquest.

The oldest level of culture in Kerala for which we have literary records is that of the Sangam age, when the Cera kings (one of the three political lineages that ruled ancient south India) dominated the political landscape. The Sangam age has been identified by scholars of Tamil literature as extending from the first to the fourth century CE, when Brahmin influence began to be keenly felt due to extensive immigration of upper-caste Aryan groups into the south following the fall of the Gupta empire (Hardy 1983: 123). A rich and sophisticated literary tradition in ancient Tamil language gives us a window into what is now called Dravidian culture, a recognizably distinct linguistic and cultural complex, different in significant ways from that of the Sanskritic culture of north India during this period.[10]

The major religious ideas which characterized Sangam culture have been succinctly summarized by various scholars. Ram lists these, based on Hardy's (1983) study, as follows:

> (a) the absence of a clear awareness of transcendence, which allows for the visualisation of the divine within the confines of earthly reality; (b) the sensual character of the worship; (c) the ecstasy of emotions in which the divine is felt to be present, which links (a) and (b); and (d) lastly the exclusively female cults of Sangam literature resurfacing

in the later *bhakti* worship in which the psychology of religious awareness is female. (Ram 1992: 69)

The concept of *aṇaṅku*, 'in many ways a very early forerunner of the concept of Śāktī' was also very important in Sangam religion (Hart 1973, 1975, 1979). Baker-Reynolds summarizes aṇaṅku as 'a malevolent, dangerous power' inhering in both the natural world and the bodies of humans and deities, particularly female (1978). Hart identifies the predominant locus of aṇaṅku in Sangam literature as in the sexual parts of the female anatomy: breasts, loins, and genitals. The goddess Bhagavati embodies all these aspects of aṇaṅku: malevolent female power that manifests as both violent and sexual energy.

Dramatic possession performances such as muṭiyēṯṯu clearly arise from these ancient forms of worship, which stressed the passionate and violent nature of supernatural energy. This power, because it inhered in the physical landscape as well as in the bodies of women, was essential for the nourishment of life and society and yet always threatened to get out of control, destroying life. Agricultural and human fertility were intimately related, so that rituals promoting the growth of crops developed using metaphors of the feminine reproductive cycle; the goddess Bhagavati herself embodies much of this symbolism. Much of ancient Dravidian religion focused on the proper evocation and management of these ambivalent powers through war, bloodshed, sexuality, and possession performance. Rituals like *teyyam* or the fire-walking cults seen in the neighbouring regions of southern India and Sri Lanka represent this strand of powerful devotionalism with direct links to the past.

Other cultural influences in the Sangam period are also important in understanding the unique development of Hinduism and the Bhagavati cult there. Buddhism and Jainism had considerable influence in Kerala from the time of Ashoka until about the sixth century CE, through the establishment of important centres of learning and religious practice. Some historians claim that the famous Kodungallur Bhagavati temple (which is referred to in Greek histories dating to second century BCE) was at one time a Buddhist nunnery.[11] The unique, unassuming architecture of Kerala Hindu temples also reflects Jain and Buddhist influence. The cylindrical shrines were inspired by Buddhist stupas, and the low, wood-latticed porticos surrounding temples imitated Jain shrines.[12] Kerala temple architecture is utterly unlike the towering *gopurams* and intricately walled cities of Tamil Nadu temples. Buddhist and Jain influences are also felt in the prevalent mythology of *yakṣis* (female tree spirits) and *nāgas* (serpent deities). These nature spirits populate both Jain and Buddhist sculpture and mythology from an ancient date (fourth century BCE). In Kerala their iconography is intimately related to that of Bhagavati, whose mythical antecedents are clearly both the malevolent feminine tree spirits and snake goddesses.[13]

Brahmins were probably present in Kerala from the second century CE, but became dominant only after about the seventh century. The contact between Sangam culture, with its Jain and Buddhist influences, and that of the Sanskrit-speaking Brahmins, forged a syncretistic cult in which neither was truly dominant. Faced with a fully developed religious system in which the control of sacred power was in the hands of the lowest castes, Brahmins were forced to delineate an alternative system of purity and pollution and to ally themselves politically with local rulers in order to retain their position of privilege and superiority (Hart 1987: 481–5). Modelling their communities on the powerful Jain and Buddhist groups, Brahmins in Kerala developed many distinctive habits and customs which distinguished them from their brethren in the rest of the subcontinent. The Nambūtiri Brahmins also developed close relationships with the martial Nāyar caste, intermarrying with and living in close proximity to them. Brahminical religion in the region was thus heavily influenced by the religious practices of the Nāyars, who worshipped the fierce goddess and serpent deities with blood sacrifice and spirit possession.

Temples, which developed after the major influx of Sanskritic culture into the south in the early centuries CE, were controlled by and accessible only to the Brahmins, Ambalavāsis (temple servants) and the martial Nāyar castes. Because of this, two distinct streams of Hindu worship developed in the ritual arts: the upper-caste Ambalavāsi arts and the lower-caste possession rituals such as teyyam. It was in this complex religious environment that muṭiyēṯṯu developed, incorporating elements of both Sanskritic and Dravidian heritage (Choondal 1981: 9, 195).[14] The texts of muṭiyēṯṯu are composed in a mixture of languages including Sanskrit, Malayalam, Maṇipravāḷam (an artificial courtly literary language combining Malayalam and Sanskrit popular in Kathakaḷi compositions), and medieval Tamil. The costumes combine elements found in the

Sanskrit dramatic forms of Chakyar Kuttu, Kathakaḷi, and Kūṭiyāṭṭam with tribal and folk styles of make-up and costuming (wooden breasts and grass skirts, black-and-white facial make-up, etc.). The dance and acting styles also combine both elementary Sanskritic forms and those used in folk possession performance. The offering of blood sacrifice at the end of muṭiyēṯṯu clearly derives from war rituals of the Sangam period as well as tribal practices.

Thus, despite many aspects of Sanskritic theatrical structure, such as the framing of the story with characters from the Sanskrit *purāṇas* (mythic texts), the careful delineation of scenes, dance steps, musical modes and rhythmic structures, and the insistence on high-caste performers, muṭiyēṯṯu also incorporates much that is alien to the Sanskritic tradition. In fact we may hypothesize that the high castes of Kerala invented muṭiyēṯṯu much as they institutionalized oracular practice in the temples, in an attempt to coopt the management of sacred power in indigenous, low-caste possession performances.

In the seventh century large groups of Muslims also settled throughout Kerala, particularly in Malabar. Their culture also seems to have had an impact on the development of muṭiyēṯṯu. Whereas until the middle of the twentieth century, Kerala women went bare-breasted, Muslim women have always covered their upper body with red cotton blouses tied at the back. The red blouse worn by Muslim women is identical to the red, long-sleeved jacket worn by Bhadrakāḷi in muṭiyēṯṯu (as well as in the Sanskritic temple dramas). Kerala Muslims followed matrilineal descent and inheritance, and women enjoyed high status in their society. Muslim queens of the Arakkal Royal House held great positions of power (Mohamed Koya 1983: 37–44, 68). Perhaps these factors impressed the muṭiyēṯṯu artists, who could have incorporated the red blouse as a symbol of feminine power. These days artificial brilliant naked red breasts are worn by the Kāḷi actor outside of the blouse, as if both to show the clothed upper body and frame the powerful breasts. No actors were able to shed any light on this matter, which must remain in the realm of speculation for the present.

The story of conquest enacted in muṭiyēṯṯu is based on the legend *Dārikavadham* ('The Killing of Dārika'). While this legend shares a number of motifs found in other goddess traditions throughout south Asia, its essential features are unique to Kerala. The story tells of the birth, deeds, and death of the demon Dārika at the hands of the goddess Bhagavati (a.k.a. Bhadrakāḷi). Elements of the Dārikavadham resemble portions of the *Devī-Māhātmya* and the *Devī-Bhāgāvata Purāṇa*, but it is the *Linga Purāṇa* (1.106) which comes closest to the Kerala story, and actually mentions the demon Dāruka. Despite the presence of cognate motifs, the full Kerala form of *Dārikavadham* does not appear in any of the Sanskrit purāṇas. Published versions in Sanskrit and Malayalam with such titles as *Bhadrakāḷi-Māhātmyam, Bhadrōlpatti*; and *Dārukavadham*, appear to some analysts to be Sanskritized versions of an oral tale.[15] Whatever its textual antecedents, the story is alive and well in oral transmission, and some version of it was known to nearly everyone I met in Kerala. Considering its importance and popularity in Kerala, the nearly complete absence of references to *Dārikavadham* in western scholarly literature is extraordinary.[16]

For muṭiyēṯṯu artists, the textual antecedents of the tale are of little interest. When I asked one veteran actor and drummer if he knew the story's origins, he replied, 'I don't know. It's a hereditary (oral) story. I don't think it is there in the *Rāmāyana* or *Bhāgavata Purāṇa*. I don't know much about this. Maybe it's from the *Śiva Purāṇa*.' Traditional artists learn the story by hearing it sung in their youth, and then carefully memorizing the ritual songs accompanying the drama during daily training. In fact in the muṭiyēṯṯu tradition, 'the rule is that it should not be written down and learned' (Choondal 1981: 156).[17]

I collected oral versions of the story of Dārikavadham from nearly every person I interviewed. In general women were far less familiar with the story than men; and muṭiyēṯṯu artists knew it in greater detail than other people. The story presented here is compiled from two oral versions collected from muṭiyēṯṯu troupe leaders.[18]

> At the time of the war between the demons and the gods, Lord Mahaviṣṇu killed all of the *asura*s [demons] except two, who escaped and managed to hide in the underworld. There were two young demon girls there too, Dārumati and Dānavati. The asuras married these virgins and begot sons. Dārumati's son was named Dārika and Dānavati's Dānava. When they grew up they came to know that their clan had been destroyed by Mahaviṣṇu, and they took an oath to take revenge upon him. To fulfil this purpose they went to Gokarna and observed austerities. Though the penance continued for a very long time, Brahma didn't appear. They were disappointed.

In desperation, Dārika began to cut off his head with a sword. No sooner had the first drop of blood fallen on the ground than Lord Brahma appeared before him and promised to give whatever boon he wanted. Dārika's first demand was: 'Every drop of my blood should give birth to a thousand asuras.' He also wanted Brahma to give him the power to overcome death and conquer the entire universe. Brahma readily agreed. Then Dārika posed a funny question to Brahma. 'Why didn't you give me assurance that I wouldn't be killed by a woman?' This insulted Brahma and, enraged, he cursed Dārika, 'A divine lady will kill you, and at that time the boons won't come to your rescue.'[19]

Dārika didn't care for Brahma's warnings and began to conquer the three worlds [heaven, earth, and the underworld], one by one. Unable to bear Dārika's cruelty, the earth goddess approached [the trinity of gods] Brahma-Viṣnu-Maheswara, and apprised them of her discontent. On hearing this, six gods created six beautiful virgins and sent them to fight Dārika. But all these six were defeated and sought asylum in the forest.

Sage Narada was watching all these events. Straightaway he went to Kailāsam, the abode of Śiva, and described the incidents to Śiva, adding that Dārika intended to invade Kailāsam. Śiva became enraged and opened his third eye which is full of fire. Out of that blazing fire Bhadrakāḷi was born. At the time of her incarnation Kāḷi wore a ferocious look with innumerable heads, hands, and legs. Even the creator became frightened. It was because of Śiva's request that Kāḷi later reduced the size of her body. Bhadrakāḷi asked Śiva for what purpose he had created her. Śiva replied that the whole universe was suffering from the atrocities of Dārika, and all the inhabitants should be saved by her.

Even after the birth of Kāḷi, Dārika remains unconquerable. Kāḷi can kill him only if she knows the mantra given to Dārika by Brahma. But Dārika has revealed the mantra only to his wife. Only if his wife reveals this to a third person will it be possible to kill Dārika. The gods think aloud and decide to create Durga. Durga goes to Dārika's house and tells his wife Manōdari that her husband is seriously ill and they must do something to rescue him. Then Manōdari gives Durga the mantra Dārika got from Brahma. This enables Kāḷi to kill Dārika. Manōdari gets the point a little late. So she curses Kāḷi: 'You shall be stricken with smallpox.' Then her face and body got filled with the marks of smallpox. For curing this smallpox Ghaṇṭākarṇan was born out of Śiva's ear. Ghaṇṭākarṇan licks Dēvi's entire body from bottom to top. When his tongue reaches her face, Kāḷi tells him that a brother should not lick his sister's face. So her face remained affected with smallpox.

To kill Dārika, Kāḷi needs the help of a ghost called Vētāḷam. Since one drop of Dārika's blood will make thousands of Dārikas, Kāḷi offers Vētāḷam lots of blood to fill her big belly. So Vētāḷam accompanied Kāḷi to the war. Vētāḷam spread her enormous tongue over the entire battleground, so that Dārika's blood would spill on it. Still Dārika's blood didn't fill Vētāḷam's belly, so she began to fight with Kāḷi. Then Mahaviṣnu sent Garuḍa [the eagle mount of Lord Viṣnu]. Vētāḷam dug her nails deep into the body of Garuḍa and quenched her thirst with his blood.

After killing Dārika, Kāḷi returned to Śiva's abode with Dārika's head. Along the way, all the people in heaven got frightened on seeing Kāḷi's anger. Even Śiva was afraid of Kāḷi. So Śiva walked naked before her, they say. As a daughter is not supposed to see her father naked, Kāḷi turned back.

This legend is believed by devotees to be a true account of events in the distant past. There are various interpretations of the identities of the *dēvas* and asuras, Kāḷi and Dārikan (see Caldwell, forthcoming (c)). Generally, Kāḷi is said to be an asura (demonic), not a dēva (divine) female. Muṭiyēṯṯu artists explain that only someone of a demonic nature could conquer an evil being like Dārika, beheading him mercilessly and drinking his blood. But she is born from Śiva, who by the medieval period was an Aryan god. This paradox is resolved by Appu Kuttan Mārār, who says, 'Kāḷi is a mixture of both dēva and asura.' This is evidenced, he says, by the fact that the musicians in the orchestra of muṭiyēṯṯu must use both 'asura' and 'dēva' forms of drum (the *uruttu* and *vikkan ceṇṭa*—actually the same drum, played either on the left or right face), for demonic or divine energies to be summoned. Only one 'divine' drum must be present, whereas two or more 'demonic' drums are required to invoke the furious energy that Kāḷi needs to kill Dārika.

Despite their differences, the various versions of legendary history all emphasize that some form of conquest of the indigenous culture took place, and that Kāḷi derives from and represents that indigenous culture. Both Choondal and Mathew suggest that Kāḷi derives from the tribal deity Koṯṯavai, a warrior goddess who delights in the blood of battle, a view shared by Hardy (1983: 223). Koṯṯavai's iconography in Sangam literature identifies her as a direct antecedent of Bhadrakāḷi in Kerala: wearing a necklace of tiger teeth, riding a tiger, and shouting in victory (*kurava*), Koṯṯavai comes to the battlefield to kill enemies, eat their flesh and drink their blood. Such iconographic details as the tiger teeth necklace (the emblem of Koṯṯavai's priests) are still seen in contemporary lithographs of Kāḷi (Fig. 2). Her blue skin (sometimes described

Fig. 2: Popular poster of Kāḷi

as black) seems to allude to the extremely dark skin colour of the residents of the mountainous regions between Kerala and Tamil Nadu.

Devotees of the ancient war goddess Kot̲t̲avai included female dancers who accompanied male warriors to battle singing, dancing, and drumming (Kersenboom 1981; Kersenboom-Story [KS] 1987). Poems of war vividly describe the rituals performed on the battlefield, which was conceived of as the locus for 'the most intense confrontation between man and the divine.... The goddess Korravai dances on the battlefield accompanied by a host of demons, ghosts, and demon women' who feast on the bodies of the slain (KS 1987: 14). Battlefield rituals included cooking of the bodies of defeated warriors: '... the king mows down the enemy forces, piles up dead bodies on the battlefield, uses elephants instead of oxen to trample the corpses, gets these "minced" corpses and carcasses cooked by a virgin, who stirs a huge pot containing blood and fat' (ibid.: 10). The demonic female spirits that attended the war goddess Kot̲t̲avai were represented by human women dedicated to the service of the king. These sacred females had 'the basic function of direct contact with the ambivalent power of the divine', which was channelled through their activities into the king's sacred power, the source of fertility in the realm at large (ibid.: 16).

Female court bards called *vir̲alis* and *pāṭin̲is* sang, danced, and played music, glorifying the bravery of the king (Kersenboom 1981). These chaste women were considered to channel supernatural forces such that they were said to have power over rain. The vir̲alis accompanied the king and his male bards at celebrations of victory in battle, dancing the wild victory dance of *tuṇaṅkai* behind the king's chariot. 'In certain instances we find the tuṇaṅkai performed during a feast ... while the hero enters on his chariot accompanied by women who glorify his erotic exploits as well, drunk with toddy' (KS 1987: 15). These female servants of the king were transformed in later eras into the *devadasis* (*nityasumaṅgalīs*) of south Indian temples. But their ritual roles included actions similar to the *veḷiccappāṭus* of today: Tamil poems of the tenth century mention the Mātaṅki, 'a female who performs simultaneously three actions: vāḷ vīci ('swinging the sword'), singing the praise of ... Murukan ..., and thirdly, beating [drums]' (ibid.: 22).

In south Indian village festivals dedicated to the goddess

performed in regions bordering Kerala, the Matangi still fulfils an important role. A virgin of untouchable caste is 'initiated as a special representative or manifestation of the goddess' (Brubaker 1978: 267).

> Most ... persons possessed by the goddess are male, for men perform most of the priestly roles in her festivals. But there is one very special role for a woman in many villages in Andhra Pradesh and adjoining areas of Karnataka, that of the Matangi. And possession is central to a Matangi's behavior and meaning. ...
>
> There is only one Matangi in a village and she usually holds her office for life. Her successor is often designated by means of a ritual in which the prepubescent Madiga girls of the village are assembled, the goddess is invoked with much singing and drumming, and she enters into one of the girls, who later undergoes testing and initiation. Her subsequent life, in Elmore's delicate phrase, 'knows no moral restrictions.' (Brubaker 1978: 267–8)

This selection through possession is exactly how the male, high-caste (Nāyar) veḷiccappāṭu is selected in Kerala temples (Thampuran 1936). The Matangi becomes possessed by the goddess, drinking toddy and dancing in 'wild frenzy', as she runs about spitting toddy on the assembled crowd, 'uttering strange wild cries', and hurling obscene verbal abuse at all and sundry (ibid.: 269). The contemporary Kerala veḷiccappāṭu's oracular ravings are muted, but clearly cognate, ritual acts.

Hardy describes the public religious activities of women in festivals during the Sangam period in south India: 'On all the streets, (young women) get into a frenzy, dance, sing, and make a loud noise. ...[T]he various forms of religion mentioned involve exclusively girls and women' (Hardy 1983: 140). Women also participated in possession trances and divination. Female shamans are found in accounts of tribal culture in the mountainous regions of the Western Ghats. Although research on these topics is scarce, existing evidence indicates that the ancient precursor of Bhadrakāḷi was Koṯṯavai, a mountain forest-dwelling war goddess; that she was accompanied by cannibalistic ghosts (*pey*); and that her ambivalent powers were recognized to inhere in young women, who performed important ritual roles embodying and expressing these powers. Frenzied orgiastic dancing, singing and drumming, eating of meat and drinking of liquor were integral parts of the ritual activities of these female practitioners (ibid.: 620). Although the veḷiccappāṭus associated with temples today are exclusively male, female veḷiccappāṭus exist in the hilly tribal areas of the Palghat region. These female oracles come to the Kodungallur Bhagavati temple at Bharaṇi and participate in the rituals of pollution, cutting their heads along with the male oracles (see Fig. 3). To my knowledge, no fieldwork has been done with these female oracles, who are reluctant to speak with outsiders. They may be the last of the female shamanic priests who perform important ritual roles in these tribal societies.[20] It is quite likely that the male veḷiccappāṭus modelled their behaviour on these female shamans, whose role was superseded in Kerala's Aryanized lowlands.

With the advent of the brahminical Aryan culture between the fourth and seventh centuries, ritual power moved out of the hands of low-caste ritual specialists and indigenous female shamans. As upper-caste art forms like muṭiyēṯṯu developed, low castes and women of all castes were denied the right to portray the deity in possession performances. This appropriation of low-caste, autocthonous religious practices by high-caste Sanskritic religion is cogently expressed in the following published legend explaining the origin of an important Bhagavati temple of central Kerala:

> The place where the temple stands today was once a dense forest inhabited by tribals. ... One day a Pulaya (outcaste) woman who had come to cut grass sharpened her scythe against a stone which started to ooze blood. The horror-stricken woman shrieked aloud and the Pulayas in the neighbourhood came running to the spot. They, in turn, informed the learned Edaṭhu Nambūtiri (a Brahmin), who, visiting the spot, realised that there was divine Chaitanya (or consciousness) of Parasakti at the place. ... It was Edathu Nambūtiri who built a shrine, performed pooja and administered the temple for several years. (Vaidyanathan 1988)

In this story the sign of the divine energy of the goddess, whose idol had been lost, is the oozing of blood from a stone when sharpened by the scythe of a low-caste female agricultural worker. This motif acknowledges the power of the originating indigenous religion by attributing the discovery of the divine image to a member of the Pulaya caste, one of the most 'polluting' groups in the traditional caste hierarchy, but also a prominent group in Kerala before the advent of the Brahmins from the north (Yesudas 1975: 34). Although it is the low-caste worker who inadvertently brings forth the 'divine Chaitanya of Parasakti' through causing the stone

Fig. 3: Female *veḷiccappāṭu* at Kodungallur Bharaṇi
(Photograph courtesy K. Gopalakrishnan)

to bleed, only the high-caste Nambūtiri priest can properly diagnose and manage the spiritual situation, converting the spot into a temple. The element of a female low-caste worker underscores the anti-structural position of the autochthonous spirituality in tension with high-caste, Aryan religion. The Bhagavati of muṭiyēṯṯu represents a kind of middle ground; she is an Aryanized, Sanskritized version of the tribal deity, who yet maintains many of her original characteristics, including possession, dancing to spirit-drums, use of fire, and blood sacrifice.

Kāḷi in the Kaḷari: the Śākta Tradition in Kerala

Tantrism, the form of worship in which deity and devotee are homologized, pervades Hindu practice at all levels of Kerala society. In its Śākta form, tantrism posits female deity (Devī) as the supreme principle of the universe. Some forms of the Śākta ritual use substances considered polluting and prohibited in orthodox brahminical religion, as a means of realization of the divine. These can include blood, alcohol, sexual fluids and meat.[21] Śākta ideas, along with ritual arts of divination (*praśnam*) and sorcery (mantravādam) are integral to Kerala Hindu worship. Kerala priests, called *tantris*, are well versed in the arts of praśnam, astrology, and certain aspects of mantravādam.

Little is known about the history of Śākta tradition in Kerala. Bharati tells us that 'Kerala has a strong Sakta and tantric element in its culture; in some form or another Sakti is the tutelary deity of Kerala' (1970: 89). He mentions the three important tantric pilgrimage places of Mūkāmbika, Hemambika, and Kanyakumari, all in or adjacent to Kerala's borders, commenting that:

> to my knowledge, there is no literature whatever, so far, on these three Kerala shrines, in spite of the fact that south Indian tantrics—by no means only Kerala tantrics—hold the shrines in high esteem and that they have been well-frequented centres of tantric worship and pilgrimage for centuries. (p. 99, fn. 11)[22]

Mūkāmbika is said to be the 'elder sister' of Kerala's Kodungallur Bhagavati; her shrine is one of the most important centres of Srī Vidyā (Śākta) worship and esoteric practice in south India. Numerous Brahmin families residing around the temple possess manuscripts detailing the rituals and meanings of the Srī Vidyā cult.[23] Despite the shrine's current location in the modern state of

Karnataka, thousands of Malayali pilgrims journey to the shrine each year, particularly for the festival of Navaratri.

Although Nambūtiri Brahmins do not always openly admit that they practise divination and other occult arts, the Tantric College in Alwaye, Ernakulam district, trains priests in esoteric Śākta practice. Many Brahmin priests are called upon by private clients to resolve personal problems. When my husband was suffering from psychological difficulties, a local doctor referred us to a well-known Nambūtiri priest, who performed an elaborate Śākta pūjā for him. As part of the ceremony, tantric mantras were inscribed onto a metal plate, which was rolled up in a metal casing for Antonio to wear around his waist at all times as protection.[24] The *kaḷam* pūjā performed by the Nambūtiri priests at the beginning of muṭiyēṯṯu also has strong tantric elements, such as the invocation of the deity through geometric designs, gestures, and mantras, and her identification with the body of the priest.

The religious practices of the 'scheduled' castes (ranked below the Brahmins and Nāyars) are also infused with śākta ideas. At Bhagavati temples managed by priests of the Ezhava caste in central Trichur district, liquor and meat are offered to the fiercer female deities (such as Oṯṯamulacci—the 'one-breasted one') populating the shrine.[25] *Mantravādins* (sorcerers) offer cures by possession and divination, and prescribe remedies requiring tantric practice.

Śākta tantrism in Kerala is also central to the *kaḷari* tradition of the Nāyar and Ezhava warriors. Muṭiyēṯṯu partakes of this martial tradition, and up to the previous generation, artists were trained in kaḷaris (martial arts gymnasia), where along with kaḷam drawing and physical training, esoteric śākta teachings were imparted. The last artists trained in this way are no longer living, and today only three kaḷaris train full time in the ancient Kerala martial art of kaḷarippayaṯṯ.[26] We visited the Chavakkad Kaḷari Sangham in Trichur district to find out more about the relationship between martial tradition and tantric practice. As we entered the small practice room for the gymnastic exercises, it was apparent that the room also functioned as a shrine. All who enter must remove their shoes, and touch the doorway as a gesture of respect before entering. In the south-western corner of the room was a seven-stepped structure with a statue of a female deity decked with serpents. In the north-western corner, resting against a red cloth, was a long curved iron sword of the kind used by oracles to represent Kāḷi. Several small square stones embedded in the earthen floor of the room were decked with red *cetti* flowers, favourite of Kāḷi. We were permitted to watch the training exercises performed by well-oiled young men, and were struck by the similarity of the swordplay to the fight between Kāḷi and Dārika enacted in muṭiyēṯṯu.

The guru (primary teacher) of the Chavakkad Kaḷari Sangham, C.S.N. Menon explained that kaḷarippayaṯṯ is a Nāyar speciality, and as such is taught by the matrilineal system, from maternal uncle to nephew. The method of education is the *gurukkul*, a traditional form of study in which the student lives with, serves, and is utterly under the control of the teacher or guru. Menon confirmed that the kaḷari also functions as an important shrine for the surrounding village. In his kaḷari, the main deities worshipped are Ganapati, Chandikesa (a form of Kāḷi), and the Saptamātrakkaḷ (the 'seven mothers', in the form of seven steps grading upwards in a triangular shape). Whatever particular deities a given kaḷari worships, the goddess Kāḷi, as patroness of war, is common to all. In the following interview, Menon details the special role of Kāḷi in kaḷari practice, and also sheds light on the iconic meaning of breasts in the costume of muṭiyēṯṯu.

Q: Why is Kāḷi related to the kaḷari?

M: There is no kaḷari without Kāḷi. Nothing can move without śakti (power, strength). So Kāḷi is really śakti. Kāḷi is actually to kill evil people and bless good people. It is to kill the evil and save the good that all these kinds of worship are performed in the kaḷari.

In every kaḷari Kāḷi is worshipped with different names. Kaḷari Bhairavi, the primary deity of kaḷari tradition, is Kāḷi. Chandika, Bhuvaneswari, Rakteśwari ('blood goddess') are all Kāḷi's forms. Bhadrakāḷi is installed in the north door. It's only there we have these *guruti* offerings. Don't you see that stone there? That is really Bhadrakāḷi. [Worshipping] this is very good for destroying your enemy, and avoiding accidents. The blessings [of these dēvis] save us; that's why we worship them before the battle.

[All around the walls of the kaḷari are hung various weapons and shields. The shields have a distinctive round shape with four circular projections that look to me like breasts with nipples in the centre. The shields are painted red; some of the 'nipples' are daubed with red kumkum powder, a form of worship.]

Q: Can you explain about the shield and the sword?
M: When we take the sword, we imagine Śiva and taking the shield we imagine Śakti. So when people see from outside, they think it is just striking and blocking. But it is not that. Actually it is Śiva and Śakti combining in the war to defeat the enemy. We imagine Śiva when we take the sword and Śakti when we take the shield.
Q: Why is the shield given a red colour?
M: Because it is Dēvi's colour. Dēvi's colour is blood. Not only that, it is a signal to show danger is awaiting. Dēvi likes red. She wears red silk.
Q: On the shield there are some circular protuberances. Do they have any resemblance to the breast of females?
M: [Reticently, surprised; laughing as if we have discovered a secret] Yes, that is why ... it's about śakti. It's to attract people. When they see it they feel attracted towards it and are distracted. When we men see the breasts, we get excited and attracted, so when this shield is kept like that on your chest, the enemy is distracted and maybe he would stop the battle also. Then to avoid getting struck also, we use this. When you have those bubbles, the sword slips away when struck on the shield and it's safe. It won't strike on our body.
Q: So the breasts of Kāḷi, do they have any power, force, or any special kind of energy?
M: As I said, people get attracted and the feeling would maybe decrease the anger and also the war can end.

Menon's remarks indicate that female breasts, as detachable icons, have the power both to attract and protect. The male warrior coopts female power to attract and kill his enemy. Female power (śakti) is simultaneously an abstract cosmic force and an immanent aspect of the human female body which arouses erotic feeling in human male bodies. This revelation explains one of the most important reasons for the male actor dressing as the female Kāḷi in muṭiyēṯṯu and other Kerala ritual arts: to cultivate power which can kill and destroy evil. The Śakta worldview in the Dravidian context focuses this force in the female breasts; and it postulates the source of aggressive, destructive power (a combination of the Sanskritic śakti and the Dravidian aṇaṅku) in the erotic attraction wielded by women over men.

Savitri, a 90-year-old Brahmin woman, also related Kāḷi's breasts to her forceful nature. However, her commentary exposed the vulnerability of women to men:

> Kāḷi has the nature of an asura woman, to kill the evil. Bhadrakali is a person who does some evil, ferocious deeds to kill the demon. *Well that's why she has huge breasts*, they say. But she is merely a woman,

> right? In olden days, men wouldn't kill women; it was considered very low. But not now. Now if women tell a lie, they can be killed.

This remark reminds us that while the cosmic battle between good and evil rages in the ritual realm, a more human struggle is also taking place between real men and women. The construction of gender in the śākta worldview, when dominated by and serving men, ironically denies to women the very sense of embodied power that the male ideology asserts they possess.

It wasn't always that way. Evidence from numerous sources strongly suggests that in ancient and medieval times, women took part in ritual and military activities of importance to society at large. Female warriors appear as characters in the *tōṭṭam pāṭṭu* (heroic ballads) of northern Kerala, sung during the worship of Bhagavati and other deities. C.S.N. Menon of Chavakkad Kaḷari confirmed that Nāyar girls were trained in kaḷarippayaṯṯ: 'Yes, in olden times our *Unni Archa* ladies [characters of northern Kerala heroic stories] were warriors. In this kaḷari females also have been taught. Even my daughter has been taught.'

The relative strength of Nāyar women as compared to Brahmins may also have contributed to the contemporary image of Bhadrakāḷi. Early Brahmin immigrants into Kerala in the fourth to seventh centuries established their superior status through assertion of their ritual purity and knowledge, and through alliances with the indigenous ruling castes. Due to the relative paucity of Nambūtiri Brahmin population, and the necessity of maintaining large property holdings intact, a system developed in which only the eldest male could take a Brahmin wife. All the younger brothers of this male were prohibited from marrying Brahmins, and were entitled to form sexual liaisons with women of the warrior Nāyar and royal Kṣatriya castes. As the Nambūtiri Brahmins followed a patrilineal system of descent and the Nāyars and Kṣatriyas a matrilineal one, these younger Brahmin men could claim no offspring, and held an insignificant status within the homes of their female companions. The majority of Brahmin women were also relegated by this system to a life of strict celibacy and seclusion.[27]

The result of this system was that husbands in the Nāyar and Kṣatriya families (usually Brahmins) held no jural authority and wielded little psychological influence. Even in the royal family we interviewed, Brahmin males appeared by the admission of all to be insecure and insignificant, at the mercy of women.[28] Ethnic stereotypes told to us by young men of lower, patrilineally organized castes, ridiculed the subservient position of Nāyar and Brahmin men, portraying them as constantly bowing and scraping before their wives and at their beck and call.[29] This was uncomfortably dismissed by the young men of male-dominated traditions, who clearly found such an idea threatening.

The strong economic and social position of Nāyar and Kṣatriya women during the medieval period was reinforced by their occasional participation in military activities and their relative sexual autonomy. Since local Bhagavatis were worshipped by each Nāyar and Kṣatriya house, the association of the goddess with women of these castes, and the attribution to her of their perceived qualities of physical strength, autonomy, and sexual potency, would have been natural. These local associations may have built upon earlier Sangam traditions of the female bards, who also combined sexuality and martiality in their persons. The combination of these various female images of power may all have contributed to the local understanding of the goddess Bhagavati in Kerala.

Bhagavati is more than a mythic figure of the Malayali imagination. Her form today is a precipitate of many centuries of historical and cultural development. On one level she represents male political struggles dating back to the ancient chiefdoms of the Sangam and feudal periods. On another level her stories are metaphors of conquest of an indigenous, female-centred religious culture by a male-dominated tradition. Finally, the iconography and rituals of the Bhagavati cult echo ancient traditions centred around fertility and enacted by human women. With the advent of brahminic religion, feminine participation in the management of the divine was marginalized. When the Sanskritic notion of purity and pollution hierarchy was superimposed upon the indigenous religious world view that cultivated ambivalent natural forces, the resultant synthesis simply could not tolerate the idea of direct feminine embodiment of divinity. Because women's natural power was now inseparable from 'impurity', women were prevented from participating in divine ritual enactments. As a result, now 'women (impure by nature) may be possessed by the inferior spirits, not by a Brahmanic deity' (Obeyesekere 1978: 471). Malevolent forms of the goddess still possess women in neighbouring regions of south India, and the ancient female ritual roles have been incorporated into peripheral rites such as the Matangi. But in Kerala these ritual roles for women have been eliminated from all but the most circumscribed contexts (for example, in the serpent cults) (see Neff 1987; Seth 1992). The unique social history of Kerala has perhaps made the image of the powerful woman too threatening to allow female embodiment of the goddess's dangerous energy to flourish. We shall explore the reasons for this and the possibilities for rediscovery of this powerful feminine tradition in chapters 4 and 5.

Performers and Patrons

The rigid social hierarchy that developed in Kerala after the early centuries placed Brahmins at the pinnacle of the population pyramid, allied by marriage with the warrior and princely castes just below them. All other members of the population were relegated to the status of *Śudra* or 'untouchable' workers and servants of the upper castes.[30] Entry to temples was restricted to Brahmins and upper castes alone; all other members of society worshipped in their own village shrines or homes. The annual temple festivals, with their elaborate processions, allowed the Śudra population to have the *darśan* (sacred sight) of the deity ordinarily hidden away in the inaccessible inner sancta. A class of temple servants, the Ambalavāsi castes, developed among the upper echelons of the warrior communities. These temple servants performed various duties within the temple walls, although they were not allowed into the inner sanctum enshrining the deity.

The artistic services of the Ambalavāsis were divided into several types. Nāyars acted as oracles (veḷiccappāṭu), and performed divining and invocation of Bhadrakāḷi. The Kuṟups specialized in visual arts and singing. They became masters at the drawing of kaḷams and the singing of the *kaḷam pāṭṭu* (songs of praise to the deity). Kuṟups were also exclusively entitled to blow the conch and sing *sōpāna saṅgītam* (temple singing as offering) at the daily worship. Mārārs specialized in all aspects of drumming. Both Mārārs and Kuṟups today claim that they once had the exclusive right to perform muṭiyēṯṯu. History books are not at all clear on the subject. In any case, the traditional system required the different Ambalavāsi groups to cooperate; they could not perform each other's work.

Today in central and south-central Kerala, the right to wear the muṭi and enact the role of Bhagavati is the hereditary and exclusive right of members of the Mārār and Kuṟup communities. In the northern regions of Trichur district, the Kuṟups have taken over all aspects of the performance, including music and visual art, whereas in the regions just to the south, now Ernakulam district, Mārārs hold these rights. Nāyars continue to fill the positions of veḷiccappāṭu at Bhagavati temples throughout Kerala, but do not generally participate in muṭiyēṯṯu. Other high-ranking castes who perform ritual dance-dramas in the Bhagavati temples of this region are the Pannikker, Unni, Nambiar, and Chakyar. Ezhavas, classified as 'other backward castes' in the current governmental scheme, as well as the 'scheduled castes' are prohibited from engaging in any of these arts in high-caste temples; however they do perform as priests, veḷiccappāṭus, and kaḷam artists in their own temples.[31]

The Mārārs and Kuṟups were considered as temple employees rather than performing artists. They were not free to accept engagements wherever they chose, but were obligated by legal contracts to perform muṭiyēṯṯu and other rituals at specific times in particular temples. Written agreements existed 'for the remuneration to be given to traditional performers. Tax free lands were assigned to the families of performing artists for the service of performing muṭiyēṯṯu and related arts in Bhagavati temples ... of Cochin and Travancore' (Choondal 1981: 198).[32] These lands could not be sold under penalty of the wrath of the goddess, who would punish the families of the artists with the death of all their children. This feudal system, while limiting the income and freedom of each family, also provided security and order.

The troupe leader, who was also the head of the joint family, received the entire remuneration of rice, oil, and cash and distributed it to the troupe members. With changes in the economic system, this unity began to break down. Today troupes are still composed largely of family members, but they no longer live in a single residential unit. Most recent disputes have arisen around issues of remuneration between family members who are no longer in the same joint family residential unit, and thus have competing interests. Even matters of style have become a problem where authority is not recognized among troupe members who are more or less equal in age and status.

Family wealth consists of the muṭi and costumes for muṭiyēṯṯu, the house and the land of the Mārār or Kuṟup family. The Mārār and Kuṟup communities follow a matrilineal inheritance system (*marumakkattayam*). According to this system, the family property as well as the knowledge and right to perform the temple arts all pass from uncle to nephew through the female bloodline. Thus, the family head is the maternal uncle to the young men in his family (his sister's sons). As *kārṇavar*, he is in charge of all property and decisions for himself and his sisters' families, and usually lives with them.

The Mārār and Kuṟup kinship structure generally follows a classical Dravidian pattern of patrilateral, matrilocal cross-cousin marriages with matrilineal inheritance. In some cases, uncle-niece marriage was practised.[33] This kinship structure leads to members of the same matriline residing together, while patrilines are dispersed. However, it also means that two matrilines are interwoven so that patrilines alternate between households (Trawick 1990b: 127). For the Mārārs, this close interweaving of families served as a guarantee that the property and knowledge of muṭiyēṯṯu would remain strictly within the matrilineal family. In effect, it created a kind of double matrilineal descent, such that consanguineal kin were also affines. As Trawick puts it, 'One crucial feature of Dravidian kinship is that it allows for the existence of matrilines or patrilines or both simultaneously, within a single marriage system' (ibid.: 121).

Naming patterns reflect this effective bilinearity. A person's first name in Kerala is the 'house' name, which is also a family name. Unlike European family names, however, this housename literally is the name of the building which houses the entire ancestral family sharing a single lineage. In the matrilineal system followed by Mārārs and Kuṟups, the housename thus denotes the property inherited through the matriline by all its consanguineal members. (In the patrilineal descent systems of the Brahmins and lower castes, the same rule applies, but to patrilines.) The first name of all siblings born to a given mother in the matrilineal system of descent will thus be her own house/family name.

The second part of the name is the given name of one's significant parent. In a true matrilineal system, one would expect this to be the mother's name for both males and females. However, the Mārārs and Kuṟups I interviewed followed a bilateral naming pattern, so that the girls took their mother's name while boys took their father's name, regardless of the lineage relationship. Women's names don't change at marriage, and they inherit from their mother and mother's brother. The third and last parts of the name are one's own given name and one's caste.[34]

This traditional pattern was complicated in the 1970s when a new law was passed requiring uniform patrilineal naming of children in schools and equal inheritance of property by all children. In the genealogies I collected, this pattern was reflected in the names of children born since the late 1960s. They no longer took their mother's house and given name (for girls), but instead were uniformly using both father's house and given name. As Appu Kuttan Mārār explained, 'Usually the Mārār community followed matriliny, but when I went to school, my father's name was put on the roster instead of my mother's. According to the modern, progressive outlook Kerala has switched over to the patrilineal system.' This remark indicates the prevalent opinion that matriliny is an outmoded, somewhat primitive system which is quite naturally giving way to the 'better' system of patriliny.

Standardized education amongst the Mārār and Kuṟup communities has been less important than it has been for other castes in Kerala. Balakrishnan Mārār's father received no formal education, but learned Sanskrit and all aspects of the traditional culture required for muṭiyēṯṯu. His mother also received no formal education, but learned basic reading of Sanskrit. In Balakrishnan Mārār's generation, third or fourth grade was considered sufficient (just enough to read and write and do simple calculations). He himself completed up to the third grade, and then at the age of eight devoted himself full time to the study of music, dance, and drumming. In his children's generation (those born since 1960), education up to the ninth or tenth grade (the end of secondary school in Kerala) is common. Some of them go on to 'pre-degree' (eleventh and twelfth grade) studies, but none has a college education at present.

Although traditionally there was no intermarriage between Mārārs and Kuṟups, or between these communities and the Nāyars, this has changed significantly in the past generation. Appu Kuttan Mārār is married to a Kuṟup, and according to the matrilineal inheritance system, his son is also a Kuṟup. According to Appu Kuttan, his family had insufficient finances; his wife's family was better off. So his family chose 'to marry up—that is, to marry girls of financially stable families. Women, on the other hand (in matrilineal communities), select for efficiency, smartness, and physique, not employment or finance. The woman realizes that he can earn by physical capacity or mental ability.' The usual Hindu rule of hypergamy, in which the male should always be superior in age, status, and financial stability, seems to be unimportant here. In a matrilineal community, hypergamy would seem to serve little purpose, since a woman's sons will inherit from herself and her brother rather than from their father. A husband who is physically attractive and pleasing would seem to be a better choice for a woman in such a community.

Nearly all the Mārārs reside at their wife's houses (wife's mother's house; matrilineal ancestral property). Houses belonging to members of the matriline tend to cluster on a single large piece of land. The houses are constructed in the traditional style of *nalukeṭṭu*, a four-sided rectangular building with an open courtyard in the centre. The house faces east, and specific activities are relegated to particular areas of the building.[35] The houses are dark and cool, with small windows and little indoor illumination. Many do not have electricity. The kitchen is a square, enclosed room with some vents at the ceiling for smoke to escape. A clay hearth with wood-burning firepits is used for cooking. These small, dark, heavily soiled, windowless rooms are where women spend most of their time. Their resemblance to the claustrophobic inner sancta of Bhagavati temples is striking. Some of the newer houses, however, deviate from this traditional pattern. These cheaper, smaller houses of brick and whitewash are designed for nuclear families, which tend to be the norm in the younger generation. Some love marriages also have taken place among the younger members of the families. In general, the traditional system seems to be changing rapidly.

Although the system of cross-cousin marriage is designed to maintain family unity, in reality it has led in some families to tremendous marital tensions. In the Punnackal family, as far back as three generations, there were accounts of deep spousal tensions leading to long separations; Balakrishnan Mārār's sister, her husband, and their son, all committed suicide due to some undisclosed terrible family misunderstanding. Although the brothers would not state the exact nature of the difficulty, they implied that there was some sexual problem between the spouses which led to a lot of hostility. Balakrishnan Mārār married his bilateral cross-cousin, following family custom, but he and his wife also were separated for some years early in their marriage due to marital difficulties (they are now living peacefully together). Sankara Narayana Mārār and Krishnan Kutty Mārār, Balakrishnan's younger brothers, decided not to marry in the traditional way. Krishnan Kutty, although he was youngest, married first, to a local girl he fell in love with.[36] Sankara Narayana's marriage was arranged to a girl from outside the family.

Krishnan Kutty Mārār (KK): We both, my brother and I, gave up the system of marrying from the same relation. We married outside.
A: You both saw your elder brother's experience and decided not to?
Sankara Narayana Mārār (SN): Well, we did not feel it nice. It was not a very interesting relation. We felt that.
KK: Only our father did not have any bad experience like that. All the others had problems.
SN: Well that is an experience we got from *cettan* (elder brother), so we felt that would be difficult.
KK: That wouldn't be good for a peaceful happy family.
SN: The main reason behind that [cross-cousin marriage] was our property and wealth. That has to stay inside the family, without going outside whatever.
KK: Yes. Earlier we married without accepting dowry.
A: Won't you have to give dowry for your daughters?
KK: Perhaps we may have to give. Now there is no alternative.

The traditional marriage ceremony which Balakrishnan Mārār and his cousin Bhargavi Amma underwent was a simple affair, in which clothing, one coin, and a ring were exchanged at the bride's home. Bhargavi Amma's recollection of the marriage was dim. It didn't seem to have much meaning for her.

> Our marriage? I forget it. A long time has passed, say forty to fifty years back. Am I going to sit around remembering all that? There were some ceremonies at the house, like garlanding each other, exchanging rings, then some presentations and all and after that we came here. Then after coming here, we went back on the fourth day. We kept moving here and there.

Their sons' marriages were conducted recently in the local temple, with the exchange of the *tāli* (wedlock) and receipt of dowry, as is the custom in other castes in Kerala. Nowadays, the daughters-in-law come to reside with their husband's parents, contrary to prior matrilineal custom. Bhargavi Amma's two daughters-in-law were living at home with her and Balakrishnan Mārār when we visited them, although both the sons were working in

Hyderabad. Thus the tradition of a woman living with her own matrilineal kin in a familiar environment after marriage has dissolved, along with the freedom from dowry and the relative autonomy which the older system provided to women. Mārār and Kuṟup brides today must marry in the same way as their patrilineal, patrilocal sisters, a change which is not necessarily to their personal benefit.

Marital relations in the families of performers were at a minimum during the festival season, when men were frequently away from home for long periods of time. Some Mārārs were required to stay at the temple all the time, getting leave to go home only one day or so a month. For these couples, sexual relations were very rare indeed. Even with such restricted relations, of course, women get pregnant. After the temple festival season ends, the monsoon rains come. Pan-Indian erotic associations to the monsoon season are thus naturally reinforced as this is the time when husbands are home and idle. With pregnancy sexual activity is once again curtailed. Although customs vary quite a bit, most Mārārs and Kuṟups we interviewed said that they avoided sexual relations after the first five or six months of the wife's pregnancy. The general belief is that women at this time lose interest in their husbands and feel unwell. Symptoms of vomiting, weakness, and food cravings are mentioned by both men and women. After the baby is born, sex is avoided for another ninety days. In the generation now in their late forties contraception was not practised. Today the younger generation practises family planning, so that most families are limited to two children. Appu Kuttan told us this change was, as with everything else, 'due to economic problems. Earlier in the times of agricultural labour it was beneficial to have more children; now with wage labour, we have to limit it to two.'

Today almost all childbirths take place in the hospital, but amongst the wives of the muṭiyēṯṯu artists now over forty-five years old, childbirths had taken place at home. Remani (Sankara Narayana Mārār's wife) and Radhamani (sister to Balakrishnan, Sankara Narayana, and Krishnan Kutty Mārār) showed me the room where everyone in the family had been born. It was a tiny, dark room about five feet square, at the centre of the house on the western side.

Radhamani (RA): This is the birth room. All the deliveries were right here.
Remani (RE): I've not gone to any hospital.
Q: Was there any light in here?

RA: There was only a *viḷakku* (brass oil lamp) here.
RE: In those days there was no electricity.
Q: So at the time of delivery was there anyone to help you?
RE: There was a nurse. A midwife (*vāyattatti*) [embarrassed laughter].
Q: Was she hospital-trained?
RE: No. Just an ordinary village midwife.
RA: The midwife was a nice person. The pain at that time would last for a whole day. There wasn't much trouble or anything. I delivered four times and all were right here. I had it right in this spot here, lying down.
Q: Is any special food taken at that time?
RA: Raisins and sugar candies are given. After ten or fifteen days there are special medicines. Some Ayurvedic syrups. Then grape paste.
Q: Was any cloth spread during the delivery?
RE: Only a mat.
Q: What do you do with that mat?
RE: That is burned.
Q: What do you do with the placenta?
RA: For that, a small thatched room is made outside [near the toilet, on the western side of the house]. We take bath only in there for fifteen days after the birth. Inside that hut the placenta is buried in a pit in the floor.

The new baby sleeps in the bed with its parents, and is breast-fed until the next child is born (usually two to three years). The Mārār women all told me that discipline was meted out by mothers, starting at 'about one and a half year old. From then they understand what is said. First we say things in a nice way. If that doesn't work, we get angry. When he starts to know what pain is, around three, at that time she starts hitting [to discipline the child].' When I asked if the father also hits the child, Radhamani replied, 'The father doesn't hit. They don't even go in front of their father. We are the people who hit.' Despite these assertions, the men in the family stressed their own mother's sweetness and consoling manner when their father had insulted or hit them. This denial in adulthood of the authoritarian aspect of the mother's persona was common among the males I interviewed, even when it did not conform to the facts as revealed by women in the same families.

All the children below the age of puberty (10–12 years) sleep either in or under the bed of their parents, on mats spread on the floor. For the Punnackal family, there were some eight children sleeping in the room when the current Mārārs were boys. Around puberty, the girls were given a separate room, and the teenage boys slept outside together on the veranda.

The baby is not given a name until around four to six months, when it undergoes the ceremony of first rice feeding. This was an important ceremony in the Mārār and Kuṟup families (as it still is in most Kerala families), at which female children had the tāli-tying ceremony.[37] According to Bhargavi Amma, the baby's mother tied the tāli around the girl's neck. When the child grew older (at puberty), the tāli would be given to the temple. Some rice was given to the baby to eat for the first time, and the mother's brother would name the child, whispering the name into the baby's ear.

One reason the child was not named until so late was the frequency of infant deaths until the last several decades. Bhargavi Amma told me that her mother 'gave birth to nine children and only four children survived. With God's mercy I did not have any trouble with my children.' Radhamani's mother also lost four of her nine children when they were young; one committed suicide as an adult. Today only Radhamani and her three brothers remain. Although she was the youngest, and doesn't remember the details, Radhamani knows that 'Amma [mother] had suffered a lot.' Balakrishnan Mārār, being the eldest, recollected that dark period of his childhood well.

> There was our eldest sister, the one that Amma delivered first. That sister died some forty years back in her fourteenth year. After that immediately elder to [Sankara Narayana] and immediately younger to me, there was a child named Raghavan that also died. I remember that also. I remember all the deaths in my family. All the deaths. There were two immediately elder than Krishnan Kutty. They died as yesterday and today [on two consecutive days]. If any diseases came then, there wasn't any hospital treatment. So some folk medical treatment would be done, and sometimes that wouldn't have any effect. So those two died because of that. It was due to the trouble from dysentery. But the eldest girl died from tetanus when she cut herself with a sickle. In those days injections were not available.

When all these misfortunes were followed some years later by the suicides of Balakrishnan Mārār's sister, her husband, and son, the family decided to conduct an astrological consultation (*praśnam*) to find out the supernatural causes:

> KK: Just to know if it was from *dēvikōpam* [the wrath of the goddess] or due to some anger of the household deities. It was revealed that it was from their anger. Their worship had not been done in the proper

manner. There was pollution in the installation of the idols. So we felt it would be better if that was fixed. After the purification rituals were over, it was very peaceful for us here in all matters.

At menarche, girls in this caste underwent the traditional puberty ceremony (*tiraṇḍukalyāṇam*).[38] As 60-year-old Bhargavi Amma explains here, the elaborate rituals marking the life cycle of the young girl have all declined over the last forty years, and few puberty ceremonies are celebrated today:

All the rituals—*kettukalyāṇam* (tying of the tāli), *pudavakalyāṇam* (giving of the dress at marriage), *tiraṇḍukalyāṇam* (puberty ceremony), *pulikudy kalyāṇam* (a ceremony observed in the seventh month of pregnancy)—that was all during the time of the ancestors. Now all those rituals don't exist. Now everything has been cut down into a single marriage ceremony. Aha! Today you people can't afford it. If you have all those ceremonies for girls and then have to conduct three or four marriages, you would become a pauper. That time is gone. Now even I don't remember it.

A muṭiyēṯṯu troupe, today as in the past, is a family unit. The troupe leader (*āśān*) is normally the eldest male in the family, and as such, makes all important decisions about the organization, management, training, income, and activities of the troupe. In communities following matrilineal inheritance, like the majority of Kuṟup and Mārār families now performing muṭiyēṯṯu, the role of āśān, with its concomitant spiritual power and temporal authority, passed from the maternal uncle (mother's brother) to the nephew (sister's son). Since the 1970s, the matrilineal system of marriage and inheritance has largely given way in the Mārār and Kuṟup communities to a father-son pattern in the transfer of authority. Accordingly, most of the āśāns we interviewed had been trained in muṭiyēṯṯu by their fathers, rather than their uncles. However, they recognized that this represented a fairly recent shift:

The transmission of this authority is through descent. Earlier it used to be from uncle to nephew [in the matriline] but now it has transformed from father to son. My father trained me, but his teacher was his uncle. From my time on it will be my son. My sister's sons have taken other kinds of employment. They are no more interested in this.[39]

The composition of the troupe still consists of closely related male kin, although some members no longer reside in the home of the āśān. Still, despite the breakdown of large joint family living groups, kin still live in close proximity to each other, usually on partitioned portions of their ancestral land. Thus, although household authority may be more diffuse than in the past, distributed among a group of nuclear households, a web of shared economic and sentimental interest still binds the group.

Of all the roles in the muṭiyēṯṯu performance, the most important is clearly the role of Kāḷi. Most āśāns agreed with Balakrishnan Mārār's statement that 'the eldest person is supposed to take the role of Kāḷi'. The troupe leader/household head is therefore often called the *Kāḷi āśān*. According to Balakrishnan Mārār, 'generally nobody takes the role of Kāḷi before the age of fifty. Before that age one is not sufficiently mature for the role. This was the advice given by my father. But he also advised me that if you are put in circumstances that require you to do it, it is okay.' Strength, maturity, and total mastery of all the technical aspects of muṭiyēṯṯu, are expected of the Kāḷi āśān. After all, it is he whose head will carry the sacred muṭi containing Kāḷi's consciousness (*caitanyam*); and whose body the goddess will actually enliven with her power.

The gravity of this responsibility is inseparable from the utter ritual purity required of the artist. It is because of these requirements that women are excluded from participation in any aspect of the performance tradition:

> Muṭiyēṯṯu must be performed with utmost purity. Women are always considered impure. So it cannot be taken over by females ritually. Muṭiyēṯṯu is a temple art. In general there is no scope for females in any of the temple arts. They are not included and they have no importance.[40]

The concern with ritual propriety and purity is integral to the tradition of temple service. As muṭiyēṯṯu is 'the most important ritual offering done in Bhagavati temples', according to the artists who perform it, 'the person who plays the role of Kāḷi has to undergo certain rules in his daily life (*noyimbu*).' These austerities must be observed throughout the six-month performance season, from December through April, when performances may run consecutively for a number of weeks. 'During this season we mostly take *noyimbu*. We never take non-vegetarian food or alcohol. We sleep next to our wife but may not have sex with her. All these instructions are given by our ancestors. When this season comes, I do it very promptly.'[41] Fasting and sexual continence are absolutely required for one day before a performance as a form of self-purification. Before beginning the make-up for the role of Kāḷi on the day of the performance, a ritual bath is taken. Only food which has been offered to the goddess (including various forms of popped or parched rice, jaggery, plantains, and milk) may be taken during the day. Only ritually washed cloths (washed by the Veluttedan Nāyar community, a high caste of ritual servants) may be worn for the costume of Kāḷi. After completing the make-up and costume, the actor is no longer a mere human being. He should neither touch nor talk to anyone at this point until after the performance is completed.

These careful ritual injunctions prepare the Kāḷi actor for the transformation his consciousness will undergo during muṭiyēṯṯu:

> While the actor adorns his head with the flower from Kāḷi's seat he gets mentally prepared, identifying himself with Kāḷi. Then onwards, till the completion, the actor will be Kāḷi. When Narayana Kuṟup plays the role of Kāḷi it is not Narayana Kuṟup on the stage but Kāḷi herself. After taking the role of Kāḷi the actor would be conscious only of Kāḷi within half an hour. No other thoughts will come to his mind. The actor who plays Kāḷi with the heavy crown on his head gets the vigour and power of Kāḷi gradually.[42]

The ritual power cultivated and released in the Kāḷi actor's performance benefits the entire community. The offering of muṭiyēṯṯu 'is performed to make Bhadrakāḷi happy and to get some useful boon. This is to get rid of diseases, to get good crops in the field, and also to get blessings' (Balakrishnan Mārār). The eradication of fever diseases is in fact one of the principal aims:

> In the past muṭiyēṯṯu was performed as a medicinal ritual. It is said that when any family got affected by smallpox they would make an offering to conduct a performance of muṭiyēṯṯu. Then the disease would be cured. In those days the significance of this performance was mainly as a ritual offering. Recently the artistic value of the performance was recognized. But the basis remains as it was. Muṭiyēṯṯu is performed for pleasing Kāḷi. (V. Narayana Kuṟup)

Muṭiyēṯṯu can only be performed in a Bhagavati temple, whether public or private. As a religious offering, it can only be undertaken with the strict observance of proper ritual procedures. If these rules are not followed, Bhagavati may become angry and heap misfortune on the families of the negligent parties. Because of this requirement, an intimate cooperative relationship exists between the communities of performing artists and the temples where muṭiyēṯṯu is performed. These relationships have been drastically altered by economic and political changes since 1947. The future of muṭiyēṯṯu will be determined by the flexibility of the system to adapt to these changes.

Before Indian Independence, all temples were owned privately by large upper caste families. These included Nambūtiri Brahmins, royal families, and Nāyars. Nāyar temples were located within their residential taravāḍus, and meant for family use. Entry to Nambūtiri and Kṣatriya temples was restricted to these upper castes. The vast properties owned by the upper-caste landlords were dismantled and redistributed to bonded labourers by the Communist government elected in 1957. This redistribution, combined with strong unions and intensive education programmes, improved Kerala's standard of living dramatically. Temples were opened to all Hindus, and lost their exclusive caste restrictions. While the egalitarian reforms vastly improved life for most Malayalis, they inevitably reduced the wealth of the temples. Patronage of ritual arts was no longer a guarantee, nor was it based on feudal relationships. Some temples did remain in private hands, but as village governing boards took over the management of the temples, the fate of muṭiyēṯṯu and other arts lay in the will of the community at large.

Although muṭiyēṯṯu is usually performed by prior contractual agreement with specific temples, individuals and families often sponsor particular performances. This may mean paying for the costs of the performance already scheduled at the temple, and receiving the blessings from the rituals. Alternatively, an individual may commission a special performance of muṭiyēṯṯu on behalf of his family during the regular festival season, even if it has not previously been sponsored at the temple. Lastly, families with large homes can occasionally sponsor muṭiyēṯṯu at their residences. Whenever muṭiyēṯṯu is performed as a special offering, the motivations are usually the same. Appu Kuttan Mārār explained, 'Muṭiyēṯṯu is performed as an offering if we are under some bad situation like diseases or financial crisis or even for getting a job. It is also done by couples in order to have children. [In these cases] it is done as an offering to Bhagavati by the required people.'

The theme of disease is very important. Muṭiyēṯṯu was frequently performed in the past to alleviate smallpox. When a family member became ill, someone would make a vow to the goddess that if the patient was cured, they would sponsor muṭiyēṯṯu at the temple.

> There is a belief among the people that if they don't sponsor a performance after vowing to offer it, there would be some bad effects on them. That is absolutely true. People especially picture that related to smallpox. Say if you offer something to Bhadrakāḷi and don't fulfil it there is a belief that you'd get smallpox. That is in the Malayali mind since very olden times. Nearly fifty years ago there was a lot of smallpox. Now there is no smallpox, only chickenpox. Even if chickenpox comes it is said to be due to Bhadrakāḷi's anger. If a Malayali gets chickenpox, immediately the family will go to Bhadrakāḷi's temple and worship and make these vows. After the disease is cured, we take bath and go to the Bhadrakāḷi temple and make some offering there.[43]

Muṭiyēṯṯu must be performed mainly because of the whims of the goddess. It is simply her desire that we do so. Misfortunes are interpreted by villagers as manifestations of Bhagavati's power. That this power is occasionally harmful to humans is simply an accident of nature, and part of the order of things. The only remedy is to comply. The account of the origin of the Kalambukavu Bhagavati temple at Kanjiramattom by an eighty-year-old man living nearby illustrates this idea.

> The Dēvi (goddess) here faces the west and she is the form of Bhadra ['the auspicious one'; an ironic epithet meant to induce the goddess's mercy]. The western orientation indicates power.[44] This temple used to be in a dense forest. The route to the temple of her elder sister used to be through the forest.[45] On Tuesdays and Fridays the goddess would be pulled by chariot to her sister's temple at midnight. People who lived on this route had a lot of problems. The astrologer was consulted and he said that people who want to prosper should live somewhere else. It's not the Dēvi's fault. She does not do that intentionally. If someone interferes with her route they will get a problem. So people do offerings and ask her not to harm them too much. It is her nature to be powerful, and it's just our bad luck if we are in her way.[46]

The ritual power evoked in muṭiyēṯṯu is concentrated in the sacred headgear, the muṭi. The muṭi and costumes are the wealth of performing families, their most prized heirlooms. As such, they must be handled and kept with great care: 'My father told me how the muṭi was made and how you have to respect it. You mustn't keep this anywhere near places where women are menstruating [a particular room used by women at that time]. It should be kept in a special room in the house' (Pazhur Damodaran Mārār). The muṭi is kept in the family store room (*ara*) in the centre of the house, along with other valuables like cooking vessels, jewellery, rice stores, and pūjā items.

The muṭi is more than a ritual item. It represents the whole lineage of ancestors (kārṇavars) whose dedication and care have preserved it. The love and regard in which the muṭi is held was eloquently expressed by Pazhur Damodaran Mārār as he showed us an ancestral headgear handed down through his family for generations:

> This is an ancient muṭi, some 500 years old. It is from my father's grandfather's time. It has been done very beautifully. I thought to repair it, but you know if we work on that it would lose its value. So I thought not to do that and leave it as our ancestors had it. I could keep the memories of our kārṇavars who wore it alive in my mind. I had thought to give it to the Archaeological Department, then finally I thought no, let that stay in our family to show our tradition. Let our children also know that they own this tradition. Let it not be destroyed, let it stay. So I preserved it.[47]

Training in all the aspects of muṭiyēṯṯu is conducted at the home of the āśān, taking place during the rainy season from June to November, when no performances are conducted. The majority of training is done in the early morning hours, with additional time spent in the evening, at dusk and even after supper:

> Generally boys start training from the age of five. The training should begin before sunrise. First they should make the body flexible by exercises. The body will be rubbed with oil and different steps will be taken as exercise. In the evening one hour will be spent on training. Training should last this way for at least five years. Then only will they be able to perform perfectly.[48]

Other artists considered the period of training to be longer: 'If you really study this it would take twelve years. Only then you can do something' (Krishnan Kutty Mārār). The reason for this lengthy training period is the vast field of arts that must be mastered by the muṭiyēṯṯu performer. 'For this art *nrttya-gīta-vādhya* (dance, song, and drumming/music) are essential. Even though acting is not a must, rhythmic footsteps with knowledge of music are essential. We did not have any other kind of education and we were deeply involved in this. We made this our life's work, to preserve it' (Pazhur Damodaran Mārār).

Starting at the age of six to eight, the boy begins to learn each of these requisite skills in a particular order: first the basics of sōpāna sangītam, the traditional style of votive singing practised in Kerala temples; then drumming and basic rhythm cycles; and lastly the roles and steps for each character in muṭiyēṯṯu. Balakrishnan Mārār described some of the rigours involved in learning the steps:

> During the night we go to some barren area where there is silence. All the students along with my father will practise spinning and the footsteps such as running, jumping, and spinning. The half-turns are of three different types—back-leaning, spinning on one leg, and going around the lamp halfway. We learn this after 8 or 9 p.m., after dinner. Once I got very ill and vomited but my father just made me get up and do it again. In this way I learned to endure it.[49]

The training in dance steps and fighting tactics is clearly related to the Kaḷarippayaṯṯ martial arts tradition still cultivated in Kerala, although the exact historical relationships have not been traced:

> It is said that the fencing or gymnastic exercises in kaḷarippayaṯṯ and the war scene of muṭiyēṯṯu are similar. It is difficult to say exactly because in kaḷarippāyaṯṯ the types of exercises are many, whereas in muṭiyēṯṯu the Kāḷi–Dārika battle passes through just eight or nine types of exercises. However these are similar to kaḷarippāyaṯṯ'. (V. Narayana Kuṟup)

Both the martial title 'Kuṟup' and the existence of Bhagavati temples converted from active kaḷaris indicate that in feudal Kerala the martial arts and ritual dramatic traditions were intimately related. It seems likely that the training for muṭiyēṯṯu and for actual war exercises was once conjoined. Balakrishnan Mārār and his brothers claimed that their father, Punnackal Kunju Mārār, was fully trained in the kaḷari tradition, including daily full-body massage for flexibility, complete weaponry training, and mastery of fighting steps and blocks. He was also initiated into tantric Srī Vidyā Śākta worship, and had full knowledge of the esoteric meaning of the Sri Yantra and its relation to the drawing of the Bhagavati kaḷam for muṭiyēṯṯu. The Śākta tantric tradition was an integral part of traditional kaḷari training, as this esoteric knowledge gave the warrior extra strength to win in battle. These days this tradition has largely been lost. Although muṭiyēṯṯu artists today must also learn some steps, sword-fighting and blocking, these techniques are very simplified. 'After father's time nobody bothered with this kaḷari and all. No one took pains for that, mainly as the income was decreasing and we were forced to take outside work. That is why people don't look into that any more' (Krishnan Kutty Mārār).

The tradition of muṭiyēṯṯu has been maintained by three different families located in central Kerala. While remaining remarkably faithful to the dictates of tradition, each of these families has inevitably developed a distinct style that can be distinguished regionally. The three styles are centred in Koratty (southern Trichur district); Pazhur and Piravom (central Ernakulam district); and Muvattupuzha (eastern Ernakulam district) (see map, Fig. 1). The troupe leaders currently affiliated with each of the three styles are as follows:

1. **Koratty**
   Varanattu Narayana Kuṟup (E. Koratty)
   Varanattu Sankara Kuṟup
   Varanattu Narayana Kuṟup (W. Koratty)
2. **Piravom**
   Pazhur Damodaran Mārār
   Keezhillam Gopalakrishnan
   Appu Kuttan Mārār
3. **Muvattupuzha**
   P. Narayana Mārār
   Rama Kuṟup[50]

The stylistic differences among these three groups are seen in: (1) the staging of the entrance of Kāḷi; (2) the makeup style of Dārika and Danavendra; (3) the use of the curtain; (4) the role of Kūḷi; (5) the role of the drummer/troupe leader in subduing Kāḷi. The texts sung by the three troupes do not differ substantially from each other, despite the fact that this is an oral tradition. But like many ritual oral traditions in India, the songs of muṭiyēṯṯu are not subject to individual modification and variation (they are not formulaic). These are memorized verbatim and consciously maintained as much as possible in their 'pure' unadulterated form. Some differences can be detected however, especially in the texts from Muvattupuzha, which appear to be older, having a larger admixture of Tamil.[51]

Traditionally, each family operates in a particular territory under hereditary agreements with specific temples. As temple service relationships have disintegrated in the decades since Independence, however, these distinct separations in territory have occasionally been transgressed. Keen competition has arisen, resulting in frequent disagreements, hostilities, and splintering of the troupes into the eight which remain today. These difficulties have arisen because of the loss of security previously provided by the feudal temple system. Although their remuneration in those days was modest, the Mārārs and Kuṟups had the leisure to dedicate themselves entirely to their art. The unquestioned authority of the kārṇavar, and the channelling of all finances directly into his hands, gave no room for disputes and accusations. As the family lived together as one unit, sharing all resources, their unity and utter obedience to the kārṇavar's will ultimately benefited all. With the advent of democratic political processes, Communist land reform, and the disintegration of the feudal system, such unity simply could not be maintained. As resources have become strained, traditional training is no longer possible:

> In the past we got food, rice, paddy, money, and different items from the temple. We didn't have to look for anything else in the family. In those times the elders could sit at home with their children and teach them. Now nothing like that is possible nor does it exist. Now if the kārṇavars (family heads) don't do any outside work, they cannot thrive. In the temple there is nothing available. In this way all the art forms are becoming extinct. It started getting extinct from 1947, when the new amendments and new bills were passed.
>
> After our generation there is no one to study this and take it over. That is the problem. Wherever you go—Piravom, Koratty, or Muvattupuzha, you won't find the younger generation interested in this. It is work requiring great sacrifice. Most people cannot afford [to dedicate the necessary time to] it. Even doing all these arts well, I am not able to take proper care of my family. No one would be willing to undertake the study of this art facing such difficulties. I don't see any further improvement in our fortunes in the future. That is the situation of this profession. Those are the facts.[52]

However great the desire and faith of the Mārārs and Kuṟups may be, they cannot live without food. The financial support of the temples is insufficient to provide them with a decent livelihood. Other sources of sponsorship must come to the fore. The cultural ministries centred in Kerala and in Delhi have attempted to provide such support in the form of stipends and scholarships to deserving artists. But this contact with government funding agencies has been a mixed blessing, apparently benefiting some artists, but not others. Most seriously, this contact has divided the few living artists irrevocably, spreading their rare talents even more thinly. Under these circumstances, the future of muṭiyēṯṯu is uncertain.

Fieldwork, Backstage

My first impressions of Kerala, as my husband, my daughter and I got off the plane in Cochin and bargained with a taxi for the two-hour drive to Trichur, were disoriented and depressed. The first hour and a half of our drive was spent on a side lane of the city of Ernakulam completely stalled in traffic due to a political rally which had completely paralysed the city. We soon discovered that our irritated frustration was useless to effect any kind of change in our luck. There was nothing to do but wait. Once we finally got moving again, and the taxi passed the outskirts of the town, I began to take in some of the scenery around us. Contrary to my expectation that I would love Kerala, with each passing kilometre the sweltering heat and utterly alien landscape seemed more and more like a prison. My heart sank as I thought, 'What am I doing here?'

Our arrival in town was no more heartening. The lanes of Trichur were a nightmare to navigate, with no street signs of any kind to direct us. Our taxi driver knew nothing of the topography, and there was not a soul to be seen. Everyone seemed to be asleep inside, out of the hot noonday sun. Somehow we found our way to the small, dark house that was to be our residence. This too was a disaster. We soon found that instead of having the house to ourselves, as I had been led to believe, we had been allocated a single dark room without a bath in the very small home of a young widow with two teenage children. Our first night, with thousands of mosquitoes, oppressive heat, and frequent trips outside to a bare stone bathroom, was a nightmare. It turned out the next day that my academic guide, Dr Thomas, was out of town—about 1,500 miles away, at a conference in Kashmir. He was not expected for about two weeks. I was desperate.

Fortunately for us, an ex-student of Dr Thomas's showed up the next morning and offered to help. He dedicated the following week entirely to helping us relocate to a new and more modern, private apartment (thereby forfeiting our Rs 5,000 deposit, which the landlady refused to return), finding an appropriate field assistant, and staffing our household with a cook, child-care, washerwoman, and other necessary personnel. By the time Dr Thomas showed up, we had our organization fully in place. Dr Thomas was not at all pleased with the situation. He pounced on my field assistant and began to quiz him, actually administering a written test on Kerala folklore. He shouted at my household help, and told me stories of the horrendous experiences he had had with previous American scholars, particularly women.

'You must have a female field assistant!' he asserted. He told me of an American woman who had come to Kerala a few years ago who allegedly had had a scandalous affair with one of her informants, become pregnant, and caused a terrible mess. 'This sort of thing must be avoided at all costs', he said. Dr Thomas then sat down to draw up lists of places I must go, people I must see, schedules and charts. I began to be a bit alarmed, as I saw that he understood our association to be one in which he supervised all of my activities and I merely provided financing and clout to achieve his goals. This was not at all what I had in mind. Yet I felt some reticence in expressing my views, being much younger, a stranger, and a woman. I knew I didn't like what was happening, but I didn't know what to do.

Through a kind of passive resistance, I ended up simply holding my ground and ignoring most of Dr Thomas's advice, while pretending to accept it. I soon discovered, by talking with another American scholar who had two decades of experience working in Trichur and knew Dr Thomas well, that he had a somewhat unsavoury reputation. This reputation seemed to hover around issues of women, alcohol, and money. There was no dearth of gossip in Trichur society, as I soon discovered, and before long I had heard it all. No matter about that, I thought. He knows his subject and I can handle him. Little did I know how vulnerable I really was.

In my efforts to be a faithful 'participant observer', I purposely cut myself off from any western network and totally immersed myself in local culture. The few foreigners I met seemed to regard me as a curiosity, with my Kerala saris and prim behaviour. Most were in Kerala to study drama, music, and dance; not being anthropologists, they felt no need to alter their western personas to accomplish these aims. This put a distance between us. My friends were all Malayalis. This gave my fieldwork great depth, as I became truly dependent upon those around me, and was not free to disregard the social network in which I was embedded. But it had the disadvantage that when I inevitably came into serious conflict with that system, I had no support to speak of. This dilemma threw me on my own inner resources in a unique way.

What became clear very quickly was that as an American scholar with a large grant, I was a commodity, to be bought, charmed, worshipped, coerced, threatened, and exploited. The very fact of my white skin (my husband, a Guatemalan, looked more like a 'fair-skinned' local) seemed to pigeonhole me immediately, no matter how hard I might try to blend in by my dress, manners, or behaviour. This of course was a blessing at times, but also an annoyance and often a hindrance. In any case, there seemed to be little hope of having any sincere or 'interest-free' interactions with people who had too much to gain and nothing to lose by their association with us. Within weeks, I began to receive cards and letters from people I barely knew, telling me their innermost troubles and requesting my assistance in getting them to the United States. A jeweller from whom I had bought a pair of ear rings sent me an effusive, emotional card with a twelve-page letter describing his health problems and asking me to assist him. People who pressed me relentlessly to come to their homes for lavish meals later complained bitterly about my failure to help get their sons into American schools. I was overwhelmed by the hospitality, neediness, and subtle coercion of those around me, whose intentions I often didn't understand yet whom I only wanted to please. I also found that people were unused to relating to one another as unique individuals. Local proverbs cynically commented on the hypocritical nature of social relations, in which no one, not even one's brother, could really be trusted. To my dismay, I soon saw that few were likely to perceive me as 'myself'; I, like everyone else, was simply a pawn in an elaborate social game.

Another serious impediment I encountered was the impression of westerners held by nearly everyone I met in Kerala. There seemed to be three major stereotypes about Americans (although these applied to Europeans and Australians as well) that I constantly encountered:

1. *Americans don't love their children.* For Malayalis, this lack of affection was clearly evidenced by the American customs of leaving kids alone at home or putting them in front of the TV; making children sleep alone in separate rooms (which was

considered abusive); putting children in boarding schools (although this is more an English than an American custom, and one which is imitated by the upper classes in Kerala); adhering to rigid bedtime and feeding schedules; and weak family ties. People spoke with disgust about rebellious American teenagers who disobey and are rude to their parents. They expressed surprise when I held Sofia on my lap and kissed her, kept her with me for fieldwork, and seemed to love her in a way that was familiar to them. I found myself saying more than once, 'Well, we are all just human beings, the same everywhere.'

2. *Americans have no morality*. This was made clear by the immodest dress of European women tourists (showing upper arms and legs); the fact that women move about independently, that western people have multiple sexual partners, that they divorce. The impression of immorality was strongly reinforced by ever-present topless female sunbathers at Kovalam beach (who all appeared to be Europeans), as well as pornographic videos and movies imported from western countries. Pictures of nude white men and women in explicit sexual postures were a common sight in movie ads, rated 'A' for adult, posted openly at bus-stands and roadsides. Nude sex scenes from American feature films are also cut indiscriminately into local Malayalam-language feature films by distributors to increase daytime business (teenage boys tend to go at that time).

3. *Americans are all very rich*. The few Americans and Europeans who visit Kerala, though not necessarily wealthy by standards of their own countries, appear totally unfettered. They stay in the best hotels, completely out of reach of most Malayalis. They don't seem to have to do any work (hippies, tourists, etc.). Again my industriousness was a surprise to them; my apparent wealth was not.

The bad press given to Americans in particular is due in part to their relative scarcity in Kerala (only a handful of people I met had previously encountered an American), and to the negative propaganda of the Communist government during the decades of the 1960s through the 1980s. Siding with the then Soviet Union and North Vietnam during most of this period, Communist sympathizers portrayed America as a grotesque, bloated exploiter. The few Americans who came to Kerala during those years often experienced problems with their work, especially if it had to do with low-caste communities, where Communism was most popular. All this created a difficult environment in which to create a good first impression. Obviously we would have to work very hard at being visibly good citizens. This mostly required me to modify my behaviour, adopting the dress, diet, and habits of an upper-class, educated Malayali woman. I could not fully achieve the desired effect, however, as my work required me to travel, be out at night, and have much more contact with men than would be acceptable for any Kerala female.

I took seriously Dr Thomas's suggestion that I try to find a female field assistant to assist me, especially in working with women. The sex-segregated nature of Kerala society made this an imperative. However, despite concerted efforts over several months, it was impossible to find anyone suitable. Young unmarried women simply would not be let out of the house to roam about with an American lady at all hours of day and night; married women had too many important duties at home and their reputations to protect. The interviews I did conduct with women were nearly all accomplished with the help of Laji, my young male field assistant. The quality of their responses is a tribute to his sensitivity and social skills. Despite his gender and youth, Laji was often able to put all kinds of people at ease and gain their trust. This worked especially well with people who were not of high status in the society; older, high-status men often treated him with disdain. In some cases Dr Thomas helped me with the interviews; and a young woman did accompany me on one occasion. Some educated women who spoke English well could communicate their thoughts to me directly, but this was limited to one or two cases.

One of the most important aspects of my research agenda was the matter of being allowed into the temples. Kerala is notoriously conservative in this regard, and does not allow non-Hindus into Hindu places of worship. This is no doubt one of the reasons for the dearth of anthropological studies of high-caste art forms like muṭiyēṯṯu by western ethnographers. I consider myself to be a believing Hindu, though cognizant of the problems inherent in such a claim, and was fully prepared to undergo the 'conversion' ceremonies offered by the local Arya Samaj. My family and I travelled to the city of Calicut to the Arya Samaj offices, where we were instructed to bathe, change our clothes, and perform a Vedic *homa* (fire sacrifice), in which we would shed our old identities and become Hindus. We took Hindu names of our own choosing (I became Amba), and as our names were being inscribed into a book, an official asked me, 'What caste do you choose?' (one cannot be a Hindu without a caste, it seems). In a moment of inspiration I chose Nāyar. I think the matrilineal history and legendary sexual freedom of Nāyar women must have played a part in my inspiration; I felt a certain defiant glee in voluntarily rejecting the status of a Brahmin. An official conversion certificate was issued to each member of my family, allowing us access into the temples. We were now—quite artificially of course—adopted members of Kerala society.

The personae that were eventually constructed for us by our host society are well illustrated in an interview that appeared in the national newspaper *The Indian Express* (Krishnan 1992). The subheading of the article, entitled 'At Home in an Alien Land', conveys the general flavour: 'They look like any Keralite family. But the American anthropologist, her husband and daughter have adopted India out of love, and Sara [sic] is busy unearthing the forgotten Keralite art of Mudiyettu.' Although I had no desire to publicize my visit, a good friend insisted on conducting the interview so his cousin could get a promotion at his new job working as a reporter for the newspaper. As I owed this friend a favour, I felt I could not decline the interview. The article received enormous attention. Wherever we went in Trichur after that, people knew our names and faces. Even my liaison officer at the Fulbright office in Delhi wrote to me that she had seen it, and why hadn't I sent them a copy? I somewhat resented having the article published at all, even though it was well written and rather flattering. I felt very uncomfortable with the publicity, as if we were movie stars. The person who wrote the article later broke off all relations with me in an offended huff, as he felt I had not shown sufficient gratitude for his efforts to publicize me (something most Malayalis would eagerly welcome). This incident illustrates the kind of misunderstandings that can arise in such a tangled web of subtle social obligations and divergent cultural values.

All of this 'backstage' drama is an essential part of understanding the process of impression management that inevitably constructed the ethnographic results I have presented in this work.[53] As outlined in the Prelude, my consistent foregrounding of this backstage area through excerpts from my own and Laji's journals, as well as presentation of direct quotes in interviews, is an attempt to open the entire project, both process and results, to view. Only by doing this is it possible to deconstruct the 'authority' of the ethnographic voice and reveal the complexity of power relations in fieldwork, especially when conducted by a woman.

A local scholar of folk arts was well aware of the tendency of scholars, both indigenous and foreign, to distort the way they collect and use ethnographic data. He made this clear as he advised me on how to go about studying muṭiyēṯṯu.

> Now what she [Sarah] should do is see the original performers. In my opinion she should not go to scholars, those who took Ph.D. and doctorate. See them only at the end. Otherwise you won't get anything. These people who get Ph.D. have got their information exploiting people like us. Then they write it down to their credit and get royalties for that. So what I tell is taken by Laji and what Laji says is only what she gets. At the same time, she is not getting into the original matter. So there is not much chance of a significant study.[54]

In such an environment, an ethnographer has a deep responsibility to behave in a fair manner towards those s/he is studying. Even unwittingly, we can seem to hurt people who have taken pains to help us, simply by failing to visit, write an occasional letter, or to do some small thing for them in return. Certainly they expect to receive some remuneration or at least a mention in the ethnographer's book. A small incident made this imperative poignantly clear to me. When after a lengthy search we finally located an aged muṭiyēṯṯu troupe leader, P. Narayana Mārār, at his home in eastern Muvattupuzha, his family welcomed us cautiously. As they asked us to sit down, someone went to call the aged actor. Well over 80 years old, Narayana Mārār had never married due to health problems in his youth. Clad only in a single tattered orange loincloth, he came out to meet us supported by a wooden stick. After being told at loud volume (he is almost deaf) of our purpose in visiting him, Narayana Mārār began to shout, 'Aha! Yes! I met one American once. He came here nearly twenty years ago and talked to me and took tape-recordings of my songs. Wait! I have his name right here.' Unrolling a grimy pouch in the waist of his loincloth, Narayana Mārār's trembling fingers rustled through a few tiny scraps of paper and coins he kept there. Delighted, he held out his gnarled hand and handed me a yellowed shred of paper. On it was the name of a scholar who had written on Kerala arts. When I expressed familiarity with the name, we had a lively exchange for a few moments. But after his initial enthusiasm, Narayana Mārār began to complain. 'You know, I've carried this paper all these years. He said he would come back and see me. He said he would write to us. We never got a copy of his book. We never heard anything from him. Why should I cooperate with you now?' I had no answer to give as I looked at the pale, watery eyes behind the great white beard.[55]

[Excerpt from a letter home]
4 January 1992

As for Trichur, our home, it is a peculiar melange of communist activists, ancient Hindu rituals, noisy auto-rickshaws, goats, chickens, and endless coconut palms waving in the hot breeze. It's a land full of poetry. There is truly no way to appreciate or understand the magnificent, mysterious rituals we are studying without being immersed in the physical environment of this place. The natural world has rich symbolic meaning in Kerala art and life. But to say it has 'rich symbolic meaning' is an irritating betrayal of the sense of the thing. The notes of the drums and cymbals, the blazing torches in the midnight hours reflecting off the golden caparisons of elephants carrying brilliant deities around a grove of trees in the temple seep into my soul, and give meaning and life to all the slides I saw of stone archways with heavy-breasted yakṣis merging or emerging from trees on temple gates, sitting in classrooms back home.

All this is not to say it's been unmitigated joy. My husband especially is having a very hard time adjusting. Besides the disorientation, loneliness, and heat, he is extremely jealous towards the men I have to work with. The attitude towards women here is extremely conservative, which is not what I expected of Kerala. This has fascinating consequences from the point of view of my studies, and the meaning of the Bhagavati cult; but from the point of view of my marriage, it's disastrous. Coming from a similar (though not as extreme) macho culture, my husband is excessively possessive of me and concerned about my image. Being here seems to have awakened all of his buried feelings about being from a 'third world' country (he has not been back to Guatemala for 14 years since he left there), and he is behaving in ways I have never seen before. He doesn't trust any young unmarried man as far as he can throw him, to be alone with me. Result: he feels compelled to accompany me everywhere every minute, and never lets me do my work with my assistant unless he is there. Would be fine, except he doesn't like the work much, the stress, the travelling, the exhaustion, the feeling of being a second fiddle, *inutil* (useless), purposeless. He gave up his job to come here with me, on my income, for my project, and he just seems to be between a rock and a hard place. He seems to try to bury his misery alternately in beer and meditation. I can only pray that with time he will mellow out a bit and find his own niche. The next four months are going to be very stressful, as we must travel and observe many ritual performances around Kerala during this festival season.

At the same time I am also developing a real love for the goddess Bhagavati. She's something wild and powerful and ancient. She holds various weapons in her hands. She is hot, full of rage, sexually dangerous, but also a loving mother whose blessing ensures prosperity and fertility. She is a mother, a virgin, and a warrior. She resides in a special tree, she loves the colour red, she loves blood, coloured powders, music and dance, and humour. She is covered with smallpox, but she is beautiful. She is evoked and feared by her devotees, who hope to control her through the performances they do. She is beautiful and fierce. She is the forest.

It will be incredibly weird to return to the US after another year of this. I truly feel I am on another planet in another *yuga* [era] altogether.

Notes

[1] The term 'Bhagavati' generally refers in Kerala to the generic Devi. It can indicate a benevolent form of the goddess, and may even refer to Pārvati, Sarasvati, or other pleasing incarnations. The name Bhadrakāḷi, on the other hand, refers unequivocally to the goddess in her violent form. I routinely heard the names Bhagavati, Kāḷi, Dēvi, and Bhadrakāḷi used interchangeably, sometimes in the same sentence.

[2] Malayali means a speaker of Malayalam, the language of Kerala.

[3] See Thampuran 1936; Obeyesekere 1984: 600–2.

[4] Before the Temple Entry Act of 1936, all devotees but Brahmins were prohibited from entering into the inner courtyard of the temple. Today, all may enter the courtyard and stand before the deity, but only priests may enter the sanctum and touch the deity's idol.

[5] See Caldwell forthcoming(a).

[6] See Richmond, Swann, and Zarrilli 1990; Konow 1969.

[7] Published studies of muṭiyēṯṯu include Choondal (1981); Chandrahasan (1989); Nāyar (1962); Venu (1984); Vidyarthi (1976); and sections of Tarabout (1986).

[8] Historical sources mention the region as far back as the fourth century BCE. For general Kerala history, see Achyutha Menon 1961; Jeffrey 1976; Krishna Ayyar 1966; Krishna Iyer 1968–70; Kunjan Pillai 1970; Leela Devi

1986; Logan 1951; Mateer 1883; K. S. Mathew 1979; K. P. P. Menon 1986; Shungoonny Menon 1878; Sreedhara Menon 1967.

[9] The Nambūtiri Brahmins are culturally distinct from other south Indian Brahmins, due to their isolation and antiquity as a group in Kerala. See Abraham 1960.

[10] Despite recent critiques of 'essentializing' constructs, the term Dravidian (which originated to describe a distinct language group found in contemporary south India) is commonly used by indigenous scholars of the region, as well as by non-Indian scholars, to describe a linguistic, cultural, and to some extent physical complex of people tracing their origin to the ancient Tamil-speaking culture area of southern India. This usage is increasingly problematic due to its association with various political, historical, and scholarly agendas that seek to reify a 'pure' Tamil past supposedly free of Indo-Aryan linguistic and cultural influences. (See Ramaswamy 1993, 1997). Scholars are increasingly coming to view the situation in ancient south Asia as one of continual admixture of different languages and cultures over very long periods of time, such that it is nearly impossible to identify a 'pure' Dravidian or Sanskrit free of mutual influence. Despite these caveats, I concur with Kersenboom's cautious identification of 'the period of pre-300 AD as ... reflecting the most "intact" picture of Tamil society we can know of historically' 1981: 32. The characteristics ascribed in the following discussion to 'Dravidian' culture and religion are meant to refer to this pre-300 AD period, which shows relatively little influence from Vedic religious ideas and practices, and to later periods in the south where the same religious ideas hold sway.

[11] Gentes 1992 and Obeyesekere 1984; chapters 13 and 14 discuss the ancient relationships between Hindu, Buddhist, and Jain ideas, and their possible interaction with West Asian religion; see also Parpola 1994.

[12] For discussion of Kerala temple architecture, see Bernier 1982; Kramrisch 1953; Vatsyayan 1989; Coomaraswamy 1938 discusses dome symbolism.

[13] For history of *yakṣas*, see Agrawala 1966, 1971; Coomaraswamy 1971; Moti Chandra 1952–3; Sutherland 1991. A similar process of transformation occurs in Bengal and Orissa, in the cults of Sitala, Manasa, and Tara.

[14] Page references for Choondal 1981 are to the Malayalam text; translations were completed by L. S. Rajagopalan.

[15] The *Bhadrakāḷi Māhātmyam* is recited daily by upper castes; the text is also called *Bhadrōḷpati* or *Saptaśati* (P. P. G. Pillai 1956: 102–3). Choondal (1981: 157) summarizes textual versions in Malayalam.

[16] Kinsley 1975; Peterson (1989) and Hiltebeitel 1991 mention the story in footnotes; an account is present under the unlikely title 'Ghantakarna' in Mani 1975. Shulman states that the Tamil text *Tirukkūvam*, contains a version of this legend 1980: 103, n. 64. Peterson 1989: 172–3, n. 82 refers to an account of the myth of Kāḷi and Dāruka in the *Tēvāram Kaḻakam* edition,

verse 6. The *Śilappadikāram* also contains a reference to 'Durga who tore apart the broad chest of Dāruka' (Ilankovatikal 1993: 188), indicating the antiquity of this legend (at least 1500 years).

[17] See also C. A. Menon 1959.

[18] Collected in Malayalam from V. Narayana Kuṟup, Trichur, Kerala, January 1992, and Appu Kuttan Mārār, Muvattupuzha, Kerala, May 1992. For full original versions, see Caldwell 1995: 33–6.

[19] In written versions it is Brahma who asks Dārika why he has not asked to be assured that he would not be killed by a woman; Dārika replies that such a thing is ridiculous and unthinkable. Brahma then curses him. In one version told to me by a woman, Pārvati appears and asks Dārika why he has not asked for the boon of protection from death at the hands of a woman; his sarcastic answer enrages her and she curses him.

[20] See Elwin (1952) for description of a tribal female priestess in central India.

[21] On the theology and practices of Śākta tantrism, see Bharati 1970; Brooks 1990; Sircar 1967, 1973.

[22] Mūkāmbika is in Kollur, a forested area in southern Karnataka; Hemambika is in Palghat, a hilly district in central Kerala; and Kanyakumari is the southern tip of India, currently part of the state of Tamil Nadu, but earlier a part of the Travancore kingdom. See Fig. 1.

[23] Personal communication, Mūkāmbika temple priest, May 1992.

[24] This talisman is very commonly worn in Kerala, particularly by infants and young children, to protect them from bad dreams or witchcraft. The metal container is strung on a thick black thread around the waist or neck.

[25] Obeyesekere (1984) suggests that Oṯṯamulacci is identical to Kaṇṇaki/ Pattini: 'The only single-breasted goddess in all of Indian mythology is Pattini' (536). However, the data I collected on her installations in Ezhava temples in Trichur district suggest that she may be an indigenous goddess with her own history. For the present the topic awaits further research.

[26] The three functioning kaḷaris are located in Calicut, Trivandrum, and Chavakkad. We visited the Chavakkad kaḷari, located within the area of muṭiyēṯṯu performance. See Zarrilli (1979, 1984) for descriptions of the Trivandrum tradition.

[27] See Yalman 1963; also Leach's (1970) critique of the same.

[28] See interview with Korratty Pakkattil House women, chapter 5.

[29] See Thankappan Nair (1969) for proverbs on Nāyar women.

[30] Some authors refer to Brahmins and Nāyars as both representing the 'higher' castes in relation to all other groups. Technically, however, even Nāyars were considered by Brahmins to be 'Śudras' (Yesudas 1975: 13–18). The numerous castes assigned to the Śudra category were ranked hierarchically among themselves as well. The degree of divisiveness between castes, and the obsessive concern with 'untouchability' in Kerala reached a degree

far beyond that of any other region of south Asia. See Yesudas 1975; Jeffrey 1976, 1992; K. P. P. Menon 1986.

[31] Elder (1996) provides a succinct account of the Indian government's contemporary categorization of castes.

[32] Choondal 1981 gives an example of such a contract in his Appendix 5. For details on economic and political aspects of muṭiyēṯṯu performance, see Caldwell 1995, chapters 2 and 4.

[33] Choondal 1981 states that Kuṟups are patrilineal, but I did not find this to be the case. The ethnographic data for this chapter are mostly drawn from the Mārārs of the Piravom family. For uncle-niece marriage in a neighbouring region, see McCormack 1958. For Dravidian kinship systems in general see Trautmann 1982.

[34] In patrilineal groups such as the Ezhava, however, women do take their husband's first name as their new last name at marriage. This practice is also being adopted by some younger, educated Nāyar women living in nuclear families. The basic four-part naming system outlined here is followed throughout the Hindu communities of Kerala. However only upper castes tend to retain the caste name at the end of their name. I did not meet anyone from a caste below Nāyar who used their caste name. But there are many Keralites with the last name 'Nayar', 'Menon', 'Nambutiri', 'Nambiar', and so on, denoting high-caste status.

[35] See chapter 3 for discussion; see also Moore 1989.

[36] Normally the eldest children marry first. See Trawick (1990b) for a sensitive treatment of the tension between husbands and wives in the Dravidian kinship system.

[37] For Nāyars and Brahmins, this mock marriage ceremony was performed at puberty. See Aiyappan 1972; Gough 1955. Apparently this ceremony was previously performed in the Mārār community, but it has now been abandoned due to the high costs involved.

[38] See chapters 3 and 5 for further description of puberty ceremonies.

[39] Pazhur Damodaran Mārār, interview, Pazhur, Kerala, July 1992.

[40] Ibid.

[41] Balakrishnan Mārār, interview, Muvattupuzha, Kerala, May 1992.

[42] Varanattu Narayana Kuṟup, interview, Trichur, Kerala, January 1992.

[43] Premnath, an Ezhava villager who attends muṭiyēṯṯu regularly. Interview, Piravom, Kerala, June 1992.

[44] Hindu deities are normally installed in temples facing the East. Western-facing deities are said to be of a demonic or harmful nature, causing spirit possession and other difficulties. This story shows that the goddess's power has a more or less amoral quality, as a part of nature.

[45] Many south Indian goddesses are said to be sisters. People would often tell me that the goddess residing at a particular temple was the older or younger sister of another specific goddess at a nearby temple.

[46] Interview, Kanjiramattom, Kerala, April 1992.

[47] Interview, Pazhur, Kerala, July 1992.

[48] V. Narayana Kuṟup, interview, Trichur, Kerala, December 1991.

[49] Interview, Muvattupuzha, Kerala, May 1992.

[50] For addresses of the artists, see Caldwell 1995: 664.

[51] We audio-recorded the complete muṭiyēṯṯu songs and dialogue from each of seven of the troupes. For detailed discussion of stylistic differences among the various troupes, see Caldwell 1995: 220–8.

[52] Balakrishnan Mārār, Interview, Piravom, Kerala, September 1992.

[53] See Berreman 1962.

[54] V. S. Paul, interview, Trichur, Kerala, January 1992.

[55] As it turned out, he did in fact give us an enormous amount of material, we paid him fairly for his time, and we continue to correspond.

2

DĒVIKŌPAM
THE WRATH OF THE GODDESS

It is the month of Kumbham in central Kerala. Late February, so hot my clothes stick to me, and so does the dirt mixed with sweat on my skin. It's pitch black with stars, long past midnight as we sit in the earthen compound of the temple of Bhadrakāḷi, the patron deity of Kerala. Outside the temple walls lie the yellow stumps of harvested paddy plants, like so many decapitated warriors, dry, upward-reaching, waiting, in neat rows. A mournful song accompanied by plodding drum beats and punctuated by deafening firecrackers tells the story of the misdeeds of the demon king Dārika, of the birth of Bhadrakāḷi from Śiva's third eye, of her virginity, her fury and beauty, of her violent battle and final destruction of Dārika by severing his head at the neck, and her triumphant return to her father, the demon's blood-dripping head dangling from her upraised hand by its long black hair.

The temple elephants, splendid in their golden head-dresses, and dazed by the deafening drums, amble back to the temple door with their sacred cargo. They kneel before the shrine as the Brahmin priests dismount holding the enlivened image of the goddess to return it to the inner sanctum. In front of the shrine stand plantain stalks heavy with fruit, ripe golden coconuts, and bunches of flowers. Two lines of women and girls, each holding a small tray of lights and flowers, stretch from the temple door to the outer compound, welcoming the goddess.

An announcement over the loudspeaker gives the rates for various offerings which can be made. The snack-sellers and bangle stalls are doing a brisk business. A woman seated on the ground near me breast-feeds an infant while staring at the elephant procession. The smell of alcohol on the breath of a man nearby who leeringly attempts to engage me in conversation is overpowering. Groups of boys gaily punch balloons and play cricket in the dirt with sticks and stones. They laugh heartily to see me jump at the roar of the firecrackers. The drums pound relentlessly. The festival of the goddess is in full swing.

Now it is the dead of night. The drama of Bhadrakāḷi and Dārika has been unfolding to the deep voices of the drums for several hours. As each scene begins, the actors dance and spin, carefully making offerings of prayers and flowers to the deity of the *kaliviḷakku*, the oil lamp at the centre of the performance area, which has been enlivened with the spirit of the goddess. The actors' movements are accentuated by the occasional brilliant green flare of the torches, made of oil-soaked rags tied to branches, onto which are thrown handfuls of *teḷḷi* powder, an indigenous medicine extracted from tree resins. It has a beautiful smell, fresh and pungent, and has an antiseptic effect which once served to eradicate smallpox germs in the area. Bhadrakāḷi is a fever goddess, and the offering of this ritual performance is said to cure any pox diseases afflicting villagers, by satiating her blood thirst and cooling her down from her raging, overheated state.

It is the deepest part of the night of the most dangerous day of the week, the time when ugly and bloodthirsty demons move abroad in search of their victims. It is a time when people should be safe and asleep in their beds, doors and windows shut, protected from the evils of the dark. But they are not in their beds. They are here, women, men, and children, in full view of the night sky, the unhealthy mists of evening, the frightening spirits of a Friday night, watching the battle of Bhadrakāḷi and Dārika on the dry, barren paddy fields of the village temple grounds. All night the actors and priests have been flirting with the dark powers at large. Everything has been calculated to call forth those powers and to invite them into the performance arena, into the person of the actor himself, into the body of Bhadrakāḷi dancing muṭiyēṯṯu.

And now it is time. Kāḷi begins to veer madly into the audience, wildly waving her sickle-shaped iron sword in blood lust for Dārika's head. People jump up from their seats and run for the safety of the shrine, as she chases Dārika erratically around the temple ground. Suddenly her heavy head-dress begins to slip, her steps falter, she swoons and begins to tremble violently, her eyes rolling up into her head, her arms flailing. She is helped to her seat near the flame, her head-dress removed, the energy temporarily contained and controlled, her body cooled.

Beginning after midnight and lasting until dawn, muṭiyēṯṯu is preceded by a series of elaborate rituals, including the drawing of a kaḷam of Bhagavati in her fierce form (kaḷam is an artistic rendering in coloured powders on the floor of the inner sanctum of the temple); invocation of the goddess through kaḷam pāṭṭu (singing and drumming), offering of light and food items, waving of indigenous lamps to exorcize evil spirits, destruction of the kaḷam by the artist, and distribution of the mass of coloured powders to the faithful as *prasad* (blessed food or offerings). These rites are accompanied by the performance of songs and instrumental music, leading up to the spectacle of the muṭiyēṯṯu drama proper.

The goddess Bhadrakāḷi (always enacted by a male actor) appears, sporting fearsome make-up, elaborate head-dress and colourful costumes. An orchestra of percussionists and singers tells the story while the actors act it out. The actor is ritually empowered with the spirit of the goddess before her shrine, and is 'possessed' by her at least once during the performance itself, causing the actor to lose consciousness. A lengthy battle scene culminates in the death of the demon Dārika at daybreak. After the drama concludes, Kāḷi blesses children from the audience, waving their bodies in circles before the sacred oil lamp. The *guruti* ritual is then performed, representing blood sacrifice (though now by law, it is done only with vegetable products).[1]

The overall structure of the rituals of which muṭiyēṯṯu is the culmination may be regarded as a gradual evocation of dangerous powers building to a climax in possession, then cooled and properly diffused so that the dangerous powers are released in a harmless form back into the wild. As such, the rituals are essentially exorcistic.[2] Once the ritual empowerment of the kaḷam has been completed and its energy infused into the fire of the stage lamp, the dramatic enactment of muṭiyēṯṯu, in which dangerous energy takes bodily form, may begin. Whatever other preliminary entertainments take place as part of the festival, muṭiyeṯṯu must always be the last item, ending at dawn. The dramatic action of the play is framed by a musical invocation at the beginning and rituals of sacrifice at the end. The drama ranges from serious, powerful possession scenes to raucous improvised comedy before its culmination in the beheading of the demon Dārika. With the performance of guruti sacrifice, the dangerous powers evoked by muṭiyēṯṯu are dispersed and order returns. The total time elapsed in all these events from beginning to end is about eighteen hours, from noon to dawn.

Muṭiyēṯṯu literally means 'the carrying of the headgear (muṭi).' Muṭi has a number of meanings in Malayalam: hair, a crown, headgear, a bale of rice paddy carried on the head. In the context of the ritual performances described herein, its technical meaning is the carved wooden headgear representing the goddess, and carried on the head by an actor playing the role of Bhagavati. It is a sacred image full of the enlivened power of the goddess. As with other sacred images, the deity's power can be invited to leave or enter the physical object. The muṭi is thus considered to be the goddess herself.

Seven fully costumed characters (all played by males) enact the story of Bhadrakāḷi's birth and the killing of Dārika through dance and speech, accompanied by the singers and orchestra. These seven characters are Śiva, Nārada, Dārika, Kāḷi, Kōyimbaṭa Nāyar, Kūḷi, and Dānavēndra. Two of these, Kāḷi and Kūḷi, are female characters; the rest are male. Śiva and Kāḷi are divine beings; Dārika and Dānavēndra are demon twins. Nārada and Kōyimbaṭa Nāyar are high-born humans serving the gods, and Kūḷi is a grotesque forest-dwelling female clown who assists Kāḷi. Kūḷi and Dānavēndra vary in prominence according to the troupe style, but the other roles are fairly consistent in make-up, dialogue, and characterization.

The play's dramatic structure consists of seven scenes, always presented in the same order. After invocations to the god Ganesh and an overture praising the goddess Bhadrakāḷi (lasting about thirty minutes), the action of the play commences, as follows (the approximate duration of each scene is given in parentheses; at times it can be less):

1. Nārada's recital to Lord Śiva in Kailāsam (Śiva's heavenly abode) of the infractions of Dārikāsura, the demon king (30 minutes)
2. Dārika's entrance (1 hour)
3. Kāḷi's birth, entrance, self-purification and setting out for war; culminating in the actor's possession, loss of consciousness, and 'cooldown' (removal of the muṭi) (1–2 hours)
4. Comic dialogue between Kāḷi and Kōyimbaṭa Nāyar, a warrior of the Nāyar caste sent by Śiva to check on the progress of the war (30–45 minutes)
5. Comic scene by the grotesque forest clown Kūḷi (a female counterpart to Kāḷi); the only scene allowing for improvisation and audience interaction (30–60 minutes)
6. Kāḷi and Kūḷi search out the demons and engage in battle (30 minutes)
7. Triumph of Kāḷi and decapitation of Dārika by removing his

headgear; blessing of children and final songs of praise (30–45 minutes)

The overall structure of serious (scenes 1–3)—comic (scenes 4 and 5)—serious (scenes 6 and 7), is demarcated by constant drumming, which stops during scenes 4 and 5. The cessation of the drums as Kāḷi's headgear is removed is very striking, after some 15 hours of non-stop sound during the festival. Drums in the comic scenes are used only to punctuate the dialogue in short rhythmic bursts at the end of each person's line.

This chapter will examine the performance as it unfolds, alternating ethnographic explanation with excerpts from my own and Laji's fieldnotes, interspersed with occasional composed narrative. (These changes of register from analytic to subjective can be identified by the accompanying change of font.) This format allows you to see each facet of the performance from a number of angles to get a feel of the whole. Moreover, the fieldnotes provide insight into the emotional tenor of the events, which cannot be separated from the drama's structural or symbolic meanings. A performance engages the audience fully in an experiential manner, providing knowledge through identification, emotion, physical sensation, and participation. This multifaceted narrative presentation engages the reader on a number of different levels in an attempt to recreate some of that experience.

In keeping with the idea of a performative narrative structure, this chapter follows a characteristically Indian, rather than traditional Aristotelian, dramatic form. That is to say, it does not present events in a single, linear manner, but circles back over the same material several times, elaborating and going deeper into the theme each time.[3] Like a classical musical *rāga* performed first slowly and then at faster and faster speeds in a cyclic time-frame, this organization leads you into the material first gradually and then more and more deeply, altering your perceptual and emotional response as you follow it along. The opening of this chapter, like the overture to an opera, provides a taste of both the subjective and analytic descriptions to come. But reading about muṭiyēṯṯu's structure in the preceding paragraphs is a bit like reading the plot summary of an opera libretto. While clear enough, it is also rather dull. Still, it has the virtue of letting you know what to expect, which is more than the ethnographer has when setting out to her first performance of muṭiyēṯṯu.

Just as it took attending many performances for me to begin to understand what I was seeing, reading the experiential narrative at the beginning of this chapter gives only a glimpse of the whole. Each performance, while sharing many features with others I attended, was unique in mood, style, and setting. Though the following summary is organized chronologically as if attending a single performance, the notes are drawn from many different performances.[4] Except for organization and minor editing, however, the text of the notes appears as it was written in the field. Two brief narrative descriptions were composed upon my return to the United States. The following account, then, takes you through a single total performance experience, providing background information at the start of each section. We begin with our arrival at the temple festival around midday, and end with the completion of the ceremonies the next morning.

Dusk

Muṭiyēṯṯu performances are scheduled as part of a temple's annual festival, which is held on a date considered to be the astrological birthdate of the goddess residing in that particular temple. These dates vary from temple to temple. Not every Bhagavati temple has muṭiyēṯṯu performances, except those that have hereditary contracts with specific troupes. The performance takes place in a dried, harvested paddy field abutting the temple proper, or else in the earthen outer compound. Villagers walk to the performance in small groups, arriving around dusk. Men and women generally keep apart, as they do at most Kerala social functions, for the duration of the evening. I travelled (usually long distances) by bus, train, or auto-rickshaw to reach performances that troupe leaders had informed me about in advance. My party generally included my husband Antonio, my three-year-old daughter Sofia and her nanny (an unmarried Malayali woman about 29 years old), my field assistant Laji, and a couple of videographers (by prior arrangement with the artists). Sometimes other friends of ours also attended. Abhilash, a friend of the family with an interest in muṭiyēṯṯu, accompanied our group to one performance. The events that followed are key to the personal story alluded to in the rest of this book. We usually stayed in local hotels where we could set our things down and rest (we often worked 18 or 24 hours straight at these events), before embarking on the journey back home the next morning.

As we get off the sweltering, lurching bus and pull our sticky clothes from our bodies, we look around the terminal. Dark vacant stares greet us from faces as exhausted as our own, arms loaded with sweaty children, packages of food and bags of clothing. One young woman stares at me with snake eyes. She turns to her friend while still glaring at us; they whisper and laugh loudly. A bus pulls in and scores of people crush madly to the single door at the rear, wildly shoving one another aside in vain attempts to enter the tottering vehicle already bursting with passengers. Not much point in our asking for directions to the temple here.

After checking into the hotel (still no washing up as there is no water at this hour), we follow the freshly bathed and cleanly dressed crowds over to the temple, walking through the village lanes, over a stone bridge, to see what's going on. Fresh fragrant flowers dangle in the women's heavily oiled, long black hair; bright gold chains, ear-rings, and bangles gleam from their necks and wrists. The older women wear simple white garments; the younger ones brightly coloured saris. The men laugh together, smoking and talking in small groups by the sides of the road as they watch the procession of festival-goers, periodically arranging and disarranging their skirt-like lower garments while talking, folding them up short, then dropping the folds to the ground again.

At the entrance to the temple ground two large plantain stalks heavy with fruit, ripe golden coconuts, and flowers welcome visitors. As we enter, crowds of people are milling in and out. Straight ahead, four musicians playing heavy drums serenade the representation of the goddess in their midst: a small metal mirror, daubed with red and yellow powders, framed by a white cloth folded in the form of an accordion fan behind it; the whole is mounted onto a large red and gold plaque.[5] This representation of the goddess, taken from inside the low, tile-roofed shrine just beyond, sits atop a majestically caparisoned male elephant, whose job it is to carry her in a slow procession around the temple grounds. As the instruments serenade the goddess, the elephant tears some leaves from a nearby tree and munches.

The energy is intense and colourful; many things are happening at once. Behind the temple, near the makeshift toilets, groups of young boys are excitedly stuffing gunpowder into stone mortars. From time to time they set off these fireworks, which explode with a brilliant blaze of light and an ear-splitting roar. Each time I jump in alarm, provoking mocking laughter in onlookers, who seem to enjoy my discomfiture immensely. Some small children react with even more alarm, however, bursting into tears and having to be comforted by laughing parents. I take a look around. Here is a toy-stall, there a balloon-seller, some kids playing with balloons. Groups of villagers enter the tea-shops, lit up in front of the temple, to buy hot milky tea and bananas. We proceed to the Bhadrakāḷi temple to meet the artists and see the preparations for the kaḷam drawing.

Suddenly several men come over to me and start shouting that they don't want me to take photos (though I am not even carrying a camera), that I don't belong here. I try to explain my motives for being here, that I have permission from the temple board, and ask them how they can truly judge whether my devotion is greater or less than their own, just by the colour of my skin. I realize I am getting too angry. They stand silent momentarily. There seem to be two factions in the temple office—one which wants to treat me well and the other which deeply resents my presence. Surendram, son of the President of the Temple Board, offers his services and defends me to the hostile ones. This place really feels ready for a fight.

A small scene is then caused by the temple authorities coming over to greet us and rather prematurely offering us an opportunity to get inside the shrine. One man is very unhappy about this and they start shouting at each other. I also feel it odd to be ushered into the sanctum sanctorum so unceremoniously, but don't know quite what to do with everyone trying to be so helpful and kind. No matter how one might wish to just 'blend in', the presence of a foreigner with a tape-recorder creates an instant uproar, and it often ends up a mess. My husband fears we'll be lynched when we return. Certainly he is over-reacting. We decide to retire from the scene for now and go see if the water for a bath has come yet at the hotel.

[From Laji's notes:] Then the committee men came, got introduced to Amba [Sarah].[6] She was taken out to a different place where they kept the costumes and muṭi. I had to go always behind her dragging my tail, always at her beck and call. Then a guy came and started a mess with the man who took us in. He said, 'It's no harm to me, but still we are not sure what kind of people they are.' He went to talk to the committee. Amba and Antonio were offered some nice seats. I did not want to follow them like a scarecrow, answering tons of stupid questions. I sat alone at a place near the committee box. There was a mess among the members. They started fighting among themselves. One gentle (or wild) man came and started scolding the president: 'Hey, what are you doing? I had asked you to pour some oil on the lamp and you never bothered. Instead, you just want to take it out and show it to these Americans (some obscene comments).' They started talking in high-pitched voices and hitting their palms against the desk. I noticed that in the temple premises there were more than fifteen policemen and realized it wasn't a safe place. People were almost drunk there. A disgusting and annoying area. I hated being there. I found it uncomfortable to sit there anymore and soon Amba came. We decided to come back to the hotel.

[Sarah's notes:] While glancing over the menu at the hotel, trying to choose between various mutton dishes and fried rice, I wonder what we can expect when we return to the festival. Mr Unnithan, the Secretary of the Trichur Kathakaḷi Club, had described the main events, taking place after the midnight hour, when the fierce Bhadrakāḷi, represented by a special actor wearing the muṭi on his head, celebrates her violent victory over the demon king Dārika.

> After the ritual drawing and song, Kāḷi will celebrate her victory. After midnight, at 2 a.m., the shrine will be opened and [the actor] will take the muṭi and wear it on his head. He will run around the temple in between the people. There will be lakhs of people there to observe.[7] There will be so many drums at that time. All the hundreds of spectators will be running around after that [actor]. See, when the muṭi is on his head he gets inspired by some unseen force, and he starts running. He gets inspired by the power of Dēvi. So everyone will think 'she is looking at me.' Thousands of people simultaneously will feel 'Dēvi is looking at me.' No matter what corner they go to, when [the actor] walks forward each one will feel that '[the muṭi] is looking at me, staring at me, and it is coming to me.' Because that Dēvi's eyes are staring at you in the audience [he chuckles knowingly].
>
> That is the perfection of that art of painting. Actually people are afraid of it. People won't even wear a red-coloured costume or shirt because they are afraid that Kāḷi will be attracted by that colour and she will rush towards them. Nobody will use even a red-coloured kerchief on that particular day in that locality. No one knows what Dēvi will do. Dēvi may attack, so they are afraid. Nobody likes to attract the special attention of Dēvi, for after Dārika's killing, she celebrated her victory in a ferocious manner. It is not the peaceful form of Dēvi you see then: such a frightful appearance! So at that moment nobody likes to attract the special attention of Dēvi. Nobody likes it.

Enlivenment

The most important preliminary ritual to muṭiyēṯṯu, without which it cannot be performed, is the drawing of a multi-coloured kaḷam depicting the goddess. A large portrait is drawn on the temple floor out of five coloured powders—white, black, red, yellow, and green. The powders are applied painstakingly, one at a time, by tapping them through a hole punched into the bottom of a coconut shell. The two-dimensional powder drawing portrays Bhagavati in her fierce state, with weapons in her many arms and the severed head of the demon Dārika dripping blood from one of her lower left hands. The number of arms can vary from a minimum of four to as many as sixty-four, depending on the sponsor's ability to pay (the more arms, the more the cost). Ordinarily six or eight are portrayed. The goddess's eyes are wide, and fangs protrude from her red lips. Her eyes, nose, and conical breasts are built up to protrude three-dimensionally from the floor. The eyes and nose are built up out of the coloured powders; but the breasts are constructed out of two different kinds of rice, heaped up to make large conical shapes before being dusted with red powder. The entire kaḷam takes three or four hours to make, involving tremendous artistic skill (see Fig. 4).

Once the kaḷam is completed, oil lamps, coconuts, arecanut flowers, rice, and bananas are placed at points around the circumference of the drawing, and offerings of light, mantras, ritual gestures, music, and food are made by a priest or the artist himself. The artist who composes the kaḷam is usually the same man who will perform the role of Kāḷi in the dramatic performance to come. He therefore spends many hours concentrating his mind on the goddess's form and attributes, which helps provide the total identification required by the role, including his eventual possession by the goddess. When the kaḷam artist also performs the rituals of worship (pūjā), inviting the goddess to enliven the drawing he has made, his worship is of a truly tantric nature.

Tantric pūjās are characterized by the mental and physical identification of the worshipper with the deity. This is accomplished through a number of mental and physical actions. As each part of the deity is touched or gazed upon, the worshipper installs that attribute into the corresponding part of his own body using specific hand gestures and accompanying mantras (secret syllables imbued with sacred force). In muṭiyēṯṯu, the kaḷam is worshipped with a traditional song of praise, enumerating the goddess's physical attributes from feet to head and back again. The song not only describes the goddess, but actually installs her physically into the drawing. The priest or artist then performs traditional tantric pūjā, installing the deity into himself.

The text of the particular kaḷam pāṭṭu (song of praise for the kaḷam) used in muṭiyēṯṯu is reminiscent of the *Saundaryalaharī*, a

Fig. 4: Bhagavati *kaḷam*

Sanskrit poetic composition attributed to the revered eleventh-century Kerala saint Śaṅkarācārya.[8] Although the text of the kaḷam pāṭṭu thus echoes elite, Sanskritic tradition, the accompanying music appears unrelated to the classical Carnatic musical tradition. The tune, the singing style, and the rhythm of the kaḷam pāṭṭu also differ strikingly from those used by the orchestra in accompanying the dramatic portions of muṭiyēṯṯu.

After the kaḷam has been enlivened and worshipped, it is destroyed. The artist wipes out the drawing with some tender coconut leaves, starting from the feet and moving upwards, but leaving the breasts and face. These are wiped out separately using the right hand and the powders presented as blessed offerings (*prasādam*) to the sponsor of the evening's rituals and a few other devotees. The sponsor is also blessed by the waving of a flame before his body, from head to toe. This waving of the flame is called *tiriyuḻichaḷ* (*uḻichaḷ* also means 'massage'), and is said to remove evil influences from the physical body.

Where does the spirit of the goddess go when the powder-drawing is erased? It is released into the immediate environment, through the powders distributed to the faithful, into the body of the artist who will enact the role of Bhadrakāḷi in the drama, and into the flame which has been offered to the goddess in the pūjā. This flame is then carried out to the stage area outside, where it is used to ignite the large stage lamp placed in the centre of the earthen performance area. Traditionally this lamp was made from a brass centre-piece attached to a banana tree stem. Sometimes the entire lamp is made from brass. In either case it stands about four feet high and illumines the stage area with a beautiful flickering firelight.

We arrive again at 12:30 a.m. Hordes of people are milling around, though nothing much is happening at the moment. On the floor inside the temple building we find the kaḷam. Her feet are shown with toes pointed downwards, straddling the prone and bloodied corpse of Dārika. His head is severed, and his entrails spill out where her long curved sword has pierced his abdomen. Bhadrakāḷi's three bulging eyes, red and white, stare out at us, the only three-dimensional protrusions other than the two small red breasts built up of raw paddy rice; her four arms hold, variously, a fistful of weapons, the head of Dārika, a snake, and a bowl to catch the demon's blood. Three folds at her middle enclose the prominent navel, necklaces hang from her neck, and stars and flowers dot her long loose black hair. A square red cloth is suspended like a tent over the kaḷam. It is fringed with tender coconut leaves into which are tied arecanuts, small bananas, and bunches of mango leaves. On the floor surrounding the kaḷam are brass lamps lit with oil wicks, plantain leaves with piles of rice, ripe coconuts with coconut flowers on top; by the Devi's feet are puffed rice and bananas. Four ladies sit opposite the shrine area, hands folded in prayer to the goddess before them. Only men, however, are allowed to mount the platform where the kaḷam is installed, to perform the ritual worship of the goddess.

Pounding drums shake the small building as the kaḷam artist draws large black circles around Bhadrakāḷi's staring eyes, rousing the goddess and calling her into the drawing. The musicians sing a mournful song describing her attributes and worshipping her, as the soul-splitting drums get louder and louder, faster and faster. The attendant priest lights the oil-wick lamps outside the doors of the shrine and opens them to reveal the main image of the goddess, a brilliant golden statue laden with garlands of red flowers and limes. As the statue of the goddess is exposed, the women are hooting loudly—ullullullullu!—and loud firecrackers and sparklers are set off behind the temple. Quietly, as more crackers go off, the kaḷam is erased by the artist, who waves a green plantain leaf enclosing a burning wick in his left hand, and with his right pulls down some coconut leaves from the hanging decorations to sweep away the coloured-powder drawing of Bhagavati, leaving only the protruding face and breasts. Then dropping the leaves, he uses the fingers of his right hand to erase the face and breasts and places the powder on a fresh plantain leaf, to be given as a blessing to the sponsor of tonight's rituals—in this case a young man—and others present. The ladies apply the powder to their foreheads. Through this sequence of acts, the spirit of the goddess has been released from the drawing and is being taken to the outer compound for further rituals.

The green-room, where the artists rest, dress, and apply make-up before the performance of muṭiyēṯṯu, is a room or building within the walls of the outer temple compound. Often it is directly adjacent to the area where the kaḷam has been prepared. Several hours before the drama is to begin, the troupe members assemble there and begin the process of putting on their make-up and costumes. Payipra Radhakrishnan, a writer from Trichur who has been fond of muṭiyēṯṯu since his youth, pointed out that at festivals 'children are more interested in the green-room than the stage. They want to know how a man is transformed into Dārika. There is drama in the green-room also.'[9]

Before the actors can begin their make-up, a small pūjā is set up in the centre of the green-room. On a straw mat a brass lamp, similar to that used in the worship of the kaḷam,' is lit. One senior artist explained its significance:

> We keep a lamp in the dressing-room. This lamp is supposed to be the supreme deity. Paddy, rice, and coconut are kept in front of such a lamp as offerings to Ganapati, and we suppose that lamp to be the goddess herself. Then a pūjā is conducted there. After this we tie the cloth with prasādam on the head. From that moment we will think only of the goddess. (Balakrishnan Mārār)

The offerings to Ganapati are placed on a rounded banana leaf tip called a *nākku*. Only this rounded tip may be used, as it represents a tongue. It is thought that Ganapati eats the food offered on the tongue-shaped leaf. Some artists told me that Vētāḷam, present in the form of a small painted wooden face resting against the lamp, is also believed to receive the offerings. After the pūjā this face of Vētāḷam will be tied to the front of the Kāḷi actor's belt.

The costumes of muṭiyēṯṯu are very similar to those used in the Kathakaḷi dance drama. Some scholars have suggested that Kathakaḷi, which is only a few centuries old, borrowed and developed the original costumes of muṭiyēṯṯu.[10] But there has certainly been plenty of borrowing back, especially in the make-up of Dārika, whose character is a *katti vēṣam* ('knife' character: a type of make-up style) in the typology of classical drama. The prestige and renown of Kathakaḷi have no doubt contributed to this borrowing, as muṭiyēṯṯu artists try to increase the popularity and appeal of their lesser known, more demanding art.

The make-up and costume of the characters varies somewhat from troupe to troupe. However, Dārika's facial make-up always includes the colours red, green and white. Kāḷi's facial make-up consists of a pure black base studded with numerous white 'smallpox' marks that stand up from the face and are liberally sprinkled with red powder representing blood. Small fangs protrude from the sides of her mouth. The dress of these two main characters consists mostly of a red blouse, white lower cloth tied up between the legs, bunched white cloths at the back in a sort of frill above the buttocks, and a large multicoloured skirt. Bhadrakāḷi wears false breasts, fashioned of either coconut or jackwood, and brilliantly coloured in either red or gold. Large erect snakes often encircle the breasts. Garlands of red flowers ring her neck and wrists.

The characters Śiva, Nārada, and Kōyimbaṭa Nāyar have simpler costumes. A crown, some eyeliner, and a few lines of ash on the forehead complete Śiva's make-up. Nārada wears a long false beard, some beads like those worn by ascetics, and a saffron or white lower cloth. Kōyimbaṭa Nāyar wears the typical medieval martial dress of his caste—a red or white head-cloth, plain lower cloth, sword and shield in his hands. Dānavēndra is similar to Dārika, only less elaborate. Kūḷi has a most interesting costume, which also varies from troupe to troupe. She generally has a black top, grass skirt, ugly matted-looking hair entwined with grass and leaves, and in some troupes, long pointed red breasts and a large stomach indicating an advanced state of pregnancy. Her facial make-up is dominated by black-and-white, and must be asymmetrical and ugly. Artists say her make-up is reminiscent of tribal rituals, and indeed photographs of such rites do show similar designs (Khokar 1987: 96).

The muṭi or wooden headgear is the most important item in Kāḷi's attire. A sacred representation of Bhadrakāḷi herself, the muṭi is treated with great respect and care in the green-room. A red cloth covers the face of the goddess. Fresh strands of tender coconut leaf are attached to the back of the muṭi at each performance to represent the goddess's long hair. The muṭi can weigh up to 75 pounds and is thus both difficult and dangerous to wear. The muṭi should not be worn inside the dressing-room; it can only be placed on the actor's head in front of the temple. Its mounting on the actor's head is a critical moment of ritual empowerment.

As we move to the green-room a bunch of boys follow and perch beside us. All the costumes are hung up on a rope stretched across the room. Some troupe members are sleeping on mats on the floor. We wonder how they can sleep so deeply and then just jump up and perform.

A lighted lamp sits on a straw mat at the centre of the room. A plantain leaf with rice, coconut, and some coins is placed before the lamp. A small rectangular mirror rests on the coconut. Nearby I also see a brass vessel for pouring water, grinding stones with colours, and various tiny brushes of coconut frond. A ceramic roof-tile holds the blackened soot of the coconut oil fire, which will be used in Kāḷi's make-up. The artists offer us some weak coffee from an aluminium pot. The atmosphere is sombre and quiet.

The son of a member of the temple board committee introduces himself to Laji, quizzing him on muṭiyēṯṯu. Then he chases some of the gawking boys away. Antonio is enjoying the drumming outside by an eminent local musician. But Laji tells me that the artists are complaining about the *pancavādyam* [drum orchestra], saying 'Oh, he could do better than that', and so on.

The troupe leader is taking a break for some snuff. He smiles at us. He is cutting Kāḷi's fangs from tender coconut leaves. The troupe members gossip among themselves, smoking beedis. Now they are cheering up a bit, laughing, discussing their next performance. The party is warming up.

Someone brings out stacks of freshly laundered cloths and props. One man folds the endless cloths needed for the back portion of the costumes in accordion folds. The props (crowns, breastplates, gaudy necklaces) we saw at the artists' house earlier have been repaired. They are so shiny and pretty, glowing with their new layers of coloured foil.[11]

Other men prepare small brushes of coconut frond, burning the ends to break them. One man who had been making the coconut-frond brushes folds his hands in prayer before the lamp, then begins to mix the white pigment, made from rice flour and thickened with limestone powder. It is stored in a dried arecanut palm leaf, mixed in a half coconut shell with water. He bows to the knife which he then uses to cut the white paste. He smells the paste, then mixes it with his right index finger. When it looks ready, he tests the consistency of his product by making test 'smallpox' on his left thumb.

Now they bring out small grinding-stones to prepare the pigments for the make-up. The raw materials include:

Cāyilyam—a small glassy stone which they crush on a stone mortar and mix with coconut oil to make red colour.

Manayōla—A yellow stone with a pleasant fragrance.[12] They place it in a rag and pound the stones to powder, then mix with indigo (blue commercial dye) to make green. One artist tells me the more traditional green colour is made from crushed mango leaves, but it is not as bright.

Lime and rice powder for white—mixed with water. To dry thick and stand up.

Black—burnt coconut oil carbon collected on a pot or tile.

The troupe leader does pūjā to the lamp. A rather dirty-looking red cloth is laid before it with some bits of red flowers (*cetti* and hibiscus). He does some *mudras* (ritual gestures) three times, and with his eyes closed, he carefully lifts the cloth so the flowers don't fall off and ties it around his head. This cloth, he tells me, is a special one passed from one Kāḷi āśān (troupe leader) to another, and should not be washed. It seems to both protect and empower the wearer to undertake the role of Kāḷi and don the immensely heavy wooden muṭi.

Before starting to apply his make-up, the Mārār touches the mirror and says some mantras with more mudras. When the mirror is not in use, he places it face down before the oil lamp, resting on the plantain leaf near the coconut and Kāḷi's ear-rings. It looks to me as if it is important, although when I inquire about it he says it has no ritual significance.[13] Then he begins to apply the black carbon grease which forms the base of Kāḷi's facial make-up. After the black is applied to his whole face, the Mārār takes some white rice paste and draws the first round white dots on his face—one on the nose, then forehead, then left cheek, right cheek (one dot each). In the centre of each white dot, he sprinkles some red kumkum powder (the kind commonly used in Hindu pūjās), making the dots look like eyes. These represent smallpox, bursting with blood, which should appear all over Kāḷi's face. After this part of the make-up dries, another member of the troupe will painstakingly apply small cones of white paste in neat rows around the Mārār's face, like so many little mountains, to achieve a horrific effect.

Now Kāḷi must wait half an hour for the make-up to dry. Kāḷi lies down on a white cloth towel, puts the mirror, face down, on his chest, folds his hands over, goes into meditation. I see his eyes rolling up, the whites showing. He seems to be in a trance. The whole way they are doing this is slow, quiet, concentrated, serious, simple, devotional, powerful.

Dārika also starts his make-up by holding the mirror to his chest and touching it with mantras. Then he begins to apply red to his nose, then his right cheek, then left, forehead, and around the upper portion of his face. He surrounds this red area with a frame of pale green all around. Now Dārika paints tiny white dots outlining the red and green areas, and a round white circle on the tip of his nose.

This Dārika has been performing the role since he was twelve years of age. He looks to be about fifty or more now. Now Dārika lies down with a mirror face down on his chest, his arms folded and eyes closed.

Outside on a stage there is break-dancing going on to Michael Jackson's 'I'm Bad'.[14]

[From Laji's notes:] One of the troupe members tells me about the schedule of the performance. He says they were to start at 12 a.m., just after the drama [a soap opera dealing with contemporary themes]. But since the drama is not yet staged, they have to wait longer. Muṭiyēṯṯu must be the very last thing to be performed. 'There should not be any performance after muṭiyēṯṯu,' he says.

On asking him about the function of the mirror, he said that it is just to see whether any small insects are landing on his face and messing up the make-up. I understand that there is no special folklore behind keeping this mirror on the chest. Only to look once in a while to see if insects are disturbing them.

The muṭi is really fantastic and alive. The hair is different—it is thin. They have only two snake heads above Kāḷi's head on the muṭi. When we asked about it the man said some time ago there were three, but it created some disasters or danger to the artist doing the performance. They felt it was a bad omen, so they took one of the snake heads off.

[Sarah's notes:] The muṭi, to be worn by the actor specially privileged to impersonate Kāḷi, sits facing the wall in a corner, its back towards us. Now some men are tying thin fresh coconut frond 'hair' onto the back of it. The smell of Kāḷi's 'hair' is wonderful—so fresh. The muṭi is a brilliantly coloured headpiece of painted jackwood, depicting the head and torso of the ferocious deity Bhadrakāḷi, her eyes bulging terrifically, large fangs protruding from her reddened mouth, snakes coiled tightly around her heavy, protruding red breasts. As I stare at the muṭi, the remarks of Mr Unnithan, made over tea in his cool, dark house a few weeks back, come to mind:

> There is a muṭi there made in a traditional way from jackwood. Actually, that muṭi is not a mere crown. It is Devi's head with a crown. See, when that Kāḷi idol is carved, when it attains perfection, it becomes Kāḷi; it is not wood. It's not just a piece of timber.
>
> That muṭi was carved on the top of the tree itself. A temporary platform was erected around the tree, and the craftsman started his work. He took months to finish it. And when it was almost complete, it was a belief of the local people that this muṭi started trembling. When it was on the top of the tree, it was not yet cut, separated; even then on the top of the tree it started trembling and shivering. Actually that craftsman wanted to make some more finishing touches to that headgear, so he chiselled and tried to fix it. As he pulled out the chisel, it started shivering again. It started some sort of movement as if it [wanted] to get separated as early as possible. Ah! That was the belief. It did not want to remain on the top of the tree as a part of the tree. It had a life of its own. It wanted to get separated. So breaking that chisel, it got separated. That craftsman took it and gave it to the *tantri*, who is the chief priest of the temple. Even now that broken portion of the chisel is visible on it. So [the actor who is to wear the muṭi makes] a thick cotton pad and places it on his head before carrying it, because this projecting chisel piece is projecting downward. It is still there, in it.[15]

Garlands of red cetti and white *alari* flowers are being prepared. The red flowers will be tied onto the wrists of the actors playing Dārika and Kāḷi, and also placed around Kāḷi's neck. These flowers are said to be the goddess's favourite. I recall reading an account of the war between the goddess and Dārika, which described the bloody entrails of the demons hanging from the trees; it is for this reason Bhadrakāḷi is said to like red-coloured flowers. The alari is white with a yellow centre and a strong, sweet smell. Snakes like it, says Laji. P. Narayana Mārār, an aged troupe leader of Muvattupuzha, told us the flowers were created by Bhadrakāḷi's shouts of victory at the end of the war: 'The flowers which fell then are called *alaripoova* (alari flowers). Bhagavati's yelling and screaming went up and came down as flowers. So the alari was created from then on.'[16]

Two ladies appear at the door and ogle me a while. They whisper to each other and sidle away. We decide to go back outside now as the performance is about to begin.

Setting Forth

Sometime after midnight, when it is time for muṭiyēṯṯu to begin, a small flame is brought out from the kaḷam area inside the temple and the large stage lamp is lit. A clearing about twenty feet square in the temple compound or a paddy field abutting it forms the simple stage area. As the orchestra begins the overture and the stage curtain is held up, people begin to gather. Men and women sit separately around the boundaries of the stage area, quietly talking. Women tend to sit close to the temple walls, on its steps and under its eaves, while men press closer to the stage, smoking and chatting amiably.

The stage curtain may be anything from a plain white muslin cloth (like those used by men as a lower garment) to a brilliantly coloured satin blanket. The latter style seems to be popular in most performances, with the exception of the Muvattupuzha troupes, who prefer plain white cloth. In either case, the curtain is held up behind the stage lamp by two men, one on either side, screening the orchestra and actors entering from offstage. The invisible area behind the curtain is said to represent the supernatural realm, from which the gods and demons emerge into the earthly plane of the stage.[17] As such, it is an important area where entering characters dance out of sight of the human audience.

The musical ensemble required for muṭiyēṯṯu consists of three drummers, a cymbal player, and one or two vocalists. The drums used are called ceṇṭa, classified into two types: dēva (divine) and asura (demonic). The cylindrical drums, carved out of jackwood (*plāvu*) are distinguished only by which of their two skin sides is played: the asura ceṇṭa is played on the left side, and the dēva or vikkan ceṇṭa ('weak' ceṇṭa) on the right.[18] The muṭiyēṯṯu ensemble contains two asura centas and one vikkan ceṇṭa. The drum is suspended vertically from a belt around the waist of the drummer and is struck with two hardened twigs of tamarind wood. Drums have great ritual significance in south Indian temple music, and are believed to contain sacred power.[19] As the drum summons the deity, its proper treatment and use is crucial. The *tāḷam*, or cycle of beats, is the rhythmic basis of the musical accompaniment. Specific tāḷams must be played at different times during the performance. The heavy, plodding beat of *triputa tāḷam* is associated with the onset of spirit possession.

The overture (kēḷi) to muṭiyēṯṯu consists of drumming and the singing of a stage benediction, including Sanskrit prayers to Ganesh and Bhadrakāḷi. The style of singing is called sōpāna sangītam ('singing on the steps [of the temple]'), an ancient form of musical worship still practised in Kerala. Although this singing style is close to that of classical Carnatic music, it is somewhat harsher and more piercing, following a simpler melodic line.

Here are excerpts from the stage benediction in praise of Bhadrakāḷi:

Oh lady shining like tender leaves
Oh holy one
Oh lady with a shining body I shall praise you
To cut the throat of the living demon (asura)
I have kept a seat for you
Oh Maheshwari please come and sit
I salute the tender leaf-like feet
Oh Kāḷi, the daughter of Śaṅkara
Come from the mountain, in Malanad
Reigning deity, to conduct this drama well
You must bless, I pray you.

She who with pleasure puts wild elephants on as ear-rings
She who is shaking with righteous rut[20]
She who rides the Vētāḷam, and who
Breaks open the chest of cruel Dārika
She who gives blood as food to the Kūḷis

She who cuts to pieces the enemies
She who returns to Lord Śiva with the chopped-off head
My mother who reigns joyfully
From Sri Kurumba Kāvu

Oh Bhairavi who reigns, I salute you.
With joyful hordes of soldiers
With an elephant as an ear-ring and
With weapons and swords
You come, holding Dārika's head and
The spear in your hand
Mother, sucking the blood,
Wearing the entrails as garlands
And playing in the cremation ground
Mother, who plays with her soldiers
Oh Terrifying Mother, please dance
When all people see you with affection
You should with pleasure bestow boons
Oh goddess Kurumba, Mother, Oh Lady
Oh mother, who is verily the mother
To all the people in the world[21]

After the stage benediction the drums roll and the head and torso of Śiva appear above the curtain. Śiva stands on a small stool behind the curtain and holds a model of a white bull's head at his waist to represent his mount, Nandi. The sage Nārada appears from behind the curtain, 'reading' from a palm leaf in his hand and dancing with one leg raised and bent at the knee in front of his body. He tells Śiva of the misdeeds of the demon king Dārika. The actor playing Nārada actually sings his lines, but the answering verses of Śiva are sung by the vocalists in the orchestra.

2 a.m. Beginning of muṭiyēṯṯu. Out under coconut trees and stars. Two loud firecrackers. The audience is small—maybe 200 maximum. At least 90 per cent left after the break dancing/film songs/drama show. Their attention seems to wander. Many more are leaving now. The young people we meet here tell us they don't have much understanding of muṭiyēṯṯu. They like the music concert portion, dramas, and other popular entertainments.

A white cloth is held up. Two drummers stand at the front left of curtain—singer, playing cymbals, stands behind, with opening characters. The illumination from behind due to fluorescent lights makes it look like a shadow play. We can see the silhouettes of the people behind the curtain.

A young boy about ten years old is sitting next to me drumming on his knees. I am seated on the side of the temple entrance kitty corner to Kāḷi's shrine. Some girls and young ladies are seated in front of me on pieces of newspaper. Sofia is drawing kaḷams as usual. Men have seated themselves to the right facing the stage, ladies to the left, in front of the temple. Some peer out from inside the temple foyer, through the wooden slats as if in their homes. Antonio, irritated and bored, has gone off to sleep in the field beyond the temple, leaving me with Laji and Abhilash. We are seated together between the men and women, so that I can ask them questions.

Scene 1. Śiva appears, looking rather like a Nāyar chieftain, with golden helmet, breastplate, and shoulder guards, red shirt, moustache, sitting on Nandi. Śiva has little facial make-up—black eye and eyebrow liner, a 'third eye'. He holds a small model of Nandi (cow's head) which peers over the curtain. He stands on a stool behind the curtain to give him some height (he is supposed to be in Kailāsam as Nārada approaches).

Nārada throws 'flowers' from behind the curtain, then comes out spinning clockwise circles around the lamp. Someone is singing from behind the curtain in a beautiful voice. Nārada's costume is very attractive, with large 'rudrākṣa' mala fashioned of gold-covered beads. Śiva and Narada each hold a palm leaf. Śiva only looks straight down the whole time. Narada hops back and forth on his right foot towards the curtain, stopping and looking down, reading from the palm-leaf manuscript. He has a very humble, devotional expression as he recites Dārika's misdeeds. Śiva looks very sombre, moves the wooden bull prop slowly across the curtain's edge. End of scene.

Next is the entrance (*puṟappāṭu* or 'setting forth') of Dārika. He walks out of the green-room to take his place behind the curtain as the drums begin to play complex rhythms. Dārika's entrance displays his ferocity, in the style of classical Kerala theatre, through very stylized movements developed over several cycles of drumming at an ever-increasing speed. Particularly important is the 'curtain look', a gradual revelation of the character's face above the curtain, with shaking gestures that seem to threaten to break out of their controlled regularity at any moment. The make-up also expresses the inner state of the character: the red and green of the *katti* make-up iconically convey Dārika's ferocious (*raudra*) nature.

After the curtain look is completed (which can take twenty minutes or more), Dārika breaks through the boundary of the curtain and begins to spin around the stage lamp, holding two daggers in his hands. This is accompanied by the showering of flowers and bits of tender coconut leaf. Dārika must dance completely around the lamp for the duration of three rhythm cycles in different tāḷams (rhythmic patterns), first slowly, then faster. Most audience members are unaware of these technicalities and simply enjoy his spinning and make-up. Dārika's dance steps are an amalgamation of classical Sanskrit theatre and Dravidian possession performances. He bows to the four directions and moves in a clockwise direction around the stage lamp by dancing along the four perimeters of a square. The foot and leg movements are clearly derived from the ancient Sanskrit dance-drama Kūṭiyāṭṭam.[22] Interspersed with these measured movements around the lamp are periods of spinning and the assumption of body postures which are more closely related to the dance traditions still seen in Sri Lanka and the neighbouring regions of south India. An interesting combination of counter clockwise spinning (around the body axis) while moving the entire body in a clockwise direction around the lamp makes Dārika's dance technically difficult. According to one troupe leader, Appu Kuttan, the spinning represents the spinning of chariot wheels as Dārika goes to the war.

After worshipping the four directions, Dārika sits on a small stool before the flame and offers flowers from a band at his left wrist into the lamp, while mentally worshipping the flame. This is followed by more rounds of dancing around the lamp with a lighted torch before his face. From time to time, the assistant holding the torch throws fragrant resinous teḷḷi powder into the flame, causing it to flare up brightly and illumine Dārika's face. This adds to the impression of ferocity.[23] While dancing, Dārika looks at the weapons held in either hand, then mounts the stool and shouts his challenge to Kāḷi, calling her to war:

Crush crush I shall crush now
I will break open the skull of the elephant in rut
I will blow up distant regions both inside and out
Come quickly with drawn sword amidst the great army
All those who are haughty will meet their end at once

The dēvas have no brains
I am an asura who has strength, intelligence,
Valour and ability to attack
I am Dārika the asura who has all these

Each of these lines is preceded by a long shouting call—'O-O-O-O-O-O-Oh!' yelled in a singsong voice, as Dārika threatens with his outstretched right arm; his left arm balances the wooden crown atop his haughty face, thrust back. The men in the audience cheer his shouts with an answering 'Hoo-ah!' After completing this challenge, Dārika leaves the stage and the scene comes to a close.

3:30 a.m. Dārika enters from the temple, wearing a tall, thin headgear. His skirt has thin horizontal stripes of red, blue, yellow, and green on white cloth. After saluting the drums, he does some elaborate dancing behind the curtain. As Dārika moves from side to side, coconut leaf 'flowers' are showered over the top of the curtain. Then he lowers the top, shaking it with white flower-shaped cloths held in each of his hands. The curtain goes back up. Dārika faces the drums again. It is going on a long time. People are getting restless. Dārika does the curtain look again, and a torch is ignited. The orchestra is visible now. Drummers and curtain holders are looking intently at his face. Now Dārika takes up two knives and shows them above the curtain, howling. He touches the knives to the earth in four corners, then spins holding them in his outstretched neck-cloths. The curtain goes up.

As Dārika presses forward into the curtain, they wind it up as if to hold him back. He tries to break out, they restrain him. He sways and writhes, stamps. Really looks as if he's working up to a stylized fury, wearing a trance-like expression. Torches with teḷḷi powder blaze up illuminating his face eerily during the spinning dance and frightening lurches. The audience is forced to get up and move. The audience comes alive when Dārika bursts forward—lots of murmuring and comments as his movements widen the audience and performance area considerably. A man leading Dārika with a torch yells occasionally to inspire him.

Dārika kneels towards the lamp on all four sides—EWSN. Dārika dances around the flame waving the knife in his right hand up and down rather gracefully. He appears to be worshipping the fire. Then he begins spinning in circles around the flame, as the drums become more intense and showers of flowers rain down. As he speeds up, it gets quite exciting. The drumming is excellent. Dārika keeps circling the fire, his eyes open wide with a fierce expression. Drumming speed seems to indicate intensity of emotion. The pose of his face and head looks somewhat like Sinhalese dance—back, to the side, with arm extended forward. Elegant, somewhat tragic expression—showing anger. After spinning, he looks down at the 'flowers' in his outstretched hand, sadly. Laji says he looks as if he has something in his mind which he can't get out—suffering. ([Laji's notes:] Dārika goes round thinking deeply. It seems that he has some agony inside.) Yes.

Thin hardened tamarind twigs beat out the rhythmic refrain on the taut skin drumheads—1 2 3 4/1 2/1. This is very powerful. The drums are so hypnotic. The arms and chests of the five strong young drummers shine as they bend forward and backward in perfect unison. I'm starting to get drawn inside myself—I feel different. It's hard to write or be objective. Laji also has stopped writing. Abhilash stares hypnotically at the flame as Dārika continues to dance around the flickering oil lamp. I fall into meditation from this drumbeat. There is something so sensual and masculine about the drumming—powerful, passionate, incessant. One tall and handsome drummer watches me swaying slightly to the rhythm; he seems to play to me. I lose my self-consciousness and enter the energy of the drumming with them. Somewhere I see flashing knives again. I'm lost in the drums and barely notice Dārika. The eyes of the drummers are so wild, like wolves. They look through me.

Then Dārika gets up on the stool and calls Kāḷi for fight. Scene 2 ends. Loud firecracker. People get up and take a break. The drummers leave.

People crowd around me and watch me as soon as the action stops.

[Laji's notes:] Then a discussion among some spectator ladies. The crowd is enjoying the break, seeing Amba's crazy way of sitting [leaning her head down on her lap]. 'Look, she is sleepy. Hey, daughter, why do you come for this, which you can't do? Isn't it enough for you to sit and eat and drink over there [in your country]? Do you really need to go for this?'

Only now, after more than twelve hours of preparation, is the stage fully set for the central event of muṭiyēṯṯu—the appearance of Kāḷi. The actor who is to play the role of Bhadrakāḷi comes out of the green-room and stands before the goddess in her shrine. Several men lift the enormous muṭi onto the actor's head and fasten it to the red head-cloth underneath. The coconut-frond hair, tied into a knot, is cut loose and released over the actor's back. At this moment, women hoot loudly, signalling the intensification of śakti (divine power) this act entails. The priest comes out of the shrine with some blessed water for the actor to drink, then solemnly hands him the sacred *vāḷ*, the curved sword of Bhadrakāḷi. With this act, the actor is transformed. From this moment on, he is Kāḷi, fully present to the company of worshippers assembled in the temple grove. Kāḷi's face begins to tremble, her eyes bulging and tongue protruding, as she shakes the sword in one hand and threatens, pointing with the other. Her movements are unpredictable now, and she may attack anyone at any time.

As Kāḷi moves to the stage area she is followed by groups of laughing, shouting men who hold branches and dance behind her merrily. These spectator/participants represent the army of ghosts (*bhūtas*) attending the goddess as she goes to battle. Kāḷi touches her hand to each of the drums and then to her forehead in a gesture of reverence. She stands behind the curtain with the back of her muṭi (a plain, unvarnished wood surface) facing the audience. This stance represents her birth from the forehead of Śiva in Kailāsam. She then turns to face the audience and the spectacular sight of the glimmering muṭi has its full effect in the lamplight.

Kāḷi proceeds to worship the sacred flame and purify herself. This is shown by a lengthy sequence of hair-combing, in which the goddess runs her fingers through the dangling strands of coconut-frond hair, smoothing it out. The importance of these actions is evidenced by the attention to realistic detail. For example, the actor even mimes the rolling up of fallen, loose strands of hair into a ball, which is then cast off to the side. We often observed village women in Kerala combing their hair with exactly the same motions. Why does Kāḷi spend so much time on cleaning her hair? Troupe leaders could not clearly explain the significance of this act except to say that it shows her bathing and purification (women groom their hair in this way after a bath). These actions, however, seem to have a more profound significance. In ancient Dravidian culture hair was regarded as the source of great force, intimately tied to powers of sexuality, aggression, and supernatural energies.[24] This inheritance is still seen in the loosening of women's hair during states of spirit possession, as well as in the veḷiccappāṭu's (oracle) running of the fingers of his left hand through his long, loosened hair while in trance at Bhagavati temples. The running of the fingers through the hair, especially female hair, infuses the body with wild, natural sacred power. Kāḷi's actions clearly derive from these ancient ideas, which survive in various ritual contexts in Kerala, although the actors are no longer fully conscious of their meaning.

After completing the pūjā and bath, Kāḷi takes up her weapons and challenges Dārika to war. Dārika emerges from the darkness to battle Kāḷi in a fierce swordfight. Kāḷi chases him wildly around the temple until she lapses into a frenzied state of possession, losing consciousness. The onset of possession is signalled by the muṭi slipping to the side of Kāḷi's head and by the actor lowering the muṭi towards the drums. Actors deny that these are conscious acts, stating that these are simply Kali's actions at that time, 'by which we can know possession is beginning'. They describe a kind of dual performative consciousness by which the actor passively witnesses the actions taking place in his body, while also experiencing the actions of the goddess.[25]

The actor playing Kali appears before the shrine. As the muṭi is put on, ladies howl—'ULULULULULU!,' then men make a responding call: 'ARAPPUEY-HEY!'. The coconut-frond hair is let down, and tied back as ladies do here. It looks wonderful by the oil wick-light—so mysterious. Kali faces the shrine, strokes her hair with her left hand for some time while looking at the image inside. Her breasts are large and covered with gold. A garland of red flowers hangs around her neck. She receives the sword and flowers from inside the shrine, then begins to dance and shout. Fireworks punctuate the empowering of Kāḷi, along with more ululating. The men standing around her respond with more shouts. She takes blessings from the drums, and begins a spinning dance. Under a mango tree, men wave branches of mango leaves. Everywhere there is fire. The men go behind her waving branches and wildly shouting, urging her on (some sexual element to it)—a lot of fun for the people in this. Kāḷi gets wilder in movements, more out of control, charges audience. The women are more quiet and to the sides in this part. I feel as if it is definitely a chance for men to release their frustrated emotions, sexual energy. A lot of them appear drunk.

Now ladies wail again as Kāḷi stops spinning and the drums stop. She faces the drums silently, moves the curved sword up and then down as men wave their branches and urge her on, music getting faster and faster. Flowers and tiny bits of tender coconut leaf are being thrown—drums get very intense and fast. Spinning again—actor really does look as if he's in an altered state! Fire powder thrown, spinning—she suddenly charges, almost knocking over one child, looks at people in a scary way. Women seem quiet, pensive here. Many cover their heads and mouths as they look on with a serious expression. Men by contrast are very merry, endlessly laughing and teasing, trying to provoke Kāḷi by waving branches at her. One boy standing in front of me (above Kāḷi) tries to push his friend onto Kāḷi (in jest). Finally she heads for the stage. Men are shouting '*Tey tey*!'[26] She heads back, then goes ahead, seems to try to show how unpredictable she is. Now the women come walking out, smiling, behind the men. They talk and imitate the men's calls. I find myself running away from Kāḷi, somewhat scared. The children are all still awake, though it's nearly 4 a.m.

Kāḷi approaches the curtain from behind. We see Kāḷi's muṭi just from the back now. Then she turns to face us. The muṭi is spectacular. Jackwood with gilt. The face of Kāḷi carved there is large and strong. Actually you feel she is present there. We only see the Kāḷi of the muṭi (not the actor's face yet). Her black face shines over the curtain. As the actor's hands come over it looks as if the Kāḷi in the muṭi is moving her hands, like a puppet. Eerie. Now the curtain is raised to reveal the figure of Kāḷi.

Then the curtain is lowered again and held against her body. As she challenges Dārika and calls him to fight, the wound up curtain is held against her. Kāḷi emerges, spinning, waving her curved sword in her right hand, looking around for Dārika with fierce expression. Kāḷi's movements and costume are very womanly. Heavy breasts, prominent, large nipple area; padded hips and waist. The dancing and costumes are very artful and earthy, sexy.

Now Kāḷi comes to sit before the stage lamp and does pūjā and purification. Her skirt is full round red silk with golden border, blue and coloured apron in front, white cloth bunched in back, one hanging down from the waist. After cleaning her hair, she stands and spins around the lamp, throwing sweet white alari flowers all around. Laji says the white flowers littered all over the ground look like a battlefield—like little heads. Kāḷi dances for a long time around the fire.

This truly is a beautiful setting. The colourful curtain, the flaming lamp, the singing and drums and the tall coconut trees rising up behind like silent listeners, witnesses and participants in this drama of good and evil. The wife of Nambūtiri's younger brother (whose home we stayed in overnight) asks me as Kāḷi enters the stage, if I know what is the meaning of muṭiyēṯṯu. I ask her to please tell me. She says it is a way of teaching *dharma* [righteousness] to the common person, who is unable to distinguish good from evil. Her words pierce my heart. I feel she is simply a mouthpiece for Kāḷi, conveying a powerful message to me. I probe further, asking what exactly is the nature of the lesson—what is good and what is evil? But she becomes confused and cannot say more. I realize it was just a moment of inspiration. She looks confused and excuses herself to go watch the play. I wonder what is it like to be a woman like this, who has always obeyed the rules and never known anything else. Who is Kāḷi for them?

The women around me seem oblivious to the performance—they are eating peanuts, talking, and mildly scolding their children. Some are sleeping. Kāḷi is looking furious—eyes wide, mouth open, staring intently, and brandishing an iron sword while she dances to the heavy beat.

Kāḷi is on one side of the curtain and Dārika is on the other. They can't see each other but they are doing parallel movements: threatening, sticking their tongues out. Kāḷi is putting her long iron sword over the top of the curtain and it has red on the tip, like blood. She shouts, sticks out her tongue, puts her head back and thrusts her arm forward. Kāḷi attacks Dārika very vigorously. The two men holding the curtain have to really hold her tight. She is holding her right hand on the huge, heavy muṭi now and attacking ferociously as Dārika spins away from her. It is very dramatic. She is big, stocky, and fierce looking. But her movements are very agile also. There is a sudden stir about Dārika. Maybe he's fainted or something. People start looking back towards the temple to see if he is over there. I'm not sure where he is. Kāḷi is on the stool now. Very very strong. She is shouting. Sticking out her tongue and stretching out the hand, open like a flower, her head back. Hips stuck out to the side where the hand is, as if to say, 'Come on, come to me if you dare!' Waving the sword around vigorously. The guy holding the curtain looks nervous and he is staying away from that sword. Shouting, sticking out her tongue again. The drummers are watching her very intently. Kāḷi's waving her sword and ordering people around.

[Laji's notes:] Now Kāḷi calls Dārika for war, standing on the stool and shouting. There is a dialogue. Dārika says 'I'll take your head to Kailāsam, so that Kailāsam will shake. I'll give your head to your father's feet.' She responds that she will take out his tongue and give his blood to quench Vētāḷam's thirst. They keep threatening each other and going round the lamp. Now Kāḷi has a long sword.

[Sarah's notes:] The fight is more intense now, as Kāḷi chases Dārika fiercely around the temple ground. They disappear into the back of the temple, then Kāḷi reappears. No one knows where they will go now. The audience has to get up out of their way. After some time as the drums get more and more frenzied, Kāḷi begins to falter and swoon, shouting and screaming. Sofia [my three-year old daughter] becomes quite wild watching this. She wants to imitate everything and is making quite a scene, twirling and spinning.

There is a lot of śakti in this place. Intense humidity, dense coconut groves all around. A huge shout goes up as Kāḷi swoons. Here they say when the possession is authentic, the nose of Kāḷi on the muṭi will sweat. The torches flare up with fragrant green light. As I watch Kāḷi twirling and spinning to the torches and drums, I feel like crying. Heat and emotion crowd my heart. I feel love, sadness, happiness, longing—something very powerful is happening to me. It is the goddess whom I am to fathom now, not the remote male ice gods of the Himalayas, but the intimate, earthy females of forest, earth, and tree. As she spins I feel my own soul spinning with her. I am fascinated and dizzy, empty and expectant, hot of heart—feel I mustn't get too close or I could become lost. I feel the heat of Abhilash's dark muscular arm, the scent of his skin permeating my own.

[Laji's notes:] The possession part was authentic. People gathered round him in groups. He was having a very bad feeling like he was very hot. He was fanned by different people, all making him comfortable, allowing him to breathe more air. They continued fanning him for so long; he was breathing fast and his heartbeat was very intense. He was very emotional. He was offered some water—I guess it is coconut water. He tried to talk to someone but was not able to speak aloud. He had someone to feed him water; he could not do it by himself. His legs were trembling. When he was relaxed, he started praying and doing some rituals with the flowers on his costume. The stage was reset and the curtain put up again. Some people are leaving. One lady tries to keep the people here, saying, 'Hey, it is not over yet. There is one more hour to go!'

Comic Relief

The unremitting intensity of the events up to this point is broken by the release of tension in Kāḷi's possession and 'cooldown'. The muṭi is removed and set on the ground before the Kāḷi actor's feet, as he recovers and sits silently for some time. This apparent 'breaking of character' is also quite common in the classical Sanskrit theatre and does not seem to bother anyone. At this point Kōyimbaṭa Nāyar (sometimes called simply Kōyimbaṭar), a Nāyar chieftain, enters the stage and engages the drummers in a comic dialogue. His ostensible purpose, according to the troupe leaders, is as an emissary of Śiva, who has sent him to enquire about the progress of the war. Apart from providing an opportunity for the Kāḷi actor to take rest, Kōyimbaṭa Nāyar's dialogue also provides a welcome relief from the ritual solemnity of the action so far, and prefigures the broad satire of the Kūḷi scene to follow.[27]

The dialogue starts with puns on drum syllables, and sophisticated musical satire which plays on the sounds of the Malayalam words. Much of it is quite incomprehensible to modern audiences. An excerpt from the second portion of the dialogue will suffice here to illustrate an important theme developed in the Kūḷi scene which follows. In this segment, Kōyimbaṭa Nāyar talks about a prostitute in a Brahmin house. There is biting social satire in his remarks.

K: I went inside that house called Anattu.

D (drummer): What for?

K: Because of the prostitution practised by the whore at Anattu.

D: Then everyone would like to hear the head-to-foot and foot-to-head description of the prostitute of Anattu house.

K: Yes. I shall describe her in detail. There are particles of rice bran and flour in the spaces between her teeth and pieces of twigs in her fuzzy, dishevelled hair; her clothes are torn.

D: Oh ho ho.

K: There is an empty space between the thighs [indicating that she is too thin; i.e. her thighs are not plump].

D: Yes.

K: She has a hunch in her middle.

D: Yes.

K: She has the complexion of a green leaf.

D: Yes.

K: My Kota [personal name of the woman] is a beautiful gem in a dust heap. Victory to her! Hail! Hail! Hail! Hail! Hail!

D: A first-class whore indeed. Why didn't you add four more calls to victory—Hail! Hail! Hail! Hail!

K: When she saw me she gave me a hearty welcome.

D: After all she is a whore. She would welcome not only you but anyone else as well.

K: She kept ready for me one or two measures of rice husk carbon [used to clean teeth; only a tiny amount is required].

D: Yes.

K: She kept ready for me a bundle of coconut-leaf stem [the center of the coconut leaf is used to scrape the tongue and also as a toothpick].

D: Yes.

K: She kept one full bunch of mango leaves. This is for cleaning the teeth. [Mango leaf is folded and used as a toothbrush. The chlorophyll in the leaf removes mouth odour.]

D: Is that so? So the bunch of mango leaf is not to be put as manure in the field but to be used to clean your teeth. [Mango leaves are used as plant fertilizer.][28]

K: It is for cleaning the teeth. She dug and pressed one spouted vessel full of water too.

D: What is the need of pressing water in a vessel?

K: So that the vessel can hold more.

D: Oh I see. So even if the form of her body is not good, her stupidity is great. Otherwise will anyone try to press water into a vessel to make it hold more? So Kōyimbaṭar and she match well.

This comic dialogue is significant because it portrays the women of a Nambūtiri Brahmin house, supposedly the purest and most chaste, and certainly the highest-status females in Kerala society, as low, filthy whores; a severe insult allowable only in this comic ritual setting. Such abasement is also common in the Bharaṇi festival at Kodungallur, where not only high-caste women but the deity also become the targets of obscene acts and comments (Gentes 1992). Moreover, the mention of a 'head to foot and foot to head' description of the Brahmin prostitute directly recalls the song of praise sung to the Bhagavati kaḷam in the temple, and thereby draws an insulting parallel to the goddess herself. This theme of juxtaposing the goddess with a low-status female who breaks all the rules of ritual and social propriety is taken up enthusiastically in the next scene, with the entrance of Kūḷi. As we shall see, the specific details of Kōyimbaṭa Nāyar's description of the whore of Anattu house correspond exactly to the comic routine of Kūḷi's improvisation; actions which in turn recall Kāḷi's purificatory behaviour in the scene just preceding this one. A complex series of self-referencing frames is thus set up by these three sequential scenes.

Kāḷi is cooled down. The muṭi has been removed and placed before the drums. Kōyimbaṭa Nāyar now comes in wearing a large necklace and a white lower cloth. Kāḷi looks tired. The cymbal player answers questions of Kōyimbaṭa Nāyar from behind Kāḷi, who sits impassively. The feeling lightens up significantly. It's the first time the drums stop, for one thing. You get out of the trance. The audience is listening quietly, laughing occasionally at the jokes interspersed with chanting of mantras.

After a while some men in the audience begin to interrupt the scene by shouting 'ha!' all the time in place of the drummer, who begins a rather silly shouting match with the audience. Not a very respectful group. Now instead of 'ha!' they start shouting 'ma'—deteriorating into silliness. The troupe leader (playing Kāḷi) looks annoyed. He is breathing heavily. I think he is going to die doing this role one day.

Kūḷi

The entrance of Kūḷi is the comic highlight of muṭiyēṯṯu. Although her improvisation and costume vary significantly, she always behaves as an alter ego to Kāḷi, imitating Kāḷi's actions in a grotesque manner, and acting as an intermediary with the audience.

Her make-up and costume are clearly meant to identify her as a tribal figure. Kūḷi is a forest-dweller (hence the tribal make-up, as aboriginal people of Kerala live in the hilly, forest regions of the Western Ghats). This is indicated by her grass skirt, naked upper body, and leaf-decked hands and hair. In the story of Dārikavadham, on which the action of muṭiyēṯṯu is based, Kāḷi's assistant is actually the bloodthirsty Vētāḷam. Kāḷi rides on Vētāḷam's back to go to the war. This character is not portrayed in muṭiyēṯṯu these days, but is represented only by her face on the belt around Kāḷi's waist. There is some indication that the Kūḷi character may have evolved from an earlier Vētāḷam character.[29] In any case, her black skin and asymmetrical facial make-up identify her as a barely human being without culture; yet as Kāḷi's skin is also black, they share some attributes.

As Kūḷi enters the stage area, she goes through a series of actions that directly parallel those of Kāḷi in her earlier entrance. Like Kāḷi, Kūḷi stands before the goddess's shrine and twirls as if possessed by the goddess (however, everyone knows this is feigned). She enters the stage area hooting wildly and calling, '*Makkaḷe*! [Children!]'. Her huge belly and drooping, pointed red breasts identify her as in an advanced state of pregnancy. She later tells Kāḷi her pregnancy is the result of her dual rape by Dārika and his brother Dānavēndra. It is this information which infuriates Kāḷi sufficiently to resume and consummate the war. The highlight of Kūḷi's antics is her chasing of grown-up men in the audience and carrying them to centre stage, where she seats the victim forcibly on her lap and thrusts her pointed breast into his mouth. This is repeated numerous times throughout the scene to the immense delight of the spectators, including the 'victims', all of whom laugh uproariously. Clearly Kūḷi's behaviour makes an important commentary on the meaning of Kāḷi as a 'mother' goddess.[30]

The remainder of Kūḷi's comic routine centres around self-cleaning and the performance of everyday female domestic chores, all of which she does completely incompetently.[31] First she bathes and washes her hair in a ridiculous manner (recalling Kāḷi's elaborate hair cleaning); then she brushes her teeth, eating the toothpaste and making jokes; she does laundry adding black to the clothes, then sets them on the ground to dry and walks over them, soiling them again. She sweeps the courtyard, putting more dirt in the path. In every case she shows her lack of knowledge about proper cleanliness and purity, an important theme in Kerala culture. Her illegitimate pregnancy, in fact, is another example of this lack of bodily control. Finally Kūḷi does some folk dances, making obscene puns all the while, then pretends to go fishing. The finale of her scene brings her into play with Kāḷi, as she goads the goddess into searching for the demon brothers and pretends to sharpen her sword by cutting her nipples. She misunderstands the injunction to 'finish off' (i.e. kill) Dārika with the sword as an instruction to eat the sword. This she mimes as the scene comes to a close.

It is striking how directly some of Kūḷi's actions in this scene recall the comic dialogue of Kōyimbaṭa Nāyar discussed above. The detailed enumeration of her foolish hygiene habits, including tooth-brushing and bathing, are nearly identical to the lines in the previous scene. Moreover, Kōyimbaṭa Nāyar's description of the Anattu prostitute's appearance also recalls Kūḷi, who is shown with ratty hair entwined with leaves and twigs. Her indiscriminate sexual behaviour is also obvious from her advanced state of unwed pregnancy. In short, Kūḷi's actions and dialogue reinforce the ambivalent chain of associations and oppositions set up by Kōyimbaṭa Nāyar between Kāḷi and low-status human females. The ambivalence is perhaps most keenly felt when, in the Muvattupuzha style of performance, Kūḷi takes the mūṭi upon her head and dances about in feigned possession while the real Kāḷi is 'actually' possessed behind her. Kūḷi shadows and taunts Kāḷi, mimicking while also giving expression to the goddess's dark underside, repressed in the goddess's divine persona. Taken together, these two female archetypes constitute a dramatically split portrait of independent feminine power.

Kūḷi enters from the forest on the southern side of the temple, carrying leaves in her hand, wearing a grass skirt and pointed red breasts. Preceded by a drummer and a torch-bearer, she dances from side to side, with wild howls and whoops. As she reaches the stage area, Kūḷi climbs up onto the platform around a tree and chases off the (mostly male) spectators sitting there, scolding them as her children. The audience howls back at her. Kūḷi then takes blessings from the instruments, feet of the troupe leader, and the muṭi, still resting against the drums. Then she begins her comic routine. She runs into the audience and picks up one man, carries him to her lap centre-stage. She begins her improvisation.

Kūḷi is a caricature of Kāḷi. She has ugly pointed breasts, huge stomach, a harsh, high-pitched voice. She chases the young boys, who tease her but then run away frightened. She's gone to get another guy from the audience. He is dressed in the black garb of a pilgrim to Śabarimala. He gives Kūḷi some money and she leaves him alone. Several more men in the Śabarimala group get carried up. She is clearly making fun of the mother role. Violent, crude, sexual. One man taken in her lap sucks from her pointy breast. Here it is the mother who is being aggressive and teasing the son. In Kāḷi's entrance from the temple it is the other way—boys teasing the 'mother' goddess. Now Kūḷi carries up an old man in a saffron loincloth—everybody's hysterical. Oh, it's an old hunchback! He's completely twisted and bent. Wow, that's really something. He too is made to suck her breast. He really seems to have enjoyed that. Now Kāḷi is putting her muṭi back on. Kāḷi and Kūḷi have some banter as Dārika and Dānavēndra enter. Assistants hold up the curtain as the action is about to resume.

War

The final scene of muṭiyē_ṯṯ_u now ensues, as Kāḷi and Kūḷi search for Dārika and Dānavēndra, who have hidden themselves in the underworld (*pātāḷam*). The two females unearth the demons and the four circle furiously around the firelight, clashing swords in pairs. After another bout of possession, Kāḷi rather abruptly 'beheads' Dārika. This is represented symbolically by her simply removing Dārika's headgear, which she then offers to the stage lamp. All the troupe leaders told me the reason for cooling Kāḷi before the beheading scene, and the simplicity of the ending were due to an unfortunate incident in the past. One Kāḷi actor, it is said, had actually cut off the head of the actor playing Dārika in his possessed fury. To avoid such calamities, the Kāḷi actor must always have the headgear removed when the fury becomes too great, and the decapitation of Dārika is shown in this highly stylized and somewhat anticlimactic manner. With this the play comes to an end.

Kūḷi lights the torch and Kāḷi tells her to go and find where the demons are hiding. She keeps putting out the fire. She takes Kāḷi's weapon, says it's not sharp enough, and sharpens it on her nipple. Then she goes searching and brings Dārika and Dānavēndra with a torch. Kāḷi, Dārika, and Dānavēndra move majestically around the flame as Kūḷi spins in the opposite direction in a comical counterpoint. She follows Kāḷi, pulling at her hair. Kāḷi threatens her.

She tumbles. Kūḷi tries to interfere in the fight between Kāḷi and Dārika, threatening him ludicrously. Then as Kāḷi and Dārika spin, Kūḷi and Dānavēndra also spin. Now Kāḷi is really running after Dārika, chasing him around the whole stage area. Dārika and Dānavēndra 'hide' behind the drummers.

Kāḷi and Dārika fight with the electric power out. It looks beautiful in the natural light with stars overhead, so mysterious, like spirits on the paddy fields in your dream. Dārika disappears. Kāḷi looks for him. The lights go back on. Too bad. It really is much more beautiful by natural light. Sofia is sleeping peacefully on a blanket, oblivious to everything.

There is a wild fight as Kāḷi becomes quite mad, running about and attacking everyone. They remove her head-dress, but she still won't relinquish the sword. Kūḷi sits on Kāḷi's stool and puts on the muṭi. Then she dances about with it, spinning. She appears as if possessed, dancing wildly, clutching her breast. Kūḷi then flops at Kāḷi's feet, but after a moment casually gets up and walks away. People all get up to leave, but Kāḷi is still seated and the drums are still playing. Laji has gone for a break, leaving me alone with Abhilash.

As the actor is possessed by the spirit of Kāḷi, our souls are possessed by something else. I can barely concentrate on the grotesque figure of Kāḷi, her tongue lolling, belly bulging under the red breasts, legs splayed out in ecstatic rage. As the drumming swells through my body, Abhilash, sitting beside me, speaks soothing, teasing words, hinting at forbidden pleasures. It is a thrilling game. My body is getting hotter and hotter, my mind spinning. I stare into his eyes shamelessly, drinking him in.

Abhilash turns his head suddenly as if he sees something. 'I feel him watching us. He is there somewhere.' But when I turn to look I see only the moving sea of mocking faces, gloating over the violent movements of the bloated Kāḷi in their midst. Suddenly I am afraid. Antonio's eyes are like a presence in the darkness, a cat on the prowl.

Just as Kāḷi leaps at Dārika with a bloodcurdling howl, Antonio jabs me sharply from behind. Fear grips me. I thought he had been sleeping all this time. Acting for a moment as if nothing is wrong, he steps between us. With a broad smile, his eyes dancing cruelly, he whispers, 'I saw everything'. The pitch of the drums suddenly gets louder. Faster and faster, pounding and beating all around me. I can't hear him anymore, only see his dagger eyes and gesticulating hands. Everyone is standing now, moving out of the way as Kāḷi wildly pursues Dārika through our midst. Suddenly I hear his voice: 'I'm leaving you. Right now. If you don't come with me right now, it's all over.' I reply stonily, 'I can't come now. I have to stay here until it's finished. This is my work.' He turns abruptly and stalks into the darkness. My heart is pounding. Good, he's gone.

But Antonio is not gone. He is sitting uselessly on a stump at the border of the compound, immobile in his frustrated rage. How could he go? Where? There are no buses at four in the morning. He is helpless and utterly alone, a caged tiger in the hostile darkness.

The fight is over. Kāḷi has won. Silently removing Dārika's wooden headgear in a pantomime of decapitation, Kāḷi waves it solemnly in circles before the oil lamp. The gaudy colours of the tinsel overlay glitter and gleam, at odd moments revealing the plain, rough wood beneath. Dārika stands to the side, silent, defeated, impassive, dead. The greasy green face paint slowly dribbles down his cheek, melting indistinguishably into the stiff white borders of his chin.

Blessings

As the play comes to a close, the remaining spectators bring their infants up to be blessed by Kāḷi and take blessings themselves from the sacred flame. Kāḷi waves a torch in front of the gathered spectators and showers them with red flowers from her muṭi.

After about five hours, as the dawn breaks, Kāḷi symbolically beheads Dārika, removing the colourful wooden head-dress and hair, which she waves before the oil lamp, chanting in Sanskrit. Parents bring their infants forward for Kāḷi to bless, which she does by waving them before the lamp and applying a spot of lampblack to their foreheads. Some say that the sight of the gruesome Kāḷi so startles the sleeping infant who is awakened in this manner that he becomes brave and strong for life. Others merely wish to obtain the blessings of the now benevolent goddess, at this moment of her victory, at the height of her śakti, or power. Kāḷi breaks a coconut somewhat casually before the stage lamp. The small crowd murmurs quietly. Kāḷi waves a torch as people gather close around with folded hands to receive blessings. Kāḷi waves her muṭi and receives coins there.

Blood for Spirits

The final rite after the conclusion of muṭiyēṯṯu is the offering of a blood-sacrifice, guruti. Although a vegetable substitute for blood is now decreed by law in Kerala temples, actual animal sacrifice is still occasionally practised, as the excerpt below indicates. This blood-sacrifice is required to appease Vētāḷam and the other demonic spirits who have come from the forest to assist Kāḷi in the war. By offering blood to them, peace can once again be restored.

The action now shifts to the north side of the shrine where guruti, or blood offering to the evil spirits of the forest, is about to take place. A bamboo grid, plantain stalks, coconuts, and bowls of red liquid are being prepared by the priests.

[Laji's notes:] A man in the crowd explains what is happening: 'Guruti is related to muṭiyeṯṯu. The evil spirits, the devils and assistants of Kūḷi are residing in a place nearby. Now Dēvi along with these spirits who are to accompany her for the war are brought to an area near the main temple shrine during muṭiyēṯṯu. Then there is an offering for these spirits which is called guruti. After the guruṭi is given, these spirits are sent back. Otherwise they are said to remain here, which could create problems.'

[Sarah's notes:] I see chickens being prepared for the guruti (unusual). The chickens make a horrible noise just before they are killed. They seem to know and cry horrendously with bloodcurdling shrieks that sound almost human. Sofia asks me, 'What is that sound, Mommy? Why are the chickens crying?' Tears well up in my sleepless eyes as I try to reassure and distract her. My whole being revolts against this. I feel very frightened but there is nothing I can do but try to hide my fear from everyone.

Dawn

The temple festival is over as the dawn breaks and people head for home. The artists return to the green-room to pack up their belongings and receive their payment. In a few days, or perhaps even the next night, they will perform the entire ritual once again.[32]

Mothers in the audience scoop up their sleeping children, collect their belongings, and follow dishevelled husbands through the dew-damp brown paddy fields to homes nearby. Birds fly here and there in the thin morning light, their songs brightening the cool misty air. The performers, back inside the temple, are removing their make-up and drinking hot tea. I too lift my heavily sleeping little one, take blessings from the muṭi, and shoulder my bag of notebooks and tape-recorder, heading for home.

Notes

[1] *Guruti* (in some parts of Kerala known as *gurusi*) comes from the Tamil *kuruti*, meaning 'blood'. Since the outlawing of blood offerings, guruti is made from turmeric and calcified lime, which turn a brilliant red when mixed with water. Originally used by Nambūtiri Brahmins as a blood substitute in some ancestor sacrifices, turmeric-lime guruti is now integral to nearly all temple rituals in central and southern Kerala.

[2] See Nambiar 1979.

[3] See Schechner and Hess 1977.

[4] I attended a total of fourteen full muṭiyēṯṯu performances by eight different troupes in 1991–2.

[5] The mirror is often used as a representation of the deity in Kerala Hindu worship.

[6] Amba was the Hindu name given to me at the conversion ceremony described at the end of chapter 1.

[7] 1 lakh = 100,000.

[8] W. N. Brown 1958.

[9] Interview, Trichur, Kerala, February 1992.

[10] See Choondal 1981, Nāyar 1962 for discussion of costumes in muṭiyēṯṯu and Kathakaḷi.

[11] Prior to this century, the muṭi was not painted. The jackwood headgear was stained with natural red dye and oiled to reflect the golden firelight of the stage lamp. This effect has been exaggerated with the use of brilliant paints and foils today, as well as artificial light.

[12] According to Choondal, manayōla is bisulphate of arsenic, and is used as an Ayurvedic medicine for anaemia, poison, and cough 1981: 152.

[13] Freeman (1991) describes the role of mirror-gazing in teyyam.

[14] Entertainments like break-dancing, melodramas, and film songs are presented as preliminaries to muṭiyēṯṯu at even remote temple festivals.

[15] This legend pertains to the muṭi enshrined at Adur temple in Pattanamtitta district. Similar stories were related to me by muṭiyēṯṯu artists.

[16] Interview, Muvattupuzha, Kerala, February 1992.

[17] Appu Kuttan Mārār, Interview, Muvattupuzha, Kerala, May 1992.

[18] Vikkan ceṇṭa is also used for kaḷam pāṭṭu.

[19] See Hart 1975 on the sacred power of drums in ancient Tamil culture.

[20] For a discussion of symbolism of the sexual activity of elephants, see chapter 3.

[21] Transcribed from various performances; translation by L. S. Rajagopalan, 1992.

[22] See discussion of Kūṭiyāṭṭam in Richmond, Swann, and Zarrilli 1990.

[23] Fire torches of this type are used by tribal people to control elephants and tigers in forests. The material of teḷḷi powder is the gum of the Kundu rukkam tree, available only from the mountainous forest areas, and its technology is known only to the tribal people living in the hills Choondal 1981: 158. Teḷḷi is an Ayurvedic medicine with antiseptic properties. Pazhur Damodaran Mārār told us that teḷḷi was traditionally used to cremate the bodies of smallpox victims at midnight 'in olden times', and guruti (blood-sacrifice) was also offered to the bhūtas (ghosts) who were believed to be attracted to the feast of dead flesh. Damodaran Mārār also mentioned that in times of war the dead would similarly be cremated *en masse* on the battlefield at midnight, using teḷḷi powder.

[24] See Hart (1973, 1975), Hiltebeitel (1981, 1988, 1991) for the significance of hair in ancient Dravidian culture. Appu Kuttan Mārār told us that Dārika also has long hair, and cleans it during his scene. When we asked why Dārika is shown in this manner, he replied, 'During ancient times, kings also had long hair.'

[25] Despite significant regional variations in the order of events, in all performances of muṭiyēṯṯu a specific sequence of actions by Kāḷi indicates the onset of possession: slippage of the muṭi, erratic movements, and bowing of the headgear toward the drums.

[26] *Tey* means 'god' (via Tamil, from the Sanskrit deva), possibly related to the Tamil word *tai* for 'mother'. According to the participants, the shouting invokes the goddess's fierce energy.

[27] Nāyar (1962) notes the resemblance between this scene and the comic scene of Ittikandappa Kaimal in the brahminical dramatic form known as *Yatrakali* (also known as *Sanghakkaḷi*). The opening lines of the second portion of Kōyimbaṭa Nāyar's dialogue in muṭiyēṯṯu directly refer to 'Nambūtiris [Brahmins] of the Sanghakkaḷi troupe.' The language used is a medieval Malayalam which is close to Tamil (the two languages began to diverge about 1,000 years ago), which places this scene quite far back in history. The Kūḷi scene which follows seems to be a more recent addition which reaches a wider audience.

[28] I am grateful to L. S. Rajagopalan for the explanatory comments in brackets.

[29] Nāyar (1962) describes both a Vētāḷām character and separate 'Kūḷis' or forest ghosts, in muṭiyēṯṯu.

[30] See chapter 4.

[31] Appu Kuttan Mārār explained the relationship between Kūḷi's and Kāḷi's actions: 'Kāḷi's actions mean self-purification, but not purification of the environment. But Kūḷi does the purification of the environment, not self-purification.' Appu Kuttan's remarks reflect that Kūḷi is of low caste, whereas Kāḷi is high caste; the distinction between external and internal purification being one of the key markers of caste level.

[32] During the festival season, a troupe may perform up to fifty performances in three months.

3

LANDSCAPES OF FEMININE POWER*

Throughout India, the earth is regarded as a sacred, living entity having a female nature. From the temple of Bhārat Māta in Banaras to Kāmarūpa in Assam, from the source of Gangā Mā (the river Ganges) at Gangōtri in the Himalaya mountains to the tip of Kaniyākumāri at the southernmost point of the subcontinent, the land of India is infused with śakti, female creative energy. This creative energy which is the source of life is embodied in the physical forms of trees, plants, rivers, rocks, and soil, as well as in the complex personae of the myriad Hindu goddesses.[1] According to legend, the body of the goddess was cut into numerous pieces which fell at different spots throughout the land; each of these śakti pīthas is now the site of elaborate worship at permanent shrines (Bharati 1970).

The feminine power of the natural world is expressed most dramatically in the earth's seasonal generation of food. The soil, nourished by the decomposed elements of the dead, in interaction with the forces of heat and moisture, unfailingly produces out of itself fresh vegetation which sustains life. As far back as the Rig-Veda (*c.* 1200 BCE), these forces were worshipped anthropomorphically as gendered deities subject to manipulation by the will of human beings. The earth, Prithvi, was the ready, heated female body, seeking the soothing and fertilizing seminal rains of the sky-god Indra. The successful copulation of these two was responsible for the growth of plant life necessary to human survival.

In the non-Aryan traditions of India, represented in ancient Tamil poetry and practice, as well as in the beliefs of tribal populations, the

* 'Harvest of War' (pp. 112–13), 'Elephants and Tigers' (p. 146), from *Poems of Love and War*, A. K. Ramanujam © 1985 Columbia University Press. Reprinted with the permission of the publisher.

same ideas took slightly different forms. Rather than focusing on atmospheric deities and their grandiose activities, these traditions worshipped the earth's body in the form of mountains, rocks, trees, and bodies of water. The lush growths of vegetation and impressive geological formations of India's ancient landscape were the stage for profound dramas of energy and feeling in which the human, natural, and supernatural worlds were inseparably intertwined. By the Sangam period in south India (*c.* 150 BCE to 250 CE), this complex view of nature was codified into a sophisticated poetic tradition which delineated five types of landscape and their corresponding moods.[2] A conventional 'language of signs' established a 'world of correspondences between times, places, things born in them, and human experiences.' Through this 'live vocabulary of symbols … the actual objective landscapes of Tamil country become the interior landscapes of Tamil poetry' (Ramanujan 1985: 241).

These symbolic correspondences between exterior and interior landscapes inform many aspects of traditional Kerala culture. From time reckoning and house construction to the indigenous ideology of gender, external physical features correspond to inner states. Taking inspiration from the Sangam poets, and following the lead of contemporary Malayali scholars, we focus in this chapter on 'the three natural regions of *Kurinchi* or hill, *Marutham* or plain, and *Neythal* or ,coast' in our examination of the lived landscape of Kerala as expressed in the Bhagavati cult (Krishna Ayyar 1966: 10).

Marutam: Trees and Food

From my fieldnotes:

In the outlying village areas, where we often have to go for our work, my heart expands with enormous joy and love, I don't know quite why, for the emerald paddy-fields, the deep coconut groves, the red earth. It is so very green and lush: tree on tree, green on green, a jigsaw of deep living colours. I find myself obsessed with trees—mango, jackfruit, banyan, coconut, and many more. Some leaves are round (cashewnut), some oval shaped and pointed (mango), some as delicate as touch-me-nots, closing to the brush of a finger. Coconut palm hair sways gracefully in the wind, as tall arecanut palms tease above (it is said that coconut trees are afraid of areca palms and grow away from them); grasses, ferns, and wild plants carpet the ground below. Everywhere there is life, luxuriant, cool, moist, breathing, insects and birds calling, rain pouring down in bursts. I love the deep green of the paddy-fields and coconut trees, the mounds of brown earth piled up from the rains, fertile breasts waiting to be spread out again.

One evening at dusk, as we drove to the seashore in a jeep, wind rustling through our hair, the thin skin of reality was suddenly pierced. As I turned my head, I caught a fleeting glimpse of Bhagavati, red and black, coming towards us through a grove of trees (*kāvu*—which also means temple). I went deep, deep, and then we arrived at the back-water, where we took a raft over the still waters lined with thousands of coconut trees waving in the breeze against the brilliant sky. As we glided through the silent flooded paddy-fields, we passed a tiny island with twenty coconut trees growing, miraculously, from its tiny area of soil. Just as our boat approached, a strong wind came up and rustled their leaves uncannily. Again I had the feeling of a host of Bhagavatis reaching out to greet me; tall green mothers, roots deep in the moist brown soil, heads touching the sky. Tears came to my eyes as we passed. The sheer beauty of the scene was overpowering. Like the tendrils of creepers in a snake grove, these sights and sounds weave around my soul and captivate me. I see with a ravenous look of love, a deep openness, a sweet pain that feeds and destroys, all at once.

The most visible landscape in Kerala, the one that the traveller sees, and the one where muṭiyēṯṯu is performed today, is the landscape connected with food: coconut trees and fields full of rice paddy, in an endless panorama of green. Almost all of the lowland area between the seashore and the mountains is heavily planted with small terraces of rice paddy bordered by stands of coconut trees. These two agricultural products are the staples of Kerala's diet and economy, present in some form at every meal. Between the rice and coconut fields lie house compounds, each with its garden and stands of fruit-bearing trees. In a typical house garden papayas, bananas, guavas, mangoes, cashewnuts and jackfruit provide ample crops, while turmeric, black pepper, cardamom, vanilla, nutmeg, and chillis of various colours and heat can be harvested as needed for the kitchen. Rice from the fields is kept in large storage chests for use throughout the year. Cows and chickens provide animal protein in the form of milk, eggs, and poultry flesh. Only vegetables and other staple commodities are purchased from the local markets. Each house compound, its courtyard neatly swept and garden carefully tended, is within shouting distance of its neighbour, often the home of a relative or friend. Small paths weave among the trees connecting the compounds and fields in a tapestry of growth, activity and industry. Both congested urban areas and empty barren plains are rare; by far the majority of Kerala's landscape is typified by the green web of villages and fields. This is *marutam*, the fertile plains, where life thrives.

Amongst the houses and fields lie many small Bhagavati temples. Almost every village has its local Bhagavati temple, as well as somewhat less numerous shrines to Śiva, Krishna, Ayyappan, or demonic spirits such as Chattan or others. Mosques and Christian churches are also seen in many villages. But unique among deities, the icons of Bhagavati in muṭiyēṯṯu make it clear that she is an incarnation of the fertility of the land.

Muṭiyēṯṯu was traditionally performed in a dry, harvested paddy-field, temporarily transformed into a sacred space. Even today, muṭiyēṯṯu performances often take place in the dry fields abutting a local Bhagavati temple. The word muṭi (a head-dress, crown, hair) also refers to the heavy bundle of harvested rice paddy carried upon the head by agricultural workers at harvest time. Generally, female workers cut the paddy and carry it upon their heads, while men supervise the work and carry the bundles suspended from long sticks carried over the shoulder. The connection of the muṭi with both rice and the head suggests that Bhadrakāḷi in muṭiyēṯṯu may be seen on one level as a ritualized form of the female agricultural worker who carries the harvested paddy through the fields on her head, and ultimately, as the spirit of the paddy itself. Paddy sprouts traditionally can only be transplanted on Tuesdays and Fridays, days sacred to Bhagavati. Transplanting songs sung in the rainy season are dedicated to Bhagavati, as is the first harvest of the Malayalam year, offered along with goats and chickens at her temple. Bhagavati is thus both the generatrix and the consumer of the paddy plant, the essence of its fertility.

The goddess's connection with rice is expressed in the kaḷam (ritual drawing of Bhagavati). Bhagavati kaḷams are constructed for forty-one days during the month of *Dhanu* (December–January) before muṭiyēṯṯu takes place. Ritual specialists also are unable to give an adequate reason for this practice. But the gestation period of sprouted rice paddy seedlings, before they are transplanted to the field, also normally takes approximately forty-one days.[3] Could it be that the drawing of the kaḷam both prefigures and causes a successful germination and harvest later in the year? The image of the goddess is made from rice flour and powdered leaves; the large conical breasts (the only three-dimensional part of the drawing other than the nose and eyes), are formed from piles of rice, covered with red powder.[4] (see Fig. 4). The breasts and face of the goddess are wiped out with the right hand by the artist and distributed to the devotees as prasādam, the blessed and power-filled remains of the goddess's form once she has left the drawing. These sacred breasts of raw unsprouted rice are the promise of the land's continued fertility.

Bhagavati is also the essence of the coconut palm. An important epithet of Bhagavati used in the opening and closing songs of muṭiyēṯṯu is '*kurumba kāvu dēvi*' which also means goddess of the tender coconut grove (C. M. Pillai 1976: 271). At the start of the performance, tender coconut palm leaves are attached to the back of the large wooden muṭi. The coconut leaf hair is tied up onto the headgear, and released when the muṭi is placed on the head of the actor in front of the goddess's shrine. The coconut hair is 'combed' with the fingers and two strands are tied behind the muṭi in the manner of Kerala village women. The grooming and stroking of this coconut-frond 'hair' is an essential part of the ritual empowerment of Kaḷi in the performance, the source as well as the sign of feminine power.

The coconut tree is closely associated with the fertility of young virgin girls in ritual. Coconut trees begin to bear fruit once they reach maturity at the age of 12 to 15 years, the age of human menarche. An overt comparison between the maturing coconut sapling and the young adolescent girl is embedded in the word '*taikonga*,' meaning 'a young woman' or 'the breast of a young woman': 'tai' (related to the Tamil word for 'mother') also means 'a young coconut palm' (C. M. Pillai 1976: 503). The puberty ceremony celebrating the attainment of menarche was a ubiquitous festival in Kerala until recent times, and is still performed for many village girls by their parents (though it is falling out of favour amongst urban, educated girls, who see it as embarrassing and 'backward'). As part of the ceremony, an unopened coconut bud (*choṭṭa*) is placed into a large measure of raw rice, and the bud is peeled open to reveal the immature coconut fruits within. This tender coconut bud and its hidden fruits are openly associated with the reproductive potential of the newly matured girl.[5] The number of baby coconuts counted inside the bud is said to predict the number of children the girl will have in her lifetime. In another folk divination, people say that when a coconut is split in half and the 'eye' side (where the three soft holes are located at the stem) is larger, the woman of the house is dominant over her husband (and should not be).

The homology between coconut trees and women is also expressed in folklore about breasts. The term '*tēṅṅu*', meaning coconut fruit, is used by males to refer to women's breasts, as in the following insult which may be said by one man to another: '*ninte ammate tēṅṅu*'—'your mother's coconuts (breasts).' The maturity and size of a woman's breasts may also be indicated in slang usage by using technical terms for the coconut fruit at different stages of its development, from smaller size to the large and heavy ripe coconut. This analogy between coconuts and breasts is more striking as the coconut fruit contains a sweet, refreshing liquid known as the 'milk'. The offering of tender coconut juice is a special way of honouring a guest who arrives at one's home, and the squeezing of the grated coconut meat to extract the thick white milk provides an essential ingredient in most Kerala curries. Amongst the many breakfasts made of rice and coconut, *ciratta puttu* is striking for its breast-like shape, formed from the half-coconut shell moulds used for steaming the cakes.

The breasts are a prominent feature in the costume of Bhadrakāḷi in muṭiyēṯṯu. Painted bright, shiny red, and tightly encircled by snakes with reared heads, Kāḷi's breasts are often made of half-coconut shells. The mounded breasts of Bhadrakāḷi in the kaḷam also visually echo the sprouting coconut fruits placed in the ground. Once the tender green leaves emerge from the fruit, the seedling is transplanted to a mound of earth, often located in the paddy fields. The breast like appearance of the protruding coconut-seedling hills amongst the green sprouting rice shoots strikingly reinforces the sense of the earth's feminine bounty, recalled in the shape of the Bhagavati kaḷam.

Coconut trees are a symbol of limitless fertility. The most important food and cash crop in Kerala, they bloom throughout the year, and the sight of the shooting buds splitting open to reveal the heavy fruits within is a delightful and reassuring sign of the health and bounty of the land. Every important ritual event is marked with the presence of a coconut flower bud standing in a measure of raw rice. This, along with the traditional brass lamp, is the most commonly recognized symbol of prosperity and happiness in Kerala. Almost every home, no matter how poor, can boast of at least a few coconut trees, which are a guarantee of both food and income. Larger landholders sell their coconuts at frequent intervals to manufacturers of coir, coconut oil, and other products for a good profit. Finally, they may lease the trees to collectors of another very important coconut product, toddy.

Toddy is produced from the fermented sap of the coconut palm. The choṭṭa, or bud (used in the female puberty ritual) is tied tightly with a thread or sinew, and the tip sliced off. The tapper uses an animal thigh bone to gently tap the sides of the bud up and down to 'heat it up', thus drawing the sap of the coconut flower up to the tip of the bud. A clay pot is placed mouth down and at an angle, so as to collect the dripping sap. Every few days the sap is collected and drunk as an alcoholic beverage. This beverage, favoured by village men, is said to be invigorating and refreshing. Its taste is musty and sweet. Left to ferment, it turns to vinegar. Arrack, a strong distilled liquor, may also be produced from the toddy, although its production is currently illegal in Kerala.

The action of toddy-tapping has obvious parallels to human sexuality. Toddy drains the essential fluid from the tree through its flower bud, which is metaphorically associated with the female genitals in the puberty ritual discussed above. The phallic appearance of the bud and obvious symbolic parallel of the tapping action to the production of semen from the penis, by heating and stimulating the exterior surface in order to draw the clear, milky fluid from the rounded tip, is hard to miss, but was not consciously admitted by anyone I interviewed. One tapper, however, told a folktale in which the tapping activity vied for the attention of the tapper's wife and was clearly a substitute for sex.[6] This symbolic correspondence reinforces the parallel between the processes of human procreation and agricultural fertility. Toddy is in a sense the bījam, the essential blood-seed of the coconut tree itself. It is not surprising that certain very fierce goddesses and demonic spirits in village shrines demand the offering of toddy, as well as blood-sacrifice and meat, to satiate their thirst.[7]

The association between the goddess and the coconut palm is further supported by the fact that new toddy-tapping operations may only commence on Tuesdays and Fridays, inauspicious days sacred to Bhadrakāḷi. Old tappers recite mantras and prayers to Bhadrakāḷi before cutting the bud to extract toddy. Bhagavati is the spirit of the coconut as well as of the rice paddy.

Another tree which is intimately associated with Bhagavati is the jack wood, or plāvu (*Artocarpus integrifolia*). This tall, dark hardwood tree is said to have two varieties, one male and one female. The *varikka* plāvu, or the female tree, can be recognized by its greater fertility in the production of fruits. Only this female jack tree is suitable for the important ritual uses to which plāvu is put, such as the carving of temple drums, the fashioning of *murtis* (living idols of Bhagavati), and carving of the muṭi. The sacred associations of the jackwood tree appear to be very ancient, and figure in Sangam poems of the *kurinji* landscape.[8] Worship of the jack tree is also an important part of tribal religion in the hill region bordering Kerala and Tamil Nadu.

The association of the jack tree with Bhagavati may, as in the case of the coconut tree, derive in part from its botanical features. The jack tree, like the coconut tree, matures at the age of 9–13 years, at which time it begins to bear very large, round fruits which often grow in pairs and hang from the stem and branches of the tree. The obvious resemblance of these fruits to female breasts is not lost on men, who use this metaphor in a manner similar to that of the coconut fruit. When talking amongst themselves, men may describe a woman with very large breasts as a *cekka mulacci* or jackfruit-breasted one. The jackfruits themselves only ripen during the hot summer months of *Kumbham* and *Mīnam* (February through April), which are also the time of Bhagavati's birthday and the height of the temple festival season. At this time many curries and sweet puddings are made from the seeds and sweet, strong-smelling jackfruit, which may also be eaten raw.

Jackwood, coconuts, and bales of rice all epitomize the fierce goddess as the spirit of agricultural fertility. This idea is also unambiguously expressed by the most important icon of Bhagavati, her vāḷ, the sickle-shaped iron sword which embodies her essence and power. Both the agricultural sickle and Bhadrakāḷi's weapon are made of iron, which while very durable and strong also has the power to repel and destroy evil spirits. The shorter *arivāḷ* is used to cut the ripened rice paddy at the harvest time. Grasping a small bunch of plants in one hand, the worker (often a low-caste or non-Hindu female) slices low and firmly across the bottom of the stem with the curved blade of the sickle, then lays her bunch in the dry field. As we saw in chapter 1, an important motif in temple legends links the vāḷ of the low-caste female agricultural worker with the divine power of Bhagavati, whose presence is revealed when the worker sharpens her sickle on a rock which begins to bleed. Within shrines to Bhagavati, this curved sword, with its somewhat elongated handle, is her primary representation.[9] The vāḷ represents the goddess, receives worship in temple rituals, and is often said to shake and shiver of its own accord. The presentation of the sword by the priest to the ritual actor in muṭiyēṯṯu marks the moment of enlivenment of the actor by the actual spirit of the goddess. Throughout the performance, the possessed Kāḷi waves the vāḷ threateningly in pursuit of Dārika; and using this weapon she symbolically decapitates her foe. In the iconography of the kaḷam, the vāḷ appears in one of the goddess's right hands, opposite Dārika's severed head, dripping blood into a bowl.

This strong equivalence between the implements of harvest and of ritual death at the hands of Bhadrakāḷi echoes an ancient relationship imputed in Dravidian poetry between agricultural fertility, human sexuality, and the necessity of death for the continuance of life. In the system of Sangam poetry, marutam, the fertile, settled land, was also the place of siege, of infidelity and conflict in love. The private realms of love and sexual relations between men and women corresponded metaphorically with the public sphere of battle, death, and victorious kingship, and both of these were essential to agricultural fertility, the mainstay of human life. A Sangam poem celebrating the victory of a king makes the metaphorical equivalence between agriculture and war clear even in its title:

> Harvest of War
>
> Great king,
>
> you should shield your men from ruin,
> so your victories, your greatness
> are bywords.
>
> Loose chariot wheels
> lie about the battleground
> with the long white tusks
> of bull-elephants.
>
> Flocks of male eagles
> eat carrion
> with their mates.

Headless bodies
dance about
before they fall
to the ground.

Blood glows,
like the sky before nightfall,
in the red centre
of the battlefield.

Demons dance there.

And your kingdom
is an unfailing harvest
of victorious wars.

(Ramanujan 1985: 115)

The cutting of the head provides blood, which is associated with death, but also is a form of seed, fertilizing the earth and enabling it to produce new life (Hart 1975). The multivalent symbol of the vāḷ metaphorically links the rice plants and Dārika's head. Both must be cut down in the same way, and for similar ends: a death which gives life. But the head is not merely symbolic of this process; it is literally full of seed, in the form of stored semen.[10]

The ancient Dravidian symbolism of the harvest of war, and particularly the cutting of heads to promote the health and fertility of the kingdom, is thus a performative act (in Austin's sense), not merely a trope (Austin 1962). In this system, blood becomes the central metaphor for the fertilizing fluid of life. The procreative seed is called bījam, a word which in modern Malayalam means the reproductive and sexual fluids of both men and women. Only by the spilling of this blood-seed in battle or in sexual relations can new life develop and take birth.[11] The sacrifice of the male blood-seed to the hot and thirsty feminine body of the earth is the act which enables the perpetuation of life in the ancient Dravidian worldview. The related practice of human sacrifice among numerous indigenous south Asian communities was directly associated with maintaining the fertility of the earth. For example, in Orissa, '[the Khonds] believe that Mother Earth bestows power of life through harvest and that power of life can be returned to her by offering a life, i.e. by a human sacrifice' (Bhattacharyya 1980: 97). Muṭiyēṯṯu is one enactment of this ancient drama, in which the immensely fertile blood-seed of the demon Dārika is spilt on the dry, lifeless paddy fields after the harvest, to ensure the success of the crop in the cool, rainy season to come. The final rituals of muṭiyēṯṯu, performed at sunrise, involve the splitting of a coconut, the cutting of a particular squash, and the offering of guruti, red lime and turmeric water.[12] The coconut represents the head of Dārika, the squash substitutes for the body of an animal (as actual animal sacrifice is now banned by law), and the guruti represents blood, which is spilt on the ground. These rituals magically ensure fertility by offering an actual or symbolic head, body, and blood to the earth to satiate the dangerous demonic spirits attracted to the rituals.

Bleeding Stones and Red Earth

If the trees and food-giving plants of the fertile marutam landscape are infused with the spirit of Bhagavati, the soil from which they grow is her body. Offsetting the brilliant green of the foliage is the deep red colour of Kerala's soil. The piled-up conical breasts of raw rice in the Bhagavati kaḷam echo another common sight in the season after the monsoons, just before the festival season begins. Travelling through villages of central Kerala at this time of year one may see nearly every compound studded with small red hills. The fertile soil is carefully piled into neat rows of small conical mounds in order to preserve the nutrients in the mud for the following planting season, when the mounds are spread out again to fertilize the soil. Their similarity to the red conical rice-filled breasts of the kaḷam is remarkable, suggesting that the kaḷam prefigures and magically induces the fertile, rainy season of the year.

Muṭiyēṯṯu and other ritual arts dedicated to Bhagavati are performed only during the dry season, from Dhanu (starting mid-December) to *Medam* (ending mid-May). The height of the performance season is in the months of Kumbham and Mīnam (from mid-February to mid-April), the hottest and driest time of the year. During these months no rain falls and temperatures climb steadily to an uncomfortable level before the first monsoons in early June. Before irrigation, the fields of Kerala would have lain fallow from February to May, getting drier and drier as the harvest was taken before the monsoon rains. This is the season of pustulant fevers. These hot months after the harvest delineate the temple festival season, when muṭiyēṯṯu and other rituals emphasizing violence and blood sacrifice are performed as offerings to Bhagavati. It is also the time when, until forty years ago or so, Keralites celebrated the menses of the earth goddess in an agricultural ritual called *uccāral.* For three days representing the seclusion of the menstruating earth goddess, no agricultural work was undertaken, granaries were closed, and paddy was not sold. On the fourth day the granaries reopened and landlords repossessed their fields.[13]

The red earth in this hot, dry season is the visible womb of the earth goddess in the season of menstruation. The ritual performances of this temple festival season frequently conclude with the offering of guruti, the turmeric and lime water which represents blood. The leader of a temple performance troupe from northern Kerala, E. Kalidasan, clearly related the guruti offering to both harvest cultivation and female fertility. As he explained it, this offering of guruti by sprinkling the red water on the ground 'represents the menstruation of Bhagavati. The earth gives birth to plants in the same way a mother gives birth to a child after the menstrual period. So the earth must also be mature.'[14] According to Kalidasan, all the temple arts devoted to Bhagavati are closely related to farming culture. This interpretation differs slightly from that provided by most people I interviewed, who saw guruti as a blood-sacrifice to appease demonic spirits. Here blood is the sign of the earth's female potential to procreate.

The earth goddess's feminine power is also manifested in the common legend of the bleeding rock, collected from many Bhagavati temples in Kerala. 'These myths vary in details, but the most common form ... is that a [female low caste agricultural worker], while in the act of reaping, accidentally cut a stone and then found blood on it, and this stone was later on considered to be a divine seat of Kāḷi' (Induchoodan 1969: 263). We were told this same legend about the origin of a temple where muṭiyēṯṯu was being performed.[15] When we proceeded to the inner sanctum of the temple we were able to see enshrined there not an anthropomorphic representation of the goddess, but a large flat outcropping of black granite with a long vertical slit in its surface, smeared with vermilion powder and flowers. This vagina-like red opening which had produced blood when cut with the sickle used to reap rice paddy was the very body of the fierce goddess, not different from her manifestation in the rice-powder kaḷam or in the person of the actor possessed by her spirit in muṭiyēṯṯu.

It is a common practice at centres of Śāktā worship to regard the *yoni* or female genitalia of the goddess as the supreme seat of divinity. The famous Kāmākhyā shrine in Assam houses the divine yoni of Sati referred to at the begining of this chapter. Tantric rituals associated with Śākta practice include worship of the female menstrual flow, normally considered an extremely polluting substance by mainstream Sanskritic Hinduism.[16] Such Śākta notions inform the Kerala legends, in which the goddess's body manifests as the physical earth. The blood drawn from the living stone is proof of the goddess's divine life-force, but is also her bījam, procreative blood-seed. The female agricultural worker draws this blood with the same implement and in the same manner that she uses to cut the living rice. Her act equates this blood-seed, like that present in the decapitated head of Dārika, with the life force present in food. Her sickle, like Kāḷi's vāḷ, produces blood which both destroys and gives life.

Another legend, from the central Kerala temple at Chengannur, explicitly connects the goddess to menstruating females. According to temple legend:

> … even today the deity which is cast in *panchaloha* [an alloy of five metals] gets her periods, a phenomenon which is not heard of in any other temple. … The [attendant] examines the [white petticoat of the goddess] closely and if there are signs of bleeding sends it to … the temple [priest]. … The sanctum is kept closed for three days when the Goddess gets menses. … On the fourth day, the bathing ceremony … is conducted by taking the image in procession on a female elephant to the nearby Pampa river. Innumerable devotees, especially women with *thalapoli* (holding lamps), accompany this. (Vaidyanathan 1988: 46)

The details of the rituals surrounding the menses of Chengannur Bhagavati explicitly re-enact the traditional puberty ceremony of high-caste girls of Kerala, now falling into disuse. Nambūtiri Brahmins of Kerala previously celebrated a girl's first menstruation for forty-one days. During the forty-one-day puberty celebration, a decorated pavilion is erected and decorated with flowers while the young girl is secluded in a menstrual room or hut. The examination of the first menstrual blood-stains on the white petticoat was once a form of divination, in which the future of the young woman could be read (Krishna Iyer 1981(1): 203–8). At the end of the girl's seclusion, on the forty-first day, the girl is bathed and carried, either in a palanquin or on an elephant's back, in procession to the store room of the house (*aṟa*). This room is the granary, where a large chest of raw rice is stored, as well as other family treasures. It adjoins the pūjā room, where deities are installed and worship performed. Carrying the girl to the rice store room emphasizes the connection between the girl's fertility and agricultural plenty, both manifestations of the goddess's śākti. In the *aṟa*, the girl is covered with a red silk cloth called *vīralipattu*. Vīrali means a heroic female.[17] The giving of vīralipattu ceremonially honoured victorious warriors returning from battle. With the vīralipattu covering her face, the girl is carried out once again and the red silk cloth removed to expose her face. At that time she is instructed to gaze into a special bell-metal mirror. One woman told me the purpose of this gazing is for the girl to worship her self, to recognize her own divinity.

These elaborate celebrations closely parallel the rituals honouring Bhagavati in modern temples of Kerala. The puberty rite is held over forty-one days, the time period being the same as that demarcated for the drawing of Bhagavati kaḷams and associated rituals in the winter month of Dhanu; this also approximates the germination period of rice seedlings before transplantation to the fields. The sacred image (murti) of Bhagavati is removed from her protected seclusion in the inner sanctum of the temple and is carried around the temple courtyard placed atop an elephant's back. A *pantal* is erected in the temple where the kaḷam of the goddess is prepared and worshipped. The murti of the goddess may be placed on a stool and covered with red silk cloth at the head of the sacred kaḷam. Offerings of flowers, rice, and other cooling foods will be made to the goddess. On the last day of the forty-one days of worship, muṭiyēṯṯu or other ritual drama involving possession is performed. The costumed and made-up actor embodying the goddess's spirit will gaze into a mirror at the crucial moment of his empowerment, recognizing his transformation into the goddess by seeing his face as her own. The hooting of the *kurava* by women at the moment of empowerment is also done at the puberty ceremony, as well as at marriages.[18] This remarkable one-to-one correspondence between high-caste puberty rituals and Bhagavati temple rituals suggests that, just as Bhagavati is modelled on the virgin female, the female puberty rite is the prototype of all Bhagavati rituals seen in the temples of Kerala today.

The menarche rituals of certain low-caste and tribal groups are also reflected in the lore of Bhagavati. Accounts of puberty rituals amongst the hill-dwelling peoples of the Ghats frequently mention the idea of dangerous power inhering in the advent of menstruation, and the consequent seclusion and protection of the pubertal female. The following description of menarchal rites amongst the Parayans of the Nilgiri Hills contains elements commonly found in such accounts:[19]

> As soon as the first menstruation takes place, the girl is given an iron rod, usually a sickle. While giving the sickle into her hand, care is taken not to touch her on any account. People believe that the girl during her menses is subject to the attack of the evil spirits, as the smell of the blood-discharge attracts evil spirits. Therefore, the significance of giving a sickle or any other iron material is to prevent the evil spirits from getting any power over her. ... A Balahi woman after child-birth must always keep a sickle near her bed. If she leaves the house, she must carry it on her shoulder. (James 1974: 163.)

Bhagavati worship also incorporates these themes. The image of Bhadrakāḷi as a young virgin girl carrying a curved iron sickle (vāḷ), and the injunction against touching the Kāḷi actor in muṭiyēṭṭu once he is dressed as the goddess, recall the tribal puberty rites. The actor is empowered by the spirit of Bhadrakāḷi standing before her shrine; the priest drops the iron sickle-shaped sword representing the goddess into the actor's hands without touching them, just as the sickle must be given into the menstruating girl's hands without touching them. Moreover the association of the menstrual blood with both death (as evidenced by its attractiveness to the evil spirits) and fertility (signalling the girl's sexual maturity), makes this event a manifestation of the ambivalent feminine power of aṇaṅku/śakti.

Amongst the tribal groups in Malappuram district, during the celebration of menarche, an old lady takes the young girl on her shoulders at the conclusion of her menstrual period.[20] The old woman, accompanied by beating drums, carries the girl to a nearby pond where she is immersed and bathes to cleanse herself from the menstrual pollution. This obscure ethnographic detail may clarify the motif, clearly seen in the temple art, of Bhadrakāḷi riding atop the shoulders of a hideous, haggard old woman named Vētāḷam (see

Fig. 5). Vētāḷam, represented in muṭiyēṯṯu by a grotesque face worn at the waist of the actor playing Bhadrakāḷi, is explicitly said to be a wild, forest-dwelling creature. The correspondence between Vētāḷam carrying Bhadrakāḷi into war and the tribal old woman carrying the menarchal virgin to her bath strikingly confirms Bhagavati's identity as a menstruating virgin female.

The onset of menstruation at puberty is an ambivalent event. The symbolism of the puberty rite celebrates the fertility of the young girl, likening her to the budding coconut and ripening paddy; she is presented with the auspicious items given to a bride. But menstruation, while signalling the potential for fertility and birth, also implies a danger: the intense emotions of sexual desire which are believed to accompany physical maturity may lead the girl to disaster if not restrained and controlled until her marriage. Menstruation in a married woman signals the loss of a potential foetus, a death of sorts.[21] In menstruation, then, death, desire, and heat are intimately interwoven.

A menstruating woman is considered to be 'hot', both physically and emotionally, within the Indian system of medicine known as Ayurveda (Daniel 1984: 189; Wadley 1980: 164). This heat, like that described by the Kāḷi performers, manifests itself physically in perspiration, and emotionally in unruly emotions like anger and lust. It may also manifest in pustulant fevers such as smallpox or chicken-pox, which, as in much of India, are seen as visible signs (*darśanam*) of the presence of the fierce goddess.[22] An item of folk medicine further links female sexuality and heat, for acne eruptions on a woman's face are interpreted as a sign of a 'hot' nature (i.e. excessive sexual desire). Certain liquids and foods are taken daily, both internally and externally, to cool the body and emotions, which are intimately linked together. Women of Kerala apply coconut oil to their head, hair, and entire body—an 'oil bath'—and use fresh turmeric on their faces and bodies as a coolant and cosmetic. These treatments are more important for women in a 'hot' state, such as after menstruation (a woman traditionally remained in seclusion and did not bathe during the first four days of her menses) and during pregnancy. Although men also take oil baths and eat cooling foods, they are generally considered to be naturally 'cooler' in the indigenous system, and of course do not ordinarily undergo periodic transformations in their physiological/emotional state as

Fig. 5: 64-hand *kaḷam* of Bhagavati

women do (although the Kāḷi enactment during temple rituals provides such an opportunity) (McGilvray 1982).

Bhadrakāḷi in muṭiyēṯṯu wears brilliant red, symbolic of feminine energy in south Indian ritual (Beck 1969, McGilvray 1982). Chastity is the opposite of this fiery state: calmness, obedience, silence, passivity, and faithfulness are the outer marks of a properly controlled woman, indicative of her inner coolness and lack of desire. It is interesting that white is the preferred colour of dress in Kerala, for both men and women. This is in striking contrast to the brilliant colours for which Tamil women's attire is famous. It seems that in Kerala, there is a powerful need to overcompensate for female redness (with all its symbolic concomitants) by the application of outward whiteness. The emphasis on frequent water and oil baths and application of sandalwood on the forehead also suggest a strong concern with managing heat by applying cooling substances, especially for women. The iconic image of an attractive woman, seen in films, art, and poetry, is one just fresh from the bath, her hair fully oiled, wearing a white cloth and a dab of sandalwood on her forehead. The emotional meaning of such cool images is beautifully expressed by Kattamanita Ramakrishnan in the poem 'Shanta', which appears at the end of this book.

In the poems of love written in the marutam genre, it is not the peaceful fulfilment of connubial bliss which is immortalized, but rather the unruly emotions of passion, infidelity, and conflict. In battle, marutam is the siege, the attack on the fertile, peaceful, settled regions. Inherent in life is the promise of death, which must be fulfilled for life to continue. In the symbol of the fertile virgin this entire landscape of conflict erupts. Full of potential for giving life and feeding both foetus and society as a whole, the fertile virgin embodies dangerous appetites which ultimately require the sacrifice of male life-fluids and even death for their satiation. The rituals of the Bhagavati cult emphasize this highly ambivalent state of female virginity. While modelled on the joyous celebrations of menarche, Bhagavati rites attempt to resolve the inherent conflict this event sets in motion. Because the generation of life depends absolutely upon the taking of it, in nature and in myth, Bhagavati's character is intrinsically problematic. The unavoidable conflict between two opposing forces—feeding and consuming, giving and taking, life and death—is the central problem of muṭiyēṯṯu, as well perhaps of all Hindu worship of the fierce goddess. In muṭiyēṯṯu this paradox is resolved by transforming the violent, bloodthirsty, menstruating goddess into a benevolent, breast-feeding, life-giving protectress.[23] As an agricultural rite, muṭiyēṯṯu is charged with managing and transmuting powerful energies essential to the perpetuation of human life.

From Virgin to Mother: Three Kerala Temples

The cyclic repetitions of the months and years transform the female energies of the earth from hot to cool, from fallow virgin to fecund mother, over and over as the seasons slowly advance and decline. In the human life-cycle such patterns also emerge, in the monthly menstrual periods and the series of pregnancies and births nearly all women undergo in Kerala. Each woman passes slowly through five distinct stages of fertility over the course of her lifetime. These states, with unique social and ritual values, are in turn reflected in the qualities of specific goddesses in Kerala. The management of female powers is thereby ritually compartmentalized, with different goddesses taking prominence over particular aspects of feminine energy.

One striking feature of stories of the goddess throughout India is the emergence of one form out of the body of another. At times the fierce, black Kāḷi emerges from the body of the lovely, golden Pārvati, wife of Śiva, as the pure expression of her anger. In the *Devīmāhātmya*, Kāḷi emerges from the brow of Durga as she rides onto the battlefield, manifesting the pure violence required to destroy the demons Chanda and Munda. In another chapter of the *Devīmāhātmya*, seven goddesses emerge one after an other, from the body of Durga, each holding a different weapon in her hand, and join Durga in the battle against the demons. During the Hindu festival of Navarātri, meaning 'nine nights', three forms of the goddess—Durga, Lakṣmi, and Sarasvatī—are celebrated in turn each night for nine nights. These disparate aspects of the goddess are understood by most devotees ultimately to be a single deity.

Chottanikkara Bhagavati, the goddess residing at the temple of that name in central Kerala (Ernakulam district), changes her nature three times throughout the day. She is Sarasvatī in the morning, dressed by the priests in white clothes, Lakṣmi at noon, dressed in pink, green, or yellow, and after the pūjā at dusk she becomes Durga, wearing red. At a separate shrine in the lower courtyard of the temple, the goddess manifests as Bhadrakāḷi, dangerous and bloodthirsty. The shifting form of the goddess, and the presence of several different beings who emerge from her body, may be understood in a variety of ways. One interpretation of this phenomenon is that it concretizes different aspects of the female personality—the good, obedient wife and the angry, rebellious daughter, for example. Many writers have noted the relation between such images and the expression of contradictory, antisocial aspects of the female personality.[24] Stanley Kurtz relates the theme of multiple goddesses who are really one to patterns of Indian child-rearing in which multiple female caretakers replace the one-on-one mothering common in Euro-American society (1992). Kurtz concludes from this fact that the multiform Hindu goddesses express the childhood experience of group care-taking and the diffuse, shifting emotional attachments this pattern instils.

While psycho-social explanations provide insight into the cognitive and affective grounds of the Hindu belief in multiple deities, a different explanation may augment these. Rather than conflating different individuals or splitting conflicting tendencies in the female social personality, the motif of one or more goddesses emerging successively from another's body may express diachronic changes in an individual woman's reproductive state throughout her lifetime.

Throughout the Indian subcontinent, female reproductive development is divided into discrete phases. Five distinct stages are recognized in Kerala:

menarche — menopause

little girl (neutral) A	virgin (ambivalent) B	married (auspicious) C	widow (inauspicious) D	old woman (neutral) E
non-menstruating infertile		menstruating fertile		non-menstruating infertile

Fig. A. Stages of the Hindu Female Life-cycle

Throughout the Hindu world, and as we have seen for Kerala, an important distinction is made between a female who menstruates and one who does not. Within the domain of fertility, a further division is drawn between virgins and widows, who do not have access to sexual gratification, and married women, who do. We have reviewed in detail the ambivalent status of the menstruating virgin. All fertile women must continually strive to be chaste, or self-controlled, in regard to their sexual desires. Sexually aggressive, independent, or unwed goddesses are usually regarded in Hinduism as dangerous and inauspicious; whereas properly married, passive and subservient goddesses embody auspiciousness and well-being. In Tamil Nadu, marriage is the key which converts a woman into the highly desired state of *sumaṅgalī*, the embodiment of auspiciousness (Marglin 1985b; Wadley 1980).

Of all the five stages of female life enumerated in Fig. A, only the state of marriage and motherhood (column C) has an unqualified positive valence. The fertile woman whose desires are properly satisfied in a ritually sanctioned union, and who bears healthy offspring for her family, is the embodiment of auspiciousness and goodness. Tamil myths of the goddess therefore stress the process by which the independent and aggressive virgin is tamed and properly married to her husband lord (Harman 1989; Shulman 1976, 1980). Due perhaps to the matrilineal social structure of the high-ranking Nāyar caste, in which a woman lived with her natal kin and could take a number of informal 'husbands' during her lifetime, the most common ritual icon of the auspicious woman in Kerala is the breast-feeding mother, not the subservient wife. Cool, fertile, and flowing with nutritious milk, the lactating mother is the embodiment of love and benevolence.

This benevolence is personified in the goddess of the Tirumāndāmkunnu (TK) temple, located in Malappuram district of north-central Kerala. The opening songs of muṭiyēṯṯu, as well as kaḷam pāṭṭu (songs sung at the ritual rice-flour painting) throughout Kerala specifically praise the goddess in the form of TK Bhagavati. Enshrined in her cool, wet, mountain sanctuary, surrounded by forest, rivers, and paddy fields, TK Bhagavati is the embodiment of *śānta bhāva*, or the peaceful sentiment.

We visited the TK Bhagavati temple in the rainy month of *Chingam* (August/September). The temple is located at the top of a hill, accessible by a long stairway. The surrounding area comprises flat, arable stretches and thickly forested hills. A running stream passes by the foot of the temple on the northern side, crossable by a footbridge leading to the busy fields beyond. Both the legendary environment of the original temple and the landscape visible today are cool, green, and wet. The main deity is TK Bhagavati, a form of the fierce goddess who faces north. To the south-western side of the temple are the shrines of Śiva and Pārvati, shown as a married couple united within the *Śivalingam*. Directly behind their shrine, facing west, is the image of Ganapati, Śiva and Pārvati's benign elephant-headed son.

The entire entryway to the Śiva/Pārvati shrine is crowded with images of fertility: hanging cradles, baby dolls, statues of Krishna and of couples engaged in coitus, as well as bundles of tender paddy grass, ripe coconuts, and bells. Small white circles cover the door and floor of the temple area. When we enquired, the priest informed us that these were known as *nara*—rice batter imprints made with a tube during the celebration of the first harvest in the month of Chingam (August/September). The small hanging bundles of paddy shoots were also representations of the bounty of the first harvest: the first new sprouts of paddy were brought from far-flung regions and dedicated to the temple. At Guruvayur, the famous Krishna temple in central Kerala, the same rituals are performed at this time of year.

At the neighbouring Ganapati shrine, we were informed that girls came here from all over Kerala to perform the *māngalya* pūjā, in order to obtain husbands. Ganapati is known here is *māngalya dātavu*—he who gives the opportunity for marriage to the unmarried. The rite is so powerful, according to the priest, that during a recent māngalya pūjā a suitor had arrived on the spot to propose marriage to a previously luckless young lady, who was married soon thereafter. This pūjā is specially conducted in the month of *Thulam* (September/October), at which time the temple festival also takes place on a grand scale.

The emphasis at TK is clearly on marital happiness and fecundity, both human and agricultural. Unlike the Bhagavatis of the lowland temples, TK Bhagavati embodies the auspicious state of the happily married wife. One middle-aged woman we met had visited the temple numerous times over previous months, sponsoring elaborate and expensive rituals to improve her married life. It seemed her husband had 'stopped loving her', and begun to wander afield. There was even talk of divorce, very rare in Kerala. After her fervent and generous offerings to TK Bhagavati, her husband's attention miraculously returned home, and she was now experiencing renewed marital bliss. 'My daughters are also happily married due to the grace of TK Bhagavati,' she told me.

Inside the temple proper we observed the beautiful murals and carvings which grace so many of Kerala's temples. Within the dark inner sanctum, the huge image of Bhagavati stood nearly six feet tall. She was carved entirely out of jackwood and covered with heavy, sticky black tar from head to foot. Flanking her were seven slightly smaller images, also of jackwood, depicting the *sapta mātrakkaḷ* (seven mothers) who accompany Bhadrakāḷi to war. Each of these images was anointed with a sticky black substance, a teak resin known as *candāṭṭam*. Taken from the wild stands of trees deep in the surrounding forest, this resin is the most suitable substance for anointing the goddess in the daily worship. Both candāṭṭam and sandal paste are used, each considered extremely cooling substances. Because the image is of wood, any other liquid would destroy it.

TK Bhagavati temple is a centre of power for auspicious feminine energy, associated symbolically with the months of the first harvest, Chingam and Thulam. Rain, coolness, and mountain forest are important physical features of the temple stressed by the priests and in the temple literature. Rather than symbolic blood offerings, TK Bhagavati is worshipped with the cooling resins of trees. This Bhagavati seemed to contrast in many ways with her fiercer sisters in the lowlands. The priest told us that TK Bhagavati 'has a very calm and gentle nature. She is not fierce, but has a composed nature.' We were struck, however, by the not-so-gentle looking images of the goddess which decorated the temple (see Fig. 6). We asked two priests to tell us more:

Laji: What is Dēvi's mood like?

Priest: Here it is peaceful (śānta bhāvam).

Laji: She looks as if she has weapons for killing, with Dārika's head in her hands. So how is it that she is in a peaceful form?

Priest: It is said to be the time after the killing of Dārika. After that she stands in a pleasant posture, holding the head. Kodungallur Bhagavati is her sister. She is in *raudra bhāva* (fierce mood) there.

Laji: So after the killing of Dārika, what happens to Bhagavati to calm her down?

Priest: Oh, I don't know that story very well.

Fig. 6: Tirumāndāmkunnu Bhagavati

Temple Musician: Those Kuṟups [temple artists] say that after Śiva's son Ganapati ran and sucked her breast, motherly affection came into her. Then she calmed down.

TK Bhagavati's peaceful, mothering mood, brought on by the timely breast-feeding of the clever Ganapati, is the essential spiritual feature of this temple. It is this act of sucking the breast which transforms her anger (appeased but not stopped by her killing of Dārika) into the benevolent mood which ensures fertility. The contemporary lithograph of TK Bhagavati placed over the doorway to the shrine shows the goddess wearing a bodice, raised to expose the full breasts. This is recognized by everyone as the normal way that a mother in Kerala breast-feeds a child; she simply raises her bodice to expose a breast for the baby to suckle. The coolness, presence of water, and mountain location of the TK temple are ancient Dravidian signifiers for the powers of active, licit sexuality and the renewal of life. As such, the temple is an important source of power for sexual and agricultural fertility of the surrounding regions of central Kerala.[25]

TK Bhagavati is considered to be the elder sister of Kodungallur (KD) Bhagavati, a major Kerala goddess whose temple is located in the lowland backwaters of Trichur district. The ancient town of Kodungallur (also known as Cranganore) is referred to by ancient Greek historians of the first century as a place of busy international trade in jewels, spices, and textiles. We have already referred in chapter 1 to KD Bhagavati's annual festival at Mīnam Bharaṇi, in which the shrine is ritually polluted with blood sacrifice, filth, obscenity, and possession. The goddess here, as the priest at TK indicated, is in an unequivocally fierce mood, and is symbolically linked with the menstruating virgin.

The angry mood of KD Bhagavati, which can only be alleviated with vast quantities of blood and obscenity, is also sometimes attributed to her identity as Kaṇṇaki, the ill-fated heroine of the ancient epic *Cilappatikāram*. Both Induchoodan (1969) and Obeyesekere (1984) have delineated the historical links between the temple of KD Bhagavati and the cult of Kaṇṇaki, which held great sway in medieval south India, and to some extent still does in areas south of Kerala.[26] In fact, the famous 'secret chamber' said to exist under the eastern side of the sanctum is reputed to hold Kaṇṇaki's actual physical remains. According to Induchoodan, it is said that any human being entering there would meet instant death of a most gruesome nature. No one is allowed to enter the chamber, which remains as a kind of black-box emanating Kaṇṇaki's furious power throughout the temple grounds.

Kaṇṇaki's claim to fame is her unwavering devotion and chastity to her wayward husband Kōvalaṉ, despite Kōvalaṉ's abandonment of his young wife for a torrid affair with the temple courtesan Mādhavī. Eventually Kōvalaṉ returns to his wife. When (through a series of misadventures) he is wrongfully accused of stealing the queen's jewels and therefore put to death, Kaṇṇaki's righteous wrath is immeasurable. She tears off her left breast, the locus of her divine feminine power (aṇaṅku) and throws it to the ground. The breast erupts into flame and burns down the entire city of Madurai. In the final portion of the *Śilappadikāram*, Kaṇṇaki's image is installed in Kodungallur (known as Vanchi in the poem), and begins to receive worship. As Kaṇṇaki, then, KD Bhagavati embodies the terrifying power of the chaste but fertile widow (Hart 1973; Tapper 1979).

Today at the KD temple, the legend of Kaṇṇaki seems less important than her symbolic association with menstruation and virginity. As either virgin or fertile widow, KD Bhagavati embodies the same inauspicious and heating energies of unfulfilled sexuality and anger. As we see in columns B and D of Fig. A, these two states (virginity and widowhood) are in some ways homologous. Both require ascetic control over strong physical and emotional needs, and the consequent building up of extraordinary supernatural powers. The chastity of both the virgin and the widow is a form of *tapas* as powerful as the celibate meditations of the god Śiva. This chastity, like Śiva's, is characterized by heat and anger. The rituals of KD Bharaṇi indicate that it is indeed anger, heat, and sexual desire which dominate the fierce mood of the lowland goddess. And this state is in turn a metaphor for the earth in the hot dry months of the summer season, when KD Bhagavati's festival is celebrated.

Another important Bhagavati temple of central Kerala is at Chottanikkara (CH) in eastern Ernakulam district (see Fig. 1). This temple is renowned for the constant presence of the mentally ill, who come here to perform their tuḷḷal, a hopping, frenzied dance of possession before the shrines of both Śiva and Bhagavati. On Tuesday and Friday nights at the separate Bhadrakāḷi shrine in the lower temple courtyard, the severely afflicted offer guruti and pound iron nails into a huge tree with their fists and forehead to effect a cure. But in addition to these darker functions of the temple, it is also a favourite location for weddings, particularly in the morning hours when the goddess manifests as the benevolent Lakṣmi or Sarasvatī.

CH Bhagavati is depicted as a young girl with small, bare breasts. She is the younger sister of the beautiful goddess Mūkāmbika, who resides in a remote forested mountain temple in southern Karnataka. Her features are not the refined ideal often seen in the portraits of Pārvati, Lakṣmi, and Sarasvatī; her squat body, wide nose, and dusky skin identify her as a local, perhaps tribal goddess. Her upper hands hold a conch and a *cakra*, symbols of the god Viṣnu; but Śiva and Ayyappan, not Viṣnu or Krishna, are the subordinate deities installed in her temple courtyard.

CH was the favourite temple of one highly educated young lady I interviewed, who said that she 'got no mental peace' if she did not visit CH Bhagavati at least once a month. When describing the goddess to me and showing me how she worshipped, she emphasized enthusiastically that 'she is a virgin, you know'. In her mid-twenties, this young woman was still unmarried. She clearly identified with the goddess and believed in her power to relieve the special tensions of young women. After the morning worship, virgin girls sing praises of CH Bhagavati within the temple, in the ritual of *Brahmaṇi pāṭṭu*. In the evening, CH Bhagavati is accompanied by Lord Ayyappan, whose shrine lies directly behind her own. This association with Ayyappan indicates her possible homology to the frustrated virgin goddess Mahishi at Śabarimala (see story below). The ambivalence inherent in CH Bhagavati's status as a virgin is expressed in the splitting of her form into the two goddesses of the upper and lower shrines. At the upper shrine, her auspicious, benign aspect dominates, and in the lower, her angry, heated, blood-loving nature predominates. Yet, even in the upper shrine, possessed, mad people shriek and dance wildly, expressing intense pain in a culturally acceptable manner. The dangerous power lurking behind the inscrutable smile of CH Bhagavati is let loose in the screams and flailing hair of the mad women who parade daily before her gaze.

These three important temples of central Kerala—Tirumāndāmkunnu, Kodungallur, and Chottanikkara—express the essential dilemma of female fertility. The goddesses of these three temples embody the virgin and the mother, the hot and the cool, the dangerous and the sublime. CH Bhagavati, as virgin, and KD Bhagavati, as both virgin and widow, represent the fearful feminine forces of the hot season, which the ritual specialists of muṭiyēṯṯu must transmute into the peaceful, cooling energies of the mother at TK. This polarity may be clearly seen in the following chart:

Chottanikkara/Kodungallur Bhagavati	*Tirumāndāmkunnu Bhagavati*
Lowland: paddy, coconut, jackfruit	Mountain: forest, streams, teak trees
Hot and dry	Cool and wet
Offering of blood (cocks)	Offering of teak and sandal paste (trees)
March/April (Mīnam)	September/October (Thulam)
Virgin/Widow	Mother
Menstruation, thirst and anger	Motherhood, breast-feeding, giving
Killing	Nurturing
Raudra (Fierce)	*Śānta* (Peaceful)
Kāḷi (daughter of Śiva)	Pārvati (wife of Śiva)

Muṭiyēṯṯu is performed at the lowland shrines of central Kerala, where goddesses of the virgin/widow category hold sway. The possessed actor transforms himself into the virgin goddess by donning the fearful make-up, heavy head-dress, and the red wooden breasts encircled by snakes. Marching out of the temple courtyard, the fierce Bhadrakāḷi receives the bloody sacrifice of Dārika's head on the dry, harvested paddy field, and order is restored. As the performance comes to a close, Kāḷi waves infants from the audience before the sacred flame, applying its oil to their foreheads in a gesture of blessing. The small, hot, red breasts of the virgin girl, full of dangerous power, are metaphorically transformed into large, cool, white, life-giving mountains in the ritual imagery of the songs. The passage from death to life, from virgin to mother, from drought to rain, is once again guaranteed.

Seasons, Time, Space

The landscape of Bhagavati, like the body of a woman, undergoes regular periodic changes in its qualities and capacities. The two modalities of the moist, fertile, green food-producing fields and the hot, barren, red fallow ones, each containing the seed of the other, occur in alternating cycles directly associated with the movement of the seasons through the calendar year. Because the earth is itself a divine female being, infused with life-force or śakti, the portrayal of the earth's phases in terms of the fertility of women is more than a metaphor. It is a living allegory, a visible expression of a known truth about the fundamental interconnection between all forms of life. Just as the goddess's divine power can move freely and without changing its essential nature from a statue to a tree to a lamp to a drawing and from there into the person of a possessed actor; in the same way the dancing Bhagavati of muṭiyēṯṯu does not *symbolize* the agricultural landscape but simply is that landscape expressing itself in a different form.[27]

Time in the traditional calendar of Kerala (as in most Hindu conceptions of time) is highly inflected. Each moment of the day, day of the week, constellation within the lunar month, and month within the year is unique and characterized by a set of potentialities and qualities of great significance for human activity.[28] Not surprisingly, time is also a crucial dimension in muṭiyēṯṯu. The specific hour, location and spatial orientation of the rituals allow the energies of the earth and seasons to be evoked and manipulated in the desired manner.

The most obvious temporal restriction on the performance of muṭiyēṯṯu is that it must take place in the dead of night, between midnight and dawn. One troupe leader explained to me that the war between Bhadrakāḷi and Dārika actually took place while everyone was sleeping because the world could not bear its violence. In any case the night is a dangerous time, when all manner of spirits and wild animals are freely moving about. Women light the household lamps at dusk and place them in the doorways to deter these spirits from entering the house. People, particularly women and children, should not normally go outside during the night hours.

The night is also the time scheduled for licensed sexual relations between married partners. In Sangam poetry sexual relations are often associated with war. The *Cilappatikāram*, for instance, mentions scratches as the marks of love-making, quarrels as a natural part of the passion of lovers, and the reddened eyes of lustful women like those of furious warriors exhausted from battle. The 'cruel god of death' is said to live 'in the seductive form of a girl' (Ilankovatikal 1993: 68). Violent sexuality is epitomized in the poetic descriptions of the mating of elephants and tigers. That both sexuality and the wars of Bhadrakāḷi take place in the dark is partially due to their power and danger. Both sex and war rely on the sacrifice of male blood-seed to regenerate life in the field of the female body. To properly evoke and control these dangerous regenerative forces, muṭiyēṯṯu must be performed in the heart of darkness, the source and repository of the mysterious powers of life and death.

Muṭiyeṯṯu ideally should be performed on a Tuesday or a Friday, days sacred to Bhadrakali.[29] Tuesdays and Fridays are ordinarily considered inauspicious days of the week, on which new enterprises generally should not be undertaken. Tender living things are vulnerable to intrusions by the malevolent spirits of ancestral ghosts and other unquiet dead, which move enviously among them on these days. It is said that one should not go to visit other people on Tuesdays and Fridays:

> Even if you go you have to return the same day. Say if we go from here on Tuesday our ancestors' spirits also come with us and they continue to reside there. They wouldn't come back home.[30]

These two days are specially associated with death and the hunger and needs of the spirits of the dead.

As already noted, certain aspects of toddy-tapping are also related to these two special days. One toddy-tapper in his early thirties explained to us:

> There is no special day to climb the tree. But the rubbing of the bud (choṭṭa) is only started on Tuesdays or Fridays. Also the chopping of the tip is done only either on Tuesday or Friday. Only if you do it on those days would that turn out well and prosper. That is the belief which has come from the ancestral times.[31]

The massaging of the coconut bud and the cutting of the tip are dangerous manipulations of procreative life-forces, analogous to the processes of human sexuality and death. It is fitting that this sacrificial act, analogous to the cutting of Dārika's head and drinking of his blood-seed, should take place on the days sacred to Bhadrakāḷi.

In the summer of 1993, my four-year-old daughter came down with chicken-pox, the week before we boarded an airplane for Kerala. When our toddy-tapper friend asked me on what day the first rash appeared, I remembered it had been on a Tuesday. Jay Seelan explained:

> Tuesday. Here it is also like that. In Ḳerala it is a very strong belief that chicken-pox comes when Dēvi throws some seed. When Kodungallur Amma gets angry she throws seed. So if anyone got chicken-pox here, it would sprout out only on Tuesdays and Fridays. Well I believe that strongly. This has not sprouted out on any other day here for anybody.

Seed, which normally gives life, may bring death when thrown on the field of the human body by the angry goddess. One of the most important purposes of muṭiyēṯṯu traditionally was to eradicate smallpox, which tended to erupt in the hot months of the summer festival season. Now that smallpox has been eradicated, chicken-pox has taken its place as the expression of the goddess's simultaneous anger and blessing.

Why are Tuesday and Friday specifically sacred to Bhadrakāḷi? When I asked astrologers this question, several pointed out the planetary associations to these days, which are cognate with ancient Greek astrology. Tuesday, called *cŏvvāḻca* in Malayalam, is ruled by the planet Mars. The warlike and violent tendencies of this planetary deity easily fit Bhadrakāḷi and emphasize her martial character.[32] Friday, *vyāḻarāḻca*, is ruled by Venus, a soft and feminine planetary deity who radiates love, sensuality, and beauty. The association of Bhadrakāḷi with these two polar opposites once again highlights the duality of her feminine nature. The challenge of moving the goddess from one state to the other is the continual drama behind muṭiyēṯṯu and other Bhagavati cult rituals.[33]

Held during the darkest time of night, on the most dangerous days of the week, muṭiyēṯṯu is also performed during the hottest season of the year. The year in Kerala has three distinct seasons: hot, wet, and cool. In terms of agriculture these are the seasons of harvest, rest, and planting. The hot, wet, and cool seasons are demarcated by far more than fluctuations in temperature or rainfall. Each is associated with particular foods, plants, activities, and emotional moods (Zimmerman 1987). This rich inflection of the Malayali seasons is expressed in the pattern of temple festivals and rituals which take place at specific times of year, and in the deities associated with them. Each deity has an affinity with the particular season corresponding to his or her own nature: either hot or cool. The complementarity of the festivals celebrating these hot and cool deities sets distinctive moods for the season of the year whose boundaries they demarcate. In this anthropomorphized landscape, the hot and cool deities embody profound concerns and manifest the real powers latent in the natural environment. By managing and propitiating them in the correct manner, human beings can ensure the continual prosperity and well-being of this world.

The deities who dominate the dry season from *Vrischikam* (November–December) to *Idavam* (May–June)—Ayyappan, Bhadrakāḷi, and Śiva—are those deities whose primary quality is heat. Bhadrakāḷi, the fiercest form of Bhagavati, epitomizes the hot earth in the harvest season. The festivals at the peak of the hot season induce her fertility through violence, humour, blood-sacrifice, and obscenity. These cause the symbolic spilling of the precious blood-seed, the male life-fluid which promotes continued life. The mood of such festivals is fearful, manic, and dangerous, and deadly serious even in the midst of humour.

The dry months are also the province of Śiva and Ayyappan, two male deities who, like Bhadrakāḷi, tend towards asceticism, celibacy, and heat. Śiva is an important deity in Kerala, with major temples throughout the state. His major festival, Śivarātri, is celebrated at the dark moon in the month of Kumbham (February–March). Śiva is renowned for his resistance to marriage, and for his tapas, the accumulation of powerful heat through constant meditation and celibacy. Śiva's third eye is the locus of his accumulated burning power, and it is from this hot, androgynous aperture that the fierce Bhadrakāḷi is born in Kerala legend. In addition to fire and heat, Śiva is also associated in tantric imagery with death and inauspiciousness. In fact his name, which means 'the auspicious one', is a propitiatory epithet used in the hope of inducing him to become auspicious and benevolent (Fuller 1992: 32). In Kerala mythology, Śiva is Bhadrakāḷi's father, without the agency of Pārvati or any other female.[34] The relationship between father and daughter is one of shared nature, substance, and personality. It is tinged with competitive and erotic energy. Both Śiva and Bhadrakāḷi embody destructive, anti-social forces of death, violence, and lust held tightly in control but always in danger of being unleashed.

Lord Ayyappan, a deity unique to Kerala, is the personification of celibacy and the outright rejection of women. Pilgrimage to his shrine and the temple festival take place in the month of Dhanu (December–January). Ayyappan is born from the thigh of the male god Viṣṇu disguised as Mohini, the enchantress. Her attractive form, donned to confuse the demons (asuras) during the churning of the milky ocean, excites Śiva, whose powerful semen impregnates the temporarily female Viṣṇu. The homosexual conception of Ayyappan is sometimes regarded as a conventional symbol for the union of Śaiva and Vaiṣnava religious cults, deeply hostile to one another in medieval south India. But the rest of the Ayyappan mythology leaves no doubt as to the psychological appeal of his wildly popular cult.

Among his various adventures is Ayyappan's battle with a female buffalo demon named Mahishi, whom he kills. Mahishi is really a beautiful young maiden, released from a curse by Ayyappan's slaughter of her buffalo form. She yearns to marry him, but he escapes her desire by stating that 'on whichever year a virgin pilgrim does not come to Sabari Hill to worship me, on that year I shall marry you' (Daniel 1984: 246). It is noteworthy that this story is the exact mirror image of the famous Mahiṣāsuramārdinī myth, in which the fierce goddess Durga humiliates and kills the male buffalo demon, who wishes to marry her (Shulman 1976, 1980). Established in his barely accessible shrine at the top of Śabarimala in southern Kerala, Ayyappan greets the thousands of pilgrims who brave the forest and hardships to reach his shrine each December and January. Mahishi waits patiently in her small temple nearby for a year in which no new pilgrim comes, and she may finally realize her desire. People in Kerala told me that it was the duty of Ayyappan devotees to ensure that 'virgin pilgrims' made the trip each year, but also that these pilgrims make a point of greeting the frustrated Mahishi before going to the Ayyappan shrine. If they failed to do this, Lord Ayyappan would have to give in to her sexual demands and thereby lose his celibate power.

The denial of sexuality is one of the primary goals of the Ayyappan cult. The anthropologist E. Valentine Daniel, who accompanied the pilgrims one year, has the following to say about Lord Ayyappan's characteristic iconographic pose—a squatting position similar to that used by men while defecating:

> The weight of his body rests on his toes, and his knees are held up by a strap at an odd angle. One pilgrim assured me that if I were ever to be struck by an unvanquishable ithyphallic condition, all I had to do was to get into the Ayyappan position and I would be assured of flaccid relief. In any event, it has worked for Lord Ayyappan for the last seven or eight

centuries. ...Lord Ayyappan has become the lord of celibacy par excellence. (Daniel 1984: 246)

Only males may approach the Ayyappan shrine. All females capable of menstruation—all those between the ages of about 9 and 55—are prohibited from coming near the mountain temple. The men who make the journey must furthermore undertake a vow of complete celibacy for the forty-one days before and during their pilgrimage to Śabarimala. Shoeless, dressed all in black, wearing special bead necklaces, and carrying ghee-filled coconuts in small sacks on their heads, the hordes of male pilgrims fill railway stations and temple yards all through Kerala during the month of Dhanu (December–January), as they make their gruelling trip.[35] The cult of Ayyappan is surely motivated in part by a desire to overcome the perceived sexual power of women, a power which seems to threaten male solidarity and well-being. The increasing popularity of the Ayyappan pilgrimage, which is growing annually and now drawing pilgrims from all parts of India, would seem to indicate that this fear is very much alive in the minds of Indian men.[36]

The most prominent deity of the cool season is Krishna, the seductive and playful incarnation of Viṣnu. Krishna is the direct counterpart of Kāḷi in that he represents the fulfilment of all that she lacks: fertility, in the form of rain, playfulness, babies and unabashed eroticism. Krishna is the hero of the rainy, cool time of the year, his birthday celebrated in the month of Chingam (August–September).[37] Not blood, fire, and swords, but butter, cool rain, and the sweet strains of the flute are his signs.

The profound opposition of these two polarities of heat and coolness which dominate the two halves of the year is epitomized in the qualities of the two great deities Śiva and Viṣnu. Śiva represents fire, heat, death; Viṣnu water, coolness, and life. Viṣnu is consistently associated in mythology with both water and serpents. His proclivity for taking female forms is also renowned, and many devotees of Krishna have a strong feminine identification (Carstairs 1958; Kripal 1995). Whereas Krishna, the incarnation of Viṣnu, indulges endlessly in erotic play, Śiva, Ayyappan, and Bhadrakāḷi reject sexuality, storing its potent energy within themselves as extraordinary heat. Śiva, Ayyappan, and Bhadrakāḷi predominate in the hot time of the year; Viṣnu in the form of Krishna pervades the cool months after the monsoons.

The relationship of the goddess to both Śiva and Viṣnu is crucial. The fierce goddess of the hot months is independent and unfulfilled. Her sexual desire can be quenched only by violence and, as the myths suggest, by incestuous union with her father, Śiva. The goddesses celebrated in the cool months of the year are the controlled, benevolent Laksmi, wife of Viṣnu, or the benign Sarasvati. Numerous scholars have noted that this duality in the goddess's nature is directly related to her marital status (Bennett 1983; Erndl 1993; Hawley and Wulff 1982). In many parts of India, the fierce goddess is ultimately tamed and controlled by being wedded to her male betters, gods who conquer her in battle. In Kerala, however, the ending is different. Unlike Meenakshi of Madurai in neighbouring Tamil Nadu, the fierce goddess Bhadrakāḷi never marries, is never tamed. She may be converted into a breast-feeding, benevolent mother, but not by the agency of a man. It is the appearance of a baby, sometimes Śiva himself crying to be nursed at her breast, which cools her and calms her wrath. It is as a breast-feeding mother that Bhagavati becomes the benevolent protectress of her people.

The division of the year into hot and cool seasons, with their accompanying moods, symbols, and deities finds concrete expression in the spatial organization of both temples and traditional homes in Kerala. Krishnan Kutty Mārār, an outstanding kaḷam artist whose family traditionally perform muṭiyēṯṯu, explained to me that each month of the Malayalam year corresponds to a particular directional orientation in the temple. He outlined the position of the months in the temple structure as given in Fig. B, although he could not explain the significance of this arrangement to me (see Fig. B).

Adding the cardinal directions as well as the solstices and equinoxes to the schematic shown in the figure, we can see that the temple orientation maps the path of the sun through its annual cycle, moving in a counter-clockwise direction. The top half of the diagram corresponds to the hot, bright half of the year, known in Sanskrit as the *uttarāyana* or northern path, and the bottom half represents the cool, dark half of the year, the *dakṣināyana* or southern path of the sun (Fuller 1992: 265). An additional diagonal axis divides the year into wet and dry halves, corresponding to the seasonal monsoon rains. The two seasons thus reach their peak respectively in the months of Mīnam and *Kanni*. The north-east corner, or '*mīnakoṇ*' represents the peak of the hot, dry season, with all its associated meanings as outlined in this section. Its direct

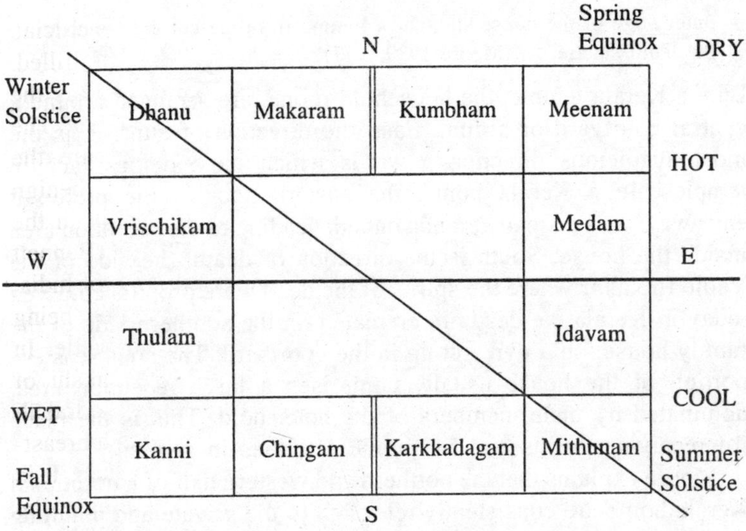

Fig. B. Correspondence of Temple Orientation with Lunar Months

opposite, the south-west 'Kanni' corner, epitomizes the cool, dry, fertile energies of life. The south-east and north-west quarters of the chart, corresponding chronologically to the solstices, represent liminal, transitional periods.

Throughout India, the cardinal directions have anciently assigned meanings, described in the Purāṇas and physically encoded in the symbolism of temple architecture as a miniature cosmos (Kramrisch 1946). Melinda Moore has presented a detailed analysis of the influence of directional symbolism in the construction of traditional Kerala homes in her article 'The Kerala House as Hindu Cosmos' (Moore 1989). Her findings agree closely with my fieldwork in central Kerala amongst both high-caste (Brahmin, Nāyar, and Ambalavasi) and lower-caste (Ezhava) families. As Moore demonstrates, individual rooms in the generally square-shaped home are assigned specific uses according to their location in the house. These divisions of utility are strictly observed, segregating activities and persons within the home. And just as in the temple, the homology between the months of the year and the structure of the house is made explicit in the Malayalam building manuals:

> In Kerala the place for 'laying the first stone' ... is determined by drawing squares for the twelve Malayalam solar months around the

> outer edge of the house site, and counting from the current month to the tenth square. ... (Moore 1989: 177)[38]

Like a Kerala temple, the household rooms are arranged around a central courtyard or atrium. East, the direction of sunrise, is the most auspicious direction, towards which most deities face in temples. In a Kerala home, the eastern door is the preferred entryway, with a small veranda outside leading to the reception area inside the house. South is the direction of death, the side of the Vedic fire altar where the spirits of the dead were propitiated. Even today in Kerala the dead are cremated on the southern side of the family house, on a pyre set up in the courtyard. The south-eastern portion of the house usually comprises a large reception area, dominated by male members of the household. This is the place for receiving guests and for public activities in general.

Moore explains that the northern and western half of a traditional Kerala home are consistently relegated to the private and polluting activities of women, whereas the southern and eastern sides comprise public, male space. Menstruation and parturition, for example, are restricted to the room at the north-west corner of the house. This position corresponds in our temple/months configuration to the month of Dhanu, in which the forty-one-day ritual offerings of kaḷams and songs are made to Bhagavati. The room at the northern door of the house is the dining-room, and the north-east room is the kitchen. Moore notes that in a smaller house, a menstruating woman would sit in the 'north-western corner of the northwesternmost room ... —a room used for family dining and for other purposes as well' (ibid.: 172). Thus the entire northern side of the house is the province of women: of nourishment and also pollution. Menstruation and birth are the key activities related to the northern side, but defecation and bathing are also accomplished outdoors on the northern side. The polluting effects of the northern door are such that 'after bathing, the house is normally re-entered by the front (eastern) door. Exiting by the northern door when going on a journey is thought to have bad consequences' (ibid.: 177).

This set of associations to the north door is intriguing when considered in light of the Bhagavati cult. The lore and rituals of Bhagavati consistently emphasize the importance of the north direction. The most striking example of this is in the north-facing orientation of Kodungallur Bhagavati, perhaps the most important Bhagavati temple in Kerala. Many people told me that their local

Bhagavati was either a form of this goddess, or her sister, and the northerly orientation of the deity's temple was considered proof of this relation. Furthermore, in several performances I attended, I was told that the actor possessed by the spirit of the goddess Bhadrakāḷi had to be forcibly restrained from running off to the north, a direction toward which she was irresistibly attracted. Once she escaped towards the north, she could never be brought back.

There seem to be several possible explanations for this emphasis on the north. One possibility is that it represents a memory of the historical link between the possession performances of Kerala and the bhūta cult of Tulunad in southern Karnataka.[39] Another clue may be the ancient Dravidian rite of *vatakkiruttal* (literally 'sitting facing the north'), in which a king or warrior would commit ritual suicide by fasting while seated in a northward-facing direction (Hart 1975: 88ff). Hart does not explain *why* the north was significant to the ancient Dravidians for this purpose.[40]

Although history and the ancient rituals of death no doubt play a part in the concern with the north in the cult of Bhagavati, it is the domestic symbolism of menstruation and birth that I believe is at its root. The northern side of the temple is the location for the offering of blood-sacrifice, or its substitute, guruti. This bloody feasting of ancestral spirits is clearly associated with death. The blood of a living creature must be spilled in order to feed the hungry and malevolent spirits of the dead. This blood is associated with the blood of menstruation, as one troupe leader clearly stated:

> After finishing [all the offerings to] Bhagavati, we arrange guruti—red- coloured water in a big pot on the northern side. This guruti represents the menstruation of Bhagavati. I read somewhere that in Africa there is also a custom of cutting the forest to plant crops, and the women sprinkle menstrual blood there for fertility. We sprinkle the red water on the ground in the same way.[41]

An image at the famous Vadakkanathan Śiva temple in the centre of Trichur town reinforces this association of blood-sacrifice with both menstruation and birth. The sanctum sanctorum housing the enormous Śivalingam [an aniconic stone representation of Śiva] is decorated with murals along its exterior circumference. This is a common sight in Kerala, but the murals on the northern side of the shrine are atypical. They are painted in a different style from the refined, muted paintings seen elsewhere in the temple. Over the closed northern door of the lingam shrine is an image of a completely naked woman, her legs parted in childbirth. Female figures, clearly midwives, stand at her side to receive the newborn infant. This female is not a recognizable deity, but a very realistic human woman of nondescript appearance (with noticeably pink skin). Above this rather unusual depiction are a series of roosters painted in profile. The blood of a cock is of course the normal sacrificial offering to Kodungallur Bhagavati and other deities who require living blood. The temple priests seemed uncomfortable when I enquired about the meaning of this image, and were unable to provide any illumination of its symbolism. But directly beyond the mural, proceeding in a clockwise direction (the prescribed method of circumambulation of Hindu shrines), one comes to a deep trench, carrying away the liquid offerings which have been poured over the lingam inside the shrine. I was admonished not to step over this trench, as to do so would be to 'cut the head of Śiva', an irremediable sin.[42] This reminder of decapitation and blood-sacrifice of the male deity directly adjacent to the image of the birthing, naked female strikingly juxtaposes blood, birth, and death, which are all associated with the northerly direction.

The northern direction, the hot months of the year, and the northern path of the sun through the sky are physically encoded in the architectural orientation of the Kerala temple. In the Kerala home, these elements are further associated with the female domains of menstruation, feeding, and birth. The offering of blood-sacrifice by male priests at the northern side of the temple symbolically links these ritual activities to the real procreative activities of women in the home. Death and pollution are rewoven into the fabric of life through the agency of bījam, the stored blood-seed which feeds new life. By this symbolic conversion the male priests manipulate the cosmic processes of the physical world, guaranteeing the prosperity and well-being of society.

Snakes and the Underworld

The central Kerala coast is a realm of wet lowlands and backwaters, weaving snake-like out of the fields and rivers of the fertile inland. Innumerable trees line the brackish waters, which rise in the monsoons to flood the simple mud-thatch homes on their banks. Fishing and water transport are the dominant economic activities of the region. Reptiles and amphibians abound. Snakes in particular are at home here, swishing silently through the dark waters and grasses, striking suddenly and bringing death. The feeling is dark, mysterious, peaceful, yet potentially threatening.

This is the ancient Tamil landscape of *neytal*, with its interior emotional moods of grief, battle, and anxiety. The realm of backwaters and seashore is the abode of snakes, the entrance to the underworld, pātāḷam.[43] Purāṇic references to the watery underworld realm of the snakes indicate that the neytal regions of Kerala could have been the geographic location of pātāḷam. Local folklore considers this to be the case. The ancient folklore of the watery underworld beings pervades every indigenous religious tradition of the Indian subcontinent—Hindu, Jain, and Buddhist (Sutherland 1991). No one knows the origin of these beliefs, which were already old at the time of the composition of the epics and Purāṇas. The main qualities embodied by the semi-divine, semi-demonic creatures inhabiting waters, trees, and rocks are fecundity and malevolence. In Kerala the nāga, or serpent deity is the ever-present reminder of these ambivalent, watery powers.

Worship of snakes or nāgas is popular in many parts of India; in Kerala it is ubiquitous. Nearly every house compound has a *sarppakāvu*, an untouched patch of wild growth on the southern side of the house reserved for the undisturbed use of the snakes. Small shrines house stone representations of the male and female nāgas in an astounding variety of forms. For many people living in the heavily forested areas of Kerala these household nāgas and *nāgayakṣis* are the deities truly empowered to determine their family fates, for good or ill. The higher Sanskritic gods housed in the temples can be worshipped directly only by Brahmin priests, but nāgas belong to everyone.

One reason for the intimacy between humans and nāgas is the physical proximity of their earthly manifestations, snakes. Krishnan Kutty Mārār, a kaḷam artist, described the experiences he and his brothers had as boys sleeping out on the veranda at night:

> It was dense forest around here. Like Śabarimala [the forest shrine of Lord Ayyappan]. Sometimes in the middle of the night when we used to lie here we would look around and we could see those snakes by the side of the [sleeping] mat. Also scorpions and other harmful creatures would come and sit around us. But we did not have any trouble from them biting or poisoning anyone, even though they have slept a lot with us. That is because of the power of the nāgayakṣis installed in our shrine.[44]

According to Balakrishnan, a member of the Pulluvan caste who makes his living singing chants for the serpent gods, physical snakes should not be confused with nāgas:

> The snake that we worship is not the ordinary snake that we see, such as the viper, cobra, etc. The real snake is different. It is invisible. We can't see those snakes in the sarppakāvu [sacred serpent-grove]. They are gods with great powers. It is just like a temple or church—we have a god installed there. That is our god.

The major offering to these nāgas is *pāḷum nūṟum*, a mixture of milk, bananas and turmeric said to be favoured by the snakes. The offering of this sweet, milky liquid is both cooling and replenishing.

Numerous studies of the symbolism of nāgas have stressed that these sub-aquatic dwellers are associated with a liquid procreative energy that has both benevolent and malevolent aspects. As dwellers in the 'moist underworld', nāgas have infinite access to both the watery sources of life and the realms of death and decay. They are closely associated in Sanskrit mythology with yakśas and yakṣis, who dwell in trees and 'symbolize the explosive fecundity of the natural world.' Trees are the 'mediating symbols' linking yakśas and nāgas, according to Sutherland. While yakśas dwell at the foot of trees, snakes are found 'in the moist dark spots' at their roots. 'The essential substance that links yakśas, nāgas, and trees is water.' Both '*contain* the life-supporting liquid they symbolize. The watery essence is manifest in trees as sap and in nāgas as venom' (1991: 39).

In Kerala these two powers of tree and water unite in the popular figure of the nāgayakṣi, a female serpent deity. Her iconography (as well as her essentially malevolent character) are also found in the figure of Bhadrakāḷi. In muṭiyēṯṯu, Bhadrakāḷi's large head-dress is completely covered with raised serpent hoods. Snakes also encircle the prominent red breasts of the actor's costume. Fangs emerge from the sides of her mouth, suggesting the venomous organs of poisonous snakes. The glazed expression of the actor in trance and the darting movements of the tongue (said by actors to express anger), also suggest the behaviour of snakes. Bhadrakāḷi moves slowly at first, turning suddenly and attacking spectators during her entrance into the performance arena. In all these ways the heroine of muṭiyēṯṯu shows her affinity to a nāgayakṣi. One veteran actor who plays the role of Kāḷi commented:

> Bhagavati is also called *Sarpabroshini*—the one who wears snakes. Śiva also has got one around his neck. So Bhadrakāḷi wears snakes too

> since she was born from him. Even on the crown (muṭi) there are lots of serpent hoods. Serpents are important for Bhagavati.[45]

Like Śiva, Bhagavati is associated primarily with the powers of anger and desire. These volatile qualities are also attributed to nāgas, as Sutherland explains:

> *Nāgas* are strongly associated with eroticism as well as fertility. This symbolism is a manifestation of the nearly universal equation of serpents with sexuality, engendered principally by their phallic form, multiple progeny, unpredictable and insidious temperament reminiscent of the emotional behaviour of the sexually jealous or obsessed (particularly women, it is thought), and in the subterranean habitation of snakes that links them paradoxically with female sexuality and genitalia as well. (Sutherland 1991: 38)

The feminine erotic associations with both nāgas and yakṣis are expressed in the belief that the serpent deities possess only females. In the ritual of *sarppam tuḷḷal*, virgin girls become possessed by the snake spirits and receive offerings.[46] At the major serpent shrine of Mannarsala in south-central Kerala, a hereditary priestess who remains celibate for life is believed to embody the serpent deities. The ambivalent power over fertility represented by the nāgas, and particularly the nāgayakṣi, is a feminine power. But only virgin, celibate, or post-menopausal women are considered pure enough to embody the sacred serpent gods. They are repelled by blood or impurities of any sort. The predominant position of Bhagavati, the fierce virgin goddess, in the spiritual life of Kerala has deep roots in autochthonous nāga worship.

Serpent worship is traditionally conducted in the month of Kanni (September–October), the cool, wet season associated with fertility. The full set of associations becomes clearer when we examine the position of the month of Kanni in the calendrical/directional symbolism of the Kerala house. The part of the house corresponding to Kanni is the south-west corner, an area of the house relegated to sexual relations between married couples: 'The southwestern-most bedroom … is the one usually given to a newly married couple to promote conception on their wedding night' (Moore 1989: 177). This position is diametrically opposed to the north-easternmost corner, symbolizing the month of Mīnam. Mīnam, it will be recalled, is the height of summer, the hottest, driest month, and the primary season for the performance of muṭiyēṯṯu and the offering of blood-sacrifice. The earth goddess in the season of Mīnam is a virgin—

infertile, menstrual, hot, desirous, and angry; in Kanni, she is an erotic wife, wet, cool, and fertile, impregnated by continual infusions of semen. The offering of milk and bananas to the serpent deities in Kanni represent the white procreative liquids of life; these are in opposition to the red blood offerings of Mīnam, symbolizing death and desire.

These two seasonal poles of the year (marked by the autumnal and vernal equinoxes) reflect the continuous cycle of life and death in the landscape of the goddess. Neither pole can exist without the other. Blood becomes milk/semen, death creates life. These extremes are united in the watery neytal regions of pātāḷam, the underworld, the coastal seashore and backwaters of Kerala. Seeking out Dārika in the depths of that watery underworld, Kāḷi brings him to the open battleground and beheads him so that the balance of life may be restored. The mood of grief and battle is a necessary prerequisite for joyous union.

Elephants and Tigers

The colors on the elephant's body
shine, as he grazes
with his herd
on bamboo shoots,
breaking down branches;
then, in thirst,
he goes to a watering place,
kills a crouching tiger
poised for attack.
Pouring rains
clean the tusks, wash down the blood on their tips,
as he walks slowly along slopes
of jagged rock.
He's arrogant
after finishing off a vicious enemy,
and with six-legged bees making lute music
over the juices of his lust
he mounts his female,
then goes to sleep in our man's banana groves...

(Ramanujan 1985: 27)

The real home of Bhagavati is not the watery realm of pātālam, but the mountain landscape known in the ancient Tamil poetry as *kurinji.* The forested, inaccessible mountain is also the dwelling place of Murugan, 'The Red One', who possesses women and men violently, and who loves the taste of blood. The scarlet *ixora* flower, known in Tamil as *vetci* (Malayalam cetti/tecci) is sacred both to the shamans of Murugan and to Bhagavati in muṭiyēṯṯu. The mountain landscape of kurinji is associated with night, passion, possession, and the prelude to war. Clandestine sexuality and violent emotions express the raw power inherent in the mountain forests. As the poem quoted above indicates, the brute strength and wild sexuality of elephants and tigers are the favourite symbols of the forest's primal power. Bhadrakāḷi embodies this power, wearing an elephant and a tiger as her two ear-rings. Bhadrakāḷi's tiger-like female vehicle, Vetāḷam, also expresses this aspect of her personality.

Legendary accounts of the birth of Bhadrakāḷi always mention her prodigious size and ferocity; even the wild elephant worn as a decoration in her left ear and the tiger in her right are conceived to be life-sized. The elephant in Kerala folklore represents a combination of sexuality and violence that is deeply in tune with the ancient Dravidian concepts of sacred power. Many hymns of praise to the goddess describe the love-making of Śiva and Pārvati in the form of two wild forest elephants in rut (one artist explained that this was the origin of Ganesh, the elephant-headed god). This emphasis in the texts suggests a wild sexuality which also appears in elephants as madness and rage. The onset of rut is unpredictable, and male elephants can kill people and go on rampages while it lasts. For this reason, the legs of temple elephants (always male) are continually chained in huge iron shackles, which only reinforces the sense of terrifying power under control. The prodigious phallus of the male elephant, as well as its phallic-shaped trunk, further reinforce its association with enormous sexual power.[47]

Folklore surrounding the female elephant is no less erotic. Several men told me that the slow, lumbering walk of the female elephant is 'very sexy'. The clanking chains on the female elephant's feet as she is led down the street (a common sound in Kerala) is likened to the jingling anklets of a mature woman. An attractive woman's buttocks are likened to the rear of an elephant in a complimentary folk simile. Folk wisdom has it that the sight of either an elephant's behind or that of a prostitute on setting out from home is a good omen. Finally, the elephant's domed forehead is compared to a woman's breasts. The songs praising Bhagavati in the kaḷam pāṭṭu preceding muṭiyēṯṯu describe her breasts as like the domed brow of the elephant; her thighs are likened to the trunk of an elephant, and so on. The entire body and behaviour of the elephant become a symbol for Bhadrakāḷi's erotic attraction as well as her latent ferocity.

Bhagavati's second earring is the head of a tiger. The tiger in Kerala folklore represents carnivorousness, cruelty, and nocturnal activity. The folklore of yakṣis as bloodthirsty, night-stalking vampires reiterates this theme.[48] The tiger is also the mount of the fierce goddess. The iconography of Mūkāmbika Bhagavati (located in southern Karnataka but highly revered by Malayalis and considered to be the 'elder sister' of Chottanikkara Bhagavati) is of a naked, forest-dwelling goddess with a tiger's head in the place of her vagina (see Fig. 7). This iconographic representation of the position of the goddess's mount makes the isomorphism between the female genitals and the carnivorous, bloodthirsty mouth of the tiger clear.[49] The teeth, fangs, and tongue are all essential aspects of Kāḷi's iconography in muṭiyēṯṯu. The ancient warrior goddess Koṯṯavai, Bhadrakāḷi's prototype, wore a necklace of curved tiger canines around her neck to indicate her ferocity and bloodthirst. Vētāḷam, the voraciously bloodthirsty assistant/mount of Kāḷi, is also referred to at times as a tiger. She is said to hook her claws into the back of the eagle Garuḍan, Viṣṇu's mount, in the ritual of *Garuḍan tūkkam* (a hook-swinging ritual prevalent in the Travancore region of Kerala). Vētāḷam is said to drink vast quantities of blood from Garuḍan's back to quench her endless thirst and violence. The tiger's cruelty and bloodthirst, as well as its beauty and aloofness, again are fitting symbols for the goddess's extraordinary natural power linked to violence and sexuality.[50]

Bhagavati's connection to the landscape of kurinji with its primaeval mountain forests and wild, uncivilized energies, mirrors the goddess's historical origins in that landscape. The goddess's primary affinity with this region appears to reflect not only a geographic, but a historical movement, as she was adopted by incoming Sanskritic cultures of the lowlands into their pantheon. But as Bhagavati began to pervade the landscapes of marutam and neytal she never lost her uncontrollable, uncivilized identity as a being of the mountain forests and the indigenous ('tribal') peoples who dwell there.

Fig. 7: Mūkāmbika Bhagavati

The Three Landscapes: Transformations of Kāḷi in Kerala

The performance of muṭiyēṯṯu is intimately tied to the powerful feminine landscape that gave birth to it. Constructed of the very materials of that earth, the various forms taken by the goddess during the rituals of the performance are woven together like a palm-leaf mat. Moving from her domain in the sap of the trees and the blood of the rocks, the goddess is coaxed by singing and drumming into the fire of the coconut oil lamp. From there she leaps into the coloured rice powders of the beautiful kaḷam drawn on the earthen floor. After she receives worship there, another fiery lamp carries her spirit to the arena of the performance. Meanwhile, the actor playing the part of Bhadrakāḷi adorns himself with the elements of her body: coconut leaves, jackwood, rice powder, and coloured stones ground into paint. Fully dressed, he looks directly into her eyes staring back at him from the dark inner sanctum of the shrine. Suddenly she enters his body and animates the iron sword he takes in his hand. Moving in the warm limbs of the possessed actor, the goddess gives voice and movement to her passions of anger at the unrighteous Dārika. Chasing and jumping, she decapitates him, her red eyes flashing. As the sunlight peeks out from the cool trees, the goddess retreats into the landscape she timelessly pervades, calmed and benevolent, ready to receive the rains and bring forth the green grass of life.

The living landscapes of marutam, neytal, and kurinji are the physical stage for this drama. Each in its turn has contributed to the formation of the goddess Bhagavati as she appears in Kerala today. As the earth goddess she is present in every part of the landscape: the mountains are her breasts, the lowland areas where rice and coconut grow her body, loins, and genitals. When the season of heat and drought inflames her, the dramas of sexuality and sacrifice bring on the monsoon rains to quench her thirst. Her breasts fill with milk, the rivers flow downward and fertilize the land. As the spirits of the dead are propitiated with offerings of food, other spirits enter new wombs where they feed on the nutritious fluids of the mother's body. At the new year, the first paddy sprouts emerge from the renewed soil. With the joyous celebrations of Onam, the drama of death and life comes full circle. In the preceding chapters, we have seen how these landscapes are intertwined through time and space, history and society. In the next two chapters we shall explore the inner psychic dramas of the men who perform this gruelling ritual; and enter the real, unseen feminine worlds muṭiyēṯṯu echoes but can never truly reclaim.

Notes

[1] For sacred geography, see Eck 1981, Kinsley 1986.

[2] See Ramanujan 1968, 1985.

[3] K. S. Prabhakaran, Trichur paddy farmer, personal communication, September 1992.

[4] One breast is constructed of paddy (unhusked, raw-rice grains), while the other is of husked, parboiled white rice.

[5] The coconut bud is in fact the genitalia of the plant. For brief ethnographic accounts of these rites in Kerala, see Gough 1955 and Yalman 1963. Extensive data for individual castes are presented in Krishna Iyer 1905–7.

[6] See Caldwell 1995: 281, n. 8 for story text.

[7] See Freeman (1991) for the ritual importance of the toddy pot, drinking at rituals, etc.

[8] Peterson 1989: 171, n. 81. The Bhagavati images used for worship at the temples of Kodungallur, Tirumāndāmkunnu, and Paramekkavu are all made of varikka plāvu.

[9] The technical term for the scythe is arivāḷ, the sword used to cut rice (*ari*). The word denoting the ritual weapon of the goddess may be spelled either aruvāḷ or aravāḷ. In either case the meaning is a sword used for cutting, and the associated verb implies cutting, sawing, reaping, severing, and killing. This ambiguity built into the linguistic term for the ritual sword expresses the conflation of harvesting and death (more specifically decapitation and the spilling of blood-seed) which forms the basis of my argument here.

[10] See Cantlie 1977; Carstairs 1958; LaBarre 1984; O'Flaherty (1980). The concept of the brain as the locus of semen is well-documented for Indian culture as well as for many other cultures. In head-hunting ideology in many cultures, semen is equivalent to the fertilizing seed which produces plant life, and the supernatural power or life-force inherent in human sexual fluids is not different from that required for the successful germination of plant life. See discussion in Caldwell 1995: 287–9.

[11] For ethnomedical understandings of semen as refined blood, see O'Flaherty 1980; Daniel 1984.

[12] *Kumbalañga*, a long, thick green squash about a foot long, is used.

[13] See Krishna Iyer 1981(2): 78. Marglin 1985a: 234–5 and 1995 describes a similar festival in Orissa.

[14] Interview, Calicut, Kerala, November 1991.

[15] Kurumbakavu Devi temple, Angamaly, Trichur district.

[16] Bharati 1970; Brooks 1990; Marglin 1985a: 239–40; Schoterman 1980; Sircar 1973.

[17] The term here appears to derive from the Sanskrit root, 'vīr-' meaning 'heroic', rather than the old Tamil 'viṟali,' although both roots suggest a connection to war. See chapter 1 for a discussion of viṟalis in ancient Tamil culture.

[18] Hardy 1983: Appendix IX discusses the possible origins of the kurava in ancient tribal bullfighting rituals that were related to marriage ceremonies. In the teyyam ritual performance, the actor is empowered with the spirit of the goddess at the moment he gazes into the mirror and sees the transforming make-up (Freeman 1991). Perhaps this act mimics the puberty ceremony, underscoring the symbolic identity of Bhagavati and the menarchal girl.

[19] See Krishna Iyer 1928–36, 1937–41, 1981, and Luiz 1962 for extensive reports on this topic.

[20] In the town of Tuvvur, near Perintalmanna. Personal communication, Payipra Radhakrishnan, 1992. See Sattar 1979 for an identical tribal custom in Assam and Bangladesh: 'Menstruating girl is carried on shoulders in a victory parade throughout the village. The girl holds aloft a blood stained flag at the head of the procession' (111).

[21] This concern was expressed as far back as the *Upanishads*; see Altekar 1956[1938]: 67.

[22] One young woman who had suffered a severe case of chicken-pox in her eighteenth year told me that white-coloured pox is considered a blessing from the goddess, but black pox pustules represent a curse and the goddess's anger. Her pustules, luckily, had been white.

[23] Erndl 1993; Kinsley 1986; Marglin 1985a; O'Flaherty 1980. Ramanujan 1986 characterizes these polarities as the tooth-mother and the breast-mother.

[24] Babb 1970; 1973; Bennett 1983; Bradford 1983; Brubaker 1977, 1978; Carstairs 1958; Chaudhuri 1956; Coburn 1991; Erndl 1993; Gatwood 1986; Hawley and Wulff 1982; Hershman 1977; Kakar 1978; Kondos 1986; Kurtz 1992; Ramanujan 1986; Robinson 1985; Shulman 1976, 1980; Tapper 1979; Thompson 1983; Wadley 1975, 1977, 1980, 1992; Wulff 1982. Recent studies have begun to question the simplicity of such equations, suggesting ways women resist and contest their roles while remaining within them (Harlan and Courtright 1995; Pintchman 1994; Raheja and Gold 1994; Ramanujan 1991).

[25] This temple also had great political significance in the medieval period (C. A. Menon 1959). For the erotic implications of such breast-feeding images, see chapter 4.

[26] See also Blackburn 1988.

[27] In tantric practice and philosophy, different forms of divinity (essence, sound, image, *yantra*) coexist and are interchangeable. The knowledgeable practitioner merely draws on the form most appropriate for the need at hand. The same is true for muṭiyēṯṯu as well. We should not attempt to reduce one sign to its referent, or to foreground one meaning against another.

[28] Two calendars coexist in Kerala. One is the solar Sanskrit calendar,

which has as its first month Medam (Sanskrit *caitram*—April–May). This new year date is celebrated in Kerala with the festival of Vishu. The Kerala solar calendar is similar to the Vedic calendars used throughout India, but its year is dated from the tenth century, and is known as the Kollam Era. Thus, at this writing the Kollam year is 1172 (1997 CE). Another Malayalam year organized around the lunar cycle begins with the month of Chingam in mid-August, and this is the true Malayali new year, celebrated with the festival of Onam. Onam always falls on the Tiruvonam star date in the month of Chingam. The 'star dates' are thirty asterisms of an older Dravidian lunar calendar that repeat within the larger solar calendrical system. In addition to these two, several other calendars are also in use in Kerala. Muslims, Christians, and Hindus all follow unique calendars with different originary dates; furthermore, individual days are counted from different phases of the moon. The result is that a typical Kerala calendar sold in shops shows four different years and four different dates for each day of the year.

29 In practice muṭiyēṯṯu may be scheduled on whatever day the temple festival is to be held. However, veḷiccappāṭu performances, kaḷam drawing, *pāna*, and many other Bhagavati rituals are prescriptively held on Tuesdays and Fridays.

30 Jay Seelan, interview, 25 August 1993, Chazhur, Kerala.

31 Ibid.

32 The word 'martial' of course is itself derived from its associations with the planet Mars in the Graeco-Roman calendar.

33 Hart (1975) states that the conjunction of Mars and Venus was believed to bring drought in the Sangam period.

34 Occasionally, as in the rest of south India, Śiva is described as being married to Pārvati, with Ganesh and Skanda as his two children. But in the Bhadrakāḷi myths, Pārvati and these additional children are marginal or not present.

35 See Daniel (1984: 245–53) for a vivid description of this pilgrimage. Other references on the Ayyappa cult include Nāyar 1972, Srinivas 1955.

36 While the Śabarimala pilgrimage is rapidly gaining in popularity, drawing men from all over south India in increasing numbers each year; the ancient Tiruvātira festival, which celebrates women's erotic desire and pleasure, is dying out. The male insistence on celibacy throughout the '*mandalam*' period of November–December, in preparation for the pilgrimage, occurs at exactly the time of year traditionally devoted to the women's celebration of sexuality in the Tiruvātira festival. It is almost as if the Śabarimala pilgrimage is a competing event to drown out the voice of feminine desire expressed in the Tiruvātira songs.

37 For association of Krishna and the monsoon, see Kinsley 1975.

38 The significance of the tenth square is no doubt that it symbolizes birth; the term of pregnancy, dated from conception, is traditionally said to last ten months in India.

[39] For descriptions of the bhūta cult, see Claus 1975; Upadhyaya and Upadhyaya 1984.

[40] Jains also ritually fast to death facing north.

[41] E. Kalidasan, interview, Calicut, Kerala, November 1991.

[42] In most temples this liquid is poured out into a small tank for pilgrims to take. From there it is drained directly downwards so that it does not create any obstacle for circumambulating devotees. The obstruction of this path was a unique feature which I encountered at other Kerala Śiva temples as well. The circumambulating devotee is thereby forced to retrace his or her steps backwards and view the remainder of the shrine in a clockwise direction.

[43] The *Śiva Purāṇa, Koṭirudrasaṁhitā* 29: 4 identifies the realm of Dāruka as the 'fertile and flourishing forest ... on the shores of the western sea'; Shastri identifies this as the Arabian Sea (1969: 1373, n. 163). The *Śatarudrasaṁhitā* 42: 2–4 identifies a *jyotirlinga* of Śiva as 'Nagesa in the forest of Dāruka'; the editor's note states that 'Daruvana is placed on the Himalayas near Kedara in Garhwal on the Ganga', but the clear identification of Dāruka's forest in the previous citation as located on the western sea throws Shastri's interpretation into doubt (ibid.: 1254). Dāruka's forest is however identified in Shastri's chapter with the realm of Śiva in the form of the lord of snakes. Reference is also made to Śiva as Kirāta, the hunter form extremely popular in Kerala (Śatarudrasamhitā 41: 43, Shastri 1969: 1251).

[44] Interview, Piravom, Kerala, August 1992.

[45] Balakrishnan Mārār, interview, Muvattupuzha, Kerala, May 1992.

[46] See Neff 1995 for a complete study of these rituals.

[47] When the male elephants occasionally get erections during the temple processions, jokes and nervous giggling among females draw attention to this 'fifth leg'. The trunk may also be seen as a symbolic 'eating/drinking phallus'—see chapter 4 for the significance of the drinking phallus image.

[48] See chapter 4 for discussion of yakṣi stories.

[49] Of course this symbolism is unconscious; the ostensible meaning of the lion's position in Fig. 8 is that it is the goddess's mount, on which she is riding. However, the physical location and depiction in the artist's rendition leave little doubt as to the subconscious association with the vagina.

[50] An important motif in the traditional story of Lord Ayyappan told in Kerala is his journey to the forest to obtain a tigress's milk, to satisfy the demands of his evil stepmother who secretly wishes to destroy him. The taming of the female tiger by the celibate Ayyappan, and obtaining of her milk, reverse and neutralize the debilitating sexuality of the voracious female (evil, desirous stepmother), represented by the female tiger. The re-enactment of this conquest of feminine desire is an important theme of the annual Śabarimala pilgrimage, as discussed earlier in this chapter.

4

MALE EXPERIENCES

The picture painted by the previous chapter, of a vibrant living landscape infused with the feminine power of Bhagavati, seeks to explicate the underlying symbolic meanings of the muṭiyēṯṯu drama. Yet such seamless, intricately woven interpretations, while ringing true, seem lacking. It remains to be asked: *for whom* is the account in chapter 3 true? Cultural anthropology of the last two decades has consistently drawn our attention to the complexities of power, process, and reception which are masked by such ahistorical symbolic/structural accounts. In fact it is no longer hermeneutically possible simply to speak of Bhagavati as a symbol of fertility and growth, or to see conflicting images of female sexuality worked out in myth, without asking who is telling the myths to whom and under what circumstances.

When we look at muṭiyēṯṯu in this way, we can see that it is almost exclusively a male domain. The real and imagined spaces where the dramas of Bhagavati are played out are populated almost entirely by men. The images of dangerous feminine power we have been exploring turn out to be male constructions of femaleness, in which women play very little part. The Bhagavati cult's compelling emotional quality also seems to resonate in quite different ways for men and women. This chapter will explore the intense psychological involvement of men in the ritual, mythic, and dramatic process of the Bhagavati cult, showing how muṭiyēṯṯu expresses and resolves male cognitive and emotional conflicts particular to Kerala. The next chapter will look at the same material from the women's viewpoint, and in doing so present yet another, radically different facet of this complex whole.

Ball of Fire: The Angry Mother

The essence of muṭiyēṯṯu is heat. Heat is everywhere in the performance: in the oppressive summer night air, in the large oil-wick lamp holding the sacred presence at the centre of the drama's action, in the fire-torches that accompany the actors wherever they move, and within the body of the actor, as sweat and anger. In the words of veteran troupe leader Koratty Narayana Kuṟup:

> The actor who plays Kāḷi with the heavy crown on the head gets the vigour and power of Kāḷi gradually. When rage overcomes him the crown must be removed to calm him down. He will become physically heated. The actor suffers under the suffocation of 30–35 cloths tied tightly to his body. Besides, there is a heavy crown and facial paint. On the stage in front of him there will be two drummers. Throwing the teḷḷi powder also makes heat. Anger accelerates the amount of heat. For cooling down the actor is given water to drink after the crown is taken off, and he will be fanned.[1]

The actor's experience of possession, as the divine enters his body, is also experienced as physical and emotional heat.

> [When possessed by Kāḷi, I feel] that I've lost my self-consciousness. My head feels heavy. It is a great feeling. After losing self-consciousness, we experience a lot of heat in the body. That feels (just like) sweating in the hot sun. Along with the sweat and heat our emotions also change. We feel so angry towards the other actors. Our eyes also will appear red. Then the headgear and the weapon will be taken away and that spirit will go off on its own. When the weapon and the headgear are removed, she [Kāḷi] gets cooled and comes down to normal.[2]

This accumulation of heat is no accident, for the goddess herself is of the form of fire. The male actor must deeply identify with this female, heated form:

> After putting on the dress and make-up, we feel that we are Kāḷi. That feeling is there in our mind always as a special excitation. We fix the picture of Bhagavati in our mind, and her supernatural power enters our body. Bhagavati was born from the third eye of Śiva. Śiva puts all his anger into her. It can only be called a fire ball. To represent that fire ball, we light a fire torch on both sides. When you light that torch and throw the incandescent powder onto it, it blazes up with a loud noise: boo! boo! When we talk about Kāḷi's power ... she is the power born from Śiva's anger.[3]

The experience of the goddess is of a heat that moves from one space to another, in and out of physical bodies and containers, pervading the entire sacred performance space. Management of this heat, through its evocation, containment, and release, is the essential performative act of the ritual. The heat of the land, the body, and emotions are indivisible expressions of a single principle of energy. In the previous chapter we saw how the imagery of feminine sexuality, violence, and heat is integral to the agricultural symbolism of wet rice and coconut cultivation. In the symbolic dimension of agriculture, the dangerous heat of summer, drought, and fever must be managed and cooled. External and internal forms of heat in this system cannot be separated from each other: hot temperatures outside imply high body temperatures inside.

In the south Indian view, an imbalance in an individual's psychological/physical/humoral state generates too much heat; this excess of heat inside the mind/body manifests itself in strong extroverted emotions, in the physical signs of perspiration and skin eruptions, and in fever illnesses. One might even say that the emotions of anger and desire are actually the cause of fever; just as the goddess's anger and desire actually are the cause of the hot season. Just as excessive atmospheric heat is disruptive to the cycle of agricultural fertility, anger and desire disrupt both social and individual equilibrium, causing a person to put him or herself before others. In Kerala, such a situation is undesirable, and must be remedied. The medical diagnosis of this state of imbalance is achieved by reading the external signs of bodily heat, and by prescribing the external and internal application of substances which will cool it. The unruly emotions of anger and desire are associated with abnormal psychological states such as possession, and must be handled by ritual specialists in order to restore social and psychological balance.

From my journal:

Last week I came down with a vicious viral fever. On the sixth night of this cruel, aching fever, I lay swooning in a rage of heat, anger, desperation, and delirium. Images of Kāḷi began to fill my mind: millions of hideous demonic things vomiting forth from her eyes, nostrils, ears, mouth, breasts, navel, fingers. Like the cosmic vision of Krishna in the Bhagavad Gita but more vile and loathsome, yet somehow extremely comforting to me in that state. I just let myself go, opening to it more and more, feeling the hideous memories and feelings exploding out. I began to feel I was on fire: my face, hands, body getting hotter and hotter without stopping, a terrible pressure in my head, a feeling of anger and desperation, rage, wildness, and thirst, terrible thirst; being cut off from the outside, too weak to speak or move. I suddenly thought of the Mārārs in muṭiyēṯṯu: how they describe these same symptoms in the possession scene, and the misery they undergo which none can imagine. I started weeping with compassion, feeling in my body (because it's only when we feel it like that that we truly understand) the kind of suffering they described. I wanted to tell them, now I know what you go through, now I understand a little. I also understood how potent the metaphor of fever illnesses is in the goddess cult. It has meaning on so many levels. Heat, of course, the first: shivering and trembling, the signs of possession; delirium, dryness of mouth, sweating, spots on the skin like eruptions of heat to the surface, visible manifestations of the energy within like tiny volcanoes; the symptoms of possession as shivering, shaking. All this easily conveys the idea of divine energy which is dangerous and malefic, must be asked to leave, cooled down, given something to eat or drink, something to entice it from the body. Why a female? Because it is the female which they see as hot and angry and vengeful (as in the barren, unmarried, wronged, or those who died in childbirth). Fever is the primal battle. Feels like a war inside the body and our body actually is fighting an invader.

Physical, environmental, or psychic imbalances signify a state of 'hotness' which is considered (by men at least) to be essentially feminine. This is reflected in the metaphoric persona of Bhadrakāḷi. As a 'ball of fire', Bhagavati combines both the physical power of fire and the emotional qualities of anger and lust. These two components of emotional/physical heat—anger and desire—seem to be inextricably related. Yet muṭiyēṯṯu actors insist that lust is entirely irrelevant, and it is only anger which motivates their goddess. They explain that Bhagavati's murderous heat is analogous to the righteous, protective anger of a mother, whose strength and power, and even cruelty, is always marshalled in service of her children. Actors openly identify Bhagavati as a mother, sometimes displacing even their own personal mothers in their affections. As such, it is not surprising that the themes of frustrated sexual desire which are attributed to the goddess in other ritual contexts are downplayed in muṭiyēṯṯu.

Why is Kāḷi angry? The stories tell us she is angry at Dārika, for his evil deeds. Her anger is righteous and correct: she wants to destroy Dārika for his antinomian pride, greed, and rapaciousness. As such, she represents the force of *ṛta* (cosmic order) in the

Sanskritic universe. This interpretation of the Dārikavadham story is the one I heard most frequently from Brahmin informants. They explained to me that if a person behaves badly, the goddess will have to punish that person, just as she punished Dārika. It is precisely in this quality that many people see her mothering capacity.

When I asked people in interviews how a mother shows love to her children, the two characteristic responses most often given were: feeding and beating (another common response was self-deprivation on the mother's part). As an American, this surprised me. My response to the same query would likely include such behaviour as kissing, praising, holding, listening and spending time together, providing good schooling and clothes, and perhaps as an afterthought, giving good food and discipline. But the themes which consistently emerged in my discussions with the families of actors were of mothers as a source of strength and power, protecting and correcting children. Savitri, a 91-year-old Brahmin woman who delivered eight children and raised six (two died when they were young), was quite straightforward in expressing this viewpoint:

> Of course you have to beat your children. My goodness, I don't know how much I've beaten my children. Look. When we see children doing something mischievous or wrong, at once he is given a severe beating to correct him. Otherwise if you neglect it, he starts behaving the same way with strangers and they would beat him. I can't stand to see my children being beaten up by strangers, so it is good to nip that in the bud. I discipline my children myself.[4]

Others, perhaps expecting my disapproval, seemed to try to protect me from this aspect of their child-rearing practices. Although in my presence, local children were treated indulgently with smiles and proddings of food, I often heard violent screams coming from neighbouring houses in the late evenings before bedtime. My three-year-old daughter often reported seeing her friends beaten with sticks for misbehaviour, and began to incorporate this disciplinary action into her play. Many people casually commented that beatings have to be administered to children for numerous reasons, including getting them to study, eat, or obey. But although such corrective action was apparently routine, it was seldom public.

Many men whom I interviewed drew a stark contrast between the behaviour of mothers and fathers. Mothers were portrayed as unfailingly devoted to their children, sacrificing anything for their welfare, and protecting them at times from the wrath of distant or cruel fathers. A prominent Kāḷi Tiyāṭṭu artist of Vaikom (V) explained in one conversation with me:

V: We cannot define the word 'mother' in a single word, but its basic meaning is great love. Mother is so patient, mother is the teacher, mother is everything for a child. For example, sometimes when there are quarrels between father, mother, and children, the father may tell the boy, 'Get out! Don't enter in my house!' But the mother will never say that. When he comes through the back door she will give food and shelter; but father will not give. The love of mother is very big. Not like father. Father can abandon him, but mother cannot abandon the child. And that is the place of goddess as Dēvi.
Q: Sometimes Kāḷi appears very violent. Is that like our mother also?
V: Yes, she is blessing us. She punishes her children, to make them go into the right way. Mother is the complete food for a human being. There is no barrier for mother's love. We cannot imagine. She is so patient. At the same time, very cruel. According to circumstances.[5]

George, married and in his mid-thirties, expressed a similar point of view:

> In almost every case children love their mothers and mothers their children. Men may take some liquor and are a little rough, but mother's thoughts are that children should flourish and be brought up well. Mothers believe they are born for that only and they die for this cause. Otherwise what pleasure do they have in this world? Wives think that they should bring up their children, look after their needs only. They even forget their own life fulfilling that desire. Even if there is not enough for themselves, they devote all their time and resources to see that the children are always happy and full.
>
> When they are small they are always picked up and carried with mother. After that stage is over, when they start going to school, she kisses them when they come back, and gives them tea and snacks she has made for them. In that way a special love is generated in children. Father is rarely seen, right? It's late night when he comes back after work. So mostly children have more affection towards mother. Then when mother is starting to eat something, we snatch it and eat. So truly saying, mothers get only the half portion of the food. Of course, this is among people who don't have money. The rich can have as much as they want. But in poor homes you can see the real love.
>
> When she gets angry she at once gives a whack or pinches the child. But very soon she feels sorry and fondles it, grabbing it up in her arms, embracing and fondling the child. Mother has only one thought: children should be brought up prospering. I loved my mother more than anything else. I loved my mother most. Wherever I go, I feel like returning to my mother and seeing her. I couldn't stay away from her. Even now

> it's like that, though she is gone. When I wake up first I see my mother—I've kept her picture by my bed. I wake up from my bed seeing that only. So I've had no misfortunes till now. I am successful always.[6]

Many men thus openly idealize their mothers. Every man I interviewed admitted his mother beat him when he was a child, but regarded this as a positive expression of her love and concern for his character. Feeding and beating were the constant motifs of motherly love in the interviews, and clear connections were drawn between Bhagavati and real mothers. Kāḷi's maternal anger can be provoked by the misbehaviour of her children, and is a tonic which cures us of evil tendencies. As soon as she has beaten us, she will soothe the wounds and reward us grandly.

This portrait of affect resembles that painted by Margaret Trawick for Tamil Nadu (1990a, b). Her study reveals the multiple valences of love in a family setting, which may include behaviour some would regard as violent or aggressive, but which for south Indians expresses concern and intimacy. Mencher's (1963) account of child-rearing and family relations in the 1950s clearly demonstrates a similar combination of harsh discipline and enveloping, sensual presence. Her study also underscores the emphasis in Kerala on repression of hostility towards authoritarian figures. Thus, although the mother is clearly an authoritarian figure in the upper-caste Kerala household, sons deny feeling any hostility towards her. Mencher suggests that the child's repressed hostility may turn inward as aggression toward the self, or outward as the child torments others weaker than himself (such as younger siblings, servants, or animals).

This pattern of affect in Kerala families is projected into the image of Bhadrakāḷi as a punishing, aggressive mother who can be calmed by the child's self-punishment or dependency. The 'heat' of real beatings is re-enacted in the Kāḷi actor's rage towards Dārika. Kāḷi's gestures—left hand upraised to strike, accusatory right index finger pointing, popping eyes, and rolled back tongue—are easily recognized by Keralites as the gestures of an angry mother punishing her children. Traditionally, actors playing Kāḷi were the maternal uncles of younger actors playing Dārika; their relationship was in fact structurally analogous to that of mother and son. The maternal figure of Kāḷi, played by the mother's brother, fictively kills the son-victim figure of Dārika, played by the sister's son. The popular legends of Kāḷi actors actually having killed actors playing Dārika undoubtedly reflect tensions inherent in the matrilineal social structure in which maternal uncles held jural authority over nephews, but they also re-enact the intense intimacy of the mother-son relationship.[7]

On a conscious level, traditional Kerala men understand a mother's anger to be a positive expression of love and intimacy, and of concern for the formation of one's character. But the myths and rituals associated with the worship of Bhagavati also suggest that the goddess's anger arises from her frustrated sexual desire. The actors' conscious denial of the goddess's sexuality is belied by the explicitness of the theme in myths and rituals. The powerful identification with Bhagavati, and ultimately with the mother, that male actors undergo in muṭiyēṯṯu cannot be properly understood without further exploring these undercurrents of feminine desire, frustration, and revenge.

Journal notes:

At this point I am unable to continue the interview as Sofia starts crying hysterically and says she wants to go to sleep. So I bathe her, change her, try to put her to sleep for one hour with no luck. I become irritable, angry, and frustrated in the process because I can't observe anything. The more she complains the more enraged I become. I can hear the family talking animatedly in the house but am stuck here with Sofia. After changing into my nightgown, I realize dinner is being served in the other building and I can't go. So I miss more of the action. I guess it is like being a Kerala woman—always in the interiors, never in the action. But it's so frustrating to have to deal with Sofia all the time. It's hard enough just coming here. Perhaps I need an 'attitude adjustment.' How did Margaret Mead manage it?

Yakṣis: Dangerous Virgins

Whereas maternal anger is a form of feminine 'heat' ultimately believed to be beneficial to children, the 'heat' imputed by men to unmarried females is quite the opposite. Virgin girls are considered in folk conceptions to be overheated due to their lack of access to sexual satisfaction, posing a danger to males. Frustrated sexual desire leads to a different kind of anger which is equally a part of Bhagavati's persona.

The mental suffering of young women, particularly their frustration and anger over repressed sexual needs, is a vital theme in

Kerala folklore and popular culture. Malayali films and novels present updated versions of the pervasive and ancient folklore of yakṣis, unhappy, seductive and bloodthirsty female tree spirits out to entice and destroy virtuous men.[8] The legend generally follows the same pattern. A Brahmin man is walking home from the temple on a moonlit night, when he encounters a beautiful, voluptuous maiden standing alone on the road before him. Her bewitching smile and fragrance of jasmine utterly dazzle him, and she shyly requests his protection to accompany her home. On the way the man's amorous desire grows intense and the lady seems willing. In the morning the bloody entrails of his body are discovered hanging from the trees and the yakṣi is nowhere to be seen. In a version of this legend published in *Temples and Legends of Kerala*, the Brahmin escapes by ducking into the home of his guru, who instructs his disciple to touch the guru's body while looking at the enticing female: 'Lo! It was an apparition, a fiendish woman with fierce eyes and protruding teeth. Little did Guptan Nambūtiri realise that he was in the clutches of a terrible yakṣi out to entice men and devour them' (Vaidyanathan 1988: 103). In this version of the story, the Brahmin seeks the help of Bhagavati, who destroys the yakṣi and throws her into a pond, the water of which turns red as blood.

Virgin girls are openly associated with yakṣis in the male imagination. Most men I interviewed believed that unmarried women, as well as married women whose husbands are away (30–40 per cent of the adult male population leave Kerala to work for long periods in the Persian Gulf, returning home only briefly each year or two), are voraciously sexual, and that they secretly desire the attentions and teasing of men. George, a married man in his 30s explained to me through a male translator:

> in the olden days people believed that when they slept ... these [virgins] would come in dreams and have [sex] with us ... [producing] nocturnal emissions. ... This kind of people enter our body, and cause us to ooze [fluid]. They drain us and drink it. That's the belief.[9]

Bhadrakāḷi is conceived of in Kerala as an unmarried, virgin girl—beautiful, hot, and dangerous. Her heat arises from her virgin state, and, like the yakṣis and virgins of dreams, her desire and anger make her thirsty for male life-fluids. In folk-tales and legends, the yakṣi is a vampire, drinking the blood of her victims while seducing them; but George's statement makes the symbolism more explicit: it is *semen* which the virgin demoness wants from her victim. This fluid fertilizes and cools the hot female womb but weakens and drains the man who gives it—in the yakṣi stories, even to the point of death. The motif of drinking blood is clearly a symbolic displacement of the intake of semen by the vagina, and in some stories and medical pronouncements the two fluids are interchangeable (O'Flaherty 1980: 33–5; Shulman 1980: 103). In the Dārikavadham story, for example, the demon Dārika has the boon of reproducing himself *ad infinitum:* each drop of his blood that falls upon the earth immediately springs up into a thousand more of himself.[10] Because of this ability, he is known as *raktabījāsura:* blood-seed demon.

Bījam in Malayalam (the language of Kerala) means the reproductive seed or semen. It is possessed by both males and females and is closely related to blood. In folk conceptions of reproductive physiology, it is by heating the body and arousing sexual desire that both males and females produce (or 'ooze', in George's words) their sexual fluids—women in the form of blood, and men as semen. The mixing of these two emotionally-generated fluids leads to fertilization and life. Thus the heat of the female's desire is requisite to conception, but this process inevitably requires a 'sacrifice' of the male to the female, an offering of his life-fluids that leaves him somehow less vital, closer to death. This sacrifice of essential male fluids is enacted in the remainder of the story: Dārika is conquered by Kāḷi, who takes the help of the insatiably bloodthirsty Vētaḷam, a horrible female forest ghost. Her enormous tongue spreads over the entire battlefield and as Kāḷi kills Dārika, Vētaḷam laps up the endless river of blood so that no more Dārikas can be born from the contact of his blood with the earth. Thus Darika is destroyed by the direct controversion of his infinite autofertility: his yakṣi/demon/vampire/virgin opponents 'drain and drink' his precious life-fluids (to recall George's phrase) thus destroying his vitality and killing him.[11]

The rituals and folklore of the Kodungallur Bhagavati temple in central Kerala reinforce the association of the fierce goddess with the image of the sexually aggressive and insatiable virgin woman. As we have seen in chapter 3, KD Bhagavati is identified with the sexually deprived, overheated virgin/widow. At the annual Bharaṇi festival, drunken dancing and obscene songs and gestures are directed towards the goddess, while vast quantities of cocks were sacrificed (today, simply thrown over the temple walls). These polluting practices continue largely unabated, despite objections from various reform-oriented Hindu groups.[12]

George discussed the Kodungallur Bharaṇi with Laji:

L: So are obscene songs sung at Bharani?

G: Yes. She is an unmarried lady, right? (Very secretively:) So she is pleased or made happy at least by singing these obscene songs.

L: Kāḷi, right?

G: Yes, this Bhagavati. There is a belief that Bhagavati remains unmarried. So, singing these obscene songs, she can be made happy. These songs are sung with tuḷḷal (dancing). People go there and please her and come back once a year. It is for this reason that they dress up and go.

L: Those who have not married—virgins—do they have more interest in sex (*kāmam*)?

G: That's right. If she had been born as a human being she would have all those interests.

L: So it is to fulfil her lust that these enactments are done, these oracles' performances, obscene songs, etc.?

G: Yes, they sing to extinguish her desire. These songs and other activities, like tuḷḷal, calm her lust.[13]

George mentions songs sung to the goddess during Bharaṇi festival. At the temple one can purchase the official texts of the 'Bharaṇi songs', which are devotional compositions by well-known poets. These publications bear little relation to the infamous Bharaṇi songs sung by drunken pilgrims at the festival at Kodungallur. Although everyone knows of the existence of these songs, and they are often alluded to in published studies of the festival, their obscene content is never disclosed. Even the mention of 'Bharaṇi songs' seems to raise titters and embarrassed glances. One young man was willing to sing a few lines of these songs for me. Although they are incomplete, these fragments serve to illustrate the theme:

1. *If you have to fuck Kodungallur Amma, you'll have to have a penis like a flagpost.*[14]

2. *Didn't you see that Brahmin girl in Palghat? Didn't you see her cunt? It's like a cut Christmas cake* [a European style dark fruitcake].

3. *There's a Brahmin lady in Palghat. This lady was fucked by a dog when there was no male Brahmin.*

4. *Hey, guy, why are you sitting like that. If you don't have any song to sing come and suck my cock.*

These songs bluntly assert the sexual desire of both the goddess and Brahmin women, traditionally regarded as pure, sacred, and inaccessible. High-caste women who venture out to the festival may be mercilessly teased and grabbed by lower-caste men (Gentes 1992). Gentes cites a number of sources alleging that 'orgiastic rites' and baring of the female breasts regularly took place within the shrine during Bharaṇi (ibid.: 306–11). The combination of sexual display, head-cutting, and the decapitation of cocks suggests that Bhagavati's sexual desire is the source of her heated, angry state, giving her an insatiable thirst for blood-sacrifice, the characteristic ritual of Kodungallur Bharaṇi.

The obscene Bharaṇi songs bear a distinct resemblance to traditional south Indian puberty songs, which also have seldom been published. Again, the very mention of 'puberty songs' seemed to cause alarm and insistent denials of any knowledge of their content. I was therefore never able to collect any (unfortunately, no one I knew reached puberty while I was in Kerala). But the following excerpts from published texts of some Tamil puberty songs from the turn of the century suggest clear similarities to the ballads for Kodungallur Amma at Bharaṇi:

Tell me! O dear girl!
Have you attained puberty? Will you tell me?
Our parts are very fuzzy.
Placing it at the cunt, placing it at the twat.
Thrust it into the cunt, thrust it into the upper hole!
How does it feel to you?
Does it feel nice to you? (Ucida 1977: 53)

You have attained puberty, O girl!
They have bathed you, O girl!
They have performed the puberty oblation, O girl!
They have pushed you into a cracked hovel.
You kept on farting in the course of fucking.

Come into the eggplant field!
Come! I'll give you a handful of money!
Tell me whether this will go in or not!
I shall very slowly thrust this in and draw it out, come dear!
Go away! This cunt has just brought forth a baby.
I shall very slowly thrust this in and draw it out, come dear![15]

These songs were sung to the young girl by female relatives during the puberty ceremony and had the explicit goal of teaching her about sexual life. In Tamil Nadu as in Kerala, the songs are seldom sung as 'nowadays talking about sex is regarded as very indecent, probably due to the influence of Western prudery. Even an aged person blushes when he hears the word ... (puberty song)' (Ucida 1979: 79). The explicit references to sexuality in both Kodungallur Bharaṇi and puberty songs lends further credence to the theory (advanced in chapter 3) that the image of Kodungallur Bhagavati, as indeed Bhadrakāḷi in general in Kerala, is that of a young menstruating female.

Although most people denied any direct relation between the sexuality of virgins (or any other female emotions) and the nature of Bhagavati, George's statements imply that Kāḷi worship in Kerala does address such concerns. Bhadrakāḷi is modelled on a virgin female, who suffers from unfulfilled desire for sex and procreation, whose lack of fulfilment is one source of her anger, and who requires the blood-sacrifice of a male to cool and satisfy her 'thirst'.

Two episodes in the Dārikavadham story shed further light on the goddess's insatiable and unconventional sexuality. These are (1) the affliction of smallpox and its cure; and (2) the calming of Kāḷi's anger through incest. Consider the following oral version of the Dārikavadham story, as told by an elderly *tiṟayāṭṭam* troupe leader from northern Kerala in November 1991:

> Dārika was being wicked. The dēvas (gods) went to Śiva to complain about Dārika. Śiva said, 'Wait, I'll make arrangements for that,' and he opened his third eye and Kāḷi was born. She came out full grown and went to kill Dārika with her curved sword. Manōdari, the wife of Dārika, went to Śiva and cried, 'Kāḷi has come to kill my husband. Save us.' Śiva was in deep meditation. But Pārvati was there. She asked Manōdari, 'What happened?' Manōdari told the story and made her request. They tried to get Śiva's attention so many times but he was immersed in *tapas* (austerities). Pārvati took a pot, put her sweat in it and gave the pot to Manōdari. She told her, 'Spill this sweat on the body of Kāḷi. Kāḷi will get smallpox on her body and she will die.' When Manōdari came [to the battlefield], Kāḷi had just killed Dārika. As [Kāḷi] came with Dārika's head, Manōdari spilled the smallpox on her. Then Kāḷi prayed to Śiva: 'Father, I am sick.' Śiva heard her prayer in his mind; [he thought,] 'My daughter is [in trouble].' He took his hair and hit his hair on the floor. From that, Ghaṇṭākarṇa appeared. He said, 'Yes,

father, what do you want?' 'See son, your sister Kāḷi is ill. You go and lick all the bubbles of smallpox off her body.' He does this. But when he starts to take [the pox] from her face—in our culture, brothers don't touch the face of sisters—she turns her face away saying, 'You are my brother.' So Kāḷi keeps the smallpox marks on her face. She went to Śiva on a cheetah in a horrible fierce state. He asked her to calm down and drew so many [caricatures] in front of her on the ground. Then Śiva lay down and asked her to dance on his body saying, 'Release your temper.' After that, she released her temper. Then people worshipped her as Bhagavati because she killed Dārika and made all the people happy.[16]

One peculiarity of the Kerala story, distinguishing it from other Purāṇic versions, is Kāḷi's birth directly from Śiva's third eye. Śiva is thus said to be Kāḷi's father. This is significant as so many other south Asian variants of the Kali story claim the goddess to be either a spin-off of Śiva's wife Pārvati when she is enraged, or Śiva's consort in competition with Pārvati. While the sexuality of Kāḷi's relationship to Śiva is not diminished in the Kerala version, the structural relationship is starkly altered. As Śiva's daughter, Kāḷi is thrown into competition with the female characters in the story, Manōdari (Dārika's wife, whom Kāḷi tricks into revealing a secret mantra), and Pārvati, Śiva's wife. The rivalry between daughter and mother for the father's attention is made explicit when Pārvati cooperates with Manōdari to kill Kāḷi by throwing her own sweat on the goddess's body, thereby afflicting her with smallpox.[17] Śiva, who has steadfastly resisted Pārvati's efforts to arouse him for sexual relations, hears Kāḷi's distress in meditation and comes to her aid, creating a brother for her by slapping his matted locks on the ground; or in some versions, from his ear wax. An incestuous theme emerges, as Ghaṇṭākarṇan is enlisted to lick his sister's body from toe to head in order to remove the smallpox. In this act skin eruptions are clear markers of sexual heat and desire: it is Pārvati's sweat (a symbol of her frustrated sexual desire for Śiva) which is cast onto the virgin daughter, who then is made repulsive by the obvious signs of heat/desire disfiguring her entire body. The brother (a taboo but highly desired sexual partner; see Gough 1955) must lick her body to relieve this discomfort, an action suggestive of cunnilingus; but when he reaches her face, modesty prevents him from completing the task, and so she is left disfigured, with blood-bursting pox pustules an essential feature of her facial make-up in muṭiyēṯṯu.[18]

The incestuous theme intensifies at the end of Kāḷi's battle with Dārika, as she returns enraged and excited to Kailāsam, the home of Śiva, with the blood-dripping head of the demon in her hand. Even Śiva is terrified as he sees her approaching in this aroused state. He tries to amuse her with pleasing portraits painted on the ground (kaḷams) and grotesque comical caricatures to make her laugh.[19] But even this technique fails to cool Kāḷi. Finally, in another version collected orally from a middle-aged man:

> They say that Śiva—actually it is said that he is fully naked. He lies down fully naked in front of Kāḷi, saying 'Daughter, release your temper.' She did that and afterwards was calmed a little.[20]

The exact nature of Kāḷi's releasing of her temper is not specified here. Most versions concur with Kalidasan's (above), concluding that Kāḷi dances on her father's body. The theme of 'dancing' on Śiva's naked body thinly disguises the well-known tantric versions of the story in which Kāḷi has sexual intercourse with the prone figure of Śiva in the cremation ground. The following version, collected orally in Orissa, is a clear example:

> Kāḷi ... went on a blind destructive rampage, killing everything and everyone in sight, regardless of who they were. The gods and the people became extremely worried and appealed to Śiva for help. Mahadev [Śiva] agreed and lay himself down, sleeping, on the path on which the furious, black and naked Kāḷi was coming. In her blinded anger she did not see him and stepped on his chest. At that moment Śiva's penis became erect and entered Kāḷi. At that instant Kāḷi recognized her husband and pulled out her tongue in ecstasy ... and her anger disappears. (Marglin 1985a: 215)

Both versions recognize that the goddess's anger is inseparable from her excessive desire, and that sexual contact with Śiva is the key to calming her. The striking difference in the Kerala story is the assertion that Kāḷi is Śiva's daughter and that she consciously agrees to an incestuous sexual act. The Dārikavadham story asserts the aggressive sexual desire of the goddess, and in particular, her desire for illicit sexual relations with brother and/or father.

In another important variant of the ending of the story in Kerala, the goddess's anger is calmed by the sight of two babies placed by Śiva in the doorway of Kailāsam; in some versions these are Ganesh and Nandikeśan (Tirumump 1975). Milk begins to flow in Kāḷi's breasts and her mood is suddenly transformed from one of anger to one of peaceful motherly love as she picks up and suckles the two male babies. She is depicted in this mood at the temple of Tirumāndāmkunnu, discussed in chapter 3. It is perhaps significant that all women told me this ending to the story, whereas men tended to tell the incestuous union/dancing/nakedness ending. In any case, the motif of the breast-feeding goddess also has implicit incestuous meaning, as we can clearly see from its textual variant in *Liṅga-Purāṇa* (106). In this purāṇic version Kāḷi is born from Śiva's third eye and is thus his daughter; but here, to calm her wrath after killing Dārika (Daruka in the text), Śiva himself takes the form of a baby boy and cries to attract Kāḷi's attention: 'On seeing the boy, who was actually [Śiva] the goddess was deluded. ... She took him, kissed him on his head and suckled him at her breasts. Along with her breast milk the boy quaffed up her wrath also...' (*Liṅga-Purāna* 106: 22–3 [Shastri 1973]) The father here becomes the son of his own daughter and sucks her breasts to remove her wrath.

The variant endings—Śiva dancing naked, lying beneath, sucking the breasts, or in sexual union with his daughter Kāḷi, are what Dundes has termed 'allomotifs', story elements whose direct substitutability implies their structural identity from a symbolic point of view (1962). The sucking of the goddess's breast by Śiva is thus psychically equivalent to his penetration of her vagina with his erect penis; in either case the goddess's anger is subdued by incestuous body contact. The erotic meaning of breast-feeding as a regressive form of sexual union with the mother is amply demonstrated for south Indian/Sri Lankan materials by Gananath Obeyesekere in *The Work of Culture* (1990: 114–22). The sexual meanings of breast-feeding are key to understanding the power dynamics of the Bhagavati cult drama, and gender relations in Kerala.

Fellatio and the Self-feeding Breast

Bhagavati's sexuality is expressed in a vividly oral idiom. Her phallic sword and outstretched tongue express her anger, and the authoritarian pole of the mother's personality, which punishes transgression by inflicting physical pain. Balakrishnan Mārār said, for example: 'I put my tongue out while playing Kāḷi to show the anger. It is told that Bhadrakāḷi always has her tongue hanging out for this reason.' The outstretched tongue can also signify eating.[21] The goddess's protruding tongue thus also marks the desire pole of the mother's personality, a reminder of her insatiable blood thirst. As a yakṣi prototype, she is a vampire. Her primary means of sexual satisfaction is the oral ingestion of a man's vital life-fluid, bījam (blood/semen). The rituals of the Bhagavati cult all point to aggressive and fatal drinking of the male by the female: the orgy of blood-sacrifice of male 'cocks' at Kodungallur; the male veḷiccappāṭu's cutting his head in a symbolic act of self-castration; the offering of guruti; and the story of Vētāḷam all emphasize Bhagavati's erotic, killing thirst.

Two types of psychoanalytic interpretations have been proffered to explain the common imagery of the fierce goddess seen here. One is that the goddess represents a 'phallic mother' redolent of the aggressive image of the primal scene. Alternatively, she represents the envied mother's introjection of the father's penis. Wulff summarizes this argument:

> [Kāḷi] is herself, first of all, a phallic being, the mother-with-a-penis: she stands triumphantly erect on Śiva's body, sword raised, fingers pointed, and eyes and tongue protruding. At the same time, draped with severed heads and hands, she is the bloodied image of the castrating and menstruating (thus castrated) female. (1982: 290–1)

In this interpretation, the phallic attributes of the goddess disguise male castration-anxieties ultimately directed towards the father, as well as homosexual desire for the father's penis. Following Freud, such analyses stress the father–son polarity of the Oedipal conflict as the central trauma seeking expression (Carstairs 1958; Chaudhuri 1956; Obeyesekere 1981; Spratt 1977 [1966]).

A second type of psychoanalytic framework stresses the mother–son dyad of the Oedipal triangle. Sudhir Kakar (1978) follows Klein in interpreting Kāḷi's desire to devour male semen/blood as a reversal of the infant male's desire to devour the mother's breast, and his fear of her retribution for his cannibalistic impulses. Kakar's account emphasizes the mother's erotic tendencies towards her son as a substitute for insufficient sexual satisfaction in her marital relationship; the breast-feeding relationship becomes the site of this intense, intimate erotic tie.[22] Kakar also clearly points out the ambivalent reaction of the boy, who both desires to sate his mother's erotic needs and is frightened by her inappropriate affect. Although this position is controversial, there is a great deal of evidence for the highly eroticized mother–son tie in most psychoanalytic studies of south Asia.[23]

If Kakar's position is valid, the veḷiccappāṭu's self-mutilation can easily be seen as a super-ego punishment for his taboo erotic desire for the mother.[24] His cutting of his own head in a symbolic act of self-castration provides the goddess/mother figure with the male life-fluids she requires to sate her aggressive sexual desire. The mother's excessive sexuality is perceived in infantile terms, as an oral need. The goddess needs to drink male fluids because the boy needs to drink maternal ones; as the oral is the only erotic idiom known to the child in this early pre-Oedipal dependency phase, the reverse projection takes on a sado-masochistic oral dimension.

A posture of dependency keeps the mother from getting angry and forces her into a conciliatory mood. This seems to be the message of the Ganapati/breast-feeding ending to the Dārikavadham story: the fierce goddess is cooled down when she sees a crying baby. She *must* give up her anger and suckle the male child when he is helpless and weak.[25] In this view, ritualized masochistic behaviour (symbolic self-castration, beheading of sacrificial male animals, actual self-punishment) offered to the goddess is a powerful form of psychic manipulation. The masochistic worshipper inflicts suffering upon himself to compel maternal love and nurturance (Asch 1988: 95). This strategy makes sense when we recall George's remarks about mothers who strike their children in anger and then immediately cuddle and soothe them upon seeing their distress. Trawick's evidence from Tamil Nadu also supports such a possibility. She describes the 'torturing' (unrelenting teasing leading to tears) of the most beloved children as a form of intense interaction which is at the core of the Tamil concept of family love (Trawick 1990a: 47–50). Such child-rearing practices no doubt create a deep unconscious association between suffering (physical and mental) and nurturance, acceptance, and love. Masochistic, dependent behaviour could easily become erotically exciting in such a context of affective training.[26]

The goddess's breast-feeding also has a strong erotic component which resonates with the personal experience of many adult Kerala men. All of the troupe leaders and artisans I interviewed who were over the age of forty recalled having been breast-fed at least until the age of four; some until eight years of age. Appu Kuttan recalled:

> I drank until I was seven. I was the last child. When I came back from school I'd have to get on [mother's] lap and drink. She wore no upper clothes, only a light towel. Women did not wear blouses then.[27]

Until the 1950s, most women in Kerala did not cover their breasts, but wore only a simple lower cloth tied at the waist. In fact covering the breasts was a prerogative of upper-caste women; lower-caste women were prohibited by law from doing so in the presence of upper-caste men, as baring the chest is a traditional sign of respect and submission to superiors in Kerala (Hardgrave 1968). Even today, one can see elderly women (over seventy) walking with breasts uncovered. Although the sight of female breasts would thus have been more or less commonplace, their erotic importance was not diminished by their nudity. The contemporary intensity of male erotic interest in women's breasts (now modestly covered by saris and blouses) which was revealed in observation, interviews, and folklore does not seem likely to be a recent phenomenon. Evidence from early-twentieth-century novels suggests that gazing at a woman's exposed breasts has always been erotically stimulating for young men (see V. Nair 1975).

For a young boy of seven or eight, daily breast-feeding cannot serve much of a nutritional function. In fact this sensual physical contact might be one of the only forms of positive engagement with the mother if child-rearing accounts from the region are accurate. Trawick and Mencher both emphasize the need to hide and avoid overt expressions of parental affection, for instance (Trawick 1990a, 1990b; Mencher 1963). Under such conditions one would imagine that the sight of breasts would be highly arousing, being the major form of physical contact expressing maternal attachment at this age.

Vasan Achari, an accomplished painter and sculptor who recently created a new muṭi for the Pazhur muṭiyēṯṯu troupe, often paints the goddess as a young, erotically appealing mother with a raised bodice, a young boy sucking her exposed breasts. In fact such a painting graces the street sign at the entrance to his studio. When we asked him to explain the image, Achari said:

> The meaning of the painting is that she is like a mother. She is depicted as Sarasvati, who is the mother of the arts. So that artist who is drinking from that mother's breast, that's myself.

Achari had also produced a very erotically appealing painted wooden breast-piece as a costume to be worn by a male in a ritual performance offered to the goddess in a nearby temple. Again the huge, round, firm breasts were portrayed bulging out from beneath a raised tight blue bodice. Many iconic portraits of Bhagavati in

Kerala temples show her in this fashion, with a raised bodice exposing the breasts, or with no breast covering at all (e.g. Tirumāndāmkunnu Bhagavati, Fig. 6). When asked if the goddess's breasts have any special power or significance, Achari related the following story:

> No special power (śakti), she doesn't care to cover them, that's all. She doesn't try to hide them. The breasts have a special beauty, too. Maybe that's why they have been exposed by the artists. Then in Chenganassery there is a temple. The deity installed there is Bhadrakāḷi. The idol there was made with naked breast. So there in a neighbourhood house, a Christian boy made a comment, in fun, 'This is good to hold, and good to suck' when he saw that. So that same night in his bedroom a very beautiful lady appeared. He was scared. She forced him to suck her breast. Of course she forced him and after he drank it he died. After that those people abandoned that place. It is a true story, a recent incident that happened in the temple.[28]

Achari's account reiterates the themes of sexual desire for the mother's breast (displaced onto a Christian, whose lack of respect is thus understandable if still reprehensible), and death as punishment for this desire, just as Kakar suggests. The oral themes of desire, drinking, and death constantly converge in the body of the goddess.

The breasts of Bhadrakāḷi in the muṭiyēṯṯu costume are often encircled by wooden snakes, with reared heads poised at the neckline of the actor. We have explored the goddess's close association with nāgayakṣis (female snake deities) in chapter 3. Snake worship is ubiquitous in Kerala. Almost every home has a snake grove, and milk, eggs, and other substances are offered there to avert sarppa *kōpam*, the anger of the serpents. Sarppa kōpam can manifest as general misfortunes afflicting a family, as rashes of the skin, blindness, or other eye illnesses. More seriously, a person may be bitten by a snake and most likely die. Snake-bites are quite common in Kerala, and in fact, a woman well known to me died of snake-bite during my stay there. In the ritual of sarppam tuḷḷal, frequently conducted in southern Kerala to avert sarppa kōpam, virgin girls are possessed by the snake-deities. P. S. Ramachandran, a sarppam tuḷḷal artist, states that 'the girls' minds are identical with the snakes' minds.'[29] Many people I interviewed expressed similar sentiments, saying that snakes normally possess only females, especially youthful, unmarried ones.

What connects these seemingly disparate features of the snake cult: young girls, anger, possession, skin and eye diseases, and offerings of milk? Alter's treatment of similar themes in his illuminating discussion of Nāg Pañchamī in Maharashtra help clarify their logic in Kerala. Alter notes that for celibate wrestlers, snakes symbolize insatiable female passion:

> Wrestlers regard snakes as the symbolic equivalent of lustful women. ... In this aspect snakes are associated with rabid female sexual energy which, in the view of many Indian men, is both physically and psychologically debilitating. That women are not allowed to enter the *akhara* [gymnasium] precinct is witness to the threat they pose. (Alter 1992: 146)

Alter explains that wrestlers consider both women and snakes to be orally dangerous, sucking out precious life-fluids: 'From a wrestler's perspective, having sex with a women [sic] is like being sucked dry by a snake' (ibid.). In male fantasy orality becomes the dominant erotic paradigm, the female genitals become mouth-like, and the discharge of semen into the vagina becomes a kind of drinking act. The snake, with its prodigious orality, is an ideal symbol for sexuality in such a context: the snake takes its prey whole into its mouth, kills it by swallowing it, and also kills by biting or spewing poison.

In Kerala, these same themes surface in the association of virgin girls with snakes. The symptoms associated with sarppa kōpam (wrath of snakes) now become comprehensible. Virgin girls, like yakṣis and snakes, are uncontrollably sexual and 'thirsty' for male semen, and their anger is aroused when they are denied satisfaction. The somatic symbolism of possession, with its heat, loss of body control, shouting of obscenities, and loosened hair, clearly expresses uncontrolled dangerous passion. The entering of the snake spirit (a phallic entity) into the body of a woman, is also a concrete metaphor for sexual intercourse (Sered 1994; Obeyesekere 1977a, 1981). The word for possession, *āvēśam*, means 'possession by a deity or spirit', 'inspiration by a deity', and also 'entry' or 'penetration' (C. M. Pillai 1976: 120). Veḷiccappāṭus whom I interviewed described the cause of the possession as 'spirits going inside' the body of the victim. The reaction is stupor, speechlessness, and shivering or shaking, *tuḷḷuka*. Obeyesekere has suggested that this shivering has an orgasmic quality in Sri Lankan possession, and that it releases sexual tension (Obeyesekere 1970, 1977a,

1981). One veḷiccappāṭu's comment to me that 'it feels like your hormones are working' confirms the sexual association.

Veḷiccappāṭus in Kerala called this symptom *uṟaña tuḷḷuka*. The meanings of the verb *uṟayuka* are enlightening in this context. As an intransitive verb, urayuka can have any of the following meanings: '1. to solidify; to set; to get possessed of; 2. to liquefy; to ooze; 3. to sit, subside, reside.' As a transitive, the verb means 'to curdle; to coagulate'. The noun form, *uṟa*, means 'butter-milk added to milk for curdling; rain, moisture; residence, seat' (C. M. Pillai 1976: 165). The root metaphor for the shivering symptoms of possession is the curdling of milk by the addition of buttermilk. The addition of the curdling agent (the spirit who enters the body) results in the settling or coagulation of something, and the oozing out of liquid. The image of coagulation is often applied to the heating of seminal fluid, associated with both milk and butter, when it is retained by the ascetic male (Cantlie 1977; O'Flaherty 1980). In the story of Dārikavadham, as we have seen, it is this fluid (bījam) which is desired by Bhadrakāḷi and her demonic female assistants. Moreover, George used the same word when he described the entry of the spirits of virgin girls into the bodies of sleeping men, resulting in nocturnal emissions (see beginning of this section): 'These kinds of people *enter our body*, and cause us to *ooze* [fluid]. They drain us and drink it.' This chain of metaphorical associations to the word '*uṟaña tuḷḷuka*' used to describe the symptoms of possession leaves little doubt as to its sexual connotations.

What are we to make of the other symptoms of sarppa kōpam? Skin and eye ailments are said to be the snakes' punishment for the selfish emotions of pride, envy, and desire. The skin and eyes are of course receptive organs, whose potential for erotic arousal is well developed in Indian literature and art. In folk medicine, itching skin indicates repressed desire, as do the pustulant eruptions of pox diseases and acne. Scratching is also a common form of love play described in ancient south Indian erotic literature. Eyes too are highly erotic. Desire and love are conventionally communicated through the meeting of eyes throughout India, and seeing is a form of 'touch' (Eck 1981). Bhadrakāḷi in Kerala is born from Śiva's fiery third eye, which also is the site of the fire which punishes the god Kāma (lust) when he attempts to arouse Śiva from his meditations (Cantlie 1977: 250). The third eye contains the destructive fire of desire, but as a procreative organ is also a kind of supernatural male vagina.[30] The 'evil eye', so frequently attributed to barren females and jealous people, also makes sense in this light as an overheated, desirous female organ.

In Kerala eyes are common symbolic equivalents of breasts in the costumes of *paṭayaṇi*, a southern art form dedicated to Bhadrakāḷi. In fact enormous eyes cover the entire figure of the goddess. In Malayalam, the term for the nipple is *mulakaṇ*, 'eye of the breast'. Under the male erotic gaze the breast becomes a receptive, devouring eye, homologous to the vagina in its ambivalent potential. As Roland (1988) suggests, this motif expresses in vivid metaphor the idea that 'all eyes are upon' the young, attractive female body, whose very attractiveness is then somehow its own fault (Roland 1988: 264). In male fantasy, the breasts, vagina, and eyes equally share the frightening properties of female erotic organs: all contain the feminine heat of desire which can be destructive to males, all are receptive and 'take in' (devour) their objects.

What of the offerings of milk? The snake's thirst is quenched, and its dangerous passion neutralized, by the ingestion of milk. Alter explains that mother's milk, as a sign of fertility and nurturance, is the 'inverse of erotic sexuality [as] energy is redirected away from sex to nurturing growth' (Alter 1992: 146). The purpose of feeding milk to snakes is to neutralize and cool the 'dangerous female passion' they represent (ibid.: 150).

Milk and breast-feeding are auspicious female symbols of maternal nurturance and fertility, opposed to the heated, desirous, draining and drinking orality of the passionate virgin female. But as Alter and O'Flaherty amply demonstrate, milk and breast-feeding are symbolically transformed in the male imagination into semen and phallus. Milk and semen are both considered refined forms of blood, and are symbolically interchangeable forms of condensed human energy. The ascetic male who retains his semen becomes like a pregnant female with breasts and swollen belly; the semen rises like cream to his head and produces extraordinary psychic powers (Cantlie 1977; O'Flaherty 1980: 43–8). Not only are the fluids of milk and semen symbolic equivalents, but the act of 'milking' or breast-feeding becomes a symbolic equivalent to the draining of semen from the phallus in intercourse.

We can now begin to unravel the strange symbolism of Vētāḷam's tongue in the Dārikavadham story. Śiva Raman Mārār narrated the story of Vētāḷam's tongue this way:

> The blood of Dārika shouldn't fall on the ground. If one drop of blood spills on the ground, one thousand asuras [demons] will be born. That is why Bhadrakāḷi takes help from Vētāḷam, who spreads her tongue on the battlefield. Only then the whole asura family will be destroyed. Otherwise each drop will give birth to a thousand asuras. A face of Vētāḷam is tied on the waist of the actor. In this, you can see only the head of Vētāḷam and the tongue hanging down. There is no limit for the length of Vētāḷam's tongue. It can elongate to any extent. It is a sort of monster like that. So Vētāḷam is brought to the battlefield with the agreement that she will be given any amount of blood she needs. Bhadrakāḷi fights standing on Dārika's neck. That is the significance of tying this on the waist. When the war starts, all the blood will be falling only on Vētāḷam's tongue so no more asuras will be born. It is for this that Vētāḷam is brought.[31]

Vētāḷam here seems to be closely related to the mythical demoness Long-Tongue, identified by O'Flaherty as a precursor of Kāḷi (O'Flaherty 1985: 101–3; cited in Kripal 1994: 156, n. 10). In the *Jaiminiya Brāhmaṇa*, Long-Tongue aggressively ingests the juice (*soma*) offered to the gods in the Vedic fire ritual. Her aggressive sexuality is graphically expressed in the presence of vaginas all over her body; she is slain by a male who is magically granted multiple penises 'on every limb' and who thus locks her down and kills her (Kripal 1994: 156–7). Vētāḷam clearly represents Bhadrakāḷi's most out-of-control, sexually threatening, and bloodthirsty side.

Several features of Śiva Raman Mārār's version alert us to an important meaning of Vētāḷam's long tongue. First, the tongue hangs in the vicinity of the female character's vagina; but as the actor is actually a man, its shape, location, and inexhaustible length identify the tongue as an obvious phallic symbol. The iconography of the fierce goddess throughout India shows her sitting astride a lion, tiger, or other carnivorous cat. The lion mount of one goddess closely related to Bhagavati, Mūkāmbika Dēvi of southern Karnataka, is shown in a frontal position which makes it appear as if the mouth of the lion is her vagina. I would suggest that this is the meaning of the Devi's carnivorous feline mount: it symbolizes the uncontrollable, devouring, killing hunger of the female organ.[32] Vētāḷam's carnivorous, voracious tongue seems to be equivalent to an exaggerated clitoris, a sign of the goddess's excessive, aggressive sexuality. The tongue is phallic but it also drinks. The tongue licks Dārika's bījam from his severed neck, preventing his auto-procreation by the ingestion of the blood-semen. What we have then is a form of oral sex conducted by a drinking phallus. Vētāḷam/Kāḷi's licking of Dārika's blood/semen is thus an act of symbolic magical fellatio.

Kāḷi/Vētāḷam's long tongue bears no real relation to feminine sexuality—women don't have long, erectile organs. The phallic imagery of Kāḷi reflects male sexuality imagined into a female body. It is a transsexual fantasy, not spiritually transcendent androgyny, which Kāḷi expresses in this context. For males, the positive valence of the breast, exuding life-giving milk, is opposed to the negative valence of the vagina, which is perceived as a hot, thirsty, destructive, snake-like mouth, drinking precious male semen and emitting the poison of menstrual blood. Furthermore, the phallus is equated to the breast, semen to milk, ejaculation to feeding. The next step in this symbolic process is that fellatio is functionally equivalent but affectively superior to breast-feeding.[33]

Alter's discussion of the folk motif of the suckling snake once again illuminates the symbolic underpinnings of this transformation:[34]

> In this imagery, ... [t]he breast becomes the phallus from which semen rather than milk is sucked out. ... On one level the snake sucks out the mother's nurturing milk, but on a parallel symbolic plane it sucks out vital male energy. ... As the snake drinks milk it is associated with both the good mother's flowing milk and the bad mother's passion. On one plane the suckling snake is a potent symbol of erotic fantasy, but it is also, on another plane, emblematic of the non-erotic, symbiotic relationship between mother and child. (Alter 1992: 147)

In other words, the snake can have its milk and eat it too. Phallic in shape, the snake ingests milk/semen as a neutralization of female passion. The impressive orality of the snake, which takes its prey whole into its mouth and swallows it, suggests a fellatio image. Offerings of milk and eggs, androgynous semen substitutes, further reinforce this association. The snake's phallic shape, combined with its drinking, fellating capacity, make it a perfect symbol of a 'self-feeding breast'. The snake eating milk is like a phallus which retains ('eats') and thus restores its own semen. Alter (1992) and Cantlie (1977) both impressively demonstrate the importance of this retention of semen for celibate and ascetic males, who paranoically avoid contact with females; and Alter, quoting O'Flaherty, points out that such semen-withholding ascetics are believed to have power over snakes (as symbols of aggressive female sexuality) (Alter 1992: 150).

The act of feeding milk to snakes achieves this self-contained system. As Alter explains, 'the snake reingests ... the symbolic semen that it has been milked of' (ibid.: 149–50). The mythic serpent Ananta, a snake sucking its own tail, symbolizes this perpetual motion of life-fluids without loss of fluid to the female. For wrestlers, as for yogis over millennia, this male self-control awakens the enlightening *kuṇḍalinī* power (the serpent energy within the human body) in a kind of 'internal ejaculation ... equivalent, on a symbolic plane, to the alchemical recycling of milk/semen/milk' (ibid.: 150). The snake with its tail in its mouth achieves the desired ingestion of positively valent life-fluids, love, nurturance, affect, and food, without losing anything to females psychologically or physically.

Alter draws the connection between this image of the snake with its tail in its mouth and the 'self-feeding breast' discussed by Klein (1948, 1957) and O'Flaherty (1980, 1984). Klein sees the self-feeding breast as the prototypical image of envy. By fantasizing his own penis as a feeding, breast-like organ, a male appropriates the good qualities of the loving mother without the negative qualities he fears: the desirous, engulfing, milk-withholding mother. While O'Flaherty stresses the spirituality inherent in the metaphor, regarding this 'recycling' of semen by the 'ouroboros snake [as] a symbol of the paradoxical Mobius universe which is infinite but self-contained' (1984: 242–3, cited in Alter 1992: 150), it also, more prosaically, may express a gynophobic homosexual fantasy of fellatio which ingeniously cuts women out of the sexual loop. In Sambia, New Guinea, similar psychological motivations result in a cult of actual homosexual fellatio (Herdt 1981). Is there any evidence for such behaviour in Kerala?

On a mythical level, we can certainly answer in the affirmative. The cult of Lord Ayyappan, discussed in chapter 3, is redolent with homosexual and gynophobic themes, from the transvestite homosexual pairing of Śiva and Viṣṇu which results in Ayyappan's conception, to the fanatical celibacy of devotees, and the collusive denial of Ayyappan's feminine suitor gleefully performed by the male pilgrims to the shrine.[35] In muṭiyēṯṯu, the grotesque female clown Kūḷi aggressively chases young males in the audience, places them in her lap, and forces one of her huge, pointed red 'breasts' into the victim's mouth in a parody of breast-feeding. Of course Kūḷi is played by a man, her 'breasts' are sharp, pointed, and phallic in appearance, and her passive, hysterically laughing victims are very often the black-garbed, celibate Ayyappa pilgrims during the month of Dhanu (December–January).

It is difficult to make conclusive statements about homosexual activity and practice in Kerala. My impressionistic view, based on friendships, observations, jokes and folklore I collected, as well as extensive interviews with young unmarried men, is that homosexual activity is not only present but quite common in Kerala. As in Sambia, it tends to occur in the adolescent phase of life, giving way to heterosexual relations after marriage. Only for a few does homosexuality become a permanent life-style; and, as in most of India, it is absolutely socially unacceptable and must be conducted in secret.[36]

One twenty-one-year-old male (unmarried) with whom I had established a trusting relationship, was willing to comment on this question. The interchange follows:

Q: Would you say that homosexual relations are very common here in Kerala?
A: No. I have not seen them very often. But in Trichur in that round in [the centre of town], there are people in a certain space. They go and suck this thing and all.
Q: How can you recognize a homosexual here?
A: They walk and talk in an effeminate way. We call them 'flutes'. There was a guy who used to tutor boys from 9:30 at night until 2:30 in the morning. So when I used to come from home to go to this guy's tuition centre, I would get down from the bus in the round and walk. And one day a guy came up to me saying, 'Brother, brother!' He was begging, 'Can I sing for you? Can I sing for you? I sing well.' It means: 'Can I suck your cock?' I was afraid of him. I ran away from there.
Q: But it seems from what you told me earlier that most men have had at least one homosexual experience, that it's not uncommon at a certain phase of your life for people to have it.
A: If he has lived in a hostel. When I was in school, when I was in the tenth standard, I was forced to lie for the senior students. They just bully you, 'Come on, lay, otherwise ...' You'll have to lay like a vegetable, otherwise they're going to kick you. You can't go and complain also. They just say, 'You go and complain.' They don't care.[37]

Another friend in his late twenties (unmarried) told that he had been introduced to sex by his older male cousin, who molested him and his brothers every time the cousin stayed over at their house. 'We all had to sleep in the same bed and we dreaded it because he would always seduce us.' He never told anyone. Another young man had learned about semen from a teenage male cousin who had him perform fellatio under a table or behind a couch. Young boys who hung around this man, now in his late twenties, seemed to fall in love with him. He claimed these boys wanted to fellate him; he just allowed that 'to satisfy them'. The same man also said that in his journal he had often referred to his frequently angry mother as Bhadrakāḷi. Yet another young man revealed that his cousins, a group of five brothers, had regularly 'abused' a boy in their neighbourhood for satisfaction of sexual needs while in their teens and young twenties.

This spotty, impressionistic set of remarks is not meant to prove anything definitively, but simply to convey the voices of some young men who have observed or experienced homosexual relations in Kerala. Their comments reveal the abusive nature of many of the contacts, forcefully and secretly propagated on them as children, as well as the almost 'pathologically excessive restrictions on [adolescent] libidinal life' (Masson 1976: 624) forced on young people in Kerala which perhaps encourage homosexual contacts in lieu of access to heterosexual ones.[38] It is interesting to note in the context of this chapter that the homosexual behaviour described is not anal but *oral*; that is to say, fellatio is the preferred mode of its expression, as evidenced in the epithet 'flutes' for homosexual fellator/prostitutes in the Trichur round. The service proffered by the homosexual prostitutes is sucking (fellating their clients). This suggests that it is being sucked which men find most erotically exciting.

The preference for fellatio as a mode of sexual pleasure continues after marriage. My younger male informants admitted that most men really like fellatio, and want their wives to do it. Folk knowledge is that soon after her marriage, a young woman starts to get fat because 'she is drinking a lot of semen and it is very nutritious, so they get fat.' One young man even described the proper technique for fellatio, saying it should be 'like the way a baby drinks from the breast—a strong sucking motion.' When I asked this man if he had heard that breast-feeding gives a woman sexual pleasure, he was unfamiliar with that idea. But about fellatio, he asserted, 'Most women love to do that.'[39]

A case of overt homosexuality was related to me by a married man in his mid-thirties. He told me of a veḷiccappāṭu from the Kodungallur Bhagavati temple who felt revulsion for his wife and divorced her. He became completely identified with Bhagavati, and became an active homosexual. My friend explained: '*He performs fellatio and he gets a special energy from that.* He becomes intoxicated and furious. During Bharaṇi, while under vows, he wanders and attacks people [with his curved sword], and cuts his head until it bleeds.' This veḷiccappāṭu was, according to my informant, one of the most powerful and gifted oracles associated with the Kodungallur temple.

Whatever the truth value of this account, the motifs of revulsion from women, homosexual fellatio and its magical power to infuriate and enliven, in association with the cultic worship of Bhadrakāḷi at Kodungallur, are striking proof of the symbolic processes we have traced here. Vētāḷam's 'drinking phallus', the long tongue lapping up semen, is the snake with the tail in its mouth, eternally ejaculating into itself in a male fantasy of omnipotence. The fact that only males may dress as and enact the female roles of Kāḷi/Vētāḷam and Kūḷi is no coincidence, but further proof of the fantasy of androgyny for which homosexual fellatio is a clear resolution. Both heterosexual fellatio and breast-feeding from the female, although very pleasurable to the male, involve psychologically dangerous and 'life-threatening' interactions. In actual or fantasied homosexual fellatio, the male becomes the mother with her omnipotent, life-giving breasts, and the loss of semen to the male partner is not problematic in that the female is avoided and only male sexual energies are involved.[40] In heterosexual fellatio, the threatening female becomes the sucking, dependent baby; at the same time the male experiences the satisfaction of penetrating her (oral) cavity with his penis, and thus avoids the vagina.[41] In either case, for the gynophobic male, fellatio may be the best of all erotic worlds.

The imputing of destructive power to the natural biological impulses of women, the avoidance of female genital relations, and the fear of adult sexuality are by now common themes in the psychological literature on south Asia. The cult of the goddess as enacted in muṭiyēṯṯu, far from empowering or glorifying either female qualities or actual women, is a transsexual drama of male oral fixations and regressions. Fascination and envy directed towards the female body, imagined worlds of virgin lust and anger, may come as the faintest of echoes to a woman watching from the sidelines, strange shadows on a screen behind which she can never tread.

Kūḷi: The Voice of Protest

Towards the middle of the muṭiyēṯṯu performance, providing relief from the intensity of Kāḷi's possession scene, the comical character Kūḷi enters the arena and amuses the crowd with her antics. Kūḷi is a grotesque caricature of a 'tribal' female, often shown in an advanced state of pregnancy. Gopi Nāyar, an unassuming man in his mid-thirties, is one of the best Kūḷi actors, having performed with two major muṭiyēṯṯu troupes since 1985. He never formally trained for the role of Kūḷi but simply had a knack for it and observed various actors until he developed his own style. Gopi Nāyar explained that Kūḷi 'is depicted as a tribal woman' through the donning of leaf-skirts: 'In the olden days, they never had any woven clothes. They used to make clothes out of tender coconut leaves.' The face is made up with asymmetrical black-and-white pastes in imitation of the ritual face-painting used by aboriginal populations of the Western Ghats. A red or black shirt is worn under the leaf skirt. An advanced state of pregnancy is mimicked by stuffing a large pillow under the costume. Gopi Nāyar considers the black colour in the make-up and costume to be essential: 'The real colour needed is black since [Kūḷi] is a ghost.' Black make-up is also indicative of tribal identity, according to Gopi.[42]

The aboriginal population of Kerala lives in the remote forested mountains of the eastern borders of the state. The forest and the people who live in it have for thousands of years represented powerful sacred forces of fertility, possession, and danger to those living in the lowland areas.[43] Such an association survives in the popular imagination even today. Although many aspects of aboriginal culture survive syncretically in the lowland caste society, 'tribal' people are considered by lowlanders to be degraded, animal-like and without culture. They are also considered to be sexually promiscuous, lacking the strict marriage rules and virginity taboos of caste Hindus. Tribal people are reputed to have knowledge of black magic, and control over the powerful forces of nature and the mountains. 'Kūḷi' is the name of an important tribal goddess who shares many of Kāḷi's attributes: she is a likely indigenous forerunner of the Sanskritic deity. A ritual called 'Kūḷiāṭṭam' is performed by Irula groups in the seventh month of pregnancy to ward off evil influences and spirit possession (C. Choondal, personal communication, 1992; Luiz 1962). Vētāḷam, the leader of the forest-dwelling ghosts, is represented indirectly through the person of Kūḷi. The portrayal of Kūḷi in muṭiyēṯṯu thus evokes the force of wildness associated with the forest, with tribal people, and with bhūtas or ghosts said to accompany Kāḷi to war.

Kūḷi is foolish, ugly, and pregnant. As Kāḷi's alter ego, she represents the vile and ridiculous. Kūḷi's ugliness is said to inhere in her blackness, her lack of social graces, and her pregnancy.[44] In every way she controverts the demure, contained modesty of the ideal Malayali female, whose smooth oiled hair, neat and clean dress, and quiet demeanour are her ornaments. Kūḷi's hair is a tangle of leaves and feathers in an ungainly pile atop her dark, misshapen face, which is disfigured by thick lips and inhuman features. Huge pointed breasts, elongated red cones attached by strings to the male actor's body, dangle naked over the swollen, ten months pregnant belly, itself meagrely covered by dirty bunches of leaves.[45] Her only ornaments are leaves and flowers, nowadays augmented with balloons and paper scraps. Kūḷi enters the arena whooping and shouting, calling to the audience members as her children, 'Ooooeee! Makkale! [Hey kids!]' in the voice of a street fishmonger. She speaks in a whining, high-pitched voice and crude, obscene *double-entendres* which delight the audience. Her informal comportment invites a barrage of male teasing and heckling, which she invariably returns in kind, shouting back at her tormentors, and then chasing them lustily through the audience. When she catches a victim (always a male), she carries him like a baby, limp in her arms, to the seat by the stage lamp, and proceeds to thrust her pointed 'breast' into his mouth. This 'breast-feeding' is repeated several times during her scene, to the great enjoyment of the crowd, who laugh uproariously.

All of Kūḷi's actions directly parallel the entrance of Kāḷi earlier in the play. As she enters the stage area, Kūḷi passes in front of the temple shrine, paying homage and spinning as if in possession. In some performances she even lifts and dons the sacred muṭi of Kāḷi, which has been removed from the actor's head after the authentic possession. In one performance Kūḷi donned the muṭi and feigned possession while Kāḷi was undergoing authentic possession, dancing around her in exaggerated postures. This 'fake' possession served to underscore the authenticity of the real possession, just as all of Kūḷi's foolish actions emphasize the correctness of Kāḷi's. Upon entering the stage area, Kūḷi seats herself on Kāḷi's stool in front of the oil lamp and proceeds to enact a series of inverted 'purifications', including bathing, tooth-brushing, and laundry, in a comic parallel to Kāḷi's self-purification before the war with Dārika.[46] While Kāḷi's actions are solemn, silent, and sacred, Kūḷi's are absurd, loud, and funny. Each act is done incorrectly, with emphasis on body functions, uncleanness, ignorance of proper rules of purity, and 'dirty' jokes. Like the complex wit of Kōyimbaṭa Nāyar in muṭiyēṯṯu's other comic scene (just preceding the Kūḷi scene), the dialogue pokes fun at people who don't know how to perform brahminical rituals properly, thereby encouraging an elite identification. Following the 'cleaning' routines, a series of 'breast-feeding' runs are completed, which punctuate the play with its greatest hilarity. As each victim is good-humouredly humiliated, Kūḷi 'blesses' him by applying lampblack to his forehead. This action prefigures the very important blessing of children by Kāḷi which ends the drama in the dawn hours.

The cause for Kūḷi's pregnancy is revealed when Kāḷi reappears on the scene, and the two enter into a dialogue. Kūḷi compares her body to Kāḷi's. She irreverently teases Kāḷi, pulling at her clothes and hair, and mocking her every action. This infuriates Kāḷi further. Upon interrogation by the goddess, Kūḷi reveals that she has been raped by both Dārika and Dānavēndra, resulting in her ungainly pregnant state. This revelation prompts Kāḷi into irrevocable aggressive action, searching out the two demons in earnest. Her ridiculous sidekick trails behind, goading her on. As the two females unearth their twin male adversaries, the fight begins in earnest. The four dance around the flame, chasing each other in swordplay, until Kāḷi 'decapitates' Dārika by removing his head-gear and waving it before the flame in a somewhat anticlimactic finish to the fight.

Several themes converge in the dramatic device of the Kūḷi scene. First and foremost, Kūḷi's antics foreground aspects of female sexuality and mothering which are only implicit in Kāḷi's personality. While Kāḷi is a virgin who never is attracted to or touched by any male, Kūḷi is a mature human woman who has been raped. She clearly enjoys her body and sexuality, with frequent references to penises and sex in the *double-entendres* of her repartee. Kāḷi's fury is calmed by the appearance of male infants at the threshold of Kailāsam; as she holds and breast-feeds them, her violence is muted and converted to benevolence. Kūḷi breast-feeds aggressively, hunting, capturing, and humiliating her adult male 'victims', pressing her ugly, phallic breasts into their mouths in an act of forced dependency. Both Kāḷi and Kūḷi are males dressed as females. Kāḷi's aggressive virginity and castrating sword and tongue reify the yakṣi image, accentuating the horrific danger of the virgin female, placated with the male's blood-sacrifice. Kūḷi's breast-feeding, as discussed in the previous section, symbolically converts female nurturance into homosexual fellatio. Both Kūḷi's parody of mothering and Kāḷi's threatening virginity repudiate and vilify the real feminine sexual body. Anxiety-producing heterosexual relations are converted into safe, homosexual transactions.

Kūḷi's identity as a low-caste, tribal female conflates gender inequality with caste prejudice, in a familiar ideological move noted by numerous scholars of south Indian expressive culture (Berreman 1993; Freeman 1991; Krygier 1982; Ram 1992). By identifying Kūḷi's repulsiveness with her characteristics as both a human, pregnant female and a lowly, ignorant, black-skinned outcaste, and by encouraging us to laugh at her, the drama marginalizes while it structurally equates low status with feminine gender. As a tribal woman, Kūḷi is doubly cursed and doubly rejected. In rejecting her, we despise our own biological femaleness and aspire to the values of high-caste males who embody status, ritual, power, and economic superiority.

But there is another feature of Kūḷi's scene that is worthy of note. Kūḷi gives voice, however marginalized and ridiculed, to real feminine anger provoked by male abuse. For the twenty minutes that she alone dominates the stage, Kūḷi can expostulate freely on her maltreatment at the hands of her rapists. (Significantly, this is the only scene that is fully improvised.) In fact, it is Kūḷi's rape and humiliation that finally infuriate Kāḷi sufficiently to search out and kill Dārika. All of Dārika's evil deeds come to little compared with this violation of the female body, an act which virtually all Malayalis would regard as a heinous crime.[47] Although it is a cross-dressed man who gives it voice, Kūḷi's protest suggests truly feminist concerns. But the voice is only briefly heard, muffled in the hilarity of Kūḷi's buffoonery. The voice of real feminine distress is ultimately silenced in favour of high-caste male images which serve male psychological needs.

Kinds of Power

The rituals of muṭiyēṯṯu are oriented around sacred power (śakti), its invocation, embodiment, management, and control. The Śākta worldview that informs the Bhagavati cult generally and muṭiyēṯṯu specifically regards śakti as an organic force lodged in the bodies of women and lower-caste male ritual specialists. Productive and violent, the Dravidian concept of śakti is both dangerous and essential to the maintenance of life and the world. This organic, feminized conception of power appears to be at odds with European-language concepts. The latter tend to split power into political, ritual, and psycho-erotic components, which are not necessarily seen as related. In fact the relationship between these different kinds of power is only murkily understood for south Asia and other parts of the world, due in part to the flattening effect of recent univocal uses of the term in Marxist-informed and Foucauldian analyses.[48]

Scholars have often noted the identification of political power with warrior goddesses as a feature both of the south Indian Śākta worldview and a characteristic of matrilineal, matrilocal societies. Erotic themes in the relationship of the fierce goddess to demons are interpreted as symbolic representations of structural tensions between lineage groups dominated by males.[49] This highly structural and socio-political view, which speaks of the 'feminization of violence' and the conflation of gender and caste as abstract conceptual transactions, while analytically elegant, fails to adequately account for either the personal emotional power of the dramas to actors and audiences or their obvious inegalitarian gender structure. The exclusion of women from the embodiment of female deity is not adequately explained by such structural analyses; nor is the intense psychological affect which surrounds the performance, rituals, and folklore of the goddess. While acknowledging the relevance of structural models for understanding the socio-political realm, I prefer to focus attention on the *experience of gender* evoked by the rituals. When we look carefully at the psychological reality of the goddess for men and for women, we discover that it is men who impute violent supernatural power to women's biological bodies, and men who imaginatively experience, respond to, and reify this power, while women appear to experience these matters very differently, if at all. In any case, women are prevented by cultural fiat from ever experiencing the divine possession of Kāḷi or enacting the violent decapitation of Dārika in muṭiyēṯṯu, so that the entire discourse of power, however conducted, is by necessity a male one.

When the feminine becomes a metaphor for low-status males, it also further disempowers women. In fact in the rituals of Kerala, all marginalized and disempowered groups are conflated and rejected while their śakti (sacred power) is appropriated and used by high-caste males. This uniquely south Indian, Śākta ideological process, while frequently noted by those with Marxist leanings, has been insufficiently explored with a feminist lens.[50] My interpretation here explores the juncture of psychoerotic and socio-political power under the guise of ritual power, and the ways that males mystify these to the detriment of women. The supernatural śakti of the goddess becomes the property of males, who thereby compensate for their envy and fear of the mother's sexual, procreative body. By coopting this power in transvestite possession performance, males reclaim the envied feminine procreative power within their own bodies, while denying actual social, sexual, and political power to women. By portraying those aspects of imputed feminine sexual power that they most fear and desire, males master their ambivalent feelings and assert their dominance in the social sphere. The rituals, rather than allowing women to express distress and anger, model for women their own dangerousness and the need for them to continue to bind and control their bodies for the benefit of their husbands and sons (Ram 1992, Crapanzano 1973).

At the beginning of this chapter, we saw that the male experience of Bhagavati in muṭiyēṯṯu is of the heat of the female divine. This heat, with its components of anger and sexuality, is intimately related to indigenous psycho-medical concepts of fertility and health. The intense pre-Oedipal ties to the mother which characterize Kerala males (and possibly south Asian males more generally) lead to a fixation on the feminine body as both irresistible and murderous. The mother's persona is split into authoritarian/nurturing and sexual polarities, the former expressed in the persona of Bhadrakāḷi and the latter in the personae of Vētāḷam/Kūḷi. Similarly, the feminine body is split into two zones of power. Erotically stimulating and nurturing breasts, while giving intense pleasure also function as organs of domination over the boy, and are hence a site of fear as well as desire. The *vagina*, *mouth*, and *eyes* are conceived of as devouring oral sexual organs. These are represented symbolically by Vētāḷam's tongue, Śiva's third eye, the pustules of smallpox, and the blindness produced by snake anger.

Male feminine identification focuses on the oral potentiality and threat of the entire feminine body, converting the breasts and vagina into phallic, self-feeding organs in a homosexual fantasy of fellatio which eliminates females from the loop of sexuality entirely while coopting the oral/sexual pleasures their bodies provide. The guilt of desire for the mother's body is punished by the motif of self-beheading/castration in the guise of the transvestite mother herself and the assumption of a posture of infantile dependency which converts the mother's sexual anger into benign nurturance.

We have also identified sado-masochistic elements in the Bhagavati story and its enactments. The intense erotic tie to the mother, combined with guilt over incestuous feelings and harsh physical regimes of punishment are the stimulus for masochistic pleasure in south Indian rituals devoted to the goddess. By assuming a position of suffering, need, humiliation, or dependency, the devotee regains the love of his mother.[51] Whether by becoming an infant at her breast or a supine, inert sexual partner (or preferably, both), the stories of Kāḷi assert that the male must be dominated and subsumed under feminine control. But such postures of submission to the female occur only in the world of fantasy and ritual, or in the privacy of the bedroom, having no apparent relation to the strongly patriarchal family structure of most Kerala families and of society in general. In daily life, defensive hypermasculinity rears its head to mask the deep feminine identification which muṭiyēṯṯu reveals. While powerful goddesses rage, social empowerment of living women remains elusive.

Notes

[1] Interview, Trichur, Kerala, December 1991.

[2] Śiva Raman Mārār, Interview, Muvattupuzha, Kerala, May 1992.

[3] Balakrishnan Mārār, Interview, Muvattupuzha, Kerala, May 1992.

[4] Interview, Alwaye, Kerala, January 1992.

[5] Interview in English, Vaikom, Kerala, March 1992.

[6] Interview, Trichur, Kerala, January 1992.

[7] Spiro 1982 and Obeyesekere 1990 debate the Oedipal complex in matrilineal societies. I follow Obeyesekere's line of reasoning that the emotional charge inherent in certain structural relations can be displaced onto other members of the family group, thereby fulfilling taboo desires while preserving social norms.

[8] See M. Ramakrishnan 1991[1967] for a contemporary novelistic treatment.

[9] George (a pseudonym) is a Christian, but has a very intense interest in Hindu religion and folklore. He has an outstanding collection of folk masks, and is a local authority on folk religion.

[10] This motif obviously replicates the story of Raktabīja in the second episode of the *Devīmāhātmyam.*

[11] Studies of the theme of male sacrifice in the mythology of the Hindu fierce goddess include Shulman 1980: 176–316; and Kinsley 1986: 95–122, 200–8. Often this theme is given a psychoanalytic interpretation, as castration anxiety, or reverse projection of infantile male desire to devour the mother; see Carstairs 1958: 156–69; Gough 1955; Kakar 1978; Obeyesekere 1981; O'Flaherty 1980: 81–129.

[12] See chapters 1 and 3 for a discussion of the Kodungallur temple. In April 1993, the obscene songs were successfully banned from the festival, due in large part to the influence of the Bharatiya Janata Party (BJP), India's major fundamentalist Hindu political party. Similar attempts were made in the nineteenth century.

[13] Interview, February 1992, Trichur, Kerala.

[14] Also quoted in Obeyesekere 1984: 481.

[15] Ucida 1979: 82–3. Ucida is at a loss to explain the significance of the eggplant motif in the last song except to suggest that it is a penis symbol. The song strongly suggests a kind of sexual education in which eggplants (which in south India are slender and about 6–8 inches long) might have been used to masturbate the young girl and teach her what to expect in marriage. This seems all the more likely as I was told by young men in Kerala that women are sometimes teased at the vegetable market for buying eggplants; men believe that women use them to masturbate with.

[16] E. Kalidasan, interview in English, Calicut, Kerala, November 1991.

[17] For connection between sweat and lust, see Cantlie 1977: 255.

[18] See Kripal 1994, 1995: 126–30, for a discussion of the theme of the thousand vaginas on the body or a thousand eyes, as well as of the significance of licking vaginas in tantric meditations of Ramakrishna.

[19] The rituals of paṭayaṇi in southern Kerala enact this portion of the Dārikavadham story, with participants dressing in outrageous satirical costumes and singing obscene songs to the goddess.

[20] Interview, Muvattupuzha, Kerala, May 1992.

[21] For a different interpretation in the cultural setting of Bengal, see Menon and Shweder 1994.

[22] Kakar does not mention the physiologic reaction of the woman's body to breast-feeding; breast-feeding has been shown to cause uterine contractions, resulting in pleasant sexual sensations, even orgasm for some new mothers Martin 1987. Such a physiologic reaction strongly supports his theory.

[23] See Carstairs 1958; Kakar 1990.

[24] Crapanzano 1973 interprets a nearly identical ritual in Morocco as a feminization which serves passive homosexual needs vis-à-vis the father. Although it may be accurate for Morocco, this traditional Freudian posture, emphasizing the male-male dimension of the Oedipal conflict, is precisely what we wish to controvert in the south Asian context presented here.

[25] Obeyesekere 1990: 114–22 explores this defensive/regressive posture in the folklore of Ganapati in Sri Lanka.

[26] Coen 1988; Galenson 1988: 196–203; Kernberg 1988.

[27] Appu Kuttan Mārār is particularly talented at the role of Kāḷi. He can enter into the role at any time and his possession is both vivid and extremely fierce. He is said by other actors to have an alcohol addiction, although I have no evidence of this. His name means 'Father Baby'.

[28] Interview, Chenganassery, Kerala, June 1992.

[29] 'Lord of the Dance', in the series 'Dancing'. KQED television, 1993. See Neff 1995 for ethnography of sarppam tuḷḷal.

[30] LaBarre 1984: 97. See Dundes (1980) for an extensive discussion of the evil eye, with a somewhat different psychoanalytic interpretation.

[31] Interview, Muvattupuzha, Kerala, May 1992.

[32] cf. E. F. Fuller 1993: 290. An interesting bit of obscene folklore told to me by a young man sheds light on the depth of this association. He told me that women keep house-cats to perform cunnilingus. He was utterly convinced that girls and women who have no access to sex enjoy this form of bestiality, and always chuckled knowingly when he saw images of women with purring cats on their laps.

[33] Such an equation is most spectacularly demonstrated by Herdt for Sambia, New Guinea male initiation 1981. For a comparative discussion of the New Guinea and south Asian contexts, see Obeyesekere 1990: 61 and Caldwell (forthcoming(b)).

[34] The suckling snake is a common motif in folklore of south Asia and the Mediterranean region. The belief is that such a snake sneaks up to a sleeping mother and suckles milk from her breasts, thus depriving the human child of its food. See Alter 1992: 146–7.

[35] O'Flaherty 1973 documents a plethora of fellatio-pregnancies (both hetero- and homosexual) in Sanskrit myths. But in a footnote, O'Flaherty mentions that actual fellatio was taboo in scriptures.

[36] For nuanced discussion of homosexuality in India, see Cohen 1995 and *India Tonite* (manuscript in preparation).

[37] Interview, Trichur, Kerala, January 1992.

[38] Sedgewick 1985 has suggested the term 'sexualized male homosociality' for certain kinds of homo-erotic contacts in sex-segregated societies. Most of the relations described here do not appear to exemplify Sedgewick's categorization, since they are primarily motivated by aggression and satisfaction of sexual desires where heterosexual relations are not available.

[39] However Mary Mohan, a Delhi gynaecologist of Malayali parentage who practised for fourteen years in Kerala, states that although 'men both young and middle aged enjoy oral sex, women, especially wives, do not like or encourage it. It is an act which most men indulge in out of confines of marriage' (Personal communication 1994).

[40] Herdt describes a similar attitude on the part of Sambia men: '... heterosexual intercourse is, as men see it, more draining than homosexual fellatio. Tali said, "A man loses *all* his semen in vaginal intercourse. ...In fellatio with boys he loses only *half* his water"' 1981: 249.

[41] Mary Mohan commented that 'It is in fact a long-standing joke that Keralite women are the aggressive partners and so prefer being on top of the men [sic] with him suckling her breasts during intercourse' (Personal communication, 1994). That such a sexual position should be 'a long-standing joke' implies that it is not fully acceptable to the conscious morality of Kerala society, but reveals an underlying anxiety and desire such as described in this section.

[42] Interview, Muvattupuzha, Kerala, May 1992.

[43] Hart 1975. I use 'tribal' here in its standard anthropological sense to designate small-scale social groups with distinctive language and culture, and lacking centralized hierarchical political organization. Despite the controversial nature of this term in south Asian cultural politics, it seems to me to usefully describe people with a very distinct lifestyle. Furthermore, the term 'tribal' has a clear referent for lowland Keralites, connoting a definite constellation of cultural attributes, even if these are stereotypical or inaccurate. The relationship between the image and the reality must for the present remain murky; but it is the cultural image that we are discussing here.

[44] Kāḷi of course is also black, suggesting that she too has tribal origins. Dark skin colour throughout India is regarded by caste Hindus as a sign of ugliness and low birth.

[45] The traditional term of pregnancy is said to be ten months, counting from the date of conception as the first month.

[46] See chapter 2, n. 39, regarding Kūḷi's purification as opposed to Kali's.

[47] See chapter 5, sec. 6 for further discussion of the theme of violation. Rape is a very common theme in contemporary television melodrama and cinema, both in Kerala and throughout India.

[48] Freeman 1991: 41–6. Dirks 1987 and Freeman 1991 do explore the relationship between emic and etic conceptions of 'power', albeit in very different ways.

[49] Examples are numerous; Freeman 1991: 434–8; C. A. Menon 1959; Tarabout 1986 are just a few. While structural analyses no doubt illuminate certain aspects of conflictual rituals dedicated to the goddess, my point here is how glaringly they fail to account for other, more subjective aspects of experience. It is perhaps noteworthy that the majority of these structural analyses have been championed by male theorists.

[50] See Ram 1992 and Kapadia 1996 for outstanding exceptions.

[51] The Tamil emphasis on masochistic rituals devoted to the male god Murugan suggests a somewhat different psychodynamic model. Tamil culture is predominantly patrilineal, unlike the matrilineal structures of jural authority we have outlined for Kerala. More traditional Oedipal models centred on father–son conflict would seem applicable here. Ramanujan (1983) and E. F. Fuller 1993 provide nuanced treatments of gender, masochism, and Oedipal conflict.

5

FEMALE FRUSTRATIONS, WOMEN'S WORLDS

So Much for Matriarchy

'What I find puzzling is that all the books I read before I came to India said that the women of Kerala were very advanced and independent because Kerala was a matriarchy. They said that women here were freer than in North India. But I do not find this true at all. Your women are not independent. You do not permit them many freedoms. ... And yet your inheritance laws have been traditionally matriarchal.'

Anand explained. 'Matriarchy,' he said, 'means *nephew* inherits, not son.'

'That doesn't make sense!'

'But yes!' Anand was patient. 'A man can never be certain beyond all doubt that he is the father of his wife's children. But his *sister's* son must carry the family blood even if the sister has been with many men.'

Juliet laughed sourly. 'So much for matriarchy.'

(Hospital 1982)

Like Juliet in Janet Turner's novel *Hospital*, I had read before embarking on my fieldwork that women in Kerala had a great advantage over their north Indian sisters, coming as they did from a matrilineal social system.[1] The much touted autonomy of upper-caste Nāyar women was something of a legend in the ethnographic literature. But, also like Juliet, I soon discovered that whatever vestiges of power and choice this unique social system had once bestowed upon women had dwindled. The lives of women in Kerala from many classes and castes have, if anything, taken a turn towards the conservatism and restriction of the north over the last several decades.[2] Kerala's remarkable progress in literacy development, health care, and land reform have made it a model for the rest of India; with these sweeping reforms naturally have come an increase in the standard of living for women as well as men. Longer lifespan, access to education and good medical care have made a real difference in women's well-being. But alongside these very real benefits, increasing standards of modesty, restricted social interactions, and delayed marriage have imposed new constraints on women's lives which are in some ways just as difficult to bear as the trials of illiteracy and inadequate health care which previously plagued them (Ramachandran 1995). As Robin Jeffrey states in his recent book, *Politics, Women and Well Being: How Kerala Became 'A Model'*:

> To go to school, read a newspaper, attend an office, draw a salary or seek trained medical care are widely approved activities. To contest an election and give orders to men are not. In this, the parallels with the days of matriliny remain: women may do more things in Kerala than elsewhere in India; but they do not enjoy equality with men. If they leave the accepted spheres ... they face innuendo, ridicule and disappointment. (1992: 216)

The traditional matrilineal system of the upper castes involved both inheritance through the female line and informal, multiple marital liaisons known as *sambandham.* Accounts of huge female-centred households in which visiting husbands came for conjugal pleasures in the night, leaving their sandals outside their wife's bedroom door to indicate to any other visiting lovers that she was already engaged, both shocked and titillated early European observers. Today these practices continue to conjure up an image of a romantic, idyllic, courtly past in contemporary Malayalam films. Of what women's experiences actually were we do not know very much. But Nāyar and Kṣatriya women I interviewed indicated that economic, sexual, and social decisions lay predominantly in the hands of the male head of the household, the brother of the eldest female in the family. Women's movements in the public sphere were very restricted, and inheritance, while passing through the female line, went from uncles to nephews, not mothers to daughters.[3] This social system led to unusually strong ties between brothers and sisters, who resided together and made many joint decisions; husbands meanwhile lived in the households of their own sisters. The role of the father was negligible from a social standpoint; in every respect except procreation, her brother was the more important partner in a woman's life.

Even the 'glory days' of Nāyar matriliny and sambandham marriage apparently did not necessarily mean autonomy or control by women; furthermore, these practices were strictly limited to the Nāyar and Kṣatriya castes, due to their unique relationship with the Nambūtiri Brahmins. The lives of women belonging to other castes in Kerala, organized around patrilineal, patrilocal, and patriarchal principles of residence, inheritance, and authority, differed little from those described in the ethnographic literature for much of south Asia. These women were, of course, the majority. Nur Yalman's (1963) account of Nambūtiri Brahmin social life in Kerala's traditional society goes so far as to call the treatment of their women 'sadistic'. The obsession with female chastity and sexual control which characterizes patrilineal social organization everywhere was thus also prevalent in Kerala's traditional society.

Traditional lower-caste women, by contrast, although also living in patrilineal and patrilocal families, were probably less restricted in their movements and behaviour than they are today. Prior to the 1940s, Kerala law prohibited low-caste women from covering their breasts in public (all women in Kerala normally went without upper breast coverings before that time, but upper-caste women alone had the privilege of covering their upper body in the presence of men or strangers).[4] Unlike upper-caste women who had servants to market and do chores for them, lower-caste women moved outside their homes to some degree in this minimal attire. These women often had to submit to the sexual advances of upper-caste males. The lifestyles and behaviour of lower-caste women, though not characterized by freedom or autonomy, was nonetheless somewhat less restricted and constrained than it is today.

Contact with European society and the enormous social upheavals of the last fifty years in Kerala brought about many changes, many of them for the good of women. As huge matrilineal families began to break up with land reform, women were forced to become involved in legal matters. Education, literacy, health care, and awareness of political process all changed the social scene for both women as well as men in Kerala (Jeffrey 1992). But on the heels of this huge shift came a wave of Western values and ideals, including the amassing of material commodities and the imitation of Victorian models of female behaviour. This meant the adoption of blouses or full white saris, and in the present generation, the adoption of north Indian-style coloured saris and blouses. In one household in Kerala, women of different generations can be observed wearing these three types of dress, each peculiar to her age: the old women bare-breasted, the middle-aged in waistcloth and blouse and the younger women in white or coloured saris. This rapid, dramatic shift in external dress reflects more profound changes in attitudes towards femininity as well.[5]

Structures which enclose and delimit the social sphere of women leave them free to behave as they wish within the walls of those enclosed spaces. With the disappearance of these traditional enclosing structures due to modernization, new forms of social control develop in their place. Gossip, competition, and the internalization of media images of femininity increase. In modern Kerala, as in much of India, ideals of feminine behaviour revolve around modesty, reticence, and self-control. Women should not speak with, look at, walk with, befriend, or laugh in the presence of men outside their families, except in rare circumstances. Even working women told me of the humiliating gossip that arises should they behave familiarly with a male colleague or go so far as to shake his hand in the office. Except in the most liberal urban settings of Trivandrum and Ernakulam, a woman cannot ordinarily walk alone in the street or arrive home after dark without being the target of gossip attacking her moral character.[6] Sexual mores are, as in most of India, conservative, with no dating or cross-sex socializing permissible (although groups of young people of the opposite sex may talk together in a college setting), and nearly all marriages are arranged by parents or guardians within the caste. Owing to higher education and the frequent travel of young men to the Gulf states for work, marriages are often delayed—until the late twenties or early thirties for men, and for women, until somewhere between 22 and 30. Large dowries are also expected from the bride's family, further delaying and limiting marital opportunities for many young women from less wealthy families. During the entire period from puberty to marriage—a minimum of seven years and as many as 18 or more—a girl is expected to remain a virgin, pure in mind as well as body; males are also denied sexual outlets with women of their own status and age group.

The impact of the 'Gulf boom', while raising the living standard of Kerala households markedly, has taken a toll on the mental health of women married to emigrant workers. Educated girls married at a mature age (sometimes as late as 28 or so) to husbands working in the Gulf States, find themselves isolated in their in-laws' homes for the majority of their young reproductive lives, raising children and caring for their in-laws without access to regular conjugal relations. After impregnating their brides immediately after marriage, emigrant husbands return to their jobs abroad, returning home for a few weeks once every year or two. Remittances are normally sent to the in-laws, the wife often receiving very little. This leads to frequent quarrels and misunderstandings, with wives succumbing to mental illness and depression (Chengappa 1980; Chib 1988; Gulati 1987).

Apart from the economic strain of this situation, other serious social problems have arisen as well:

> Psychiatrists ... believe that prolonged post-marital separation leads to deviant sexual behaviour by both partners, ending in guilt and tension. With sexual frustration building up, many wives have entered into extramarital relationships. In Nilambur, a 25-year-old woman married to a construction worker in Abu Dhabi seduced her 21-year-old brother-in-law. The result is that the boy has become psychotic because of his guilt feelings. To overcome their frustration many of the emigrants to the Gulf have become homosexual or have started going to prostitutes. In a recent case in Dubai, an emigrant took his brother-in-law over by promising employment but kept him as his lover. The prolonged separation has also led to sexual impotency and premature ejaculation in men, leading to more mental tension. (Chengappa 1980: 59)

With one-fourth to one-third of the young male population emigrating to the Gulf for jobs since the 1970s, Kerala now 'has the dubious distinction of having the highest frequency of mental disorders [in the country]... Tragically most of the mental instability has occurred amongst women aged between 15 and 25 years' (ibid.:58–9).

The denial of sexual outlet during the most sexually active stage of a person's life must be considered highly restrictive and both physically and psychologically hard to endure. The hot and humid climate, very minimal attire of young men in villages (often just a thin, short cloth tied around the waist), and extended family groups living in close quarters make this enforced abstinence an even greater austerity.[7] This is particularly true for middle-class women, who in many cases spend their leisure hours watching suggestive romantic movies, serials, and dances on the television, but are strongly discouraged from showing any interest in sex.[8] Girls are encouraged to keep busy, told that too much sleep is 'unhealthy', and are carefully watched and guarded by both family and prying neighbours for any signs of romantic or sexual involvement, real or imputed, which could destroy their chances of a suitable marital alliance.

Living as a woman in a society that imposed the most stringent standards of feminine self-control and self-denial gave me some insight into the level of mental anxiety which both men and women may experience in such an environment, especially in matters relating to the control of female sexuality. Complaints about this situation or even any open acknowledgement of female feelings and frustrations are generally taboo, and a tense silence on such topics is nearly always maintained. Nonetheless, when I brought the subject up in conversation, several young women did express their dissatisfaction and suffering to me.[9] Two young women in their mid-twenties, one an English teacher in a cosmopolitan town, and the other the eldest daughter of a performer of traditional Kerala folk arts living in a remote village, expressed similar dissatisfaction, longing, desire, and even anger at their respective situations, which they felt quite powerless to change. In both cases, lack of family finances was the bottom line preventing them from achieving fulfilment in either marriage or further studies. A woman who is one of many sisters, and whose family cannot afford her dowry, may well have to accept a life of celibacy, living at home and caring for her parents until their death. Unlike most married women I interviewed, these two mature unmarried women were both fervent devotees of the fierce goddess Bhagavati, enthusiastically relating her legends and stories to me, and frequently visiting her temples 'for mental peace'.

The image of the sexually frustrated, voracious young woman so prevalent in the ancient folklore of the yakṣi is now fuelled by different social conditions. The paranoid male fear of female sexuality displayed in folklore surrounding the goddess continues to hold great power over the imagination of people in Kerala under these new conditions. As has occurred perennially in India, very ancient metaphors adapt to new meanings. But these meanings still mask the true relations of power which they reinterpret. The enactment of the bloodthirsty and lustful Bhadrakāḷi reinforces images of females as aggressors in the very contexts where they have the least control.

Notes from my journal: two weeks at a friend [Rajiv's] village home.[10]

This is the hardest thing I've ever had to do in my life. My behaviour is never right. I am experiencing the frustration and anger and depression of being so restricted all the time—like walls pressing in on all sides. Each day I can move with less and less freedom. Living here in this house for almost two weeks I have gotten to see things more deeply: watching how Surabhi can't move outside at all, even to go to the market or town; having a husband who scolds you like a child, criticizes and cares for you, but wields total control; feeling really afraid and totally dependent on men. Surabhi told me last week she was very angry when her husband forbade her to join the women's dance practice for the village festival. She has no control over her life, only over the kitchen. Gossip is the social control mechanism to keep people doing the accepted things. There was big gossip just because I came off the bus at night with Rajiv, the unmarried young man who lives here. Rajiv told me I shouldn't go out without his permission as it reflects badly on the family.

A neighbour died from a snake-bite recently. All the women of the family were seen wailing and weeping hysterically for several weeks following the funeral. But none was so affected as the deceased woman's daughter. Nineteen-year-old Usha seemed to drift in and out of a kind of catatonic state. When we went to see her she lay on the bed with loosened hair, unconscious, moaning and breathing shallowly. She did not seem to hear anyone around her. Everyone sat watching her, keeping near her, but no one touched or held her. She lay miserably in a heap.

After a few months, Usha's marriage was arranged. The day of her engagement, I went to congratulate her and give a small gift. She sat in her tiny bedroom, surrounded by female relatives and children, impassive and silent. She said nothing in response to my cheery good wishes, but simply took the gift from me. Was it lack of emotion, desire to show respect, or a surfeit of feeling which prevented her from answering?

The make-up and beauty preparations of the bride began around 8:30 a.m. She sat in a sari slip and blouse with a towel draped over her shoulders as a neighbour painted her eyes and face with eyeliner and powder. A maroon bindi was pasted onto her forehead. Her hair was done up into a small top-knot, with circles of jasmine flowers draped around and dangling down to the sides, a braid down the back encircled with more flowers. Red roses were placed on the top of the knot, and gold jewelry with pretty white and red stones. They bring a mirror and small oil lamp (it reminds me of the green room pūjā in muṭiyēṯṯu). I'm struck by the small, smoky, hot, claustrophobic feeling of this room where the bride has been enclosed since last night, except for a bath this morning. It's like the sanctum where the deity is kept. All female spaces are like this—kitchens, house interiors, menstrual and birth rooms, and the dressing room for this bride.

When the women are about to put the bride's red sari on her body, some ladies start to ululate—mostly the older ladies and some little kids trying to imitate them. The mother of the bride takes no role at all. She only sits, watching. As the sari is opened and draped, the ululation is very strong (like putting on the muṭi before Kāḷi's shrine). There is some power, ritual significance to the red sari, the change of status for the girl.[11] She has been calm till now, but as at least five ladies begin to fuss over the pleats, she begins to weep. No one comforts her or pays any mind—all the ladies are busy and cheerful, and basically seem to ignore her. Finally someone wipes her eyes matter-of-factly with a hankie, without saying a word, in order to fix the dripping make-up. There are at least twenty or more ladies in this tiny room now. The smell of perfume, the heat of bodies, the crackling intensity as the time approaches are tangible. All the married ladies are laughing and joking. The bride looks miserable. What is she feeling? Is it her first time to wear a sari? I remember my wedding, feeling so nervous, full of anticipation and fear. Is she thinking about leaving her family?

'The Place of Delivery and All'

Sometimes, watching the bloated, bloody figure of Bhadrakāḷi as she groaned and loped around the muṭiyēṯṯu arena in the flickering lamplight, I experienced a strange feeling of alienation and incongruity bordering on hilarity. In my daily efforts to comport myself as an acceptable appropriation of a Malayali lady, I was constantly conscious of every curve of my body bespeaking its sexual potential, under the devouring gaze of men and boys in public. Were my breasts too noticeable, were they properly covered? Was I moving my hips too much as I walked, or was I sufficiently restrained in my body language to imply dignified propriety? I hoped I wasn't smiling or laughing too broadly, encouraging immodest thoughts in the minds of males I met. My sari, God knows, was never pulled down far enough to cover my ankles and feet sufficiently—my lady friends would always tug at it to get it just a little lower. This constant attention to my dress and muting the sexual speech of my female body had sensitized me to the importance of control in every aspect of womanhood in Kerala. Who in the world was this Bhadrakāḷi, shouting and running with long protruding teeth and tongue, her naked red breasts bouncing, chasing men wildly in the middle of the night? The sheer impossibility of Bhadrakāḷi's femaleness, combined with the reverent concentration of the audience as they watched her movements, seemed to cry out to me that something was very odd in this picture of female gender.

Naturally, I was curious to discover how Malayali women felt watching the male performances of Bhadrakāḷi. Did they sense the same incongruity that I did? Or were they enraptured in the kind of devotional trance actors and male spectators described? Perhaps the problem was merely cultural; I wasn't perceiving things as they did. Whenever I got the chance (that is, when the men of the house would allow me to talk to their wives, usually after exhaustively hearing their own points of view), I tried to question the women about their experience and understanding of muṭiyēṯṯu, and of Bhagavati in general. Almost always, they would demur and defer to the greater knowledge of their husbands. At first I took this as a posture of wifely humility and decorum commonly encountered by female fieldworkers in south Asia (Kishwar 1990; N. Kumar 1994; Raheja and Gold 1994). But even as I got to know some women better and gained their trust, few seemed to have much to say about these matters. They were quite eloquent and vociferous on other topics, once they got started—topics such as ancestral deities, the behaviour of their neighbours, or their daily workaday lives. But when it came to Bhagavati, the majority of women seemed fearful, respectful, and somewhat distant in their attitudes. There was none of the intimacy and devotion, the personal feelings for the goddess that men expressed.

The ladies of the royal Pakkattil House, privileged with much more freedom than many other women, explained:

> We actually worship Bhagavati out of fear. See if we do anything wrong, if we commit any mistake, we fear she will punish us. It is for that reason we have devotion for her. [Actually] it's not devotion, it's a kind of fear. It's something inside...an anxiety inside the mind.

In what did that anxiety consist? Was it the repressed anger and sexual desire males imagined to lurk within the female body? Women I interviewed consistently denied that they felt any personal identification with the fierce goddess, insisting that she was nothing like a human woman. Even women who appeared to me to be tense and frustrated denied ever experiencing anger. The matriarch of the Pakkattil royal family and her daughter-in-law commented:

Ratna Tamburati (elderly lady): Do you think there is anyone who never feels angry? Well, normally women should have a shade less anger, right? Shouldn't it be like that?

Q: What do you think? Do you ever feel like getting angry like Kāḷi?

RT: (Laughing) Oh no! Nothing like that. Ha!

Daughter-in-law: It's not a pretty picture (giggling).

Clearly Bhadrakāḷi embodies all that a Malayali woman should *not* be. In folk speech, a woman who shouts or expresses anger is referred to as 'a real Bhadrakāḷi', a negative characterization. In social relations, people value selflessness, cooperativeness, and stoicism in the face of adversity. Women especially are not encouraged to verbalize negative emotions and receive little comfort if they do. I was chastised by my friends more than once for 'making a mess' (getting angry or crying) when things got unbearable. Such behaviour is considered disruptive, antisocial and childlike, and for women, is only permitted in very formalized settings such as in the intense weeping at death ceremonies or in the culturally accepted avenue of possession by lower spirits.

The distance between the goddess and women was also expressed in their peripheral roles in the cult itself. It was striking to me that women were prohibited from participating in the public rituals of Kāḷi, except in the initial welcoming of the goddess with a procession of lights, and as spectators. Even in homes, I found that women tend to shy away from the worship of Kāḷi, often directing their faith towards more benevolent deities such as Krishna, Śiva, Pārvati, or family ancestors. This had not been my expectation, based on recent studies elsewhere in India (e.g. Erndl 1993). Although female spirit possession was recognized and even ritually encouraged in certain lower-caste art forms, these female possessions are distinctly devalued and differentiated from the male temple performances. The fact remains that women may never enact the role of Kāḷi or perform as oracles. I asked the wife of one prominent muṭiyēṯṯu performer who specializes in the role of Kāḷi about this, and she explained:

Women can't perform muṭiyēṯṯu because of menses. I have much bleeding and sickness at each period. I can't touch any food. People think menses is bad. We can't enter the temple. My mother told me if a woman goes in the temple when she is menstruating, she will fall to shivering, have epileptic fits, or be possessed. The old women say that if a woman goes in at that time, she will lose her eyes and go mad. Women don't have much power. If we ask small things from Dēvi, we will get them—not big things. Men have more power. For work and such, men have more. Only at the time of birth do women have power. At other times, men dominate.[12]

Male muṭiyēṯṯu artists continually emphasize that Bhadrakāḷi is not an ordinary woman. Her perpetual virginity, fury, and unconventional behaviour are signs of her non-human identity. The following comments by a muṭiyēṯṯu troupe leader and fine Kāḷi actor, emphasize the goddess's divine power by negating her physiological femininity:

Kāḷi was not born in the usual manner, from a vagina. She was born from the third eye of Śiva to kill Dārika. There is no mention of [Kāḷi having] monthly periods or pregnancy and childbirth. It is not told anywhere. *I think all these things happen only if she is born from a vagina.*[13]

Menstruation and birth are the visible signs of women's reproductive power, the essence of their identity as females in this culture. Yet, it is these very features of their being which preclude women's ritual intimacy with the goddess. That which makes them female disqualifies them from embodying the divine feminine, or even from coming near the goddess at such times. This irony is beautifully acknowledged in the following story narrated to me by Savitri, a 91-year-old Brahmin matriarch whose family sponsors muṭiyēṯṯu annually in their family temple:

An ancestor from here worshipped Bhagavati. He brought her here from Kodungallur and installed her. Bhagavati told him, 'I shall come walking towards the [temple door] here and face towards the north.' The temple door in Kodungallur is towards the north. She is the saviour of all the people in this area. She is very powerful. [It happened like this.] An old Nambūtiri [Brahmin priest] worshipped her image at Kodungallur and brought it from there. She went to the [Brahmin's house]. Remember I told you about the place of delivery and all? It is said that she immediately ran in there. So one woman of the family said, 'Look, delivery and menstrual blood are here. You cannot stay here.' 'Okay, place my sword somewhere, build an abode for me wherever you find the sword', the goddess replied. Then when the Nambūtiri returned after his bath, he saw the sword on the red stone there. At that he remembered that Bhagavati had said the temple door should face north, so he built a temple to her in that way.[14]

This story illustrates a more homely, sympathetic view of the goddess than the vampire-like yakṣis or bloodthirsty warriors of the men's imaginations. Savitri refers to 'the place of delivery', a small room in the house where menstrual seclusion as well as childbirth take place. In her story the goddess is strongly attracted to this exclusively female and highly 'polluted' space. Savitri's story thus makes Bhagavati a covert ally of women, who nonetheless must help the goddess to assume her proper place in the male ritual world. The goddess may not remain in the 'place of delivery', but must be forcibly relegated to the pure, male-controlled temple where she is eventually installed. Yet when she does so, it is not as a living, breathing female, but in the symbolic form of her sword that she agrees to be installed. The distance implied by this transformation suggests that something is lost as the female experience enters the male imaginative realm. The performances and stories of Bhagavati, rather than providing role models of female defiance and independence, serve rather to reinforce cultural ideas about a woman's inherent danger vis-à-vis men, which she is responsible for containing and controlling.

In my dealings with Kerala women, I was not convinced that they had fully internalized these negative roles, although they outwardly acquiesced in them. They seemed rather to be tolerating a system they accepted as unjust but unchangeable. Nalini Bekal, a well-known female writer of the Nāyar caste, has expressed this frustration in her short story, 'Ottakalam [Single Figure]' (Bekal 1990). The story, based on an incident from the author's youth, tells of a little girl who is not allowed to see the performance of teyyam (a ritual art akin to muṭiyēṯṯu performed in northern Kerala) at her family compound. The story and Nalini's account of the life of Nāyar women reveals that women even in this 'matriarchal' caste were subject to the same norms of pollution that applied to high-caste women throughout Kerala. In an interview, she commented on these restrictions:

N: Normally females don't go to that [performance] area. It's for men only. Look, these Parayan and Malayan people who perform teyyam are intense drunkards. So maybe it's because they are drunkards that the society keeps women away from them. Not only that, in those days it was not appropriate

for ladies to go before the men, or outside the house much. They were reluctant to go out, and they were forbidden too.
Q: In your story you say that women are also prohibited from entering the sword room [a room in the Nāyar house where ritual weapons are kept for use in the enactment of teyyam]; is that right?
N: Yes, both there and in the snake grove just outside, are special places that must be maintained with utmost purity, where women are not permitted. There in the evening a lamp has to be lit. Boys go there. Women are not allowed for any reason. It's very strict. The belief in those areas is that women are not pure after puberty. So what is behind that belief? If I am asked that I am not sure. I am afraid I don't know the answer.

Like you, I was very curious to understand [these men's] ways. I was very anxious to know about the rhythms, customs, and everything [about teyyam]. I even wanted to write a novel about it. For that you have to keep close contact. Without getting in touch with them you can't do that, right? But I was restricted from going out. It was impossible for me to know and understand more about their life rhythms and their experiences in teyyam, since it was strongly prohibited for the ladies of Nāyar [families] to talk to the scheduled caste people. Those men were liable to be punished also. It's that way even now. Even the smartest woman will find that very difficult. Look, however liberal or independent our thoughts may be, we are bound by these social and family restrictions. We can't do anything staying in the society we live in, and our family. It has to be respected. Especially when you are a girl. Not for boys. So I've seen a lot of teyyams being dressed and enacted, but not got a chance to study what lies behind it, what it means.
Q: So how did you see it?
N: I saw it from very far. We ladies stand in our porch, or some place close to the house, surrounded by fences. You can watch teyyam standing there.[15]

Nalini Bekal also told us about the puberty ceremony she underwent as a girl. Again, her personal feelings about the meaning of menstrual pollution were in conflict with the cultural ideology embodied in the rite, and generally adhered to by women, including herself.

> On the first day, she is dressed up well. It's a special occasion, a kind of celebration. That is a very happy day, you know why? It's because the girl is mature. She is ripe. The girl is big enough to be a mother. That is the belief. But then after that, each month when it occurs, it is considered as a period of impure, polluted days.
>
> So for four days she has to sit in a special room by herself and she shouldn't go outside that room. Nobody should touch her either. All the ladies come to inquire about and see, but not touch her. Very close relatives bring snacks and different eatables.

> As far as I was concerned, it was the worst day of my life. I disliked it intensely. During the menses period girls are secluded in a special room, because they are considered impure. Even now I totally object to this kind of treatment towards girls. I hate that.[16]

The fetishized image of the heated, dangerous female body represented in the stories of yakṣis and Bhagavati does not seem to resonate with women's ordinary experiences of their own fertility and sexuality. In interview after interview, when I asked women about their reproductive lives, marriages, and relationships, they expressed a more straightforward, positive, and self-accepting body image than psychologists often find in American women. I never heard women express concern over their weight, age, or beauty, as American women obsessively do.[17] Although social restrictions placed on women can lead to mental problems, these do not normally take the form of fixations or fantasies about their own bodies. The male obsession with breasts, vaginas, orality, and fellatio and their imaginative transformations in ritual, as well as the ideology of the heated female body, seem irrelevant to women, who are unable to articulate any such distinctions clearly.[18] While they acknowledge and acquiesce in the cultural rules regarding menstruation, childbirth pollution, and restriction from temple performances, these rules appear to most women to be fairly arbitrary, incomprehensible, and imposed from without. None could explain their logic to me. Thus, women's deference to men in such matters indicated much more than wifely politeness; it signified that the fetishized female body is a male construction with little relevance to women's daily lives.

The real world of women, where I spent many lazy days after the hectic performance season ended, seemed sweeter, gentler and more relaxed than the frenetic and terrifying world of muṭiyēṯṯu's Kāḷi. Female frustration, anger, and desire, although certainly present, erupted only in occasional possession 'fits' and illnesses not typical of women's daily demeanour. When they did occur, such expressions of imbalance almost always seemed to be responses to intolerable restrictions imposed by males, not natural emanations from the depths of a supposedly volcanic female nature. The world of women, though sometimes tense and silent, was more often a calm, quiet world of confident mothers, shy, laughing young girls, and mischievous infants. Afternoon massages, joke-telling sessions, mutual hair-care, and crowded smoky kitchens provide village women with companionship, physical closeness, and relaxation—qualities not particularly prominent in their more formal, restrained relations with men. These are women's worlds where men do not belong.

In the homes of the royal castes descended from the rulers of the erstwhile Cochin and Travancore states, men seemed almost superfluous. The Pakkattil House of Koratty, descended from a line of Cochin princes, owns and operates its own very exclusive Bhagavati temple (of our research party, only our videographers were allowed to enter its premises as unquestionably high-caste Hindus); they also patronize the local muṭiyēṯṯu artists and have a close relationship with them. The family follows a strictly matrilineal inheritance system, in which only daughters inherit property. When we visited there, the women of the house behaved very confidently and gave forthright opinions, often interrupting and contradicting male family members in the room. This contrasted strongly with my experience at the homes of muṭiyēṯṯu artists, where women were reticent and demure. Ratna Tamburati, the family's matriarch, is an energetic and attractive woman in her mid-fifties. She and her daughters joined the men of the house in describing relations between the sexes in their family:

Soma Varma Tampuran (Brother of Ratna Tamburati): The matrilineal system means that only the female offspring have the right to property. My son will have no family rights to anything.
Old Man (Brahmin husband of RT; we were not told his name): He [Soma Varma's son] is not considered as a member of the family. Only the daughters are counted. The men have no power.
Ratna Tamburati (RT): The uncle is more powerful in our family, not the father. The father has no importance.
[The men are requested by me to leave the room for an interview with the ladies alone; Laji is translating]
Young lady (RT's daughter-in-law): Father means nothing. Only for [sexual] production [Big amusement as all the ladies laugh loudly]. The husband has no power at all.
Q: So who takes the major role in decisions in the house?
RT: The mother's brother. Sister and brother live together. Even though girls get married, they don't go along with their husbands to the husband's house. Instead the husband comes to the lady's house to live. Or he lives with his own sister and just comes here once in a while.
YL: So when the present husband dies, nobody observes any pollution or mourning for him. The children don't observe anything, or do any cremation

ceremony. Because he is a Brahmin, we shouldn't do that. Only their people [Brahmin family] should observe it.[19]

But the confident, royal ladies of the Pakkattil House are not typical of all Kerala women. Despite the comfort and relaxation women find in each other's company, their stories often reveal a painful awareness of the inevitable suffering which is their due at the hands of men. The Panayannarkavu Bhagavati temple near Chengannur is renowned for the extreme ferocity of its goddess, as well as for the miraculous closure of the shrine's eastern door. Temple lore accounts for this custom in the following way:

> The veḷiccappāṭu of the temple told in an oracle that for 41 days elephants, goats, and chickens should be offered to Dēvi as *bali* [sacrifice], and on the final day human sacrifice should be done. For the sacrifice a virgin girl should be offered. So the people knew that prosperity would come only if they did this every year for 41 days. So they did this every year. ...
>
> Many years passed by. One year there was a surprising event. ... The virgin girl who appeared for the human sacrifice on the 41st day was found to be very happy. She ran around laughing and ṭalking joyfully. So the veḷiccappāṭu did tuḷḷal and gave an oracle [from the goddess] that 'This girl need not be offered as a sacrifice. Let her stay as my attendant here. Not only she, but no one else need be sacrificed hereafter. As the sign of this, close the eastern *naḍa* [temple door]. That should not be opened hereafter. If it has to be opened, it can only be opened after an elephant sacrifice. Otherwise danger will arise.' So after taking Dēvi's command, the door has not yet been opened until now. (Krishnaswami 1993; Malayalam newspaper article, Summer 1992)

On a visit to the Panayannarkavu Bhagavati temple, we met the temple sweeper, a woman of the Ezhava caste (previously an untouchable caste), who narrated the following, somewhat different version of the story to us:

L: Do you know who is the deity enshrined here?
EL [Ezhava Lady]: Bhadrakāḷi, the one who is facing the east. She's the one whose door (naḍa) never opens. You saw her inside—that door won't open.
L: Do you know why?
EL: Here, it was a place where guruti was done by human sacrifice. That is, the cutting [killing] of humans for the goddess. A pregnant lady was the last person who was taken to be offered as guruti.
L: Ladies were offered?

EL: Yes, ladies were sacrificed here. That was a ripe, pregnant lady. When [the priest] started to cut her she asked the authority, 'Should I be offered?' as if to say, 'I who am fully pregnant, should this be done to me?' With that the door was closed (by itself). So when that lady asked back you know, the guruti did not take place. She was not sacrificed. So from then onwards it was decided, like, no more women. After that livestock, like cows and goats were offered. Then it became chickens. Now it's this turmeric water with lime. Only that is existing now.

PL [another lady standing nearby]: That deity is bloodthirsty.

L: So the temple door closed by itself?

EL: Yes it closed by itself and it was not opened thereafter.

PL: This is because the lady was to be sacrificed and she was a pregnant lady and what she asked was—should this child and mother be sacrificed? So when she asked, Dēvi was sad. She was unhappy. Maybe she felt like 'I was challenged, now I won't repeat it anymore.' Only when [Bhagavati] decided that, the door was closed forever.

L: What kind of girls were being sacrificed? Were they normally virgins, or pregnant women?

EL: Earlier it used to be virgins. Only the last one was a pregnant lady.

Here again, the goddess represents male authority, but her underlying solidarity with women is aroused by the pregnant woman's protest. The sacrificial victim is not a virgin, but a pregnant woman. She is not happy and joyous, but sad and terrified. By appealing to the goddess's feminine sensibility, the male priests are made to repent their cruelty to women—a cruelty, we should note, which is institutionalized in the cult of the goddess, with its male priests and blood sacrifices. The Ezhava lady's story graphically represents the metaphorical sacrifice of real women and their fertility to the male goddess's ferocious, dominating cruelty—a theme that the published, male-authored version carefully masks.

The women's stories about the Bhagavati temples suggest another fascinating theme: that the goddess has *forgotten* her identity as a woman and her original solidarity with women. We have interpreted this female recognition of the male control of the cult as a metaphor for the gender politics of religion in Kerala. But perhaps there is more to the story than mere metaphor. We have argued in chapter 1 that the Bhagavati cult in ancient historical times was actually the provenance of female shamans, and that upper-caste males wrested control of the rituals from women and the lower-castes after the fourth to seventh centuries . The recognition of the role of low-caste females in so many of the origin myths of the goddess and her shrines seems to preserve a historical memory of this prior role of women, a role which is now almost entirely lost as women attempt to raise their status by distancing themselves from everything connected with Bhadrakāḷi.[20]

The study of the Kodungallur Bhagavati temple may shed light on the role of women in the evolution of Bhagavati's worship. Gentes (1992) has suggested that this temple preserves ancient West Asian rituals related to the ecstatic Attic cults, in which women apparently figured prominently. Most of this remains speculation at present; but two strong clues suggest these connections. One is the presence of female veḷiccappāṭus at the infamous Bharaṇi festival (Fig. 3). These extraordinary women come *en masse* from the foothills of the Palghat region for this festival alone. They are reputed to be of tribal origin, and I was told that they are very reluctant to speak to outsiders. Their mere presence is very significant, as no other temple in Kerala has such female ritual specialists, to my knowledge (although they are fairly common in neighbouring south Indian states). It seems obvious that the male veḷiccappāṭus clearly modelled their dress and demeanour on these women, who are now prohibited from performing the role in all other temples.

Another group of female ritualists resides at Kodungallur. These are the priestesses of the Māriyamma<u>n</u> shrine, a small and unimpressive looking installation to the west of the main temple. I know nothing of these women but the uneasy feeling I had when I visited the shrine. A group of rather masculine-looking women, all dressed in white, were seated inside the shrine as I entered. One woman, older than the rest, was seated in a corner, and I was ushered over to her to pay respects. The control these women wielded over the small Māriyamma<u>n</u> shrine was in striking contrast to the male priests and officiants in the Kodungallur Bhagavati shrine overshadowing it.[21]

Notes from Kodungallur Temple, 4 February 1992.

People stand expectantly outside the huge, closed temple doors. When they open at the stroke of noon everyone surges inside. We stand in front of the door to Bhagavati's shrine, sweating profusely. The women are in front, chanting 'Amme Nārāyaṇa, Dēvi Nārāyaṇa, Lakṣmi Nārāyaṇa, Bhadre Nārāyaṇa ...' We repeat the names over and over, palms folded, sweat dripping down, hot bodies on every side, a woman's oiled hair catching in my fingers. We stand like that for a long time, swaying gently. Some women close their eyes and seem to be deep in meditation, others have hands outstretched. The chanting, which was fairly coordinated, begins to fragment into separate streams, each starting and stopping at a different point, and we are like many spinning-wheels turning in tune with the mantra. We stand like that for half an hour.

Suddenly the doors open and the priest steps out and showers us with holy water. I receive the splashing drops directly on my face. As the doors open, the people cry out and surge forward. The goddess is huge, golden, and imposing, dressed in a blood-red skirt. Her large eyes and breasts open to us as we press closer to her in a mass. The priest pours water into our cupped hands and passes out packets of hibiscus flowers and sandal paste on a plantain leaf.

Standing, sweating, chanting Amme, Dēvi ..., I felt suddenly sad and full of longing for motherly love. We had to beg and suffer to get Dēvi's darshan. The closed door made me think of the days (not so very long ago) when women were kept secluded behind the doors of the houses, inaccessible, taboo but enticing, hard to get a glimpse of. Maybe this fuels the male fascination with peeping.[22]

To the southwest is a small shrine to the goddess of smallpox, Māriyamman̲. People worship her by throwing turmeric, peppercorns, paddy, and dried red flower petals over her stone image from in front of the white protective grille. The peppercorns litter the floor of the shrine, like pox. Some women in white sit on the platform in front of the shrine. It seemed to be a women's place—the men stayed around the outside, not mounting the steps, and Antonio and Laji went away and sat under a banyan tree.

Hysteria and Bādhā

The ancient ecstatic female cults no longer exist in central Kerala, today, though vestiges of them survive in low-caste possession rituals like sarppam tuḷḷal, muṭiyāṭṭam, and some tribal shamanistic rites. In the high-caste temple world of the Bhagavati cult, women's possession is understood as being of a completely different order from that of male specialists. The divine possession of men is referred to as dēva āvēśam (divine inspiration). Opposed to this divine possession is possession by demonic spirits, known as 'bādhā' or bādhā āvēśam (demonic inspiration).[23] Bādhā normally afflicts women but occasionally men, and is considered quite different from the trembling and shaking of divine visitations. Victims of bādhā often behave aggressively, utter obscenities and curses, and fail to observe normal rules of decorum. Their frantic hopping movements during these fits are known as tuḷḷal, a term which also refers to the artful, learned temple dances.

On numerous visits to the Chottanikkara Bhagavati temple in Ernakulam District, I witnessed the daily tuḷḷal performed by the mentally afflicted in front of the shrines of Śiva and Bhadrakāḷi. The tuḷḷal of the mad women at Chottanikkara was overpowering to me in its expression of extreme anguish. All rules of female propriety were controverted by the wild screaming and shameless jumping of the women, their matted hair flying about loose, dirt clinging to their faces, obscenities pouring from their angry tongues. Anxious family members hovered about the young women and girls, watching their movements sadly, in hopes of a cure, only interfering when they seemed to be in danger of injuring themselves in their violence. As I watched the group of hopping, screaming dancers before the shrine, one girl suddenly broke from the pack and tore madly into the temple compound, running and screaming until an older male relative gently restrained her. While I wondered what suffering could drive a woman to such extreme anti-social behaviour, the obvious parallel to the dancing of Bhadrakāḷi in muṭiyēṯṯu, which I had witnessed at so many temple festivals, came painfully to mind.[24]

A visit to Chottanikkara temple, Friday night around 7 p.m.:

The mad ladies walk alongside the Bhagavati, astride her elephant. They scream wildly as the *śīvēḷi* (serenading of the goddess) begins. We circle the temple faster and faster. The insistent drums are punctuated by screams and the clanging of elephant chains. The women seem intent on moving around the temple as quickly as possible. Then as we sit among the small groups chatting in the dark, some sleeping stretched out on the ground, a woman makes choking, strangling noises, rolls on the ground with her matted hair. She stretches her hands out as if reaching for something desperately, then hunches over in a foetal position as if very ill. Another woman is sitting and simply swinging her hair back and forth. A boy stamps his feet and sways his head, his loud shouts piercing the heavy darkness from time to time. Another woman who is holding a banana behind her back while hopping up and down starts to sing: 'Hey, who is this broad in Chotta-YONI-kkara [Chotta-VAGINA-kkara, a play on the name of the temple]?'[25] People stand around looking amused, as if it's a show.

Now we proceed to the lower temple, where Bhadrakāḷi is housed. We pass the huge temple tank where Bhagavati is said to have thrown the evil yakṣi who tempted a Brahmin, her blood staining the water a permanent red. This is where the possessed come to be cured by banging a long iron nail into a tree with their foreheads. My guide is a young man who is learning to play the part of Kāḷi in muṭiyēṯṯu; his brother is a priest here and has a small house just below the temple. He explains: 'During the fit of possession (bādhā), the patient will tell which spirit is troubling them. Then they go to the astrologer, who tells how long the nail should be. Power is put into the nail and the person has to bang it into the tree with his head.' We circle the enormous tree full of pain and spirits, fairly groaning under the weight of its thousands of iron nails. We pay our respects to Bhadrakāḷi, gleaming and ferocious within her shrine, and pass by the priest to receive what looks like water. As I approach I see with a shock that it is deep red guruti. With some revulsion I take the red 'blood' in my hand. I hesitate—am I supposed to drink this? Some spills on my white sari as I hastily try to imbibe the liquid. It's salty and heating. A rush of energy passes through me. My hands and tongue are stained orange, like Kāḷi herself. I feel horrified at the thought. The huge tree outside the shrine is hung with bats. It's amazing the fear I feel going to this temple. I don't understand how B. feels such 'mental peace' when she comes here.

Despite the obvious resemblance of the possessed Kāḷi dancer's behaviour to real female possession and madness, women are prohibited from participating in the public rituals of Kāḷi. A strange counterpoint is set up between real, female possession and male ritual interpretations of it. The symptoms which will be suffered by a woman who enters the temple while menstruating (described above) are the *very same symptoms* which the male representatives of Bhagavati manifest during the temple rituals. Shivering, fits, and possession are the signs that the fierce goddess is entering the performer and enlivening the ritual. They are the form in which Bhagavati reveals herself, and reflect the ambivalent powers of female sexuality. The performer enacting the role of Bhadrakāḷi dons a female costume (with emphasis on prominent breasts) and adopts a stylized female demeanour, including voice modulation, posture, and movements. The goddess's oracular representative, the veḷiccappāṭu, grows his hair long like a woman, ideally does not have a moustache, uses turmeric all over his body as women do, and dons the archaic ritual dress of a high-caste female (Thampuran 1936: 82). One troupe leader put it clearly: 'He should be like a lady.'[26] This is a remarkable prescription: the ritual representative of the goddess must be *like* a lady, but must not actually *be* a lady.

One clue to this conundrum may be found in glosses of the Malayalam word tuḷḷal, commonly used to refer to possession dances in Kerala. Tuḷḷal describes a wide variety of things, including those artless displays of pure misery at Chottanikkara, the possession dances of professional oracles, as well as the highly trained temple arts taught in government-supported institutions. The dictionary defines tuḷḷal as 'jumping, leaping, hopping, skipping;... fretting and fuming with anger; tremor; involuntary motion as of demoniac possession; dance; a kind of stage-play with the accompaniment of rhythmic dance and music, usually performed in temples.' Related terms denote fever with fits, trembling with anger or demonic possession (C. M. Pillai 1976: 493). This series of glosses suggests an underlying cognitive relation between certain emotions, their physiological manifestations, and spirit possession. It appears that uncontrollable anger can lead to shivering and trembling, fits and possession, and manifest itself physically in fever, uncontrolled dancing, and jumping. The ritual tuḷḷals of temple arts would appear not only to mimic, but actually to invoke these states of uncontrollable emotion, in order thus to control and remove them. In the performance of muṭiyēṯṯu this is demonstrated by the repeated exciting and cooling of the goddess, which culminates in possession.

One entry in the glossary is particularly intriguing. A *tuḷicchi* is 'an unruly or ungovernable sort of woman; a flirt' (ibid.)—all that a Malayali lady should not be. These adjectives aptly describe the behaviour of Bhadrakāli in the performance, as well as that of the mad women at Chottanikkara. The lack of control displayed by all of these undesirable female models centres around the double taboos of anger and sexuality. The yelling woman scornfully reproached as 'a real Bhadrakāli', the errant female who enters a temple while menstruating, the disobedient daughter, the flirtatious girl: these are punished with bādhā, shivering, fits, and possession. It is a woman's sexuality and potential anger that is taboo, and that must be controlled.

Yet the extremes of self-control and self-denial women in Kerala are expected to undergo, repressing sexual and aggressive feelings nearly all of their lives, can easily lead to the madness of bādhā. With little or no sex education in schools, and no discussion between mother and daughter of either menstruation or sexual intercourse, the traditional Kerala girl's reproductive life can be fraught with painful discoveries. One woman told me how at her first menstrual period she thought she had a terrible intestinal disorder and that she would die of internal bleeding. Other women, experiencing the double shock of first intercourse on their wedding night with a virtual stranger, and adjustment to a demanding, subservient role in a new home, resort to bouts of illness or 'fits' as an expression of their misery and fear. A twenty-year-old friend of mine, carrying her second child in only fifteen months of marriage, was troubled by recurrent hysterical 'fits' which also bothered her after her first delivery. These women were not normally depressed or dysfunctional in any way. In fact most women I met in Kerala, particularly mature, married women, felt that their lives were satisfying and pleasant. They were outwardly cheerful, hard-working, and contented. Yet many had suffered at some time in their lives from 'fits', 'voices', or more serious nervous disorders. Upon questioning them further, I usually found that these episodes had occurred at times of sexual deprivation or emotional stress: prior to and shortly after marriage, during pregnancy, and when husbands were away, but seldom when living in a stable nuclear household.

Many scholars have noted the relationship between women's possession and repressed sexual and aggressive emotions. Gold (1988) clearly demonstrates how possession performances she witnessed in Rajasthan allow sanctioned expression of female sexual frustration. Data from the Freeds and the many studies by Obeyesekere also focus on the sexual dimensions of female possession, but follow orthodox Freudian wisdom in attributing these frustrations to repressed Oedipal desire.[27] Lewis's classic study (1989) outlined the many parallels between social marginality and female spirit possession, suggesting that it is a form of 'protest religion'. Ram's rich study(1992) of female possession in southern Tamil Nadu exemplifies this thesis.[28] In bādhā too, female emotions of rage and desire, which are taboo, find expression in stylized behaviour. Anti-social feelings are experienced as external invasions of the body by agents embodying desire, envy, and anger. But the cure often involves beating, hurting, or degrading the body of the woman, exacerbating the original injury. By qualitatively distinguishing demonic, female possessions from divine, male ones, women's experience is further devalued. The goddess can only vanquish the evil beings who possess girls and women; she can never enter them.

Notes from my diary: a hotel in Ernakulam, April 1992.

Tonight I feel as if I am losing my grip on reality, going down a tunnel of despair and pain. Maybe there really are strange spiritual forces trying to get me—or maybe those forces are metaphors, projections of our own inner demons. Which is not to say they're not real, but perhaps they're not *outside*. Once we know this we have a way to tackle them. My head feels as if it will explode; a terrible pain at the back, top of my spinal cord where it meets my skull, my two arms aching with pain ... something heavy in my brain torturing me as if my head will drop to the floor it's so heavy. Suddenly in the midst of it, lying in the dark, I see him, beating me. I can't bear to look at it fully. It is so terrible, terrible, terrible. Pummelling my ears, breaking my glasses, relentless, cruel, punishing, the crashing cracking sound of his fists thudding on my bones, the sparkling lights of disconnected brain synapses flying, my own voice somewhere screaming out for mercy, a feeling I might pass out and be unconscious and no one would know.

It was one of the worst moments of my life and one I never expected to live to see. The weeks dragged on, I with my black eye having to face the neighbours and accept everyone's scorn, everyone pitying poor long-suffering Antonio. He had a right after all, I was his property: people even said that. One night he awoke in sweat: he had dreamed that I was Kāḷi, straddling him naked with wild hair, trying to cut his throat. He says I am possessed by the evil goddess herself.

Seductive Virgins: Whose Lust?

We have seen how the violent, lustful yakṣi-vampire is homologized to the virgin girl in the male imagination. Fully mature, but unmarried, she lurks desperate for sexual congress, luring men to their doom and death. The fear of adult female sexuality is expressed in menstrual taboos, in the marginalization of women from the Bhagavati cult generally, and in the restrictions placed on feminine sexual behaviour in daily life. As we might expect, this concern also emerges strikingly in traditional puberty rites performed for girls in Kerala.

High-caste puberty and defloration rites have been exhaustively documented by Krishna Iyer, Gough, Yalman, and others. A number of studies examine the unique tāli-tying rites, structured as mock marriages prior to the onset of menarche.[29] These appear to have been particularly important among the Nāyars who did not practise permanent, monogamous marriage. The tying of the tāli (usually by the girl's maternal uncle or other father-substitute; although sometimes by a boy of similar age) thus protected the traditional Hindu girl from dying a widow (considered a most inauspicious fate), no matter what her future sexual life held in store. Most studies of these and other rituals marking girls' sexual maturity tend to focus on their social-structural implications, neglecting both subjective experience and psychological implications.

One exception to this general rule, however, is Kathleen Gough's 1955 essay 'Female Initiation Rites on the Malabar Coast'. In this essay, Gough breaks with British social-structural tradition and attempts a strictly Freudian analysis. She suggests that many features of the Bhagavati cult as well as puberty rituals of young girls express repressed incestuous desires between matrilineal kin. Gough interprets possession as a symbolic physical entering of the girl's body by totemic male ancestors in the form of snakes, in a kind of incestuous supernatural rape. However, following Freudian wisdom of her time, Gough considers this possession to 'reflect the incestuous desires of women towards men of the parental generation ... and secondarily towards their brothers' (1955: 66). This statement supports the indigenous male ideology of the vampiric yakṣi: the virgin girl is the raging, sexual seductress out to corrupt men. Bhadrakāḷi, after all, could only be calmed after the war with Dārika by incestuous sexual congress with her father/son.

Gough's interpretation clearly intuits an unconscious desire present in the culture and expressed by the ritual. Themes of incestuous sexual desire between matrilineal kin definitely seem to surface at every turn in the data she presents. But do the rites reflect the unconscious desires of women or of men? Without more information about the personal histories and experience of the individuals involved, it is of course impossible to say for certain. However, the general disjunction we have found between male images and female experience in the Bhagavati cult suggests we would do well to question the directionality of the desire posited by Gough. Perhaps more to the point is Gough's later observation that rites centering on the ambivalent powers of female sexuality may in fact represent 'the unconscious fear ... of women for [sic] sexual attack from a male parental figure' (Gough 1955: 65).

Sered has recently suggested that women's possession cross-culturally may be a metaphorical expression of the female experience of sexual intercourse as being entered bodily (Sered 1994: 190, citing a personal communication by Kraemer). Perhaps the entry into the female body of an ancestor spirit, causing bādhā, metaphorically represents the act of incest itself. The connection between female spirit possession, anger, and sexual anxiety suggests that some women may feel highly ambivalent about even licit sexual congress, perceiving it as an attack. In the case of bādhā the entering is a form of supernatural rape, as male ancestor spirits (father figures) take hold of her body from the inside and cause her to shake and behave orgasmically (cf. Obeyesekere 1977a: 1981). But does the puberty rite and its associated folklore express the girl's unconscious desire for sexual congress with her father, as orthodox Freudians would suggest, or does it simply mask through reversal a male incestuous desire to taste the young girl's budding sexuality? Evidence points to the latter view.

The theme of father–daughter incest is prominent in South Asian folklore (Ramanujan 1983). At the same time, many Indian analysts have noted the male fear of mature female sexuality, which arouses Oedipal desires and guilt in the male and causes impotence.[30] Slater (1968), addressing similar social conditions in ancient Greece, suggests that the custom of fully mature males marrying prepubescent females resolves both problematic aspects of male Oedipal desire: unconscious fear of his mother's sexuality (in which he is powerless and will be engulfed) and his desire for sex with his daughter (who is herself his property, powerless, an extension of his own body, and boyish in appearance; a narcissistic object).

In Kerala, as in the ancient Greece analysed by Slater, a large age difference between spouses frequently applied, both in the past and present, accentuating the dominance of the male and providing him with a youthful partner who is more like a boy than a mature woman (Tapper 1979). In fact, male folk physiology frequently stresses the thinness and unwomanly bodily features of virgin girls, who quickly metamorphose into curvaceous women upon initiation into sex. Some boys told me that girls with large breasts have been fondled excessively; the very touch of a man makes the girl's body larger and sexually more mature. In the times prior to this century when girls were married prior to menarche, their physiques would certainly have been boyish. The folk belief accentuates the immaturity of the virgin girl's body while imputing to it the potential to get out of control as soon as her sexuality is awakened. The custom of depilating the pubic hair, which Slater refers to for Greece and the Mediterranean at large, is also found in Kerala as a normal part of women's body hygiene (cf. Kamani 1995). Slater suggests that this practice also reflects male fear of the mature female genitalia, and an attempt to preserve their prepubescent appearance.

The widespread Hindu cultural practice of marrying adolescent girls to much older men is also explicable in this light. Much has been made of the pre-twentieth-century practice of marrying girls before menarche; indeed this prescription in Hindu religious law appears to have been at the root of the tāli-tying ceremony as analysed by Yalman (1963). Although modern Indian constitutional law prohibits the marriage of girls before the age of fifteen, and common practice in Kerala is to marry girls somewhat later, matches between partners more than sixteen years separated in age are not uncommon. In the matrilineal Mārār and Kuṟup castes which perform muṭiyēṯṯu, marriages were sometimes arranged until the present generation between maternal uncles and nieces, rather than between cross-cousins (McCormack 1958). This unusual arrangement led to even larger age gaps between spouses than were common for other young girls in India, who were married at or before puberty to men significantly older than themselves. While the consequences of such age discrepancy have been bemoaned in discussions of early widowhood and satī, few have considered the physical and psychological violence that such legal matches perpetrated upon young girls. Medical reports chronicling the traumatic physical effects of premature, often violent sex and birth on immature female bodies alert us to these dangers (B. D. Miller 1981; Castillo 1994a, b). This suggests that even jural marriage relations might prove physically and psychologically traumatic for young girls in traditional castes. Although such marital arrangements are by definition not incestuous, still the enormous age and power difference between the spouses might well qualify as child abuse by today's standards.

Gough insightfully observes that many elements of the Bhadrakāḷi cult in Kerala express repressed socially forbidden sexual desires. In adopting the Freudian position, Gough asserts that immature females repress desire for their mature male kin. In contrast, I believe it is males who project their own sexual desire for immature, taboo females onto the young girls. Perhaps the male who is 'possessed' by the ,virgin girl in his dreams is simply engulfed by his own uncontrollable fantasies of desire. Yet he externalizes this obsession into a demonic succubus who invades his own body. What is the reality which the yakṣi image masks and perverts? That males seduce and rape females, not the other way around; that males with power use females (and other males) who are young, vulnerable, and powerless for the satisfaction of their own frustrated desires. In fantasy these victims are proclaimed to be the aggressors.

A similar reversal of facts is documented for Freud's own treatment of female child abuse data. Masson, in *The Assault on Truth* (1984), details the process by which Freud rejected his initial assessment of hysterics as victims of actual child sexual abuse, and instead developed his theory of infantile sexuality, the basis of psychoanalysis as we know it today. Thus Freud came to regard the hysteria of Dora, an eighteen-year-old girl who had memories of violent sexual assault by her father as a child, as a reflection of her repressed feminine fantasies of seducing her father. Without delving here into the historical morass surrounding Masson's controversial book, we note that this same reversal, which accuses the female victim of being the seductress, has taken place in the Kerala male folklore regarding women. And as in the case of Freudian analysis, such ideological reversals have serious moral and psychological consequences for real men and women.[31]

Males desire young girls, in Kerala as elsewhere, and institutionalize this desire in asymmetrical marriage rules and puberty rites (Tapper 1979). These rituals satisfy male unconscious fantasy and preserve insecure masculine sexual identity. The necessity for wives to be sexually inexperienced, young, and subservient also protects this male fear of inadequacy. But what are we to make of the theme of male incestuous rape of the female which is suggested in Gough's puberty rites and in women's possession more generally? Does this reflect male fantasy, or perhaps more sinister female reality?

Unlike Gough, I interviewed women and men specifically to probe their feelings and experiences about this difficult topic. Many people admitted to knowing about incestuous behaviour. One Pulluva woman (an itinerant caste that performs serpent rituals) told me that in joint families such sexual exploitation of children was fairly common. In her words, 'Say an uncle feels like going to that child and he gets involved with her. Some children agree or some children won't agree. Even if they lose their control to some extent, they won't really agree. If the child doesn't agree, they do it by force.'[32] According to her, girls who suffer such experiences often are forced to get abortions and are kept at home to prevent others from finding out about it.

Although many scholars have noted the prevalence of incest motifs in literature and folklore, to my knowledge no one has suggested that real adult-child sexual relations may play a role in these images. Upon examination we find such interactions to be much more common than has previously been disclosed. Adult–child pairings were institutionalized in the traditional Kerala marriage system in which mature males routinely married female children. It thus seems plausible to suggest that more than male fantasy may be at the root of the images in ritual and folklore. Perhaps the presence of incest motifs in expressive culture is a covert recognition of maladjustments embedded in a social structure that serves mainly male psychological needs.[33]

In order to evaluate the relationship between sexual behaviour and images in folklore and ritual, it is necessary to know more about incest in Kerala as well as in south Asia more generally. Such information is difficult to come by, as few analysts have sought it. Yet, a growing body of evidence over the last two decades suggests that incestuous relationships crossing generational and marital lines are indeed a fairly common, though socially taboo, means of sexual gratification in many parts of India.[34] Even with its higher standards of living and education, Kerala has not escaped these unpleasant realities. We have already related some anecdotal evidence of male and female child sexual abuse in Kerala. Boys told me of coerced sexual relations with married aunts and older male cousins; girls with uncles; and always these encounters were initiated by the older party. Mary Mohan, a Delhi-based gynaecologist with fourteen years of experience in Kerala villages, states:

> Incestuous relationships among first cousins, uncle and niece, aunty and nephew, children and adults are usually never reported until some medical problem occurs. However, [incest] does exist in abundance in villages, because dating and talking to someone one likes is not a way of life in the villages. These relationships are maximized during festivals when members of the family come together under one roof, during

weddings, religious functions, etc. Society condemns it publicly though very often it is the loudest voices who are involved in such activities under cover. Individuals who experience these relationships do develop a guilt complex which they try to hide, but when questioned evade the issue altogether as if it is someone else's problem. (Written personal communication, December 1994)

Incestuous child abuse in Kerala, then, may result, as in much of south Asia, from cultural conditions valuing strong restrictions on sexual behaviour, combined with very intimate and affectively charged family relations, close living conditions, shared sleeping arrangements, and a tropical climate where minimal clothing is the norm. Reactions to the development of illicit love affairs within the family are apparently tolerant so long as social secrecy and family honour are maintained. There is little evidence in most of the reports we have quoted that there is much concern for the possible harmful effects of these episodes on children.

In addition to the sexual abuse of girl children, another type of abusive sexual contact which seems to occur frequently in Kerala is the seduction of young boys by adult married women.[35] Most teenage and young adult males I interviewed stated unequivocally that there are 'plenty' of married women who engage regularly in sex with teenage boys. At first I suspected that this might be another version of the yakṣi stories, representing more male fantasy than reality. But a number of young men reported having had such experiences in their early teen years. Often these were their first heterosexual encounters, and reinforced their cultural stereotypes of aggressive and voraciously sexual mature women.[36] It became clear that such occurrences of women seducing boys were due to female sexual deprivation. In the cases I collected the accused women were in the prime of their sexual lives (in their thirties), and living apart from their emigrant husbands, who returned briefly once every year or two. In gossip, the existence of this form of unofficial mutual satisfaction was acknowledged (some referred to it as a form of prostitution); but as long as the women involved conducted their business in secret, no one really seemed to object. The general attitude was of humorous cynicism, as if to say, 'Well, what can you expect?' Yet, no one was willing to openly acknowledge that the social system might not be functioning at its best, or that there could be harmful psychological consequences for the parties involved.

It seems conceivable that some might argue the positive, adaptive function of such a system, in fulfilling a natural biological need by the only means available. But boys who had experienced such contacts were extremely ambivalent about them.[37] The large age differential, and in some cases, asymmetrical family relationship between the parties (usually of different generations) often created serious psychological conflicts. Coming from the 'top down', in terms of the authority and respect for the elder generation by the younger in Kerala society, such adult–child seductions could not be viewed as arising from mutual consent. It was never possible for me to interview women who had been accused of incestuous seduction of their nephews or other boys, although I did observe several such women in their daily life. Living frustrated existence in joint households with their married sisters-in-law, or if they were quite wealthy, as solitary household heads, such women struck me as sometimes angry, desperate, and miserable, struggling to uphold an image of respectability and cheerful calm.

Today Abhilash's friend Rajiv told me something very personal. He knew I was interested in the possibility of illicit sexual relations in Kerala, and how women manage under the circumstances they are forced to live with. So he told me that when he was thirteen, he used to hear his mother having sex with his cousin (a young man of about twenty) in the next room. His father was working abroad at that time. He used to want to kill her for it, but as an adult he could understand the desperation which drove her to such extremes. Soon afterwards, his aunt (mother's brother's wife) seduced him one night, fellating him and having sex with him. He used to sleep in the same room with his aunt (whose husband was working abroad) and her little daughters when visiting his uncle's house. She just woke him up that way one night. They kept having an illicit relationship on and off for several years until the girls got too big and his aunt was afraid someone would find out. He felt shocked and guilty but he also enjoyed it. Besides she was older and he felt she really needed that. So he had to do it. Antonio told me that Rajiv, in a friendly mood, had once offered to take him to have sex with a married woman, if he was curious to 'have it with a Malayali lady'. Rajiv told Antonio that Kerala ladies are 'very hot'. No wonder he sees it that way. I wonder what he would have done if Antonio had said yes.

Psychological research with perpetrators of sexual abuse in Euro-American countries frequently finds that these aggressors were once victims of sexual abuse themselves. I wondered if this could be the case for some of the women who had resorted to these illicit gratifications. The spotty but provocative data I obtained, and the prevalence of the theme in gossip and folklore, while inconclusive, suggest an important area for further study. It seems clear that although it may be atypical, and although it is not socially acceptable, some women seduce boys in Kerala; and some men seduce girls. Often these contacts are intergenerational and intrafamilial, between aunts and nephews or uncles and nieces. Are these incestuous episodes a recent phenomenon, or could they have played a part in the development of traditional culture? Are they more typical of one social class or another? All these questions are impossible to answer definitively with so little data and so much cultural resistance to discussing sexual topics. Only future research can hope to flesh out these preliminary hypothetical remarks.

In interviews with the married men who participated in muṭiyēṯṯu performances, conducted through a mature male interpreter whom they respected, I got a picture of traditional sexual life which differed in some respects from that of younger men, but not in others. Most of these artists, who spent the greater portion of their lives serving in temples (as musicians or visual artists), were more sexually innocent and, one might suggest, repressed, than the sophisticated youngsters of the modern towns, who have been exposed to Western-style pornographic movies, videos, and magazines. I could clearly conclude from my interviews that males suffer significant sexual deprivation. It was not possible for me, with my limited access to traditional women, to find out the intimate details of women's sexual lives and fantasies directly. But to some extent the deprivations both men and women undergo due to their very restricted sexual lives seem to reproduce the modern 'emigrant' situation to some extent. This suggests that sexual frustration may have played a significant part in Kerala's traditional culture, at least for ritual artists who are engaged in intensive temple service. When ordinary, licit avenues for sexual gratification are blocked, it appears that people resort to a wide variety of other means to achieve that gratification, including sexual abuse of children in the home.[38]

Psychologists are only starting to understand the severely debilitating effects of child sexual abuse, particularly on women. Most research to date has focused on female victims, as statistics in America and Europe indicate that the vast majority of abuse cases are perpetrated by male relatives against female children (Ryan-Blaney 1989). Until such studies are conducted in India, we cannot assume this is the case there; however, the extremely hierarchical nature of South Asian family structure, and the total dependency of traditional women upon their male family members, would suggest that statistics on abuse there will follow Euro-American patterns in this regard. On the other hand, the frequent reports of seduction of boys by older female relatives in Kerala may point to a different pattern that must also be investigated.

H. S. Narayanan, a psychiatrist from Bangalore, identifies the symptoms found in female Indian abuse survivors as follows: 'depression, anxiety, suicidal tendencies, long term personality problems, damage to self-esteem, self-mutilation and acute feelings of guilt, disgust and inferiority' (R. Menon 1992: 107). Such symptoms closely resemble those postulated by Euro-American scholars of child abuse syndrome, who report long-term effects of childhood sexual abuse that include depression, anxiety, suicide, anger, substance abuse, low self-esteem, interpersonal difficulties, sexual difficulties, re-victimization, dissociation, and somatization (Van Kley 1992: 1). Abuse victims tend to experience impaired self-image, guilt, low self-esteem and self-blame far more than non-abuse victims (Briere and Runtz 1991: 5). More serious affective and cognitive disorders have also been reported, including multiple personality disorders and schizophrenia (Kaufman 1982: 503). Many other related symptoms are present.

The relationship between post-traumatic stress disorder (PTSD) and the child abuse syndrome has become clear in recent research in the US (Briere and Runtz 1991). PTSD is defined as a set of symptoms typically following an extraordinarily traumatic event. Essential features of PTSD include 'recurrent and intrusive recollections of the event; anxiety; a reexperiencing of the trauma through dreams, nightmares, or daydreams and dissociative states. Constricted affect; hypervigilant or avoidant behaviour; startle reactions; persistent feelings of guilt ...; withdrawl [sic]; depression; and depersonalization' (Ryan-Blaney 1989: 16). Along with these emotional and cognitive disturbances, physiological responses including muscle tension, sweating, rapid breathing, palpitations, dizziness, fainting, nausea and vomiting, and disturbed sleep, eating, sex, and excretion are commonly present (Jehu 1988).

Ellenson (1985, 1986) furthermore describes a consistent grouping of symptoms in patients with incest histories; these are postulated to comprise an incest syndrome. This group of symptoms includes nightmares, phobias, and dissociative episodes (these can include disengagement or 'spacing out' during times of stress, detachment or numbing, out-of-body experiences, fugue states, and MPD (Briere and Runtz 1991: 7). Some unusual perceptual distortions also were frequently reported: recurrent auditory, visual, and tactile hallucinations, such as seeing shadowy figures or objects in the periphery of vision, hearing intruders or booming sounds, feeling the presence of an evil entity in the home, physical sensations of being touched, pushed or thrown down. Recurrent nightmares frequently contained scenes of catastrophe, violence towards family members, children being killed or harmed, and scenes of death and violence (Ellenson 1985, cited in Ryan-Blaney 1989: 13, 49). Ellenson cited 'the presence of two perceptual disturbances, either auditory or visual, ... as being the most powerful single indicator of incestuous abuse' (Ryan-Blaney 1989: 49).

These symptoms typical of abuse victims bear a striking resemblance to the cultural manifestations of bādhā or spirit possession which afflicts women in Kerala. Anxiety, depression, withdrawal, low self-esteem, victimization, experiencing unseen presences entering the body, tactile and visual hallucinations, hearing of voices, and many other symptoms bear strong resemblance to spirit possession. While such discussions are at an early stage in the West, and barely incipient in India, the possible links between female spirit possession and post-traumatic stress disorder associated with child sexual abuse merit careful further study.[39] One woman I knew in Kerala who had a recurrent history of 'fits' suffered from symptoms of hearing voices, fugue states, and biting people, including her children.[40] Frequent episodes of fainting, dissociation, numbing, and depression were also typical manifestations of bādhā amongst village women I knew well.

Richard Castillo (1994a, b) has suggested that the frequent association of spirit possession symptoms (labelled 'hysteria' by psychoanalytic observers) with sexual dysfunction in south Asia be reinterpreted along these lines. Rejecting both traditional psychoanalytic theory and biological reductionism, Castillo draws on dissociation theory to suggest the etiology of south Asian dissociative trance in child sexual abuse. Castillo reinterprets the famous cases of Somavati and Daya in the south Asian psychoanalytic literature, in both of which the female spirit possession sufferer's symptoms were seen as indicative of her own repressed incestuous sexual desires and masochistic tendencies (Freed and Freed 1985, Obeyesekere 1977a, 1981). Castillo draws on data presented in the original ethnographies which strongly suggest sexual abuse in the childhood of both women, and he pleads for a more enlightened analysis of women's spirit possession in south Asia.

Where child sexual abuse is allowed to flourish, and personal psychological dysfunction not given space for overt verbal and physical expression, possession, hysteria, and similar states may sometimes be the only expression possible. The frequent recourse of female possession victims to images of oral aggression (either turned inward against themselves or outward against others, as in the case of Somavati) and debasing, defiling, self-mutilating behaviour also suggests the symptomatology of sexual abuse victims. Compulsive or indiscriminate sexual behaviour, eating disorders such as binging and purging, and self-mutilation including cutting, carving, burning the body, or 'hitting of the head or body against or with objects' are characterized by Briere and Runtz as 'tension-reducing activities' which 'serve primarily as attempts to moderate or terminate painful affect' (1991: 8–9). These, along with numbing and spacing out strategies, 'provide temporary distraction, anes thetize psychic pain, restore a sense of control, temporarily "fill" perceived emptiness, and/or relieve guilt or self-hatred' (ibid.: 8). The symptoms of bādhā often include obscene language, sexually provocative bodily display (including loosening of hair and clothes, as well as sensual body movements), and dissociation; the cure requires the banging of an iron nail into a large tree with the forehead. The veḷiccappāṭu's head-cutting, so essential to the Bhagavati cult, may be another manifestation of these same symptoms.

These similarities suggest that sexual abuse experiences may be a contributing factor in bādhā (female spirit possession by demons). Through bādhā, traumatic experiences may be expressed in a culturally sanctioned religious idiom. The culturally specific symbols provided by the religious idiom of spirit possession give both meaning and expression to the symptoms; and thereby enable cognitive processing of trauma (A. Miller 1983: 7). Despite the culturally relative form of expression, the similarity of psychobiological response (i.e. symptoms) in both Western sexual abuse cases and south Asian bādhā suggests the possibility that both may arise from similar sources.

Like Obeyesekere and other psychoanalytic scholars of spirit possession in south Asia, I believe the symptoms may arise in part from traumatic, repressed sexual and aggressive feelings. But unlike these scholars, and in agreement with Castillo (1994a,b), I believe these arise not from repressed Oedipal fantasies on the part of the female, but from traumas associated with actual childhood abuse experiences. The theme of guilt and acting-out of provocative behaviour and orgasmic trembling which is so often seen in spirit possession (both male and female) is not incompatible with this interpretation. Child victims of sexual assault often internalize guilt and aggress against themselves, cutting and mutilating their bodies in an expression of self-hatred. Oral sadistic themes can be a reenactment of forced fellatio experiences, common in child sexual abuse. Obscene language and eating of repulsive substances are a culturally specific expression of this oral sado-masochism which in the United States more frequently manifests as eating disorders like bulimia, compulsive overeating, or anorexia.

If spirit possession does in fact reflect a cultural expression of childhood abuse trauma, we still are left with the troubling question of gender roles in Bhagavati ritual and their possible psychological origins and functions. Though the original veḷiccappāṭus were females, males have enthusiastically supplanted them in the ritual sphere. Perhaps women originally developed this form of religious behaviour to give meaningful expression to their traumas. Yet, we know that at some point men began to dominate the cult and marginalize women's participation in the ritual arena. What was the motivation for this change? Were men simply imitating women, whom they secretly envied? Although we could take a feminist political perspective and attribute the male co-optation of the cult to the sheer desire to dominate women, it seems unlikely that men could become possessed on a regular basis and undergo such intense physical deprivations as the Bhagavati rituals require merely as a political statement. There must be some deeper personal motivation at work for males in order for such a vast change to have taken place.

If PTSD is a source of women's possession in bādhā, it may be a contributing factor in male spirit possession as well. If the female's possession by aggressive male demons re-enacts actual memories of childhood rape, then the male's possession by Kāḷi could likewise recall either a sexual seduction by an aggressive maternal figure or threatening homosexual contacts in childhood. Whatever the historical factors leading to co-optation of female possession rituals by male veḷiccappāṭus and muṭiyēṯṯu artists, the intensity of male interest in and willingness to perform the gruelling rites dedicated to Bhagavati suggests that the rites may serve to express male psychological traumas as well.[41]

While this explanation may account for male adoption of the 'personal symbols' of spirit possession, it does not account for the simultaneous marginalization of women's possession to the realm of the demonic.[42] The sadistic treatment of female victims of spirit possession, while simultaneously dressing as and becoming possessed by a threatening female deity in the culturally valued realm of sacred performance, reflects a sexist splitting of this religious tradition. The predominant attitude towards the female in muṭiyēṯṯu is hostility rather than empathy, and the actor appears to identify with the threatening Kāḷi only in an attempt to pacify and control her. While identifying with and acting out female desire (in the persona of Kāḷi/the aggressive mother), the muṭiyēṯṯu actor also symbolically punishes himself for submitting to that desire by decapitating (castrating) the demon Dārika (his nephew or son, i.e. his child self). Actual females meanwhile are literally controlled through their marginalization from the sacred cult; their threatening sexuality is accentuated by a phobic concentration on the dangers of their menstrual pollution.

The relationship between the male and female abreactions in spirit possession and their complex historical relations in the development of the Bhagavati cult may be further illuminated by Freud's early discussion of hysteria and obsession (Freud 1896a, b). Freud suggests that both hysteria and obsession are ego defences which invariably originate in 'a *sexual* experience of a traumatic nature—in the case of hysteria a *passive* experience, in that of obsessions an *active* one, though even here an earlier passive experience lay in the remoter background. In other words the ultimate cause was always the seduction of a child by an adult' (Strachey 1962: 160; emphasis in original).[43] Obsessional neuroses, which Freud claims are much more common in 'the male sex', are characterized by 'acts of aggression carried out with pleasure and of pleasurable participation in sexual acts'; whereas hysteria (found more in his female patients) is associated with sexual passivity and fear. Yet both defences have an identical origin in 'sexual experiences of early childhood' (Freud 1896b: 168). This is because they are merely chronological elaborations of the same 'infection in childhood' (Freud 1896a: 209):

> In all my cases of obsessional neurosis, moreover, I have found a *substratum of hysterical symptoms* which could be traced back to a scene of sexual passivity that preceded the pleasurable action. I suspect that this coincidence is no fortuitous one, and that precocious sexual aggressivity always implies a previous experience of being seduced. ... The nature of obsessional neurosis can be expressed in a simple formula. *Obsessional ideas* are invariably transformed *self-reproaches* which have re-emerged from *repression* and which always relate to some *sexual* act that was performed with pleasure *in childhood*. [Freud 1896b: 168–9]

In 'The Aetiology of Hysteria', Freud makes the nature of this vicious circle even more explicit. Reviewing a group of eighteen severely neurotic patients (six men and twelve women), Freud found that all of them had experienced traumatic sexual assault in childhood, and were at the base of suffering from the resultant hysterical symptoms. Moreover, male aggressors had once been passive victims:

> ... I was sometimes able to prove that the boy—who, here too, played the part of the aggressor—had previously been seduced by an adult of the female sex, and that afterwards, under the pressure of his prematurely awakened libido and compelled by his memory, he tried to repeat with the little girl exactly the same practices that he had learned from the adult woman, without making any modification of his own in the character of the sexual activity.
>
> In view of this, I am inclined to suppose that children cannot find their way to acts of sexual aggression unless they have been seduced previously. The foundation for a neurosis would accordingly always be laid in childhood by adults, and the children themselves would transfer to one another the disposition to fall ill of hysteria later. (Freud 1896a: 208–9)

Studies of adult sexual abusers of children, both in India and in the West, as we have discussed above, clearly show that most abusers were once themselves victims. Freud's remarks in these neglected essays are prophetic and profound, and deserve serious re-evaluation in the light of recent knowledge about the pervasiveness and power of child sexual abuse experiences. In the context of our current discussion, Freud's remarks illuminate both the male adoption of spirit possession symptoms (much like the Victorian 'hysteria' of Freud's female patients) in apparent imitation of females; and the obsessional, aggressive degradation of females which accompanies it. If some males had been seduced in childhood by adult females, they might well suffer post-traumatic stress reactions, with all of the psycho-biological symptoms we have discussed. This complex of symptoms appears in the Kerala context as 'possession' for both males and females. But a cultural elaboration takes place in which female symptoms (Freud's 'hysteria') are interpreted as bādhā, or demonic possession; while male symptoms (also an abreactive 'hysteria') are considered in the context of sacred performance to be caused by dēva āvēśam or possession by a deity. The obsessional character of male neuroses in this culture, due to the hyperstimulation of the mother-child relationship and concomitant oral/narcissistic fixation on the ambivalent female sexual body, leads to the aggressive, hostile, and hypermasculine domination of women and to a denial of women's eligibility for sacred experience. In private life, such male obsessional neurosis could conceivably lead to actual molestation of girls and boys (a compulsive re-enactment of the aggressor's own childhood seduction by an adult); or the obsession could be temporarily relieved by the cathartic performances of the Bhagavati cult rituals. The south Asian cultural practice of hypergamy in marriage, coupled with large age disparity between spouses, could be seen in this light as an institutionalized male obsessional neurosis.

To summarize the argument using Freud's terminology, women's possession in bādhā appears to be a form of hysteria with etiology in a passive experience of child sexual abuse; male possession and enactment of Kāḷi is an obsession resulting from an active seductive experience, itself based on an earlier passive experience of maternal seductiveness or possible early homosexual seduction. What is clear from this picture is that, although both males and females may be suffering from a maladaptive vicious circle of deprivation, overstimulation, and trauma, females appear to be getting the worse end of the bargain.

Obeyesekere has sensitized us to the interaction of cultural symbols and personal experience, and the need to distinguish carefully between them (1981). Whatever the etiology of the stories and symbols of muṭiyēṯṯu, there must be sufficient resonance with the personal experiences of individuals within the culture to make the drama meaningful, for both actors and spectators. One might expect that persons who have especially severe childhood abuse or sexual/aggressive traumas would respond strongly to these symbols and have a high degree of emotional interest in the ritual drama and accompanying stories (Obeyesekere 1990: 25). Individuals without such traumas might attend the rituals for other reasons: as an entertainment, a way to fit in, a chance to show off a new sari, to look at girls, or to get out of the house. This explains why certain members of the audience are bored or find the muṭiyēṯṯu performances amusing, while others are riveted or terrified.

Performers themselves may also have different degrees of personal motivation. Although muṭiyēṯṯu is a hereditary profession, it is not an obligation. Moreover, within the troupe there are numerous roles an individual can fulfil, including musician, make-up expert, manager, or actor. Only one member of the troupe normally performs the role of Kāḷi—usually, but not always, the eldest and most experienced man. Although portraying Kāḷi is a hereditary profession, not everyone takes it up. The Kāḷi actor must be capable of becoming possessed, while at the same time remaining sufficiently in control to conform to ritual expectations in the performance. Some individuals show a particular interest or talent for this role.

Why do particular individuals get more attracted to and identify strongly with Kāḷi? We cannot yet answer this question definitively. Although I interviewed Kāḷi actors in depth on a number of topics, my relationships with them did not allow probing of such delicate topics as child sexual abuse or other traumas. In all cases I treated the artists as respected, older persons with vast stores of valuable cultural knowledge. They in turn were willing to share some of that knowledge with me once they adjudged me sincere in my respect and interest. Under these circumstances, probing into their personal weaknesses or secret traumas would not have been appropriate. In terms of transference, I was a daughter figure to most of the artists, and therefore not a person to whom such 'backstage' material could ever be revealed.[44] But by gaining the confidence and friendship of other members of the society, I did find out about some of these hidden areas.

Although I cannot make clinical assessments of the unconscious motivations of individual muṭiyēṯṯu performers, certain common themes in their personal lives do suggest the possibility of significant psychological tendencies relevant to our discussion. Dr Chummar Choondal, who became intrigued by my theory, stated that in his lifelong experience, he had noted a particular cluster of problems which seemed to afflict the families of some muṭiyēṯṯu performers. These included latent feminine identification, very late marriage (typically around age 40 to a much younger woman) or lifelong bachelorhood, homosexual tendencies, impotence, alcoholism, and mental illness. In one family a history of intermarriage seems to have resulted in a high frequency of genetic disorders including mental retardation and physical disfigurements.

By no means were these problems universal or even predominant in all of the eight muṭiyēṯṯu families I surveyed. However, they were certainly more common in the lives of at least four different actors who regularly play the role of Kāḷi. One young actor who currently plays Dārikan, but is anxious to learn the role of Kāḷi, has a history of seizures and memory lapses, as well as presenting a noticeably feminine demeanour. He is quite obsessed with Kāḷi, writing devotional poetry to her in great volume and studying every aspect of her mythology and cult in detail. Two actor/troupe leaders who are particularly gifted exponents of the Kāḷi possession scene were chronic alcoholics, had marital difficulties, and were characterized by other (competing) troupe leaders as difficult, unreliable and dishonest individuals. Yet another had remained a lifelong bachelor due to some sexual dysfunction. Even those Kāḷi actors who appeared to be happily married, well adjusted, and confident turned out to have had significant marital problems earlier in their lives. The presence of latent feminine identification and possible psychological dysfunction (by indigenous standards) does suggest that it would be rewarding to collect detailed personal case histories. The actors who show particular talent for playing the part of Kāḷi, being possessed by her on demand, might well be individuals with an abuse background.[45]

On a broader cultural level, where our analysis must remain for now, I suggest that certain general themes exist in this culture which seek expression through ritual. Although the traumas thus expressed may be common to both males and females, a distinct hierarchy of value separates the male and female realms of possession in Kerala. In Crapanzano's (1973) study of a markedly similar cult in Morocco, he suggests that for women, performance of ritual possession provides direct expression of socially repressed personality aspects. Women temporarily embody the same aggressive and sexually provocative alter ego (the female *jinn* Aisha Qandisha) who torments male cult members. But such an outlet is denied to women in Kerala, except in the cruel displays of bādhā and their sadistic cures (performed by male ritualists).[46] In his study of the mythology of ancient Greek society, Slater comments that 'sex segregation both causes and mitigates social pathology' (1968: 59). This seems to be true of Kerala too. Both sexes suffer significant deprivation from the cultural repression of sexuality and aggression. These drives appear to find acceptable expression only when directed towards inferiors (women to boys; men to women; older children to younger) (Mencher 1963). The rituals of bādhā and muṭiyēṯṯu (and other male Bhagavati rituals) may provide an outlet, even a transformative spiritual experience, but they do not change the fundamental social causes of trauma, which remain hidden and flourish in secret.

The Theme of Vengeance Revisited

One morning in Kerala I read an article in *The Hindu* (a national newspaper) about a group of women in the nearby state of Andhra Pradesh who, fed up with abusive and drunken husbands, had taken matters into their own hands. A photograph showed a poster the women had designed to express their anger. There stood a village housewife in a dishevelled sari, hair askew, with a paddy-reaping curved iron sickle in one hand and a bottle of arrack (distilled coconut liquor) in the other. Her furious face expressed vengeful anger towards unjust men, and the raised sword threatened violence if husbands didn't give up their drinking immediately.[47]

This rather commonplace incident struck me for the wonderful adaptability of the Kāḷi image, so clearly manifest in the persona of the angry housewife. Yet it was also striking how most women I interviewed never imagined Kāḷi as a role model, or even as a human female. Though myths, legends, and folk speech clearly drew such parallels, for the vast majority of women in Kerala this ready-made image of feminine vengeance and independence remained an untapped psychological resource.

David Kinsley has identified the twin themes of humiliation and revenge as essential aspects of the worship of village goddesses. In his book *Hindu Goddesses*, Kinsley reviews numerous south Indian myths in which village goddesses have suffered injustice at the hands of men. In his words:

> It could be said of these fiercely independent goddesses that they have learned that they only receive injustice from males; consequently they are determined to remain independent from men in their transformed positions as goddesses. ... The goddesses still need males to invigorate them, but they ensure that the males will not dominate them or threaten their powers (Kinsley 1986: 202).

Similar conclusions were reached by Brubaker in his study of village goddesses in south India: 'The most constant theme in this whole body of mythology is ... the grievous wrong the goddess or goddess-to-be has suffered, a wrong so outrageous that it *demands* violent retribution' (Brubaker 1978: 309). The familiar fiery wrath of the goddess is retributive, unpredictable, and ferocious, 'a quality "accounted for" in the myths by the goddess's history of being personally victimized' (ibid.: 148). It is in fact this victimization which spurs the goddess into independent, aggressive action: 'These independent goddesses are to be feared, and their fearfulness is "explained" in the myths by their earlier mistreatment' (ibid.: 142).

Moreover 'village goddesses are created through violence arising out of men's mistreatment of women' (ibid.: 122). This mistreatment is nearly always of a sexual nature. The demons in village goddess mythology are invariably male, and their violations of the goddess usually involve her sexual disgrace or humiliation (by disrobing, false accusations against her chastity); or, more often, rape and actual sexual assault. Whether the characters are human or supernatural, 'the essence of their relationship in both cases is sexual assault, whether accomplished or only threatened—i.e. sexual approach perceived [by the female] as overwhelmingly disgusting, defiling, and damaging—which must be repulsed or punished with a flaming death' (ibid.: 92). Brubaker has rightly identified the repugnance the female victim seems to feel for the rapist/demon, who sometimes is portrayed as her brother, husband, or father figure. '[W]hat is central to their relationship in either case is an illicit sexuality that is loathsome to the female and fatal to the male' (ibid.: 94).[48]

The goddess's vengeance for her subjection to illicit and unwanted sexual assault is the death of her male victim. Brubaker clearly demonstrates that the beheaded male sacrificial victim (usually a buffalo) so common to south Indian goddess rituals is clearly considered by villagers to be the goddess's demonic foe but also her husband or lover. His subordinate sacrificial position with foot in mouth expresses his complete submission to her (Brubaker 1978: 338). The demon, or his buffalo substitute in sacrifice, 'symbolizes the evil powers of violence and male aggressiveness' (ibid.: 342; quoting Agehananda Bharati) which here are subdued and punished by the vengeful female.

A similar theme emerges in the folklore of yakṣis. The yakṣi seduces and kills an 'innocent' man; but this in turn is often the result of her mistreatment in life which led to her fate as a yakṣi in the first place. One Kāḷi actor explained that

> yakṣis are ghosts. That is what our ancestors have told us. When women die of some accidents they become yakṣis. Like if she dies because someone beats her to death or if she commits suicide because of an illegal pregnancy [due to rape] she will become a yakṣi. Then she sits on top of a tree and kills men and drinks their blood. Yakṣis have some extraordinary powers. They can change their dress and appearance and also have the power to seduce men. They bring harm to males. We never hear about females having any problems with yakṣis.[49]

The theme of rape as a violation of the sacred boundaries of the female body extends to the symbolism of the goddess's festival as a whole. According to Brubaker, the underlying symbolic structure of the festival is one of 'attraction and penetration' (1978: 353). Brubaker suggests that the villagers' concern during the festival with repelling intruding demons is analogous to a fear of rape. Invoking Mary Douglas's concept of pollution as the violation of the boundaries of the 'imperfect [i.e. permeable] vessel' of the body, Brubaker suggests we consider 'the bounded village topocosm as just such a "body". ... And the vessel that is the village is of course a feminine one' (ibid.: 349). The goddess who has been raped is coterminous with the body of the village, on whose boundaries the enemy has violently intruded. The spirit possession of the goddess's ritual representative itself suggests this bodily violation through the metaphor of rape and presentation of orgasmic physical symptoms such as shivering, shaking, and feeling like 'your hormones are working', as one oracle explained it to me.

Who is the enemy who pierces and violates the feminine body of the village? As we have seen, the myths emphasize that the demon is the goddess's foe but also her lover. Brubaker therefore suggests that 'the enemy is *male*, but he is *not only* the *enemy*' (1978: 348, original emphasis). The enemy is often called the goddess's husband, a euphemism for the fact that sexual relations are expected to ensue between them (ibid.: 351). The theme of a male demon violating the body of the village/goddess may represent in part ambivalence surrounding cross-cousin marriage rules: the male sexual partner who comes from 'outside' the lineage to violate the bride's virgin female body is simultaneously the girl's classificatory husband and structural 'brother'. As such, theirs is a technically licit but psychologically taboo sexual relationship, fraught with the overtones of incestuous desire between brother and sister (Trawick 1990a). In the Kerala context, where Mārār and Kuṟup families occasionally married uncles to nieces in a variation of cross-cousin marriage, Oedipal anxieties as well as subconscious associations with fears of sexual assault could become quite pronounced.

In this light it is interesting to take another look at the story of Dārikavadham. To recap the basic plot structure, Kāḷi is born from her father Śiva to kill the demon Dārika. Dārika wishes to destroy Śiva (and the other gods) to avenge their murder of his own father in a previous war. Dārika rapes Kūḷi, who is an alter ego of Kāḷi herself. As such he is in a structural position of husband (intruding male sexual partner) to Kāḷi. Kāḷi is afflicted with smallpox by the sweat (concentrated sexual desire and heat) of her 'mother', Pārvati, who thus expresses sexual jealousy for her daughter Kāḷi. Śiva protects Kāḷi by creating a brother for her, who licks her entire body save the face; and this due to sexual modesty. This motif expresses the father's sexual desire for his daughter, gratified in the licking of her body by Ghaṇṭākarṇan (who is created out of his father's earwax; i.e. filth from a bodily orifice); as well as the brother's sexual desire for his sister. The daughter in turn appears to both desire and punish her father upon her return to Kailāsam. Śiva experiences fear when he sees Kāḷi and calms her wrath by dancing naked before her, or lying naked on the ground while she either stamps on his chest, or has intercourse with him. In any case her 'wrath' is cooled by satisfaction of the illicit mutual sexual desire of the daughter and father.

In this story, Dārika is in the structural position of both rapist and 'husband'. He is clearly an outsider who must be punished. Yet, due to the structural similarity of the Dārikavadham story to cognate south Indian myths analysed in detail by Brubaker, Shulman and others, it is clear that Dārika, like other demons who fight the goddess, is in the positional role of husband vis-à-vis Kāḷi; although this relation is disguised in this case by displacement onto the figure of Kūḷi (Brubaker 1977, 1978; Shulman 1976, 1980).[50] Perhaps Kāḷi's vengeful anger represents the anger of the young bride, traditionally just having reached puberty, at the sexual assault of her new husband. Although she appears to prefer the Oedipal attachment to her father, in fact she shows enormous hostility toward him as well. Her sexual conquest of her father (Śiva) at the end of the story is an act of sadistic humiliation and vengeance as much as it is a satiation of her sexual desire.[51] In short, the goddess's sexual relations, both with Dārika and Śiva, appear to be coloured by the familiar ambivalent emotions of disgust, desire, anger, and vengeance identified by Brubaker. Both relationships also have a clearly incestuous character.

The themes of aggressive and incestuous feminine sexual desire are also prominent in south Indian mythology of the goddess. Brubaker recounts a number of stories in which the goddess clearly acts as a sexual aggressor; but this in turn is the goddess's response to prior victimization: 'Here the female is the bold sexual aggressor rather than the one who must keep her sexuality strictly in check, but she is still mistreated and the males who mistreat her may properly fear the consequences' (Brubaker 1978: 139). She uses her sexuality to destroy the male and punish him for his prior abuse of her. In the myths of Ellamma and Peddamma, the goddess's sexual desire is directed towards her sons. She creates male children for the sole purpose of mating with them and tries to persuade them to have sex with her against their will. The sons flee their mother until they are able to destroy her 'third eye and thus deprive her of both her power and her desire' (ibid.: 143).[52] The response to illicit seduction is once again violence directed by the victim against the body of the aggressor in a form of symbolic castration.[53]

A cycle of desire, abuse, and revenge constantly seems to emerge in the myths, whether the origin point is in male or female desire. In the Ellamma and Peddamma myths, and to a lesser degree in the Dārikavadham story, 'the fear of incest is clearly stated and clearly sets off the chain reaction of alternating fear and mistreatment' (Brubaker 1978: 143). The 'leapfrogging' relationship between fear and mistreatment between the sexes which Brubaker pinpoints as central to the goddess's ambivalence closely resembles the vicious cycle of sexual abuse discussed above: the child victim becomes an abuser, whose victim grows up to abuse someone else. Where the innocent girl is raped by a trusted male relative (father, brother, or husband), she may learn to wield her sexuality like a sword. She may later turn to sons or nephews to satisfy her sexual desire. As we have suggested, the abused boy then fears adult women and again seeks satisfaction in union with inferior, non-threatening partners such as young girls or boys. This vicious cycle unifies the two distinct patterns Brubaker finds in the myths of the goddess:

> In one of these the emphasis is on the woman as innocent and her suffering as an outrage; her attractiveness is her undoing but it is not her doing; the male is drawn to her and uses her cruelly, but she does nothing to provoke his action. In the other pattern the emphasis is reversed: here the goddess uses her attractiveness to lure him to his destruction. Sometimes, in fact, she pointedly invites him to try to conquer her. (1978: 354)

If he succumbs, of course, he also invites certain death. Like the vampiric yakṣis of young men's dreams, the goddess embodies both poles of the abused woman's experience: violation and vengeance.

In all of these related myths of the fierce goddess, we thus find themes of incest disturbingly close to the real accounts discussed in the previous section. Perhaps the myths are not mere wish fulfilment in fantasy but hint at a dark and hidden reality. It seems likely that some of these stories 'give expression, in a variety of ways, to the deep motivations that beset a plurality of individuals in a society' (Obeyesekere 1990: 25). Perhaps the erotic family dramas of myth thinly disguise real injustices which real women are rendered incapable of revenging.

In these stories we hear a muffled cry for help by women who suffer and by men, perhaps once victims themselves, who are compelled to perpetuate that suffering. Perhaps males who ritually portray the goddess Bhadrakāḷi perceive the undercurrent of female rage and frustration boiling just below the surface, and never allowed open expression. Yet the exclusively male portrayal of Bhadrakāḷi as a violent, vengeful virgin in muṭiyēṯṯu is not an act of empathy. Male spectators at the performances seemed to delight in taunting and provoking the goddess, just as they often do real girls who venture into the streets. The prohibition on female participation and the extraordinary psychological power of these enactments for the male performers and participants clearly perpetuate male dominance and resolve male psychological conflicts while further alienating women from their own negative feelings.

Of course we cannot say for certain whether some women sitting in the audience at muṭiyēṯṯu may not be experiencing a secret glee at the vengeful decapitation of Dārika by the fearsome Kāḷi. Perhaps some women secretly identify with the goddess as the champion of their victimization, and thrill to see the death of their abusers in the form of Dārika. Certainly the complexities introduced by the theme of Kūḷi's rape make this possibility quite real. However, no woman I interviewed admitted to any such emotion. Moreover, as we have seen earlier in this chapter, women's stories poignantly reveal the goddess as the unwitting pawn of men in the oppression of women. The majority of the goddess's stories and ritual enactments are today promulgated by men. If women once created or controlled these myths and rituals, they do not do so today.

However, the potential for a female to coopt the mythology of the goddess for her own empowerment lurks close to the surface in Kerala as well. One renowned female ecstatic, known by devotees as Mata Amritanandamayi Ma or Ammachi, has done exactly this with a great deal of success. Born near Quilon in southern Kerala, Ammachi hails from a poor and tiny fishing village. Although details of her early life are not well known, Ammachi regularly performs the *Devī Bhāva*, or possession by the goddess, as a public blessing for all. The mood of the goddess in Ammachi's current Devī Bhāva performances is benign and loving, reminiscent of Pārvati and other beneficent mother goddesses. Yet, directly behind her as she performs the Devī Bhāva at her ashram in Quilon, stands a powerful black statue of Kāḷi in her full iconographic rage, as a kind of shadow inspiring the more pleasing face shown to the public. I was told by devotees that Ammachi in her youth had performed a more violent Kāḷi Bhāva, which included cutting her arms and head with a curved iron sword. In other words, Ammachi's early ecstatic experiences were apparently drawn from the female veḷiccappāṭu tradition. As she achieved greater renown, including a large coterie of Western devotees, this more violent form of divine possession was replaced with the current, glittery Devī Bhāva, complete with shiny sari and golden crown. Whatever the form, Ammachi has clearly drawn on the indigenous tradition of the Kāḷi cult in her native Kerala and moulded it to achieve her own spiritual ends as well as quite considerable stature as a world spiritual leader (see Johnson 1994).

Scholars of teyyam possession rituals in northern Kerala are fond of noting the striking status reversal the ritual entails. 'Untouchable' bonded serfs have the exclusive right to become possessed by the fierce deities known as teyyams. While in this elevated state, their high-caste landlord patrons cower and place offerings of food and money before them, touching their feet and fearfully granting their every demand. Scholars of spirit possession worldwide have called this phenomenon 'protest religion', and many fieldworkers in India have demonstrated the specific relationship between low social status and possession episodes (Gold 1988; Harper 1963; Holloman and Ashley 1983; Krygier 1982; Lewis 1989; Mencher 1964; M. Moreno 1985; Obeyesekere 1970, 1977a, 1977b, 1978; Opler 1963; Stanley 1988). The wild, anti-social behaviour of the possessed low-caste Matangi of Karnataka rituals dramatically expresses multiple hidden resentments, as Brubaker insightfully recognizes:

> In the case of the Matangi, of course, the goddess is physically present, having displaced the woman's ordinary consciousness and possessed her body. And because of this the sociological and theological aspects of personal abuse become twin dimensions of a single religious event. As a Madiga [low caste female] the Matangi exults in 'the humiliation to which she is subjecting the proud caste people', while as the goddess she exults in humiliating everyone. (Brubaker 1978: 269)

Contrary to the assertion of Bloch and others, ritual reversals are not always mere stopgap measures for temporary relief of stress (see Kapferer 1991: xi; Bloch 1974). By experiencing oneself even temporarily in a position of power, the possibility of a different structural arrangement becomes a real one (Turner 1969, 1974). In Kerala, which suffered from one of the most oppressive caste hierarchies in south Asia prior to Indian independence, a radical political and economic change took place. 'Untouchable' serfs, who once could be punished for merely approaching too close to a Brahmin, received equal allocations of land and temple access after 1957. Not only did real reversals take place in the social order, but teyyam performances became the hallmark cultural symbol of Marxist egalitarian ideology in Communist government parades.[54]

If low-caste groups perform teyyam as a form of social protest against landlords, perhaps women should play Kāḷi to empower themselves. Peter Claus (1994) discusses such a phenomenon in Karnataka, where a once all-male street performance tradition portraying the fierce goddess has recently been taken up by women. Erndl (1993), Hancock (1995), and Ram (1992) have provided other recent examples of female renegotiation of subaltern status through spirit possession. Such uses of the fierce goddess's powerful imagery are quite far from the harangues of BJP leaders Uma Bharati and Sadhvi Rithambara, which merely exhort males to genocidal violence on behalf of a benighted 'mother' India while real women continue to be raped and abused.[55] I am suggesting a form of empowerment in which women imagine themselves as psychologically independent, powerful beings who refuse to take abuse, and will fight back if necessary.

Brubaker states that 'the goddess is not a champion of women's rights, nor a symbol of their suffering and revenge. She is not the deified embodiment of female protest and self-assertion' (1978: 122). I agree wholeheartedly with Brubaker's assertion that the goddess, at least in Kerala, is no feminist. But symbols are not static archetypes. They are the creation of human beings, and as such are infinitely adaptable to human needs. The fierce goddess provides a rich store of indigenous symbols to Indian women, with which they can work out some of their real anger and imagine themselves in new ways. By the process Obeyesekere calls 'subjectification', women can recreate the goddess in their own image (as done by the female ecstatics he studied in Sri Lanka):

> In the case of females, becoming a priest is a powerful source of 'liberation'. It gives autonomy and power over others, enhanced social status, and—above all—freedom of movement, which in normal circumstances is severely curtailed for women. But the cultural bias is still very strong against the idea that a pure divine being would reside in an impure vehicle. This resistance is overcome in two ways: the claim may be

> made that the spirit possessing the individual is not actually the deity but an attendant or servitor who conveys the commands of that deity; alternatively, a female may claim that she is possessed by a *female* deity like Pattini or Kāḷi. Once the woman acquires autonomy, she can then also acquire the capacity to establish within herself the spirit of male deities. (Obeyesekere 1978: 466)

How and whether this should be done is of course for Indian women to decide. The alienation of women from this avenue of expression in Kerala is an unfortunate legacy of local history. But Malayali women, perhaps more than others in south Asia, should find it possible to reconnect with the goddess's strength (Humes1997; Pintchman 1994: 211–14). The next chapter explores the rich possibilities for progressive use of the symbolism of Bhagavati to achieve personal growth.

Excerpt from a letter home:
1 June 1992

I haven't written for a long time because a terrible tragedy hit me—hit me as hard as anything in my life—and I couldn't write anyone for a long time. The short version? I fell in love with a man named Abhilash, who is a friend of ours here. After intense struggles with our consciences, we decided to consummate our relationship. I decided to leave my husband. All hell broke loose one day at a huge temple festival when a love letter I had written fell from my clothes on the ground and Antonio found it and read it. He threatened to kill Abhilash and forbade him from coming to our house anymore. One month later Antonio flew back to the US. Our marriage is totally over. In the weeks before his departure, Antonio treated me like a prisoner, searched through and destroyed my things, and refused to allow me to go out of the house unaccompanied. Finally one night he beat me black and blue. Meanwhile my academic sponsor threatened Abhilash with arrest, various forms of blackmail, and generally made it impossible for us to see each other anymore. All my staff abandoned me. The day we left Trichur, everyone hid inside their houses. Only Omana, my cook (who everyone said was a thief and a prostitute), touched my bruised cheek gently when she saw it and wished me luck, her eyes full of compassionate tears.

So on April 1st I moved with little Sofia to an enormous new house in a new town, with no husband, no research assistant, no child-care assistance, no cook, unable to speak Malayalam sufficiently to manage on my own, terrified, in shock, vulnerable. Still, it was the height of the performance season that week and I had to attend three or four all-night performances, direct video shooting, and be on the ball. Somehow the work went on.

Abhilash and I did manage to see each other again, but we are afraid of repercussions. We travel together under cover and are trying to figure out what to do. My understanding of Kāḷi has become intensely personal. After this trouble, it seems as if each day new and amazing things are being revealed in my interviews with the artists. It was as if the goddess exacted a sacrifice from us in order to test and teach me; but that experience is comparable to no pain I've ever known.

Notes

[1] *Hospital* erroneously refers to the system as 'matriarchal', a term that implies female juridical and political authority. Matriliny, by contrast, indicates only kin relation and the inheritance of property exclusively through the female line. In a matrilineal system, sons obey and inherit from their mother's brothers rather than their fathers, but neither inheritance directly from mother to daughter nor female household authority is necessarily implied by this term. For ethnographic description of Kerala's matrilineal social organization, see chapter 1. For studies of Nāyar society see Abraham 1965; Dumont 1961; Fawcett 1901; C. J. Fuller 1975, 1976, 1986; Gough 1952b, 1959a, 1959b, 1961, 1965a; Jeffrey 1976; Lawrence 1976; Mencher 1962, 1965; S. Menon 1996; Moore 1985, 1988; Nakane 1963; Panikkar 1918; Raman Unni 1956; Unnithan 1974.

[2] Nambūtiri Brahmin women are an exception. Until the present generation, Brahmin women were not allowed to receive education or to leave the house. Today they have much more freedom of movement and education, sometimes taking leadership roles in public life.

[3] In some royal families, however, exclusive mother–daughter inheritance was practised. See interview with Koratty Pakkattil family, below.

[4] Exposure of the upper body was traditionally considered a sign of respect. Even today men must remove their shirts before entering certain Hindu temples in Kerala. Today this traditional practice survives only in temples and villages. Western dress patterns, in which the upper body must be covered by both males and females as a sign of modesty, have prevailed in public life since the 1950s. Village men may walk bare-chested in their house compound, but don shirts to ride the bus, go to the bank, or attend public functions.

[5] Ram 1992 comments on the binding symbolism of the sari; in light of her comments, this change in dress reflects increasing control by men, not liberation from it.

[6] This prohibition varies according to age and status: thus a younger, higher-status female is more subject to these taboos than an older or lower-status one, who apparently has less to protect. For example, the 29-year-old unmarried

Christian woman who cared for my daughter while I worked preferred to stay overnight at our home than to leave after 6 p.m. She told me she could not return home so late because 'people would talk'. Her staying the night with our family could presumably be explained as a necessity of her employment, though walking alone after dark could not.

[7] Women, by contrast, are expected to cover the body from neck to toes at all times. When at home, women normally wear either sari or 'nightie', full-length house-dress over an ankle-length slip. Of late, young girls may also wear the north Indian *kurta pyjama* or *salwar kameez* set. In any case, the body must be covered to the floor at all times. Delayed sexual relations, seclusion of women who previously enjoyed more freedom, and increased prudery in dress appear to be attempts to raise social status through imitations of the customs of both north Indian high castes and the Victorian English. Although further ethnographic and historical research is necessary, it seems likely that the current seclusion and prohibitions on the behaviour of even Nāyar and Ezhava unmarried women (many of whom previously had more freedom in such matters) is a form of Sanskritization, gaining status by emulating the earlier brahminical custom of strictly secluding Nambūtiri women. See Yalman 1963. This phenomenon may also be observed in upper-class Muslim and Christian homes in Kerala. For a discussion of the effects of Sanskritization on women's lives, see Berreman 1993; McGilvray 1988; Obeyesekere 1984; Srinivas 1956.

[8] Obviously men also would be subject to the same psychological pressures, but the modest dress and demeanour of females, and the freer social atmosphere for young men, perhaps make these pressures somewhat less onerous than they are for women.

[9] Others just looked embarrassed and changed the subject. Although I have no reliable statistics on the matter, most Kerala women I talked to even in the United States agree that young women do not generally discuss sexual matters, especially sexual problems, even among themselves. Young brides living amongst their in-laws are even less likely to reveal their feelings on such matters to their affinal kin. Sexual worries and dissatisfactions therefore often are expressed in terms of physical complaints, which may be confided to female affines and treated medically without shame (in fact, they are an acceptable way of getting out of onerous household chores and of garnering the attention of superiors). It may be that the young women who openly voiced complaints to me perceived in me a non-threatening ally and representative of 'Western' values.

[10] Laji, knowing I was interested in experiencing village women's daily routine, arranged for me to stay for two weeks with the family of his friend Rajiv, who spoke English well.

[11] See discussion of kurava, chapters 1 and 2.

[12] Interview, Trichur, Kerala, January 1992. This woman began to weep copiously as she recounted her life-story to me through a female translator.

Her story focused on a series of losses, starting with the deaths of her father and brother, and ending with her marriage. Her open expression of grief in our private conversation contrasted strongly with her composed, controlled demeanour every time I met her in the company of her husband.

[13] Appu Kuttan Mārār, Interview, Muvattupuzha, Kerala, May 1992.

[14] Interview, Alwaye, Kerala, January 1992.

[15] Interview in Malayalam and English, Trichur, Kerala, January 1992. Recently a sixty-year-old woman of the Kaimal caste (a high Nāyar caste) living in the US told me that women could not watch muṭiyēṯṯu at all in the 1940s. Although she hailed from a town where muṭiyēṯṯu was performed, and although the men of her family attended every year, this woman had never seen a performance. She asked me eagerly if she could watch my videos of muṭiyēṯṯu, taken in her home-town.

[16] Similar sentiments are voiced in Mrinal Pande's short story 'Girls' 1990.

[17] This is probably because these are not the only relevant factors in marriage choice; a girl's behaviour, reputation, wealth, education, and family social standing are equally important to her success in finding a mate. Once she is married, it is considered immodest for a woman to be overly concerned with her appearance.

[18] This was in striking contrast to the material collected (from men) in Tamil Nadu by Daniel 1984.

[19] Interview, Koratty, Kerala, February 1992.

[20] Obeyesekere has traced a similar process of historical 'masculinization' of the goddess's cult in Sri Lanka, although recently women ascetics and ritualists have begun to proliferate again 1977b, 1978.

[21] Obeyesekere refers to this as the Vasurimala (smallpox goddess) shrine, apparently basing his account on Induchudan 1969. He states that the priestesses of the Vasurimala temple are Nāyar women 1984: 536.

[22] Peeping at bathing women is an erotic preoccupation in Kerala (and, from anecdotes I have heard, perhaps throughout India) and is a rich area for research. One young man told me of the masturbation sessions he had shared with other teenage boys while peeping at girls in this way in a school hostel setting. Many men expressed the belief that women masturbate while bathing (as men do themselves—the bathroom being perhaps the only private place available). Bathing scenes in which young women appear in various states of Onanistic ecstasy are ubiquitous in Malayali feature films. Countless photographs and letters to the editor of *Debonair* magazine (a *Playboy* clone published from Bombay) reiterate the theme. Novels set in feudal Kerala often depict a lovelorn boy following the object of his affections to the bathing-tank and spying on her during her bath. It is notable that the Kurumba tribes of Palghat region have a tradition of men choosing their wives on the night of Śivaratri by observing them swimming naked in the river. Each man chooses the woman who appeals to him and woos her. (Personal communication,

Palghat tribal officer and anthropologist, May 1992.) The erotic associations of bathing and water are also eloquently explored in Ramakrishnan 1989, translated at the end of chapter 7.

[23] Distinctions between divine and demonic possession are made in nearly all South Asian languages. See Gold 1988; Schoembucher 1993; Stanley 1988; Wadley 1976.

[24] As in other areas of India, mental imbalance is traditionally believed to be a sign of possession by an evil spirit, either male or female; but, significantly, not by Kāḷi or any other dēva (divine being). Exorcism is the remedy. Few individuals in Kerala utilize modern clinical psychiatry, which still carries a heavy social stigma. However, a common medical disorder treated at psychiatric clinics is the Victorian malady 'hysteria', the symptoms of which closely resemble spirit possession. Hysteria is considered to be a disease almost exclusive to women. Dr Jagadambika of Alwaye, a practising psychiatrist, noted the intimate relationship of hysteria symptoms and sexual dysfunction (personal communication, November 1992). Her patients described the same feelings of inner heat, trembling, and rage that typify the inner experience of possession reported by actors performing muṭiyēṯṯu.

[25] The word we have translated as 'broad' is '*ammayi* [lit. 'aunt']' used in a slang sense to mean a voluptuous, sexy, mature woman.

[26] E. Kalidasan, personal communication, November 1991.

[27] Freed and Freed 1964, 1985, Obeyesekere 1970, 1977a, 1981; summarized and critiqued by Castillo 1994b.

[28] However, see Boddy's 1989 objection to the 'status deprivation' theory; also Sered 1994.

[29] The tāli or wedlock is a necklace (once string, now gold chain) tied around the neck of the bride by the groom. Tāli-tying rites were distinct from rituals celebrating a girl's first menstruation (puberty rites). For description of puberty rites, see Krishna Iyer 1905–1907, 1909–12, 1928–36, 1937–41; Aiyappan 1972, Thankappan Nair 1976.

[30] Particularly Kakar 1978, Carstairs 1958. Kondos notes the 'isolation of the erotic impulse as a paternal proclivity' directed towards his daughter 1986: 195; this eroticism between father and daughter is also acknowledged by M. Roy 1975, who, however, feels that it remains in a repressed, sublimated state throughout the lives of both parties.

[31] See Masson 1984, introduction.

[32] Interview, Chengannur, Kerala, August 1992.

[33] I am by no means suggesting that the only purpose of social structure is to fulfil unconscious fantasy. But while exhaustive studies have been done on the economic, political, and cognitive functions of kinship organization, few have considered the psychological motivations of social structure (Trawick 1990b is a notable exception). As Chodorow and Sprengnether have pointed out, we need a 'psychology of patriarchy'. See Chodorow 1989; Sprengnether 1990. It is from this perspective that the present comments are offered.

[34] See Caldwell 1995: 513–17 for a general discussion of incest in India; Castelino 1985 is a recent sociological study.

[35] This has not been the case statistically in clinical studies conducted in Europe and America, at least so far. It is possible that sexual abuse of boys by women may be more prevalent in the particular social circumstances of south Asia.

[36] This stereotype is vividly encountered in the tales analysed by Vatuk and Vatuk 1975.

[37] *Debonair* magazine is filled with anxious confessional letters to the advice columnist about such episodes. There are rich data here (even if only fantasied) for psychological research.

[38] In addition to the rich materials on peeping (see n. 22) and bus-sex (rubbing genitals against women's backs and squeezing their breasts in crowded buses—see Kakar [1990] for a similar account), I also collected interesting material on bestiality. Sex with domestic and farm animals is a common practice, admitted to by several people and confirmed by gynaecologist Mary Mohan, who commented that 'bestiality is practised before marriage both by men and women' (Personal communication, 1994). Obscene folklore frequently refers to husbandless women resorting to being 'fucked by a dog' (see Bharani songs, chapter 4); one young man admitted to being fellated by a dog; and women were said to keep cats for sexual purposes (see chapter 4, n. 35). I never obtained any such admissions of sexual behaviour from women, who I am told don't even share this information with each other. However, homoerotic gratification among unmarried girls, as among boys, is reputed to be very common in college hostels. These anecdotal materials suggest that the societal repression of sex does not result in innocence, but only alternative taboo sexual behaviour that continues to feed back into fantasy.

[39] The fact that nearly half of the women presented in several American psychiatric clinics were found to have a definite history of child sexual abuse suggests that such a connection should always be investigated Ryan-Blaney 1989: 29–30.

[40] See Obeyesekere 1963 for similar symptoms.

[41] This is not to suggest that childhood sexual abuse is the only possible etiology for spirit possession, which has many other metaphorical and spiritual meanings. Only detailed study of individuals who become possessed can shed sufficient light upon this hypothesis to prove or disprove it.

[42] See Obeyesekere 1981 for the definition of personal symbols.

[43] Freud clearly states in, p. 168, n. 1 that by 1924 he completely rejected this hypothesis. However it is so salient and accurate from our current perspective, that Freud's remarks here bear careful rereading, despite his later re-evaluation of this early position.

[44] See Berreman 1962 for the concept of the 'backstage' in ethnographic encounter.

[45] Obeyesekere makes a similar suggestion about Abdin in *Medusa's Hair* (1981).

[46] Krishna Iyer 1981 discusses the cure by beating practised in exorcistic treatments of possessed women.

[47] See Thimmaiah and Sharma (1978) for a similar study in Karnataka.

[48] Brubaker suggests that the female's wrath and heat are sexually arousing to the male. See also Gregor's 1990 study of the psychology of rape, which again suggests sado-masochistic drives.

[49] Appu Kuttan Mārār, Interview, Muvattupuzha, Kerala, May 1992. In this context Appu Kuttan was discussing Bhadrakāḷi's role in conquering yakṣis who disturb people. While this would seem to structurally oppose Bhadrakāḷi and the yakṣi, other stories I collected made it clear that they are isomorphic. In another version, for example, the yakṣi eats her victims and hangs their bloody corpses from the trees in the morning like flowers, as Kāḷi is said to do in some versions of the Dārikavadham story.

[50] In Kerala kinship structure, this would make Dārika Śiva's son-in-law, but also his brother-in-law (in the case of matrilateral uncle-niece marriage). Kāḷi marries her uncle; her father thus becomes her brother-in-law; her son becomes her classificatory 'brother' as he is also her uncle's son. In this way incestuous desire is fulfilled by displacement on to legitimate partners (cf. Obeyesekere's discussion of Trobriand Oedipal complex, 1990, chapter 2).

[51] Sometimes she steps on him—an act of unimaginable disrespect and debasement. When P. Narayana Mārār told this part of the story, he uttered 'ugh', with an expression of disgust.

[52] Once again, the third eye appears as an overheated vagina; Brubaker interprets the male fear of the goddess's third eye as 'a fear of woman as sexually voracious (even incestuously voracious)' (1978: 144).

[53] A folk-tale of the Koya people reported in Elwin (1949) reiterates this theme: a man saw a woman 'sitting with her legs stretched out and he saw her thing and liked it.' Afraid that she would refuse his advances, he sent his long penis out through a hole in a fence, and 'the woman cut off the penis with a sickle' (Elwin 1949: 260). Similar motivations came to light in the sensational castration case of the Bobbitts in the US in 1993 Kahn 1993; Masters 1993; and in the autobiography of Phoolan Devi 1996.

[54] Ashley 1993; Holloman and Ashley 1983; Freeman 1991. This is not to say that they caused the revolution, but merely that they kept the undercurrent of protest alive.

[55] See Bacchetta 1993 and McKean 1996 for discussion of the role of the goddess in Hindu nationalist women's rhetoric.

6

Transformation Through Theatre

At a talk I gave to a group interested in folk theatre in Madras in 1992, several audience members, familiar with folklore and theatre studies, vehemently objected to my use of the word 'performance' to describe muṭiyēṯṯu. While they would have no problem classifying Kathakaḷi, Kūṭiyāṭṭam, or Bhārata nāṭyam (all classical dance-dramas with a religious basis) as 'performances', these south Indians place an art form like muṭiyēṯṯu in quite another category. Because the deity is *really present*, and the agency which enables the rite to take place effectively is divine, not human, such rituals could never be in the same category as mere 'performances'.

A similar distinction was made by E. Kalidasan, a troupe leader of tiṟayāṭṭam, a folk drama form of northern Kerala: 'this is the main difference between [art forms such as] teyyam or muṭiyēṯṯu and tiṟayāṭṭam. The god shouldn't really come in tiṟayāṭṭam—it is just acting.'[1] Yet watching Kalidasan's troupe perform the *kolam* (character) of Naga Kāḷi, complete with apparently 'acted' possession, I was hard put to distinguish any difference between this 'performance' and the nearly identical behaviour of the Kāḷi-possessed actor in muṭiyēṯṯu. Furthermore, the tiṟayāṭṭam performance included rituals at a temporary 'shrine' built out of banana stalks for the occasion, the presence of a komaran or oracle (similar to the veḷiccappāṭu), and the use of fire-torches to control the furious energy of the 'possessed' actors. At the end of the performance (I think rightly so called here) the actors smeared themselves with black sandalwood tar and ashes, running madly about as if dashing to death in the forest beyond. These actions had a powerful emotional effect on the spectators, some of whom (mostly women and children) looked frightened, others of whom (men) joined madly in the mêlée of tar-smearing and wild dancing.

For everyone the event, performed in the pitch darkness of a Kerala night in a dried paddy field, seemed to be a window into the uncanny world of powerful spiritual energies. Yet the performers themselves could draw a clear line between the nature of this 'performance' and muṭiyēṯṯu.

The problem of possible dissonances between intent and effect is for south Indians the crucial marker distinguishing ritual from theatre. Although theatrical artifice may be so great as to impart a 'true' spiritual experience to the spectator in a consciously 'performed' setting, the fundamental goal of the performance is still primarily aesthetic, and relatively mundane. On the other hand, a particular enactment of a ritual may appear relatively weak from an aesthetic point of view—the actor playing Kāḷi may not have been particularly emotionally riveting, he may have danced without much energy or technique; there may have been very few drummers; no spectators may have been present—but the ritual efficacy of the performance is not diminished so long as the artist's mental attitude remains impeccable. It is the attention to ritual exactitude and the conscious surrendering of action to the will of the deity which marks such a performance as non-theatre in the Western sense.[2]

Such ontological distinctions have not always been present in traditional theatre forms, including ancient Sanskrit drama. The *Nātya Śāstra* makes clear the spiritual basis of all performing arts, which were seen as inextricably linked both with each other and with *brahman*, the transcendental source of all consciousness and action (*Nātya Śāstra* 1987; Richmond, Swann, and Zarrilli 1990). The purpose of all classical Sanskritic art forms, including music, visual art, dance, drama, and poetry, was so to captivate the mind of the sensitive appreciator (*rasika*) that it would naturally be drawn deep into its divine source and experience transcendental bliss. Art was thus a form of meditation. This sensibility is quite different from the earthy ecstatic religion which underlies dramatic art forms like muṭiyēṯṯu. As Hardy states, there was essentially no concept of transcendence in the religion of the Sangam period; and even today the majority of south Indian folk Hindu practice reflects a love of immanence. For historical reasons we have traced in chapter 1, upper-caste Kerala arts including muṭiyēṭṭu combined features of the Sanskrit theatre with ritual arts whose essential features were possession and blood-sacrifice. Perhaps the strict distinction south Indians draw between theatre and ritual stems in part from this dual heritage. For these audiences, the transcendent concepts of Sanskritic theatre seem to produce a relatively abstract and somewhat artificial form of performance, while the immediacy of possession and sacrifice remains the only true proof of divine immanence for the devotees of the goddess in Kerala.

Performance theorists over the last two decades have examined the shared terrain of ritual and theatre in a variety of cultures, seeing these as different 'magnitudes' of performance which can alternately *transport* and *transform* both actors and audiences (Schechner 1977, 1990). While distinguishing between the *transportative* effects of theatre, which are essentially temporary cognitive states; and the *transformative* effects of ritual, which effect permanent ontological changes in the being of participants, these theorists see grounds for overlap in the two genres. Moreover, performance theory recognizes the importance of non-verbal, somatic behaviour in the creation of the transportative/transformative experience. Schechner in particular has developed an elegant brand of performance theory which engages the specifics of non-verbal performance structures and their cognitive effects. In Schechner and Appel (1990), these insights are applied in diverse cross-cultural contexts, in an attempt to tease out the 'kinesthetic basis of knowledge' underlying ritual, dance, and theatre. As in these art forms, muṭiyēṯṯu's transformative power to evoke, present, exorcize, bless, and heal, as well as its transportative power to entertain and amaze are embedded in the ritual's elaborate non-verbal structure.

By contrast, a number of important studies of the transformative power of ritual—its ability to effect an ontological change in the state of participants—focus on language. Tambiah (1979) and Bloch (1974) made important early contributions to this debate, felicitously exploiting Austin's concept of linguistic performatives as words that do things rather than merely signify.[3] In fact, these authors noted that ritual language is often characterized by incomprehensibility, archaism, and ungrammatical formal features which logically deter their meaningfulness as discourse (see Staal 1989). Tambiah and Staal use a semiotic approach, reinterpreting the function of ritual language as 'metalinguistic', closer to music or mathematics as 'pure activities'. Bloch chooses to see in ritual language a form of mystification and political manipulation. Despite their differences, all of these interpretations conclude that ritual language functions for the most part as a non-verbal semiotic element embedded in a total performative code. As such, ritual language is not merely denotative or discursive, but depends for its full meaning on the connotative, contextual cues of sight, sound, touch, smell, and hearing provided by the entire performance (Langer 1979).

In muṭiyēṯṯu, linguistic utterances make up a small portion of the total performance content. Out of five or six hours that the drama lasts, no more than a total of ninety minutes consists of singing or speaking. Except for Kūḷi's comic improvisation, these songs and speeches are strictly memorized.[4] The language used ranges from the incomprehensible to the colloquial. In general, the language of the more 'sacred' contexts is Sanskrit or Maṇipravāḷam; the 'comic' portions employ more or less colloquial, modern Malayalam.[5] This elaborate changing of linguistic registers, while typical of ritual language worldwide, triggers specific cultural cues in the south Indian context which have been examined in detail elsewhere (Blackburn 1988 Freeman 1991).

Language, then, is not the only or even the primary semiotic element of muṭiyēṯṯu. In the ten to twelve hours preceding muṭiyēṭṭu proper, a series of artistic and musical performances prepare the temple and the artists for the powerful rites to be performed after midnight (these preliminaries consist of the drawing of the kaḷam, songs of praise, and drumming performances described in detail in chapter 2). Once muṭiyēṯṯu begins, non-verbal expressive forms predominate in the performance. **Music** (specifically drumming and singing), **body movement**, **costume**, and **use of light** are the four most important elements invoking the energy of possession and making the rite effective. It is through the proper manipulation of these non-verbal elements that the goddess comes, receives the sacrifice, and is pleased.

Throughout almost the entire five or six hours of the performance, loud and relentless drumming can be heard. Only during the two comic scenes (Kōyimbaṭa Nāyar's and Kūḷi's scenes) are the drums relatively silent, used only to punctuate the dialogue. The drums embody spiritual energies essential to the ritual effectiveness of the performance. Even Kāḷi bows to the drums upon entering the stage, taking blessings from the musicians, the real holders of spiritual power (Hart 1975). A particular rhythm (triputa tāḷam) signals the onset of the possession. The musicians furiously play this rhythm when Kāḷi's head-dress begins to slip and she lowers it, seemingly uncontrollably, towards the drums. The actor loses consciousness and has to be helped to his seat on the small stool before the stage lamp.

The total environment of sound, light, and movement has a powerful effect on both actors and spectators. Balakrishnan Mārar explained his experience of possession at this time:

> It is the total sound around and also the circumstances—the drumming, sounds made by people, kurava [ululation of women], and so on. While we go around the temple, this drumming, hooting, and flaring up of fireballs all together make a big sound. At that time we are in the war. Then there is a heavy fight with Dārika. At first we will feel some weakness. Then a sudden change comes. Some power comes into us without our knowing.[6]

Not only sound, but also the play of darkness and light strongly affect the mood of the performance. Although nowadays artificial lighting is often used, the original lighting of muṭiyēṯṯu consists of nothing but the stage lamp and the torches flaring with the greenish light of the teḷḷi powder. The audience sits on the dark borders of the stage, and the actors' glittering costumes and make-up are illuminated by the firelight. The visual effect of the flickering light on the fantastic make-up and muṭi is quite other-worldly. As Choondal remarks:

> It is darkness and light that create the world of colour on the stage. Darkness has as much ability to project mood as light, and light has it in the same measure as darkness. What are the colours of darkness and light? In the depiction of moods, only these two, which have natural power, are relevant. (1981: 155–6)

It is difficult for urban Americans to imagine what it is like to be in a natural environment at night in utter darkness, with no illumination save fire. The central Kerala countryside is thickly forested, and in the night when the electric power fails (as it frequently does), one can sense the intense liveliness of the plants and animals, and one's own vulnerability. Dogs howl eerily in the moonlight, snakes emerge from their holes underground, and no one ventures outside. Pazhur Damodaran Mārar explained that this terror-inducing darkness is one reason the performance always takes place at midnight:

> It is at that time that the war between Kāḷi and Dārika really took place. The terror of this war cannot be conceived by ordinary people. So this

is the appropriate time—in Malayalam time, after the night has passed some 7½ *nāḻikas* until 7½ *nāḻikas* in the dawn.[7] To show the terror of the war it is done at the same time.

Through this complex mélange of gestures, sights, sounds, smells, tastes, and touches, the audience is transported but also transformed. The village which sponsors the rite undergoes a kind of 'corporate possession, for normal patterns of life are suddenly thrust aside and the village is inundated by a wild raging energy ... the festival is an ecstatic experience of the living goddess, plunging her people into the dark, defiling, dangerous dynamism of life, that they may partake of its power' (Brubaker 1978: 288). The festival and rituals of which muṭiyēṯṯu forms the core are truly theatre and truly ritual in every sense of the words.

Brubaker focuses on the role of 'self-affliction' in south Indian village-goddess worship to effect both psychological and spiritual transformation in devotees. For Brubaker, self-affliction rites, which voluntarily inflict pain, humiliation, or suffering upon devotees, are the essential experience of the goddess's ambivalent power. This power is essentially female and pertains to both sexuality (hence fertility, the generation of life) and death. It is simultaneously dangerous and liberating.

> Our inquiry into self-affliction practices showed devotion to the goddess plunging one into the midst of danger, anxiety, and the stark contingencies of life. Deep and intense ambivalence appears at every turn. But it is the kind of ambivalence that yields ecstasy. This is perhaps easiest to see and understand in the experience of self-affliction, where courting danger gives life new intensity and where fear can be transformed into rapture. (ibid.: 287–8)

It is easy to see how such transformation through self-affliction is possible for the muṭiyēṯṯu actors, especially the actor who plays Kāḷi. The artists who perform muṭiyēṯṯu must endure gruelling heat, weight, hunger, and exhaustion during the long midnight hours of their offering, for very minimal pay. They must dedicate their entire lives to their art form, often at the expense of their family's financial security. As one senior performer told me, 'No one thinks about what we suffer. They simply come and watch the performance and go home. Only we know what it is to live for this art.'

Suffering and anger are themes which constantly arise in the actors' statements about their inner experience during the enactment of Kāḷi. But a deep devotional sense also pervades their experience. The performance of muṭiyēṯṯu and related art forms is a divine offering, not an entertainment. Its primary purpose is to please and appease Bhagavati; the reaction of the spectators is, in theory, irrelevant. Yet, the special circumstances under which the drama is performed ideally lead actors and audience together to a heightened devotional state which transforms the actors' consciousness. One veteran, who has played the part of Kāḷi twenty to thirty times annually for over forty-five years, described his inner experience of this transformation:

> After the entrance of Kāḷi, during the war [with Dārika], we find it difficult to control ourselves. We feel lots of special energy in our mind and body. At that time we are in the war. At first we will feel some weakness. I'm telling you my experience. After this, a sudden change comes. Without our knowing, some power comes into us. At this time, all the audience will be concentrating on us, with great faith in their hearts. So when all these people are looking at us, that same divine power gets into us. We as well as they get totally immersed in it. When there is this divine power everywhere, everyone including us gets totally mixed up in the divine power of God.[8]

The ability to transform personal suffering into spiritual experience is a significant feature of ritual performances throughout the world, whether overtly dramatic in form or simply private meditation and prayer. Victor Turner noted that the symbolic structures provided by culturally sanctioned rituals allow an 'intensity of subjective states that is part of "transformation". It also includes the collective dimension, ... indicating that profound, subjunctive [sic] experiences may occur not only within isolated individuals but may be expanded to involve small groups and even communities' (Myerhoff 1990: 248). Drama itself, by allowing an individual to act 'in between identities', to use Schechner's phrase, is a prototypically liminal form of symbolic behaviour. By making room within one's own body for the consciousness of another, as in the possession performance of muṭiyēṯṯu, the actor expands his own psychological repertoire and experiences the intense physical infusion of energy and its release required by the ritual. This process, in both actor and audience, was known to the ancient Greeks as 'catharsis', a term which we now use loosely in English to refer to any intense release of pent-up emotion.

I suggested in the previous chapters that muṭiyēṯṯu actors who are particularly talented at playing the role of Kāḷi might be traumatized individuals whose particular psychological propensities and histories compel them towards this form of performance. Obeyesekere has suggested a felicitous distinction between *progressive* and *regressive* orientation in ritual enactments of this sort, and he provides a detailed analysis of the difference between individuals of both types (1990: 3–68). In short, his theory is that some individuals may be able to transform their traumas by means of available cultural symbols into authentic religious experience which liberates them in a manner analogous to a psychoanalytic cure (ibid.: 21–4). Kripal's recent study of the nineteenth century mystic Ramakrishna suggests that just such a progressive orientation allowed the saint to make use of severe psychological debilities in such a way that thousands of people were spiritually transformed by contact with him (Kripal 1995).

Of course not all individuals have such a 'progressive' orientation; many are condemned to compulsive, regressive reenactments of trauma in masochistic rituals of self-torture and expiation (see Obeyesekere 1990: 14). Without further detailed study of the life-histories of each of the individual muṭiyēṯṯu actors playing the role of Kāḷi, we cannot identify which of these two orientations is experienced in individual possession performances. However, the statements of actors imply that a progressive orientation is possible, indeed even the goal of the performance, which is deeply physical in its transformative power. This progressive orientation may be another factor in the south Indian distinction between rituals like muṭiyēṯṯu and mere 'performances'; the effective, ontologically and psychologically transformative power of ritual as opposed to the mere cathartic (hence regressive) function of drama is emphasized by such a distinction.

If some muṭiyēṯṯu actors experience transformation of a progressive sort, what can we assert about the experience of the audience? We identified a variety of audience responses to muṭiyēṯṯu, not all of which are synchronous with the 'total immersion in divine power' idealistically asserted by the troupe leader above. Obeyesekere notes this variety in audience response to collective representations like muṭiyēṯṯu, whose rigidly traditional form is not easily susceptible to individual modification: 'The audience at best identifies with the action; at worst they ignore it and go to sleep. The symbol is not and cannot be integrated into the life history of the individual' (Obeyesekere 1990: 25). But this is not to say that the ritual drama is therefore personally meaningless. On the contrary, depending on the degree of fit between the details of the drama unfolding in the ritual arena and specific personal experiences in a spectator's own history, the effect can be quite overpowering. Though audience responses may vary widely due to individual, private, even secret personal factors, belief in the 'truth value of the experience' offered by the ritual is felt by people who share the same belief system (ibid.: 26). In this sense Brubaker is right in asserting that these rituals are a kind of group catharsis; or to use Obeyesekere's more refined terminology, possibly even provide an opportunity for group transformation through their progressive effect on particular individuals.

One way that muṭiyēṯṯu accommodates these varied levels of individual response is through the incorporation of both serious and comic scenes. Troupe leaders frequently disparage the comic Kūḷi scene as a historically recent addition, not essential to muṭiyēṯṯu's structure. Although none of them could explain precisely when or how this scene came to be part of muṭiyēṯṯu, they grudgingly admitted it had gained in popularity and therefore had to be expanded in recent years to encourage audience attendance at the rituals. Whatever the origin of the comical Kūḷi scene and the Kōyimbaṭa Nāyar dialogue, comedic breaks characterized by dialogic *double-entendres*, obscenity and satire are deeply ingrained features of south Indian and Sri Lankan folk drama.[9] Kapferer identifies these portions as essential to the invoking of demonic forces, who are by nature lewd, sensual, and low-minded. In the exorcistic dramas of Sri Lanka which Kapferer studied, such comic scenes were necessary to entice demons to the ritual arena where they could then be trapped and neutralized (1991: 285-319).

Obeyesekere, analysing similar dramatic rituals in Sri Lanka, typifies the comic portions as 'cathartic rituals' in the sense of ancient Greek drama. Vulgar cathartic rituals 'that parody the numinous give a more direct expression to the anxieties that dominate the people' than the 'solemn, stately ritual' which characterizes worship of the goddess in both Sri Lanka and Kerala. These more serious and numinous ritual performances Obeyesekere calls *dromena*, from the Greek. Catharses lie close to the emotive core that motivates them, and only thinly disguise it. Much folklore fits into this category. By contrast, dromena, and 'high art' in general, are further symbolically removed from unconscious conflicts, bringing 'the psychological problems of the group ... under fine ego and cognitive controls'. Embodying cultural, religious, and philosophical values developed over long historical periods, dromena bring psychological problems 'in line with higher cultural values and [give them] idealistic representation' (1990: 27). In this sense they are progressive, allowing the transformation of personal traumas and difficult issues into meaningful forms which in turn are connected to larger religious, historical, and philosophical realities. Indeed this 'processing' of trauma through shared symbolization and expression is a fundamental form of healing common to most shamanic and even psychoanalytic forms of treatment (Cunningham and Tickner 1981).

According to Obeyesekere's model, the alternating serious and comic portions of muṭiyēṯṯu may be seen as significant variations on similar themes, each of which speaks to particular groups in the audience, enabling them to relate meaningfully to the activities of the ritual. The juxtaposition of serious and comic treatments of the same theme may also be seen as a kind of framing device (Kapferer 1991). This framing provokes cognitive distance and reflection, an essential feature of drama which makes it an authentic form of abstract thought, as well as of immediate experience.[10] Thus 'that which is camouflaged in the dromenon is laid bare in the cathartic rituals' and on some level at least, the theme is not only experienced emotively, but understood and interpreted as well. In this way dramatic rituals embedded in a shared belief system are able to transform and provide a progressive resolution of problems for some audience members. Others, bored by the dromena, and enjoying only the slapstick of the cathartic rituals, may remain in a more regressive mode (Obeyesekere 1990: 28). The unique dual structure of south Indian ritual dramas provides both possibilities.

Although ideally muṭiyēṯṯu thus provides ample scope for personal reflection, catharsis, and progressive spiritual transformation, in actuality the range of audience response tends to be somewhat delimited along gender lines in Kerala. While troupe members claim to experience deep spiritual ecstasy during the performance, and many members of the audience of both sexes appear entranced as they watch it, women in the audience observing muṭiyēṯṯu mostly expressed fear and anxiety during the dromena of muṭiyēṯṯu, though they laughed cautiously at the antics of Kūḷi in the comic scenes. No woman admitted to identifying in any way with Bhadrakāḷi. This does not necessarily mean that no women experience such an identification, but only that *they do not feel it is acceptable to do so*. They are not consciously able to integrate any socially taboo feelings they may experience, such as sexual desire and anger towards men. When such emotions become intolerable, as we have seen, women resort to dissociative behaviours like unconsciousness and demonic possession in the idiom of bādhā. Spiritual elation or cathartic liberation were not in the conscious repertoire of any young women I interviewed. It is noteworthy, however, that some older, post-menopausal women of high caste (Nāyar or Kṣatriya) did seem to have a somewhat stronger, though still disguised, positive identification with the ritual figure of Kāḷi. This is likely due to their social standing as respected elder members of an elite matrilineal social group. Past childbearing, financially secure, often widowed, such women were relatively independent and could more openly acknowledge their desire for freedom from male dominance.

But even these mature women can never take up the role of Bhadrakāḷi and know what it is like to wield the iron sword, to whoop and run after men, threatening to kill them for their wrongs. Aside from exceptional individuals such as Ammachi (see end of chapter 5) who radically reject their ordinary social roles, the majority of women in Kerala are thus denied a clear progressive orientation in Hindu high-caste ritual worship of the goddess. There are no female ecstatics or priests leading worship at the major Bhagavati temples of Kerala, although we have traced historical evidence that such phenomena occurred in the past. Yet I have suggested that Kerala women *could* theoretically make use of these progressive symbols and work out their own traumas through identification with Kāḷi. As I sat through night after night of muṭiyēṯṯu and countless other Bhagavati rituals over several months, without my intent these powerful symbols began to work on my own consciousness, wreaking a transformation in my life I could never have imagined possible.

Diary entry: 21 March 1992. Kovalam Beach, Kerala.

It's early morning and the waves are breaking on the pale shore below my balcony. The soft fringes of a coconut palm sway slightly in the morning breeze. I feel this palm accompanying me here is goddess Bhadrakāḷi, but newly in her loving form. At first I could only see her fierceness and cruelty. I identified with her anger and her wildness. I wanted to hurt someone, when I faced the abuse by my uncles—wanted to castrate them, cut off their heads and hold them high, the fresh red blood pouring out into a golden bowl so no more demon men might be born. Astride her father/husband, who is inert, loving her yet powerless except through her, she ejects her red tongue fearlessly, her garland of skulls clacking, her firm, high breasts with nipples pointed and dangerous as on a tantric shield of Kaḷaripayaṯṯ. Her deep blue skin, almost black, glistens with the light of self-realization, the eternal shining through her like the night sky with its stars. Her counterpart, surprisingly, is Krishna, the dark lord of disorderly love, night, time and destruction. Not the lovely baby or the archer Arjuna's guide, but something deeper, more primitive—a forest youth with smooth skin and enchanting eyes. They make an odd pair, like a mother and a son, different manifestations of the dark: she the midnight and he the early dawn, she the heart of darkness and he the promise of morning, she the tiger and he the peacock. They walk together into the dark forest and lie in a wild embrace secretly. This is forbidden, but a great love is born. A love that will destroy but also give birth to something unexpected and great. Is there a seed growing inside her? She does not know. But when she whispers his name there is a stirring deep in her bowels, an answering motion, a ripple in a pond which contains a wave.

The waves are relentless, blue, peaceful yet full of power. In the silence between their falling, as they draw back into their source, is the space between the breaths, a potent stillness. The waves cease for no one, and nothing can remain on the shore but is gathered into them and back to the deep.

Why do we cling to what is? There is a force inside, or maybe outside, a force drawing this karma on. I never thought it could happen this way. I was so certain my marriage would last forever, that I could sit in it as in a lovely boat, safe from the waves, cuddled like a baby in her father's arms, oblivious to everything, just wanting to be held. But there is a force, as inevitable as the waves, whose voice is repeating clear and still inside, 'Let this go ...'

How could I be called upon to cause such pain? Kāḷi wouldn't blink to sever the head—but I am full of remorse and sadness, bewildered. My mind can't grasp it at all—and there is no one to clarify it for us. When I close my eyes, Bhadrakāḷi dances before me—in intricate rosewood, in bronze, or coloured paints—her breasts like eyes, full of power and sight, but also compassion somehow.

At muṭiyēṯṯu the other night, I approached her with new respect, a deeper appreciation of her powerful nature. It was the first time I experienced that mix of deep respect and hopeful devotion. Having received her blows from within, I had a closer relationship with her. I felt her drawing me closer, closer. I was fascinated watching her dance and threaten behind the fiery torches, and I longed for his presence by my side. The one who was always with me, a sweet dark boy who holds my heart. Without him everything seems empty, dry. No joy in stars, moon, trees or green fields—everything lifeless and sad, echoing his name. I traced the beautiful curved Malayalam letters of 'Abhilash' in the sand at the beach—who is he? I don't know. But I must find him to find myself. I can say nothing more.

At the end of the muṭiyēṯṯu by Gopalakrishnan's troupe, Balan Mārār as Kāḷi came around and waved the torch before each of us, as we stood in line in front of Kāḷi's shrine. Three times he waved the light, faster each time, as we took blessings. Suddenly (s)he stopped before me, reached up and pulled some red cetti flowers from her muṭi and gave them to me. (To no one else did she do this.) I was filled with love and I felt: 'Finally the Mother is pleased with me. She will protect me but I must understand who she is. Respect and consciousness are the key.' Then we walked with her down the dark country road, torches flaming, to the house of the sponsor, where she was received with offerings and blessed those present. Watching the small procession in the dark night, marching down the road with the glittering muṭi illumined only by fire and moon, was such a moving and mysterious sight. She is the people's protectress, the incarnation of what brings them life—coconut and paddy—and she is the night.

Before leaving Kovalam we took the prasad (flowers, etc.) from Padmanabhaswamy Temple and threw it together into the sea, without looking back. Suddenly we both felt a tremendous energy inside, a discomfort like a volcano about to erupt. We sat seven hours on the sweltering train suffering and bursting. When we got home I called my mother and in the middle of that call, Antonio attacked me, hitting me hard, buffeting my head from side to side, breaking my glasses, shouting and moaning. Now we are living as if in a dream, just waiting for the days to pass until he leaves forever. Something died inside me. I am afraid.

Obeyesekere acknowledges the power of ritual symbols to restructure unconscious thought and even provoke real, dramatic change in one's personal life. But such a transformation depends upon a shared context of belief. How is it that I, a white half-Jew, half-WASP, highly educated, financially and politically privileged American female on a grant from international funding agencies, had such an experience? I was not raised in a Hindu context, nor had I been exposed to the mythology of the goddess Bhagavati in any in-depth way before arriving in Kerala. I had however undergone a year of intensive psychotherapy for sexual abuse history just before embarking on my fieldwork. I was trapped in a dysfunctional marriage which was re-enacting a lot of that history, yet I was in complete denial of the problem. Once during my therapy the image of Kāḷi had appeared in my mind as a kind of alter ego, the perfect embodiment of both the virgin and the whore personalities I felt lurking in the filthy basement of my own self. Kāḷi's unvarnished rage and murderous glee certainly gave vivid form to the anger I was beginning to acknowledge towards the uncles who had abused me throughout my childhood. Just before leaving for the field, the therapy had brought to my attention a whole pattern of my life I had never understood: why had I dropped out of Yale as a sophomore and joined a Hindu sect which required total celibacy and fanatical religious practice—a practice I devoted myself to wholeheartedly for the first five years of my twenties? Although I had never recognized the connection before, I remembered then that my dropping out of school directly followed a serious sexual abuse incident involving one of my uncles. I saw that I had sought escape from my body, from my family and culture, from the world itself, in the lap of Hindu asceticism. (I had to laugh when I read Masson's [1976] piece—it described me so exactly.) But on that path I had unwittingly entered deeply into the philosophy and spiritual reality of Hinduism. By the time I returned to school in my mid-twenties to continue my education in anthropology, I had spent five continuous years of celibacy and study in an ashram, one year of it in north India. What then, was my culture, when I boarded that plane to Kerala in 1991? No Indian would say I was truly Hindu. I certainly was not Indian in any sense, and least of all Malayali. I had chosen to work in Kerala because it had interesting religious art forms. Yet once I arrived, the symbols of those art forms sank deep into my mind and heart and caused a revolution in my life which was, I think, in keeping with the meaning of the goddess for many Indians I interviewed. In some sense I actually entered the community of belief of the muṭiyēṯṯu actors, who recognized that shared awareness in me during performances and told me they could perceive my devotion.[11] How is such a puzzle to be understood?

Luckily, I am not the first anthropologist to enter an unfamiliar religious world to such a degree. Once called 'going native' and earning Frank Cushing the ridicule and rejection of his peers in the 1930s, an attitude of devotion and shared belief has been pioneered by such anthropologists as Robert Desjarlais, Colin Turnbull, Paul Stoller, and Karen Brown (K. Brown 1991; Desjarlais 1992; P. Stoller 1989; Stoller and Olkes 1987; Turnbull 1990; Goulet and Young 1994). Each of these courageous scholars of religion and performance has allowed the boundaries of privilege, domination, and control which invisibly demarcate every white American anthropologist from his or her host community to dissolve through a relationship of apprenticeship and full participation. Such an attitude requires a willingness to be utterly transformed in one's deepest being. Contrary to the assertions of many, the concomitant 'loss of objectivity' is more than compensated for by the depth of insight this posture allows. More important and troubling, this approach fundamentally restructures the anthropologist's world and 'culture' in ways that are not at all easy to understand.

6 April 1992

After that it was like living in a nightmare. As each day dawned, new tragedies and difficulties emerged. I kept losing things, suffering ... Today I read the most amazing thing in a paper on Kodungallur Bharaṇi (Gentes 1992): the festival begins on Kumbham Bharaṇi and ends on Mīnam Bharaṇi (today). The intervening month represents the war between Kāḷi and Dārika. These two days (Kumbham and Mīnam Bharaṇi) marked the first and last days of this horrendous warlike, sacrificial drama in my own life. The day the letter fell from my dress and Antonio banished Abhilash from our house was Kumbham Bharaṇi. I took the whole experience as a punishment for my infidelity and tried to convince myself that my only salvation was to be a good, obedient, and faithful wife, and banish all thoughts of Abhilash from my mind forever. But try as I might, my whole being rebelled against it. I knew that I could not return to such a charade. And finally disaster struck when I told Antonio my feelings. When Antonio finally left for America, I was left utterly alone. I sent Abhilash a letter asking him to meet me, but he never came. Then yesterday, I finally saw Abhilash again. The day was Mīnam Bharaṇi. It seems it was all a terrible misunderstanding. He also has suffered tremendously, and stayed away because he feared for my life. At last some meagre light is beginning to creep into the terrible darkness which obscured the last few weeks for me. Bharaṇi to Bharaṇi, one month of sacrifice to her blood-thirst.

When I realized that the revolution in my own life had begun and ended on the exact dates demarcating the goddess's traditional month of destructive fury, I was both terrified and elated. On one level it seemed my life was totally out of my control, but on the other hand this meant the goddess was somehow 'running my show', and therefore, taking care of me. The events of my tragedy suddenly had meaning and cosmic significance beyond my personal lusts, fears, neuroses, and confusions. It was somehow 'meant' to be this way. This belief sustained me through weeks of suffering and loneliness I never would have imagined possible. Instead of running away and returning home (which my parents and friends all urged me to do), I plunged even more deeply into the stories and performances of muṭiyēṯṯu. Interviewing the artists, visiting their homes, travelling to temples and so on in the months following these dramatic events, I began to reconstruct my own life—or rather, to allow it to be structured by the work as it unfolded. Many things were out of my control for those final eight months of fieldwork; I depended heavily on the good will, help, and love of some, and sometimes suffered from the exploitation and cruelty of others. Yet an intense spirit of perseverance and faith guided my activities, interviews, and travels. I kept on learning more and more about the goddess.

Diary entry 23 Oct. 92:

Despite all these rather revolting sexual theories and interpretations, the fact remains that when I look at the picture of Kāḷi on my pūjā, I feel a sublime love for her. The artist has conveyed the sublime beauty and tranquillity which lie behind her ferocious and cruel mien; especially in the faces which turn to the side and gaze upward as if in *samādhi* [see Fig. 2]. There is a profound meaning below the surface, a perfect stillness which lies just beyond the piercing of the deepest dread. As there can be peace in desire, there is also mysteriously peace in violence. Perhaps in the release of all that is pent-up, or perhaps more as the eye of a hurricane or a black hole is peaceful—infinite potential yet infinitely the gateway to peace—strange. It is only by embracing all this in ourselves (as events have forced me to do) that we can enter that space of peace, if at all.

But it is also important to note George's view (and that of most Keralites), that nobody worships Kāḷi out of love or devotion but either out of (1) fear and respect and to deflect her wrath; or (2) to obtain evil powers to harm others. This view of Kāḷi is not so overlaid with spirituality as my interpretation. I think many levels coexist within Kāḷi, depending on how deep you go.

In his classic, iconoclastic tome on method, Devereux addresses problems of counter-transference in social-scientific research, plunging fearlessly into the question of whether or not sexual behaviour can be researched by the participant observation method. Ordinarily, he concludes, nothing can be gained by such a project, because the intentions and behaviour of the two participants will be so ill-matched, and the enormous store of unconscious, bodily knowledge required so lacking in the anthropologist, that any sexual experience thereby obtained will be distorted beyond recognition. Nor would direct observation of sexual behaviour of 'natives' provide even the slightest information about the meaning of such behaviour to the persons involved. In the remarkable two-and-a-half page appendix to this chapter, Devereux makes a radical, extraordinary statement.

In 'The problem of personal experiences', Devereux asserts, sexual experience is indeed 'scientifically exploitable' if it is 'obtained not in pursuit of data but of Love'. The empathy gained through love, he says, transcends the boundaries ordinarily present between ethnographers and 'informants'. 'Information based on the experience of Love', Devereux explains, 'is valid precisely because it is not distorted by an obsessive pursuit of (pseudo-) objectivity and is based not on participant observation, but on a *shared experience*' (1967: 118; emphasis added). Speaking of the great ethnologist Verrier Elwin's work on tribal India, Devereux attributes his unsurpassed data on Gond sexual life 'to the fact that Elwin loved and married a Gond girl, although, so far as I am able to determine, he nowhere mentions his personal love-experiences in his ethnological works.' Naturally not. Such an admission would have been grounds for immediate disqualification from the elite circle of social scientists. 'Yet it seems evident that what gives reality and depth to [Elwin's] ethnological data is that indirect inner illumination which his own reciprocated love for a Gond girl provided. In fact, he probably understood what being a Gond meant by experiencing how his Gond wife *phrased* their essentially human relationship' (ibid.).

Learning through love and in relationship requires the student (ethnographer) to become both deeply attached and vulnerable to his or her 'informant'. The power inequalities which inhere in the ethnographer-informant relationship, which so deeply trouble post-modern ethnographers, can in some measure be dissolved, even reversed by such a commitment of love. That is because 'what takes place on this level of interaction is not an experimental relationship ... but an interaction between two human beings. It is a basic relationship, which simply happens to be phrased—and only phrased—through the medium of two different ethnic personality types' (Devereux 1967: 119). This relationship cannot merely be terminated by the ethnographer's grant coming to an end. It is a permanent commitment which totally changes the course of both persons' lives. Often that commitment involves bonds of financial and personal assistance that reverse the one-way 'take it and leave it' tradition of ordinary ethnography.

13 October 1992 (After a tour to Konarak and north-eastern India)

Today I realize that this incredible love which makes my heart feel it will burst *is* divine love. This is God for me. This is the goddess manifest inside of me. *Saundarya Laharī*, the flood of ecstasy, the sexual bliss which is realization, the erotic longing which is utterly selfless and beyond the flesh—a pure spirit of light drifting on an ocean of sacrifice and peace. Couples pulsating in stone above my head on ancient, dead temples—phalluses full, breasts bursting, lips quivering with detached smiles; thighs turned out as if dancing. That perfect stillness in the torment of love and desire, that mothering instinct to press his dear black-haired head softly against my naked breast, that soft hand travelling gently over my body in the pale morning light; a black burning fire in the pools of his eyes which frightens me; my stomach fluttering when I hear his voice whisper 'don't be sad', so soft and high. That kind of love, which I never knew and which is so powerful that only tears can begin to express it, that makes my soul burn deep down inside and flutter helplessly like a rag in the wind, is the secret of God. Is this where my long-lost spiritual quest has led me? I give myself to him over and over again. I see the Kangra images of Chinmastami naked, delivering her own head on a plate, the hot red blood spurting from her neck like the river Ganges into Śiva's hair ... That's how much I love him—*fiercely*, capable of giving anything, even my life. Like sitting in a lake of fire.

Devereux's remarks seem to affirm the possibility of real knowledge, real 'shared experience' across seemingly unbridgeable gulfs of mind, gender, and culture. This can only be achieved, he suggests, by going far beyond both 'objectivity' and 'participant observation' towards a state of mutuality whose essence is commitment, negotiation, and embeddedness. Devereux recognizes of course, that 'the fieldworker, who is necessarily a transient, usually cannot hope to achieve such an authentic love-relationship.' Nor am I by any means recommending that others break up their marriages, wreak havoc on the social order, or betray confidences, all of which were very unfortunate consequences of the experience I underwent in Kerala.[12] I am merely pointing out the power of such a transforming love relationship to give a kind of insight that is impossible to achieve in many other ways. However, 'friendship, loving-kindness and scientific creativity' are other kinds of deeply human relationships which Devereux identifies as 'quite as able as Love is to heighten [the fieldworker's] empathetic sensitivity'. This is because 'friendship, quite as much as erotic love, is a creative phrasing of a real human relationship' (Devereux 1967: 119). This essential emphasis on committed human relationship, in which creativity, mutual concern, and real openness to being changed by the other are the foremost concerns, goes far beyond 'dialogic approaches', post-modern deconstructionist language, or endless self-reflective monologues to break through the prisons of orientalism, colonialism, sexism, and scientific reductionism which have so plagued our discipline.[13]

Many possibilities for human relationship exist beyond love and friendship. It is just as likely, if not more so, that anger, hatred, or mistrust will result between the ethnographer and members of a host culture. E. Moreno provides a terrifying case in point. Some twenty years after the fact, this female anthropologist (writing pseudonymously on the insistence of her publishers (see E. Moreno 1995: 248), shares her experience of being raped by her field assistant. This courageous essay spares nothing in its stark attention to the complexity of the field situation and the real possibility for horrendous outcomes. Moreno highlights the vulnerability of female fieldworkers without portraying herself solely as a victim. Such issues are simply not addressed in graduate anthropological training. Utterly unprepared for the nuances of emotional transference and counter-transference, much less their convolutions in a situation of unequal wealth, power, and gender in the long shadow of colonial history, most ethnographers have to go 'by the seat of their pants' in such situations, and then omit them from their ethnographies out of shame. The publication of the Malinowski diaries was a trenchant case in point; yet despite the passing of more than three decades since that moment in anthropology, few ethnographers have dared to bare the full realities of the field encounter or explore the implications of personal experience as a way of knowing.[14]

The fact is, intense interpersonal experiences in the field are an unavoidable and in fact requisite part of the 'participant observation' method of fieldwork. The erasure of such episodes, which are far more common than the reading of ethnography would suggest, is a deeply troubling epistemic move. This comes from a continued deep prejudice against 'emotion' and bodily experiences as non-cognitive and hence ultimately irrelevant to our theory-making enterprise. My inclusion of such material in this account is a kind of 'coming out' that I hope will inspire self-reflection and debate on the part of other ethnographers.

The mirroring, negotiation, and vulnerability of personal relationships are the stuff by which we first learn to be in the world as children; they are just as naturally the way we begin to make sense of another culture. As naïve members of an alien society, both our behaviour and our understanding are unusually messy, confusing, and disturbing. They are full of mistakes. The pain of such mistakes, which we call 'culture shock', *is how we learn* about a new culture. To erase this process is to deprive the ethnographic enterprise of its most fascinating and precious core. By exposing the process courageously and carefully to scrutiny, the possibility for real human knowledge emerges.

That knowledge may take us far beyond the crafting of more and more theory. We may actually have to be transformed. Such a transformation in our way of looking can enable us to extend beyond our limited academic horizons to encompass much more fully the point of view of those traditionally 'on the periphery'. Let me put it another way. One day early in my stay in Kerala, during an interview in my living-room, George criticized what he perceived to be my detached scholarly approach to muṭiyē_ṯṯ_u. This is what he said to me:

> You know, the way you are going about it you won't get anywhere. The original flow doesn't exist. Only when your studies touch your innermost feeling, will you reach a state when it pervades everything you do. You can think only of that. Then only will your mind be able to go

into it fully. Look, it's like if I love someone very much, I can't even spend one day without seeing him. Well, if you become that much attached to your subject, loving it most earnestly, then you would not be able to live without that. So after some time, when it's beyond the point of mere work or study, when it becomes your only, final resort, you would be enslaved by it. Then, after a while, you will feel like you want to stay in Kerala. You would be reluctant to leave here. There would be a big change in you, I am sure.

Notes

[1] Interview, Calicut, Kerala, December 1991.

[2] I shall continue to use the word performance herein, in the broad sense of 'actions done to accomplish some purpose'. This seems to accommodate the south Indian sensibility, although it does not draw the ontological distinctions I have explored above.

[3] Freeman (1993) also applies Austin's 'performative' sense in his analysis of teyyam possession in Kerala.

[4] The texts of muṭiyēṯṯu are passed down orally; in the six versions I collected from different performances by the same and different troupes, there was little variation.

[5] However, the Kōyimbaṭa Nāyar speech includes archaic Malayalam (closer to Tamil than the modern language) which is memorized but not fully understood by the actors. This routine includes complex jokes about music and obscene materials not fully understood by the artists.

[6] Interview, Muvattupuzha, Kerala, May 1992.

[7] One nāḻika is 24 minutes. See Wood (1985: 39–41) for an explanation of traditional Malayalam time segments.

[8] Balakrishnan Mārār, interview, Muvattupuzha, Kerala, May 1992. Note switching from first person plural to first person singular. In general the use of first person plural in Malayalam is humbler and more inclusive. It may also reflect the 'dual consciousness' of the possessed actor, who actually contains two separate consciousnesses within his body simultaneously during the possession. Although Kāḷi is dominant, the actor remains present as a passive witness to the action his body is performing. See Schechner (1985: 6, 123). Perhaps this is why he is able to coordinate the possession with the correct movements and drum-beats of the orchestra. Yet this semi-consciousness on the actor's part does not negate the authenticity of the possession for indigenous actors or spectators.

[9] See Kapferer 1991; Obeyesekere 1990, chapter 2. The Vedda Yakkam tradition of Sri Lanka includes a comic 'tribal' (Vedda) female routine that closely resembles muṭiyēṯṯu's Kūḷi scene. It is possible that this similarity is attributable to Sri Lanka-Kerala migrations over the last century. My thanks to Susan Reed for bringing this material to my attention.

[10] Langer 1979. On the artistic and cognitive function of framing in south Asian expressive culture, see Hess 1993.

[11] Linda Hess suggests that it is the social category of 'devotee' rather than any idiosyncratic perception of a spiritual state that often motivates religious celebrants in assessing the devotion of Western observers. In describing her own study of the Banaras Ramlila, Hess wrote, 'since I was there, attending every day, getting close to the gods giving so much energy and devotion to this work, people assumed I was a devotee, and told me so' (personal communication, July 1995). Although such an explanation is indeed possible here, one artist singled me out at a particular performance where I did indeed feel something very unusual. He later told me spontaneously that he had perceived a special devotional fervour in me at that moment (this encounter is described from my point of view in the diary entry above).

[12] Such behaviour also has profound effects on the next scholar to come to the region. There are serious moral issues to be confronted in thinking about such personal involvements. These difficult issues are debated in Kulick and Wilson 1995.

[13] See K. M. Brown 1991; Scheper-Hughes 1992; and Herdt and Stoller (1990) for recent outstanding attempts to achieve such a breakthrough.

[14] Notable exceptions include Tsing 1993; Cesara 1982; Crapanzano 1980; Rabinow 1977; Behar 1993, 1996.

7

AN OPEN END

The artists who draw the sacred kaḷam of Bhagavati tell us that the elaborate multicoloured powder image is really the centre-point of a larger, unseen sacred diagram, the Śrī Yantra. The Śrī Yantra in turn is an abstract representation of the goddess's world, replete with guardians, forts, fountains, and untold intricacies of cosmic meaning. The four entrances demarcating the boundaries of this sacred space all lead to the centre-point, where they explode out into the brilliant flaming form of the personified goddess. After briefly presenting herself to her devotees, the goddess departs and the drawing is wiped away.

In this work we too have entered the world of the goddess through a kaleidoscope of interpretations. Chapters 3 through 6 each enter this domain through a different door and traverse four very different pathways. In chapter 3, we have seen how the ancient south Indian cults of possession, bloodshed, and sexuality intimately linked to agricultural fertility are still alive in muṭiyēṯṯu. Explicating the symbolism of the Bhagavati cult through the dimensions of time and geography reveals the subtle, often forgotten interconnections between food, household space, seasons, gender, and human fertility. The ancient poetic conventions of Sangam poetry provide analytic categories for understanding these rich intersection of meanings rooted in the land itself.

Chapters 4 and 5 explore the symbolic world of Bhagavati through the dimensions of psychology and gender. Child-rearing, social practices of different castes, and local ideas of motherhood all contribute in complex ways to the emotional dynamics underlying the ritual performances of Bhagavati. Female power is understood to be more than a philosophical category, functioning more as a way to alleviate deep-seated male anxieties than to empower women. Attending to women's realities using a feminist lens in chapter 5, we find that women are alienated from this tradition, which once lay within their purview (as suggested by our historical overview in chapter 1). Themes of vengeance and suffering permeate both the male and female forms of possession performance explicated in chapters 4 and 5, but these are channelled by cultural ideology into the discrete realms of the divine and the demonic. Chapters 4 and 5 also demonstrate how these dramas of spiritual, political, and personal power continually adjust to new meanings over time. In recent decades, psychological traumas associated with changing social circumstances find fertile soil in the complex symbolism of the goddess's decapitation of the demon Dārika. Perhaps due to this symbolic richness, the ancient art of muṭiyēṯṯu is not, as many had thought, in imminent danger of dying out.

Chapter 6 uses the lens of performance theory to focus back upon the specific bodily and emotional features of the Bhagavati rituals that lead to spiritual and psychological experiences of transformation. While acknowledging the origins and function of many of the symbols in ecological, psychological, sexual, and political realities, we suggest that all of these are not sufficient to encompass the full meaning of the Bhagavati rituals. Shared transformative personal experience is a dimension of the whole that can only be pointed to in this text, but not re-created. Arriving at the centre point of the sacred drawing, we must break through to a different dimension altogether.

Now, having followed these four paths to the centre-point, the goddess appears as much more than the sum-total of all of these views. Superimposed upon one another, they build up a multi-layered portrait of a deity, a drama, and people who encounter themselves through her in a variety of ways. Many strands contribute to the goddess's continuing hypnotic power. She is many things to many people. Yet two conclusions seem to stand out: that Bhadrakāḷi in Kerala is primarily a deity of and for men, and that she is more feared by most people than she is loved. As one woman said, 'We actually worship Bhagavati out of fear. [Actually] it's not devotion, it's a kind of fear. It's something inside ... an anxiety inside the mind.' That anxiety has many facets. Some are historical, some political, some religious, some symbolic, and some psychological. In Bhadrakāḷi's complex personality all these facets are reflected. The perpetual evocation of that anxiety, and its placation and alleviation through suffering and sacrifice, balanced by rituals of peace and plenty in the cool months, are integral rhythms of the Kerala landscape.

We need not feel the necessity to reduce all these complex facets into a single perspective, through which we can understand the unitary meaning of muṭiyēṯṯu. Each of these interpretative views expresses and leads us to a truth about the meaning of the whole. From one vantage point muṭiyēṯṯu is a propitiatory rite which aims at invoking, controlling, and converting dangerous female energy—embodied in the image of the fertile virgin—into benevolent mothering energy for the well-being of society. But this supernatural drama also has profound implications for the self-images and real lives of its spectators. While providing a deep spiritual experience for men, the worship of the fierce goddess in Kerala may actually work in subtle ways to propagate women's negative self-image and keep them under control. In fact, as in so many things, the view one gets of the performance of muṭiyēṯṯu depends entirely upon where one is sitting.

This complicates the question of 'meaning' enormously. If we are to say what a rite or symbol 'means', perhaps we must leave behind Aristotelian notions of unilinear clarity and adopt what Ramanujan calls the 'context-sensitive' epistemology of south Asian culture. A 'context-sensitive' approach denies the ultimate truth-value of particular statements, or even their unequivocal referentiality. It says that a word is never a pure denotative sign, merely pointing to its referent, as Aristotle had insisted, but always connotes, evokes, shifts, both from context to context and from hearer to hearer. A statement can be understood only in the full context of who says it, hears it, overhears it; under what circumstances the statement is made; and even, in India, when—the time of day, the season, the planetary influences—where, why, and innumerable other subtle contextualizing factors (Ramanujan 1989). What can we know using this approach, which I have called the construction of a crystal? How do we integrate the various emic and etic points of view presented here into a meaningful whole? Whose view is correct?

Obeyesekere's complex understanding of symbolism (1981, 1990) is helpful, acknowledging the interplay of the historical, the social, and the personal. The enduring symbolic aspects of Kāḷi in south

Asia may well have originated in shared psychic conflicts, although the goddess's specific iconography may also be based on historical realities (chapter 1). Exactly how the symbolism arose or whom it served we shall never really know. But using Obeyesekere's concept of personal symbols, we can attend to how various individuals and communities make use of this rich cultural symbolism: upper and lower castes, males and females, northerners, southerners, Sri Lankans, Americans. Menon and Shweder (1994) have done this kind of cultural psychological analysis of the symbolism of Kāḷi in Bengal, emphasizing the increasing cultural role of 'shame' in recasting the goddess's iconography to match current normative messages about female behaviour (see also Kripal 1994). By collecting what Obeyesekere calls 'myth associations', spontaneous commentaries elicited about folk stories, we can tap indigenous interpretations for their deeper psychological meanings.

The personal symbolism of Bhagavati for people in Kerala seems to vary enormously, ranging from irrelevance to apotheosis. A historical development from low-caste, female shamans to high-caste male ritual practitioners appears to correspond with similar movements elsewhere in south Asia. We have examined the psychological complexities of these personal symbols for men and women, and identified their possible etiology in childhood sexual abuse trauma. We have moreover shown how male transformation of psychological trauma intersects with political domination of women to further serve male psychological needs, while perpetuating female suffering. By splitting possession into qualitatively different male and female domains, males achieve transformation and progressive orientation while women are left to cathartic, regressive behaviour of low cultural status.

The domination of Bhagavati in Kerala culture is a central fact that seems to express a deep ambivalence about women and femininity which belies Kerala's matrilineal social history and relatively high position of women. At the end of chapter 5, I have suggested that feminist theorists within Kerala could use the available cultural symbols and make them personal. By ceasing to deny that Bhadrakāḷi could ever be like one of them, by allowing themselves even in imagination, to once again take up that sword, women can perhaps imagine themselves into a life of greater possibilities and responsiveness, however they decide to construct that world. It need not be like ours.

How do all these dimensions, which we have described using such impoverished terms as 'symbolic, psychological, sociological, and spiritual', intertwine in the heart of a living, breathing human being? Can an ethnographer ever know how this feels for members of another culture? The inclusion of the personal 'subtext' in this study is an attempt to seriously address this issue. Human suffering and desire are the inescapable themes of the muṭiyēṯṯu drama and the Bhagavati cult they serve. It is only natural that a student of these arts must also face those realities in her own being. This should not be perceived as a weakness but a strength. The desire to throw off the chains of one's bourgeois existence and plunge into a sometimes painful reality is motivated by a thirst for truth, as Obeyesekere confirms: 'There are, however, the few who will be attracted to such forms of experience and thought, in spite of the physical and social environment in which they live, because they have searched, as Freud did, the dark recesses of their own lives and from there have had a vision of the dark side of life in general' (1991: 288–9). Such a journey is a beginning, not an end in itself.

I believe that the narration of my own experience does tell us something about muṭiyēṯṯu, deeply and truthfully. If culture is embodied, code-transactional, shared and bodily, then by entering into it in all these ways the culture enters the ethnographer and reveals itself in her own experience (Desjarlais 1992). If participant observation works at all, it works like this. Criticism has been levelled against the participant-observation ideal, asserting the dubiousness of this method, and its colonial Cartesian inheritance (Srinivasan 1993); yet it remains the hallmark of anthropology, and rightly so, I think. The power imbalances that concern post-modern social critics certainly were inverted in the experience of this ethnographer, both by choice and by the circumstances of my being a woman, by my personal history, and by my attitude towards the goddess. Through the impact of Kerala upon me, often unwitting, the way I saw, felt, and understood muṭiyēṯṯu was transformed from initial boredom and disappointment to final rapture and a sense of awe. In the end it seemed to me that if there is an irreducible meaning to muṭiyēṯṯu, perhaps it is simply that people hurt each other and become transformed through that intimacy. Kāḻi is the raw expression of that power of human beings to reach to their deepest emotions and inflict harm on one another, but also to break free.

But how can we know if this vision is anything like that of a member of the culture from which these symbols are borrowed?

A possible answer to these troubling questions presented itself when I discovered a poem by a well-known Kerala poet in a local literary journal. The poem 'Shanta' by Kattamanita Ramakrishnan wonderfully crystallizes all the themes my own account explores: coolness and tenderness, heat and misery; the erotic power of women like the fertilizing force of rain; the cruelty, ugliness, and pain of human relations and their transcendence through love; and most of all, the play of all these in the frenzied drumbeats of the goddess's temple festivals, those catalysts that mysteriously bring about life's renewal. The poem's ending points to an escape from the prison of social norms through the liberating experience of the possession rituals of the Bhagavati cult. In a tone redolent of Kodungallur Bharaṇi, the poet exhorts his lover to awaken from her stupor of proper routine and 'defile the shrine' of the local goddess with her wild dancing. Though the voice is that of a man, the emotions are human. In the images of rain and heat, dried tears and burning desire, are the seeds of something we all know. The troubling themes raised by the poem, like those in this book, are not fully answered, only circled through in a counterpoint of voices and moods, brought to consciousness, then left as an open end to the intensity of experience they point to. As we wipe away the vestiges of our multi-coloured painting, like a vivid dream that fades in the morning light, the coloured powders blur, and only a memory remains.[1]

Shanta [Peaceful]

Shanta,
Changing your wet clothes after the bath,
Squeezing out your long hair and draping it over the back,
Shaking your bangled hands gently,
Lining the eyes with eyeblack and darkening the flickering branches of the eyelashes,
Smearing sandal paste on the forehead and
Lighting the evening flame of your blooming smile,
Come sit near me and fill me with delight
Chanting something simple and sweet
A few verses of the hymns to Lakṣmi sung at the auspicious hour of dusk.

Let your eyes be camphor flames,
Your words as fragrant as musk.
With the tinkling bells of your fingertips
Stroke my chest and awaken me inside.
There is no dusk for us,
Other than this midnight hour we have nothing;
Let's brim with meaning these precious moments dropped before us.
I see your swollen eyelids as you knelt before the smoky stove,
    trying to set fire to the raw firewood there;
Hot tears welling up from the eyes already reddened by smoke,
Flecks of ash in the wind-blown hair,
A black mark where you rubbed your nose with your soot-covered
    palm,
The three-inch bruise under your bent shoulder smeared with dirt and
    grime;
Below your armpits, I see the ripped black blouse stained with sweat.

Oh Shanta! let's forget
Let's claim a few moments
Sitting in this little courtyard
Let's share the beauty of the vast sky together
I shall sing to you an old refrain,
On the mountain too high for man or elephant to climb
A thousand forests have flowered down
I saw deer jumping and playing
Now let me sing,
On the mountain too high for man or elephant to climb
A thousand forests have flowered to the ground.
From the sky a fawn leaped down
On its antler a crescent moon
Oh crescent moon fawn, oh crescent moon fawn!
Sandal-daubed fawn, jump playfully
Jump playfully into this small courtyard
Please jump playfully encircling my Shanta ...

What?
Is there no water for bath?
Not even to drink?
Did the children go unwashed?
Where are they?
Did they go to bed all covered with dust,
Weary and filthy, without even a bath in this intense heat?
Is it them I hear groaning and mumbling?
Poor innocent darlings!

Concerned for their dying young shoots, the wilting mango trees lining the street ask me
Hey traveller, where are you going?
To the heart of this village, weary and weakened by heat?
Why do you seek this unlucky place where there is not even the shade of a crow's leg?
I said,
In any unfortunate desert, my Shanta waits as an oasis,
Keeping her ears sharpened to hear my footsteps.
Don't you hear her scolding the stubborn children:
Mischievous children, let your father come here and
You'll get a nice beating!
The children sleep exhausted even without being beaten.
What? Did our well dry up?
All our wells have gone dry.
All the ponds and creeks and rivers have dried up.
I saw the ferry-boatman sitting on the twisted stern of his boat, lifted up onto the landing, sitting useless and idle, with his head between his knees.
His eyes lay trapped in the thorny dry sand on the riverside
He even forgot to raise his hand in greeting.
I noticed along the way I came
All those squashes you had planted and nursed, now wilted and crumbled to dust.
Even the fond moistness of the paddy fields has dried to drought,
No more the croaking of frogs.
Poor frogs who bring rain crying and crying,
What could have happened to them?
They might have died waiting in the cracks of the ridges edging the fields
I saw on my way
People gathered by the perished spring in Kanjirapara,
With pots and buckets in their hands
Lamenting and calling each other names
Each blaming the other for his lack of water.
When their throats get hoarse from shouting
They'll just accuse each other coughing
When cough and drought get tangled in the throat, suffocating,
They'll just sink to the ground and lean their heads on their hands.
Look! Even the wellspring of the winds has dried up
The trees are still
Those roots seeking water underground must all have decayed in their wanderings

How long can they survive only on sap?
Termites have broken out of their mounds
Catch one and see—
Isn't there any sign of dark rain clouds on their bellies?

With my ears pressed close to your heart
Let me remember
Let me imbibe the knowledge of your fragrance
Let me gulp the intoxication of your smile
Oh my girl, let's melt into one
Let us split open the forehead of this sorrow
And make a lotus flower bloom
Let's play and run on each and every tender petal until we are dripping with sweat
Let's melt and flare up as colourful dreams of sweat drops, as the music of clouds,
As rain let's seep down through the pores of this soil
Come on!
Come! as evergreen joy
Come as a river's overflowing music
Come as sorrow, come as strength
Come as truth, come as the song of my life,
Come, as the music of the universe—oh Shanta!

Like a corpse crawling toward its chopped-off head
The dusk fades away.
The directions stand with distorted grimaces of desperation
I can't even look at them,
How hideous everything is here.
Inside me too unpleasant images are slowly creeping in
Like a thief, stealing what remains
Of my peace of mind.
What is there to see?
What is there to enjoy?
Those abandoned eyes which pounce on sights
Those unproclaimed ears who rush after sounds
Tongue imprisoned in a dungeon of different tastes
Nose receptive to all smells
Skin which absorbs every touch and heals wounds
Mind which comprehends both wanted and unwanted,
That bird which is hovering in circles above the mind,
Makes us experience everything so completely.
Look at this sky,
Its face disfigured with smallpox scars
Only the lashes of the blind eyes occasionally flutter.

There is no laughter, no happy news,
Only the howls of lame dogs.

On yonder mountain
In the shade of that garden
Embraced by a gentle smile
Didn't we sit with our eyes entwined
Caressing the bodies of tender shoots
Bruised by the honeyed thorns of our lovers' quarrels
Drinking deep from a bowl of splendour
Do you remember
When you stood like a mischievous little girl
On the banks of the rippling river of your dreams
One moment etching something in the sand
And the next erasing it
When we joined the dreams scattered amongst the stones
And became one dream in the night,
The blooming dawn, the morning sounds,
The savour of our sweet thoughts?

Drinking the forest's intoxication
We danced splendidly, spreading the enchanting colours of our plumage,
Depicting a kaleidoscope of moods with our beautiful dances
Different colour combinations became spontaneous movements
Our panting breaths became speech
The mighty frantic dance whose frenzy melts the dancer's body
Drove us with an unbearable thirst for perfection

Finally we heaved a foul-smelling sigh
And lay down exhausted with our ears pricked
For the rising of that sun that had fallen and dissolved in the sea
Bloom like the dawn, open wonderful eyes,
Race through my veins as the forest's intoxication
Ascend serenely into the firmament
Flow down into me as the consoling river Ganges
As streams of the music of awakening
Come to me, Oh Shanta.

From the dungeons of boredom
From the hallways of hatred
From the smallpox caused by evil glances and gossip
From the lusting of mirrors
From the threat of the hours
From the cruel separations of social class
From the rape of endless words and numbers

From all these have I stolen
One moment and come to you desiring relief
Why do you sit so unresponsive?
Let's seek enthusiasm either in memory or awakening
You're not even sweating enough to moisten my lips
Please at least breathe a sigh
And end this passivity of yours
I know everything that has happened
I know that the neighbour widow's son ran away going mad
I heard that the young girl who used to gambol about like a lamb poisoned herself
I heard about those houses without even a stove destroyed by fire
I also heard about the woodcutter whose axe turned and cut into his own flesh
I heard of the new brutal pastimes of old kings
I also heard bits and pieces of stories told of young princes
Dying unable even to turn and speak to the arrows unexpectedly striking them
I saw the blind parents waiting anxiously for the sound of their dear son's footsteps returning with water to quench their thirst
I also saw decayed bodies scattered all around in this village
Without even anyone to cremate them
Numbness has covered this village like a black cloth
Won't you at least sigh and erase this numbness?
Please sweat on the dryness of this silence.
Child, nothing stays the same forever.
Anything could happen at any time.
Springs can flow suddenly, splitting rocks
So we can at least talk to each other.
Let's laugh or cry or exchange a few trivial words
If we can't even do that we will also decay like this village's heart.
Decomposed bodies will lie scattered about this village
The foul smell of our rotten bodies will lay eggs in our nostrils
From those eggs maggots of destruction will hatch
They will wriggle in our polluted blood and grow there
So let's try to talk to each other
Let's emerge breaking the hard black shell of silence
Let's deny numbness
Alas! We are lying enchained here under this palm tree[2]
Oh! Whatever we see, hear, or know, is only through these links of chain
My girl, it is only through these links that I see even you!
Let's break these manacles with a deep sigh
Alas! The moist warmth of your sigh has struck my face,

Droplets of sweat sprout on your brow
I can hear your heart throb.

Oh my overflowing, curly-haired girl, churned from the undergrowth,
Awake, arise to defile the shrine of Katammanitta
Decorate your black hair, line your moist eyes with sun rays
Hang rings in your ears, and a stone garland round your neck,
Arise, awake to defile the shrine of Katammanitta!
Paraya troops come climbing up the steps of hell in a frenzied dance[3]
An army of Parayas comes, dancing and singing to the beat of the drums
Oh overflowing, curly-haired girl bloomed on a wild vine,
Arise, awake to defile the shrine of Katammanitta!
In the whirlpool of the stretched and sunken stomach
The fire snake sheds it skin and dances
Drum beats pound upon the broad chest of the parched field
The gasping throat of the plantain tree cries aloud thinking about the tender bud
Oh! Overflowing maiden, girl who shakes palm trees by the rushing stream,
Awake! Arise to defile the shrine of Katammanitta.

Notes

[1] With gracious thanks to the poet for permission to publish the poem here. Published in English as K. Ramakrishnan (1989). Retranslated for this work by Laji P. Kattungal.

[2] *Karimpāṇa*; a type of palm tree in which murderous yakṣis are said to dwell.

[3] tuḷḷal: possession dance, see chapter 5. The term used for defiling the shrine is '*kāvu tīntal*'—the same term used for the purposeful polluting of the Kodungallur Bhagavati temple at the Bharaṇi festival.

Glossary

Ambalavāsi—temple-serving castes
aṟa—granary, storage room at centre of traditional house
alari—*frangipani*, white fragrant flower said to attract snakes
āśān—teacher and troupe leader
asura—demon
bādhā—demonic spirit possession
Bhadrakāḷi—fierce form of the goddess Bhagavati
bhūta—ghost accompanying Bhadrakāḷi to war
bījam—seed, grain, semen or sexual fluid
caitanyam—consciousness, divine force within an idol
ceṇṭa—drum used in muṭiyēṯṯu
cetti/tecci—*ixora*, red flower favourite to Bhadrakāḷi
choṭṭa—unopened coconut bud
Dārika(n)—Asura opponent of Bhadrakāḷi in muṭiyēṭṭu
Dārikavadham—traditional story of the killing of Dārika by Bhadrakāḷi
darśan—'divine sight' of the deity, often through the medium of spirit possession of a ritual actor
dēva(*n*)—divine being, god
Garuḍan—the eagle mount of Viṣnu
Ghantākarṇa(n)—brother of Bhadrakāḷi created from Śiva's earwax to lick smallpox from her body
iṭakka—a small drum played in temple worship
Kailāsam—heavenly home of Śiva and other gods
kaḷam—coloured powder-drawing of a deity in the temple
kaḷam pāṭṭu—song of praise accompanying kaḷam drawing
kaḷari—gymnasium for the Practice of martial arts
kaḷaripayaṯṯ—indigenous martial arts form of Kerala
Kāḷi—fierce Hindu goddess
kārṇavar—ancestor, household head, elder
Kathakaḷi—an operatic form of ritual theatre in Kerala
kāvu—grove or temple
Koṯṯavai—early south Indian war goddess of the Sangam period

Kṣatriya—royal caste
Kūḷi—female clown in muṭiyēṯṯu
kurava—ritual ululation by women
Kuṟup—temple-serving caste entitled to draw kaḷam and perform muṭiyēṯṯu
Manōdari—wife of the demon Dārika
Mārār—temple-serving caste entitled to play drums and conch as well as perform muṭiyēṯṯu
muṭi—hair, a crown, headgear, a bundle of paddy carried on the head
muṭiyēṯṯu—ritual dance drama performed as an offering to the fierce goddess Bhagavati in Kerala temples
nāga—serpent deity who dwells in trees, water, and the underworld
Nambūtiri—Brahmin caste of Kerala
Nāyar—martial caste of Kerala
pantal—temporary pavilion set up for ritual occasions
Pārvati—wife of the god Śiva
paṭayaṇi—folk worship of Bhagavati using grotesque comic masks and dances, performed in Pattanamtitta district
prasādam—blessed remains of worship distributed to devotees
praśnam—astrological consultation to determine the cause of a problem
pūjā—Hindu worship of a deity by waving lights and offering flowers, food, incense, and pleasing sounds
puṟappāṭu—'setting forth'; entrance of a character in muṭiyēṯṯu
Śākta—pertaining to religious cults or philosophical schools devoted to worship of the goddess as the supreme theological principle
śakti—power, force, particularly inhering in the goddess
saptamātrakkaḷ—the 'seven mothers', a group of goddesses affiliated with the fierce goddess Kāḷi
Sarasvatī—goddess of learning and work
sarppakāvu—snake grove, an undisturbed area of plant growth in which snake deities are believed to dwell, and where offerings are made
Śiva—ascetic mountain-dwelling deity who is the father of Bhadrakāḷi
tāli—leaf-shaped pendant on a chain, tied around the neck as a marriage badge
tantri—priest empowered to perform worship of Hindu deities in temples
tapas—austerities performed to obtain a boon
taṟavāḍu—traditional joint family dwelling
teḷḷi—fragrant resinous powder burnt as a firework in muṭiyēṯṯu performances; also said to have antiseptic properties
tīyāṭṭu—ritual dance drama performed to worship Bhadrakāḷi in Kottayam district
tūkkam—ritual of hook-swinging
tuḷḷal—jumping, hopping, as in demonic possession or religious dance
vāḷ—curved iron sword of the goddess Bhadrakāḷi
veḷiccappāṭu—oracle who becomes possessed by the goddess Bhagavati
Vētāḷam—forest-dwelling female ghost who drinks Dārika's blood

viḷakku—brass oil lamp
viṟali—courtly female bard and dancer in ancient Tamil culture
Viṣṇu—a major deity who incarnates on earth as Ram, Krishna, and other forms
yakṣi—tree-dwelling female vampire, succubus

Works Cited

ABRAHAM, C. M. (1960), 'Nambuthiri Brahmins of Kerala'. *Vikram (Arts)*, 5(4): 15–28.

——— (1965), 'Social Change among the Nairs of Kerala'. *Journal of Social Research*, 8 (2): 25–34.

ACHYUTHA MENON, K. (1961), *Ancient Kerala: Studies in Its History and Culture*. Trichur: Ajanta Press.

AGRAWALA, V. S. (1966), 'Yakshas and Nagas in Indian Folk-art Tradition'. *Folklore* (Calcutta), 7(1): 1–9.

——— (1971), 'Yakshas and Nagas'. *Eastern Anthropologist*, 24(1): 1–6.

AIYAPPAN, A. (1972), 'The Meaning of the Tali Rite'. *Bulletin of the Rama Varma Research Institute*, 9(2): 68–83.

ALTEKAR, A. S. (1956) [1938], *The Position of Women in Hindu Civilisation from Pre-Historic Times to the Present Day.* Reprint. Delhi: Motilal Banarsidass, 1956.

ALTER, J. S. (1992), *The Wrestler's Body: Identity and Ideology in North India*. Berkeley: University of California Press.

ASCH, S. S. (1988), 'The Analytic Concepts of Masochism: A Reevaluation'. In *Masochism: Current Psychoanalytic Perspectives*, ed. R. A. Glick and D. I. Meyers, pp. 93–115. Hillsdale, NJ: Analytic Press.

ASHLEY, W. (1993), 'Recodings: Ritual, Theater, and Political Display in Kerala State, south India'. Ph.D. dissertation, Performance Studies, New York University.

AUSTIN, J. R. (1962), *How To Do Things with Words.* Oxford: Oxford University Press.

BABB, L. A. (1970), 'Marriage and Malevolence: The Uses of Sexual Opposition in a Hindu Pantheon'. *Ethnology*, 9 (2): 137–48.

BACCHETTA, P. (1993), 'All our Goddesses are Armed: Religion, Resistance, and Revenge in the Life of a Militant Hindu Nationalist Woman'. *Bulletin of Concerned Asian Scholars*, 25(4): 38–52.

BAKER-REYNOLDS, H. (1978), 'To Keep the Tali Strong: Women's Rituals in Tamil Nadu'. Ph.D. dissertation. University of Wisconsin, Madison.

BECK, B. E. F. (1969), 'Colour and Heat in south Indian Ritual'. *Man*, n.s. 4(4): 553–72.

BEHAR, R. (1993), *Translated Woman*. Boston: Beacon Press.

——— (1996), *The Vulnerable Observer*. Boston: Beacon Press.

BEKAL, N. (1990), 'Ottakolam' [Single figure]. *Grhalakshmi* (January): 10–15.

BENNETT, L. (1983), *Dangerous Wives and Sacred Sisters: Social and Symbolic Roles of High-caste Women in Nepal*. New York: Columbia University Press.

BERNIER, R. M. (1982), *Temple Arts of Kerala: A south Indian Tradition*. New Delhi: S. Chand.

BERREMAN, G. D. (1962), 'Behind Many Masks: Ethnography and Impression Management in a Himalayan Village'. Ithaca, NY: Society for Applied Anthropology, Monograph No. 4.

——— (1966), 'Anemic and Emetic Analyses in Social Anthropology'. *American Anthropologist* 68(2): 346–54.

——— (1993), 'Sanskritization as Female Oppression in India'. In *Sex and Gender Hierarchies*, ed. B. D. Miller, pp. 366–92. Cambridge: Cambridge University Press.

BHARATI, A. (1970) [1965], *The Tantric Tradition*. Garden City, NY: Anchor Doubleday.

BHATTACHARYYA, N. N. (1980) [1979], *Indian Puberty Rites*. Delhi: Munshiram Manoharlal.

BLACKBURN, S. H. (1988), *Singing of Birth and Death: Texts in Performance*. Philadelphia: University of Pennsylvania Press.

BLOCH, M. (1974), 'Symbols, Song, Dance and Features of Articulation or Is Religion an Extreme Form of Traditional Authority?' *Archives Européens de Sociologie*, 15(1): 55–81.

BODDY, J. (1989), *Wombs and Alien Spirits: Women, Men, and the Zar Cult in Northern Sudan*. Madison: University of Wisconsin Press.

BRADFORD, N. J. (1983), 'Transgenderism and the Cult of Yellamma: Heat, Sex, and Sickness in south Indian Ritual'. *Journal of Anthropological Research* 39(3): 307–22.

BRIERE, J. and M. RUNTZ (1991), 'The Long-term Effects of Sexual Abuse: A Review and Synthesis'. In *Treating Victims of Child Sexual Abuse*, ed. J. Briere, pp. 3–13. New York: Jossey-Bass.

BROOKS, D. R. (1990), *The Secret of the Three Cities: An Introduction to Hindu Śākta Tantrism*. Chicago: University of Chicago Press.

BROWN, K. M. (1985), 'On Feminist Methodology'. *Journal of Feminist Studies in Religion*, 1(2): 73–88.

——— (1991), *Mama Lola: a Vodou Priestess in Brooklyn*. Berkeley: University of California Press.

BROWN, W. N., ed. and trans. (1958), *The Saundaryalahari or Flood of Beauty, Traditionally Ascribed to Sankaracarya*. Harvard Oriental Series. vol. 43. Cambridge, MA: Harvard University Press.

BRUBAKER, R. L. (1977), 'Lustful Woman, Chaste Wife, Ambivalent Goddess'. *Anima*, 3(2): 60–2.

——— (1978), 'The Ambivalent Mistress: A Study of south Indian Village Goddesses and their Religious Meaning'. Ph.D. dissertation. University of Chicago, Chicago.

CALDWELL, S. (1995), 'Oh Terrifying Mother: The Mudiyettu Ritual Drama of Kerala, south India'. Ph.D. dissertation. University of California, Berkeley.

——— forthcoming (a). 'Bhagavati Ritual Traditions'. In *south Asia Folklore Encylopedia*, ed. P. Claus and M. Mills. New Jersey: Garland Publishing.

——— forthcoming (b). 'The Bloodthirsty Tongue and the Self-Feeding Breast: Homosexual Fellatio Fantasy in a south Indian Ritual Tradition'. In *Vishnu on Freud's Desk: A Hinduism and Psychoanalysis Reader*, ed. T. G. Vaidyanathan and Jeffrey Kripal. Delhi: Oxford University Press.

——— forthcoming (c). 'Whose Goddess? Kali as Cultural Champion in Kerala Oral Narratives'. In *Aryan and Non-Aryan in south Asia: Proceedings of 1996 Lausanne/Michigan Seminar*, ed. Madhav Deshpande and Johannes Bronkhorst, Center for south and southeast Asian Studies, University of Michigan, Ann Arbor.

CANTLIE, A. (1977), 'Aspects of Hindu Asceticism'. In *Symbols and Sentiments: Cross-cultural Studies in Symbolism*, ed. I. Lewis. London: Academic Press.

CARSTAIRS, G. M. (1958), *The Twice-born: A Study of a Community of High-caste Hindus*. Bloomington: Indiana University Press.

CASTELINO, C. T. (1985), 'Sexual Victimization in Childhood: Its Impact on Adjustment in Early Adulthood'. Master's Thesis, Nirmala Niketan College of Home Science, University of Bombay, India.

CASTILLO, R. J. (1994a), 'Spirit Possession in south Asia, Dissociation or Hysteria? Part 1: Theoretical Background'. *Culture, Medicine and Psychiatry*, 18(1): 1–21.

——— (1994b), 'Spirit Possession in south Asia, Dissociation or Hysteria? Part 2: Case Histories'. *Culture, Medicine and Psychiatry*, 18(2): 141–62.

CESARA, M. (1982), *Reflections of a Woman Anthropologist: No Hiding Place*. London: Academic Press.

CHANDRAHASAN, K. A. (1989), *Padayani, Mudiyettu, Thiyyatt*. Tripunithura: IMPACT. [In Malayalam.]

CHAUDHURI, A. K. R. (1956), 'A Psycho-analytic Study of the Hindu Mother Goddess (Kali) Concept'. *American Imago*, 13(2): 123–48.

CHENGAPPA, R. (1980), 'The Mental Gulf'. *India Today*, 7(17): 58–61.

CHIB, S. S. (1988), *This Beautiful India: Kerala*. New Delhi: Ess Ess Publications.

CHODOROW, N. J. (1989), *Feminism and Psychoanalytic Theory*. New Haven: Yale University Press.

CHOONDAL, C. (1981), *Mudiyettu: Study in Folk Theatre*. Trichur, Kerala: Kerala Folklore Academy. [In Malayalam.]

CLAUS, P. J. (1975), 'The Siri Myth and Ritual: A Mass Possession Cult of south India'. *Ethnology*, 14(1): 47–58.

——— (1994), 'Ritual Transforms a Myth'. *South Asian Folklorist*, 1(1).

CLIFFORD, J. (1988), *The Predicament of Culture*. Cambridge, MA: Harvard University Press.

COBURN, T. B. (1991), *Encountering the Goddess*. Albany: State University of New York Press.

COEN, S. J. (1988), 'Sadomasochistic Excitement: Character Disorder and Perversion'. In *Masochism: Current Psychoanalytic Perspectives*, ed. R. A. Glick and D. I. Meyers, pp. 43–60. Hillsdale, NJ: Analytic Press.

COHEN, L. (1995), 'Holi in Banaras and the Mahaland of Modernity'. *GLQ*, 2(4): 399–424.

——— India Tonite. Manuscript in preparation.

COOMARASWAMY, A. K. (1938), 'The Symbolism of the Dome'. *Indian Historical Quarterly*, 14: 1–56.

——— (1971), *Yaksas*. New Delhi: Munshiram Manoharlal. (Original work published in 1928–31)

CRAPANZANO, V. (1973), *The Hamadsha: A Study in Moroccan Ethnopsychiatry*. Berkeley: University of California Press.

——— (1980), *Tuhami: Portrait of a Moroccan*. Chicago: University of Chicago Press.

CUNNINGHAM, A. and D. TICKNER (1981), 'Psychoanalysis and Indigenous Psychology'. In *Indigenous Psychologies: The Anthropology of the Self*, ed. Paul Heelas and Andrew Lock. London: Academic Press.

DANIEL, E. V. (1984), *Fluid Signs: Becoming a Person the Tamil Way*. Berkeley: University of California Press.

——— (1996), *Charred Lullabies: Chapters in an Anthropography of Violence*. Princeton, NJ: Princeton University Press.

DESJARLAIS, R. R. (1992), *Body and Emotion: The Aesthetics of Illness and Healing in the Nepal Himalayas*. Philadelphia: University of Pennsylvania Press.

DEVEREUX, G. (1967), *From Anxiety to Method in the Behavioral Sciences*. The Hague: Mouton.

DEVI, PHOOLAN (1996), *I, Phoolan Devi*. With M. Cuny and P. Rambali. London: Little, Brown and Company.

DIRKS, N. B. (1987), *The Hollow Crown: Ethnohistory of an Indian Kingdom*. Cambridge: Cambridge University Press.

DUMONT, L. (1961), 'Les mariages nayar comme faits indiens'. *L'Homme*, 1: 11–36.

DUNDES, A. (1962), 'From Etic to Emic Units in the Structural Study of Folktales'. *Journal of American Folklore*, 75: 95–105.

——— (1980), 'Wet and Dry, the Evil Eye: An Essay in Indo-European and Semitic Worldview'. In *Interpreting Folklore*, pp. 93–133. Bloomington: Indiana University Press.

ECK, D. (1981), *Darśan: Seeing the Divine Image in India*. Chambersburg, PA: Anima Books.

ELDER, J. (1996), 'Enduring Stereotypes about south Asia: India's Caste System'. *Education about Asia* 1(2): 20–2.

ELLENSON, G. S. (1985), 'Detecting a History of Incest: A Predictive Syndrome'. *Social Casework*, 66(9): 525–32.

——— (1986), 'Disturbances of Perception in Adult Female Incest Survivors'. *Social Casework* 67(3): 149–59.

ELWIN, V. (1949), *Myths of Middle India*. Oxford: Oxford University Press.

——— (1952), 'The Saora Priestess'. *Bulletin of the Department of Anthropology, Government of India*, 1 (1): 59–85.

ERNDL, K. M. (1993), *Victory to the Mother: The Hindu Goddess of Northwest India in Myth, Ritual, and Symbol*. New York: Oxford University Press.

EWING, K. P. (1992), 'Is Psychoanalysis Relevant for Anthropology?' In *New Directions in Psychological Anthropology*, eds T. Schwartz, G. M. White and C. A. Lutz, pp. 251–68. Cambridge: Cambridge University Press.

FAWCETT, F. (1901), *Nayars of Malabar*. Madras: Government Press.

FREED, R. S. and S. A. FREED (1964), 'Spirit Possession as Illness in a North Indian Village'. *Ethnology*, 3(2): 152–71.

——— (1985), 'The Psychomedical Case History of a Low-caste Woman of North India'. *Anthropological Papers of the American Museum of Natural History*, 69(2): 101–228.

FREEMAN, J. R. (1991), 'Purity and Violence: Sacred Power in the Teyyam Worship of Malabar'. Ph.D. dissertation. University of Pennsylvania, Philadelphia.

——— (1993), 'Performing Possession: Ritual and Consciousness in the Teyyam Complex of Northern Kerala'. In *Flags of Fame: Studies in south Asian Folk Culture*, ed. H. Brückner, L. Lutze and A. Malik, pp. 109–38. Delhi: Manohar.

FREUD, S. (1896a), 'The Aetiology of Hysteria'. *Standard Edition*, 3: 191–221.

——— (1896b), 'Further Remarks on the Neuro-psychoses of Defence'. *Standard Edition* 3: 162–85.

FULLER, C. J. (1975), 'The Internal Structure of the Nayar Caste'. *Journal of Anthropological Research*, 31(4): 283–312.

——— (1976), *The Nayars Today*. Changing Cultures Series. Cambridge: Cambridge University Press.

——— (1986), 'The Nayar Taravad'. *Man*, n.s. 21: 135–6.

——— (1992), *The Camphor Flame: Popular Hinduism and Society in India*. Princeton: Princeton University Press.

FULLER, E. F. (1993), 'Pierced by Murugan's Lance: The Symbolism of Vow Fulfillment'. In *The Psychoanalytic Study of Society: Essays in Honor of*

Alan Dundes, eds L. B. Boyer, R. M. Boyer and S. M. Sonnenberg. vol. 18, pp. 277–98. Hillsdale, NJ: Analytic Press.

GALENSON, E. (1988), 'The Precursors of Masochism: Protomasochism'. In *Masochism: Current Psychoanalytic Perspectives*, ed. R. A. Glick and D. I. Meyers, pp. 189–204. Hillsdale, NJ: Analytic Press.

GATWOOD, L. E. (1986), *Devi and the Spouse Goddess: Women, Sexuality and Marriage in India*. Riverdale: Riverdale Co.

GEERTZ, C. (1973), *The Interpretation of Cultures*. New York: Basic Books.

GENTES, M. J. (1992), 'Scandalizing the Goddess at Kodungallur'. *Asian Folklore Studies* 51(2): 295–322.

GILL, M. M. (1994), *Psychoanalysis in Transition: A Personal View*. Hillsdale, NJ: Analytic Press.

GOLD, A. (1988), 'Spirit Possession Perceived and Performed in Rural Rajasthan'. *Contributions to Indian Sociology* n.s. 22(1): 35–63.

GOUGH, E. K. (1952a), 'A Comparison of Incest Prohibitions and the Rules of Exogamy in Three Matrilineal Groups of the Malabar Coast'. *International Archives of Ethnography*, 46: 82–105.

——— (1952b), 'Changing Kinship Usages in the Setting of Political and Economic Change among the Nayars of Malabar'. *Journal of the Royal Anthropological Institute*, 82: 71–87.

——— (1955), 'Female Initiation Rites on the Malabar Coast'. *Journal of the Royal Anthropological Institute*, 85: 45–80.

——— (1959a), 'Cults of the Dead among the Nayars'. In ed. M. B. Singer, *Traditional India: Structure and Change*, pp. 446–78. Philadelphia: American Folklore Society.

——— (1959b), 'The Nayars and the Definition of Marriage'. *Journal of the Royal Anthropological Institute*, 89: 23–34.

——— (1961), 'Nayars of Central Kerala'. In *Matrilineal Kinship*, ed. D. Schneider and K. Gough. Berkeley: University of California Press.

——— (1973), 'Kinship and Marriage in southwest India'. *Contributions to Indian Sociology*, n.s. 7: 104–34.

GOULET, J. and D. YOUNG (1994), 'Theoretical and Methodological Issues'. In *Being Changed by Cross-cultural Encounters: The Anthropology of Extraordinary Experience*, ed. D. E. Young and J. Goulet, pp. 298–335. Ontario: Broadview Press.

GREGOR, T. (1990), 'Male Dominance and Sexual Coercion'. In *Cultural Psychology: Essays on Comparative Human Development*, ed. J. W. Stigler, R. A. Shweder, and G. Herdt, pp. 477–95. Cambridge: Cambridge University Press.

GULATI, LEELA (1987), 'Male Migration from Kerala: Some Effects on Women'. *Manushi*, 38: 14–19.

HANCOCK, M. (1995), 'The Dilemmas of Domesticity: Possession and Devotional Experience among Urban Smarta Women'. In *From the Margins of Hindu Marriage: Essays on Gender, Religion, and Culture*, ed. L. Harlan and P. B. Courtright. New York: Oxford University Press.

HARDGRAVE, R. L. (1968), 'The Breast-cloth Controversy: Caste Consciousness and Social Change in southern Travancore'. *Indian Economic and Social History Review*, 5: 171–87.

HARDY, F. (1983), *Virāha-bhakti: The Early History of Kṛṣṇa Devotion in south India*. Oxford: Oxford University Press.

HARLAN, L. and P. B. COURTRIGHT, eds. (1995), *From the Margins of Hindu Marriage: Essays on Gender, Religion, and Culture*. New York: Oxford University Press.

HARMAN, W. P. (1989), *The Sacred Marriage of a Hindu Goddess*. Bloomington: Indiana University Press.

HARPER, E. B. (1963), 'Spirit Possession and Social Structure'. In *Anthropology on the March: Recent Studies of Indian Beliefs, Attitudes and Social Institutions*, ed. L. K. Bala Ratnam, pp. 165–77. Madras: Book Centre and Social Sciences Association.

HART, G. (1973), 'Woman and the Sacred in Ancient Tamilnad'. *Journal of Asian Studies*, 32(2): 233–50.

——— (1975), *The Poems of Ancient Tamil*. Berkeley: University of California Press.

——— (1979), 'The Nature of Tamil Devotion'. In *Aryan and Non-Aryan in India*, ed. M. M. Deshpande and P. E. Hook, pp. 11–33. Michigan Papers on south and southeast Asia, No. 14, Ann Arbor: Center for south and southeast Asian Studies.

——— (1987), 'Early Evidence for Caste in south India'. In *Dimensions of Social Life: Essays in Honor of David B. Mandelbaum*, ed. P. Hockings. Berlin, Mouton: Gruyter.

HAWLEY, J. S. and D. M. WULFF, eds (1982), *The Divine Consort: Radha and the Goddesses of India*. Boston: Beacon Press.

HERDT, G. (1981), *Guardians of the Flutes: Idioms of Masculinity*. New York: McGraw-Hill.

HERDT, G. and R. J. STOLLER (1990), *Intimate Communications: Erotics and the Study of Culture*. New York: Columbia University Press.

HERSHMAN, P. (1977), 'Virgin and Mother'. In *Symbols and Sentiments: Cross-cultural Studies in Symbolism*, ed. I. Lewis, pp. 269–92. London: Academic Press.

HESS, L. (1993), 'Staring at Frames till they Turn into Loops'. In *Living Banaras*, ed. B. R. Hertel and C. A. Humes, pp. 73–101.

HILTEBEITEL, A. (1981), 'Draupadi's Hair'. In *Autour de la déesse Hindoue*, ed. M. Biardeau, pp. 179–214. *Purusartha: Recherches de sciences sociale sur l'Asie du Sud, Pt. V*. Paris: École des Hautes Études en Sciences Sociales.

——— (1988), *The Cult of Draupadi. Vol. 1: Mythologies: From Gingee to Kuruksetra*. Chicago: University of Chicago Press.

——— (1991), *The Cult of Draupadi. Vol. 2: On Hindu Ritual and the Goddess*. Chicago: University of Chicago Press.

HOLLOMAN, R. E. and W. ASHLEY (1983), 'Caste and Cult in Kerala'. *South Asian Anthropologist*, 4(2): 93–104.

HOSPITAL, J. T. (1982) [1966]. *The Ivory Swing*. New York: E. P. Dutton.

HUMES, C. A. (1997), 'Glorifying the Great Goddess or Great Woman? Hindu Women's Experience in Ritual Recitation of the Devi-Mahatmya'. In *Women in Goddess Traditions*, ed. Karen King. Minneapolis: Fortress Press.

ILANKOVATIKAL (1993), *The Cilappatikaram of Ilanko Atikal: An Epic of south India*, trans. R. Parthasarathy. New York: Columbia University Press.

INDUCHOODAN, V. T. (1969), *The Secret Chamber: A Historical, Anthropological and Philosophical Study of the Kodungallur Temple*. Trichur, Kerala: Cochin Devaswom Board.

JAMES, V. (1974), 'First Menstruation Ceremonies among the Parayans of a Nilgiri Village'. *Man in India*, 54(2): 161–72.

JEFFREY, R. (1976), *The Decline of Nayar Dominance: Society and Politics in Travancore, 1847–1908*. New York: Holmes & Meier.

——— (1992), *Politics, Women and Well Being: How Kerala Became 'a Model'*. Oxford: Oxford University Press.

JEHU, D. (1988), *Beyond Sexual Abuse: Therapy with Women Who Were Childhood Victims*. New York: John Wiley & Sons.

JOHNSEN, L. (1994), *Daughters of the Goddess*. St. Paul, Minnesota: Yes International Publishing.

KAHN, A. (1993), 'The Bobbitts: Post-Freudian Sex Symbols?' *San Francisco Chronicle*, 27 October, p. E7.

KAKAR, S. (1978), *The Inner World: A Psycho-analytic Study of Childhood and Society in India*. Delhi: Oxford University Press.

——— (1990), 'Stories from Indian Psychoanalysis: Context and Text'. In *Cultural Psychology: Essays on Comparative Human Development*, eds J. W. Stigler, R. A. Shweder and G. Herdt, pp. 427–45. Cambridge: Cambridge University Press.

——— (1996), *The Colors of Violence: Cultural Identities, Religion, and Conflict*. Chicago: University of Chicago Press.

KAMANI, G. (1995), 'Waxing the Thing'. In *Junglee Girl*. San Francisco: Aunt Lute Books.

KAPFERER, B. (1991) [1983]. *A Celebration of Demons: Exorcism and the Aesthetics of Healing in Sri Lanka*. Reprint. Washington D. C.: Smithsonian Institution Press.

KAUFMAN, I. (1982), 'Father-daughter incest'. In *Father and Child: Developmental and Clinical Perspectives*, eds S. H. Cath, A. R. Gurwitt and J. M. Ross, pp. 491–507. Boston: Little, Brown.

KERNBERG, O. F. (1988), 'Clinical Dimensions of Masochism'. In *Masochism: Current Psychoanalytic Perspectives*, eds R. A. Glick and D. I. Meyers, pp. 61–80. Hillsdale, NJ: Analytic Press.

KERSENBOOM, S. C. (1981), 'Virali'. *Journal of Tamil Studies*, 19: 19–41.

KERSENBOOM-STORY, S. C. (1987), *Nityasumangali: Devadasi Tradition in south India*. Delhi: Motilal Banarsidass.

KHOKAR, M. (1987), *Dancing for Themselves: Folk, Tribal and Ritual Dance of India*. New Delhi: Himalayan Books.

KINSLEY, D. R. (1975), *The Sword and the Flute: Kālī and Kṛṣṇa, Dark Visions of the Terrible and the Sublime in Hindu Mythology*. Berkeley: University of California Press.

——— (1986), *Hindu Goddesses: Visions of the Divine Feminine in the Hindu Religious Tradition*. Berkeley: University of California Press.

KISHWAR, M. (1990), 'Learning to Take People Seriously'. *Manushi*, 56: 2–10.

KLEIN, M. (1948), *Contributions to Psychoanalysis, 1921–45*. London: Hogarth Press.

——— (1957), *Envy and Gratitude*. London: Tavistock.

KONDO, D. (1986), 'Dissolution and Reconstruction of Self: Implications for Anthropological Epistemology'. *Cultural Anthropology*, 1: 74–96.

KONDOS, V. (1986), 'Images of the Fierce Goddess and Portrayals of Hindu Women'. *Contributions to Indian Sociology*, n.s. 20(2): 173–97.

KONOW, S. (1969) [1915], *The Indian Drama: The Sanskrit Drama*, trans. S. N. Ghosal. Calcutta: General Printers and Publishers.

KRAMRISCH, S. (1946), *The Hindu Temple*. Calcutta: University of Calcutta.

——— (1953), *Dravida and Kerala in the Art of Travancore*. Ascona: Artibus Asiae.

KRIPAL, J. J. (1994), 'Kali's Tongue and Ramakrishna: Biting the Tongue of the Tantric Tradition'. *History of Religions*, 34(2): 152–89.

——— (1995), *Kali's Child: The Mystical and the Erotic in the Life and Teachings of Ramakrishna*. Chicago: University of Chicago Press.

KRISHNA AYYAR, K. V. (1966), *A Short History of Kerala*. Ernakulam: Pai.

KRISHNA IYER, L. K. A. (1905), *Ethnographical Survey of the Cochin State*. Ernakulam: Cochin Government Press.

——— (1928–36), *The Mysore Tribes and Castes*. Mysore: Mysore University.

——— (1937–41), *The Travancore Tribes and Castes*. Trivandrum: Supt., Govt. Press.

——— (1968–70), *Social History of Kerala*. Madras: Book Centre Pub.

——— (1981) [1909–12], *The Cochin Tribes and Castes*. Madras: Higginbotham, for Govt. of Cochin. 3 vols.

KRYGIER, J. (1982), 'Caste and Female Pollution'. In *Women in India and Nepal*, eds M. Allen and S. N. Mukherjee, pp. 76–104. Canberra: ANU.

KULICK, D. and M. WILSON (1995), *Taboo: Sex, Identity and Erotic Subjectivity in Anthropological Fieldwork*. London and New York: Routledge.

KUMAR, N., ed. (1994), *Women as Subjects: South Asian Histories*. Charlottesville: University Press of Virginia.

KUNJAN PILLAI, E. P. N. (1970), *Studies in Kerala History*. Trivandrum: The author.

KURTZ, S. M. (1992), *All the Mothers are One: Hindu India and the Cultural Reshaping of Psychoanalysis*. New York: Columbia University Press.

LABARRE, W. (1984), *Muelos: A Stone Age Superstition about Sexuality*. New York: Columbia University Press.

LANGER, S. (1979), *Philosophy in a New Key: A Study in the Symbolism of Reason, Rite, and Art*. Cambridge, Mass: Harvard University Press.

LAWRENCE, J. H. (1976) [1811], *The Empire of the Nairs* [Vol. 1]. Delmar, NY: Scholars' Facsimiles and Reprints.

LEACH, E. R. (1970), 'A Critique of Yalman's Interpretation of Sinhalese Girls' Puberty Ceremonial'. In *Échanges et communications: Mélanges offert a Claude Lévi-Strauss a l'occasion de son 60ème anniversaire*, ed. J. Pouillon, & P. Maranda, pp. 819–28. The Hague: Mouton.

LEELA DEVI, R. (1986), *History of Kerala*. Kottayam: Vidyarthi Mithram Press.

LEWIS, I. M. (1989) [1971]. *Ecstatic Religion: A Study of Shamanism and Spirit Possession*. 2nd edn. London and New York: Routledge.

LOGAN, W. (1951) [1887], *Malabar*. Reprint. Madras: Government Press.

LUIZ, A. A. D. (1962), *Tribes of Kerala*. New Delhi: Bharatiya Adimjati Sevak Sangh.

MALINOWSKI, B. (1967), *A Diary in the Strict Sense of the Term*. New York: Harcourt, Brace, & World.

——— (1987) [1929], *The Sexual Life of Savages in North-western Melanesia*. 3rd edn. Boston: Beacon Press.

MANI, V. (1975), *Purāṇic Encyclopaedia*. Delhi: Motilal Banarsidass.

MARGLIN, F. A. (1985a), *Wives of the God-King*. New York: Oxford University Press.

——— (1985b), 'Female Sexuality in the Hindu World'. In *Immaculate and Powerful: The Female in Sacred Image and Social Reality*, ed. C. Atkinson, C. H. Buchanan and M. Mills, pp. 39–60. Boston: Beacon Press.

——— (1995), 'Gender and the Unitary Self: Looking for the Subaltern in Coastal Orissa'. *South Asia Research*, 15(1): 78–130.

MARTIN, E. (1987), *The Woman in the Body: A Cultural Analysis of Reproduction*. Boston: Beacon Press.

MASSON, J. M. (1976), 'The Psychology of the Ascetic'. *Journal of Asian Studies* 35(4): 611–25.

——— (1984), *The Assault on Truth: Freud's Suppression of the Seduction Theory*. New York: Farrar, Straus and Giroux.

MASTERS, K. (1993), 'Sex, Lies, and an 8-inch Carving Knife'. *Vanity Fair*, 56(11), November: 169ff.

MATEER, S. (1883), *Native Life in Travancore*. London: W. H. Allen & Co.

MATHEW, K. S. (1979), *Society in Medieval Malabar*. Kottayam: Jaffe Books.

MATHEW, V. G. (1984), 'Cultural Factors Related to Mental Illness in Kerala'. In *A guide to Clinical Psychiatry*, ed. V. M. D. Namboodiri and C. J. John, pp. 224–38. Kolenchery, Kerala: Department of Psychiatry, MOSC Medical Mission Hospital.

MCCORMACK, W. C. (1958), 'Sister's Daughter Marriage in a Mysore Village'. *Man in India*, 38: 34–48.

MCGILVRAY, D. B. (1982), 'Sexual Power and Fertility in Sri Lanka: Batticaloa Tamils and Moors'. In *Ethnography of Fertility and Birth*, ed. C. P. MacCormack, pp. 25–74. London: Academic Press.

——— (1988), 'The 1987 Stirling Award Essay: Sex, Repression, and Sanskritization in Sri Lanka?' *Ethos*, 16(2): 99–127.

MCKEAN, L. (1996), 'Bharat Mata: Mother India and her Militant Matriots'. In *Devi: Goddesses of India*, ed. J. S. Hawley and D. Wulff. Berkeley, CA: University of California Press.

MENCHER, J. P. (1962), 'Changing Familial Roles among south Malabar Nayars'. *Southwestern Journal of Anthropology*, 18: 230–45.

——— (1963), 'Growing up in south Malabar'. *Human Organization*, 22: 54–65.

——— (1964), 'Possession, Dance, and Religion in North Malabar, Kerala, India'. *International Congress of Anthropological and Ethnological Sciences*, 9: 340–45.

——— (1965), 'The Nayars of south Malabar'. In *Comparative Family Systems*, ed. M. F. Nimkoff, pp. 163–91. Boston: Houghton Mifflin.

MENON, C. A. (1959) [1943], *Kali Worship in Kerala* (2nd edn.). Madras: University of Madras.

MENON, K. P. P. (1986), *History of Kerala*, ed. T. K. K. Menon. New Delhi: Asian Educational Services.

MENON, R. (1992), 'Sexual Abuse of Children: Hidden Peril'. *India Today* (31 October 1992): 101–7.

MENON, S. (1996), 'Male Authority and Female Autonomy: A Study of the Matrilineal Nayars of Kerala, south India'. In *Gender, Kinship, Power*, ed. M.J. Maynes, A. Waltner, et al. New York: Routledge.

MENON, U. and R. A. SHWEDER (1994), 'Kali's Tongue: Cultural Psychology and the Power of Shame in Orissa, India'. In *Culture and the Emotions*, ed. H. Markus and S. Kitayama, pp. 241–84. Washington, D.C.: American Psychological Association.

MILLER, A. (1983), *For Your own Good: Hidden Cruelty in Child-rearing and the Roots of Violence*, trans. H. & H. Hannum. New York: Farrar Straus Giroux.

MILLER, B. D. (1981), *The Endangered Sex: Neglect of Female Children in Rural North India*. Ithaca: Cornell University Press.

MOHAMED KOYA, S. M. (1983), *Mappilas of Malabar: Studies in Social and Cultural History*. Calicut: Sandhya Publications.

MOORE, M. A. (1985), 'A New Look at the Nayar Taravad'. *Man*, n.s. 20: 523–41.

——— (1988), 'Symbol and Meaning in Nayar Marriage Ritual'. *American Ethnologist*, 15(2): 254–73.

——— (1989), 'The Kerala House as a Hindu Cosmos'. *Contributions to Indian Sociology*, n.s. 23(1): 169–201.

MORENO, E. (1995), 'Rape in the Field: Reflections from a Survivor'. In *Taboo*, ed. D. Kulick and M. Wilson, pp. 219–50. London and New York: Routledge.

MORENO, M. (1985), 'God's Forceful Call: Possession as a Divine Strategy'. In *Gods of Flesh, Gods of Stone: The Embodiment of Divinity in India*, ed. J. P. Waghorne and N. Cutler, pp. 102–20. Chambersburg, PA: Anima.

MOTI CHANDRA (1952–3), 'Some Aspects of Yaksha Cult in Ancient India'. *Prince of Wales Museum of Western India, Bulletin*, 3: 43–62.

MYERHOFF, B. (1990), 'The Transformation of Consciousness in Ritual Performances: Some Thoughts and Questions'. In *By Means of Performance: Intercultural Studies of Theatre and Ritual*, ed. R. Schechner and W. Appel. 245–9. Cambridge: Cambridge University Press.

NAIR, V. (1975), *The Legacy*. Delhi: Vikas.

NAKANE, C. (1963), 'The Nayar Family in a Disintegrating Matrilineal System'. In *Family and Marriage*, ed. J. Mogey, pp. 17–28. Leiden: E. J. Brill.

NAMBIAR, A. K. (1979), 'Structure of an Exorcistic Ritual of North Kerala'. *Malayalam Literary Survey* 3(2): 48–54.

NARAYAN, K. (1993), 'How Native is a 'Native' Anthropologist?' *American Anthropologist*, 95: 671–86.

The Natya Sastra of Bharatamuni [1987]. Translated into English by a board of scholars. Delhi: Sri Satguru.

NAYAR, S. K. (1962), *Keralattile natoti natakangal* [Folk dramas of Kerala], Madras University Malayalam Series, No. 12, Madras: Madras University. [In Malayalam]

——— (1972), 'Ayyappa Cult'. *Annals of Oriental Research*, 24(1): Malayalam section 1–19.

NEFF, D. (1987), 'Aesthetics and Power in Pambin Tullal: A Possession Ritual of Rural Kerala'. *Ethology*, 26(1): 63–71.

——— (1995), 'Fertility and Power in a Kerala Serpent Ritual'. Ph.D. dissertation, University of Wisconsin, Madison.

O'FLAHERTY, W. D. (1973), *Asceticism and Eroticism in the Mythology of Siva*. Oxford: Oxford University Press.

——— (1980), *Women, Androgynes, and Other Mythical Beasts*. Chicago: University of Chicago Press.

——— (1984), *Dreams, Illusions, and Other Realities*. Chicago: University of Chicago Press.

——— (1985), *Tales of Sex and Violence: Folklore, Sacrifice, and Danger in the Jaiminiya Brahmina*. Chicago: University of Chicago Press.

OBEYESEKERE, G. (1963), 'Pregnancy Cravings (dola-duka) in Relation to Social Structure and Personality in a Sinhalese Village'. *American Anthropologist*, 65(2): 323–42.

——— (1970), 'The Idiom of Demonic Possession'. *Social Science and Medicine*, 97–111.

——— (1977a), 'Psychocultural Exegesis of a Case of Spirit Possession in Sri Lanka'. In *Case Studies in Spirit Possession*, ed. V. Crapanzano and V. Garrison, pp. 235–94. New York: John Wiley.

——— (1977b), 'Social Change and the Deities: Rise of the Kataragama Cult in Modern Sri Lanka'. *Man*, n.s. 12: 377–96.

——— (1978), 'The Fire-walkers of Kataragama: The Rise of Bhakti Religiosity in Buddhist Sri Lanka'. *Journal of Asian Studies*, 37(3): 457–76.

——— (1981), *Medusa's Hair: An Essay on Personal Symbols and Religious Experience*. Chicago: University of Chicago Press.

——— (1984), *The Cult of the Goddess Pattini*. Chicago and London: University of Chicago Press.

——— (1990), *The Work of Culture: Symbolic Transformation in Psychoanalysis and Anthropology*. Chicago: University of Chicago Press.

OPLER, M. E. (1963), 'The Cultural Definition of Illness in Village India'. *Human Organization*, 22(1): 32–5.

PANDE, M. (1990), 'Girls'. In *The Inner Courtyard: Stories by Indian Women*, ed. L. Holmstrom, pp. 57–64. London: Virago.

PANIKKAR, K. M. (1918), 'Some Aspects of Nayar Life'. *Journal of the Royal Anthropological Institute*, 48: 254–93.

PARPOLA, ASKO (1994), *Deciphering the Indus Script*. Cambridge: Cambridge University Press.

PEARCE, J. C. (1982), *The Bond of Power: Meditation and Wholeness*. London: Routledge & Kegan Paul.

PETERSON, I. V. (1989), *Poems to Siva: The Hymns of the Tamil Saints*. Princeton: Princeton University Press.

PILLAI, C. M. (1976), *NBS Malayalam English Dictionary*. Kottayam, Kerala: Sahitya Pravarthaka Co-operative Society.

PILLAI, P. G. (1956), *Malayalabhashacharithram* [*History of Malayalam Literature*]. Kottayam: NBS. [In Malayalam].

PINTCHMAN, T. (1994), *The Rise of the Goddess in the Hindu Tradition*. Albany: State University of New York Press.

RABINOW, P. (1977), *Reflections on Fieldwork in Morocco*. Berkeley and Los Angeles: University of California Press.

RAHEJA, G. G. and A. G. GOLD (1994), *Listen to the Heron's Words: Reimagining Gender and Kinship in North India*. Berkeley: University of California Press.

RAM, K. (1992), *Mukkuvar Women: Gender, Hegemony and Capitalist Transformation in a south Indian Fishing Community*. New Delhi: Kali for Women.

RAMACHANDRAN, T. K. (1995), 'Notes on the Making of Feminine Identity in Contemporary Kerala Society' *Social Scientist* (New Delhi) 23(1–3): 109–23.

RAMAKRISHNAN, K. (1989), 'Shanta'. *Malayalam Literary Survey*, 11(4): 52–9.

RAMAKRISHNAN, M. (1991) [1967]. *Yakshi*, trans. P. Jayakumar. New Delhi: Penguin.

RAMAN UNNI, K. (1956), 'Visiting Husbands in Malabar'. *Journal of the Maharaja Sayajiro University of Baroda*, 5(1): 37–56.

RAMANUJAN, A. K. (1968), *The Interior Landscape: Love Poems from a Classical Tamil Anthology*. Bloomington: Indiana University Press.

——— (1983), 'The Indian Oedipus'. In *Oedipus: A Folklore Casebook*, ed. L. Edmunds and A. Dundes, pp. 234–61. New York: Garland.

——— trans. and ed. (1985), *Poems of Love and War*. New York: Columbia University Press.

——— (1986), 'Two Realms of Kannada Folklore'. In *Another Harmony: New Essays on the Folklore of India*, eds S. H. Blackburn and A. K. Ramanujan, pp. 41–75. Berkeley: University of California Press.

——— (1989), 'Is there an Indian Way of Thinking? An Informal Essay'. *Contributions to Indian Sociology* (*special issue*), n.s. 23(1): 41–58.

——— (1991), 'Toward a Counter-system: Women's Tales'. In *Gender, Genre, and Power in south Asian Expressive Traditions*, ed. A. Appadurai, F. J. Korom and M. A. Mills, pp. 33–77. Philadelphia: University of Pennsylvania Press.

RAMASWAMY, S. (1993), 'Engendering Language: The Poetics of Tamil Identity'. *Comparative Studies in Society and History*, 35: 683–725.

——— (1997), *Passions of the Tongue: Language Devotion in Tamil India, 1891–1970*. Berkeley: University of California Press.

RICHMOND, F. P., D. L. SWANN, and P. B. Zarrilli, eds. (1990), *Indian Theatre: Traditions of Performance*. Honolulu: University of Hawaii Press.

ROBINSON, S. P. (1985), 'Hindu Paradigms of Women: Images and Values'. In *Women, Religion, and Social Change*, ed. Y. Y. Haddad and E. B. Findly. Albany: State University of New York Press.

ROLAND, A. (1988), *In Search of Self in India and Japan: Toward a Cross-cultural Psychology*. Princeton: Princeton University Press.

ROSALDO, R. (1984), 'Grief and a Headhunter's Rage: On the Cultural Force of Emotions'. In *Text, Play, and Story: The Construction and Reconstruction of Self and Society*, ed. E. M. Bruner, pp. 178–95. 1983 Proceedings of the American Ethnological Society. Washington, D.C.: American Ethnological Society.

ROY, M. (1975), 'The Oedipus Complex and the Bengali Family in India (A Study of Father-Daughter Relations in Bengal)'. In *Psychological Anthropology*, ed. T. R. Williams, pp. 123–34. The Hague: Mouton.

ROY, R. L. (1963), 'Social Position of Music and Musicians in India'. *Indo-Asian Culture* (New Delhi), 11(3): 233–41.

RUBY, J., ed. (1982), *A Crack in the Mirror: Reflexive Perspectives in Anthropology*. Philadelphia: University of Pennsylvania Press.

RYAN-BLANEY, B. (1989), *An Analysis of Variables Associated with Post-traumatic Stress Disorder among Adult Women Incest Survivors*. D.Ed. dissertation. Boston University.

SALIBA, J. A. (1974), 'The New Ethnography and the Study of Religion'. *Journal for the Scientific Study of Religion*, 13: 145–58.

SATTAR, A. (1979), 'Place of Menstruating Woman in Tribal World'. *Folklore* (May and June): 111–18.

SCHECHNER, R. (1977), *Essays on Performance Theory 1970–1976*. New York: Drama Book Specialists.

——— (1985), *Between Theater and Anthropology*. Philadelphia: University of Pennsylvania Press.

——— (1990), 'Magnitudes of Performance'. In *By Means of Performance: Intercultural Studies of Theatre and Ritual*, ed. R. Schechner and W. Appel, pp. 19–49. Cambridge: Cambridge University Press.

SCHECHNER, R. and W. APPELL, eds (1990), *By Means of Performance: Intercultural Studies of Theatre and Ritual*. Cambridge: Cambridge University Press.

SCHECHNER, R. and L. HESS (1977), 'The Ramlila of Ramnagar'. *Drama Review* 21(3): 51–82.

SCHEPER-HUGHES, N. (1992), *Death Without Weeping: The Violence of Everyday Life in Brazil*. Berkeley: University of California Press.

SCHOEMBUCHER, E. (1993), 'Gods, Ghosts and Demons: Possession in south Asia'. In *Flags of Fame: Studies in south Asian Folk Culture*, ed. H. Brückner, L. Lutze and A. Malik, pp. 239–67. Delhi: Manohar.

SCHOTERMAN, J. A., ed. (1980), *The Yonitantra*. Delhi: Manohar.

SEDGEWICK, E. (1985), *Between Men: English Literature and Male Homosocial Desire*. New York: Columbia University Press.

SERED, S. S. (1994), *Priestess, Mother, Sacred Sister: Religions Dominated by Women*. New York: Oxford University Press.

SETH, P. (1992), 'A Dialogue with Serpents: A Snake Ritual of Kerala'. *Asian Art*, 5(3): 53–79.

SHASTRI, J. L., ed. (1969), *Śiva-Purāṇa*. Delhi: Motilal Banarsidass.

——— (1973), *Liṅga-Purāṇa*. Delhi: Motilal Banarsidass.

SHULMAN, D. (1976), 'The Murderous Bride: Tamil Versions of the Myth of Devi and the Buffalo-demon'. *History of Religions*, 16(2): 120–46.

——— (1980), *Tamil Temple Myths: Sacrifice and Divine Marriage in a south Indian Śaiva Tradition*. Princeton: Princeton University Press.

SHUNGOONNY MENON, P. (1878), *A History of Travancore from the Earliest Times*. Madras: Higginbotham.

SIRCAR, D. C., ed. (1967), *The Sakti Cult and Tara*. Calcutta: University of Calcutta.

——— (1973), *The Sakta Pithas*. Delhi: Moṭilal Banarisidass.

SLATER, P. E. (1968), *The Glory of Hera: Greek Mythology and the Greek Family.* Boston: Beacon Press.

SPIRO, M. E. (1982), *Oedipus in the Trobriands.* Chicago: University of Chicago Press.

SPRATT, P. (1977) [1966]. *Hindu Culture and Personality: A Psychoanalytic Study.* Bombay: Manaktalas.

SPRENGNETHER, M. (1990), *The Spectral Mother: Freud, Feminism, and Psychoanalysis.* Ithaca: Cornell University Press.

SREEDHARA MENON, A. (1967), *A Survey of Kerala History.* Kottayam: Sahitya Pravarthaka Co-operative Society.

SRINIVAS, M. N. (1955), 'A Brief Note on Ayyappa, the South Indian Deity. In *Professor Ghurye Felicitation Volume,* ed. K. M. Kapadia, pp. 238–43. Bombay: Popular.

——— (1956), 'A Note on Sanskritization and Westernization'. *Far Eastern Quarterly,* 15: 481–96.

SRINIVASAN, A. (1993), 'The Subject in Fieldwork: Malinowski and Gandhi'. *Economic and Political Weekly,* 28(50): 2745–52.

STAAL, F. (1989), *Rules Without Meaning: Ritual, Mantras and the Human Sciences.* New York: Peter Lang.

STANLEY, J. M. (1988), 'Gods, Ghosts, and Possession'. In *The Experience of Hinduism: Essays on Religion in Maharashtra,* eds E. Zelliot and M. Berntsen, pp. 26–59. Albany: State University of New York Press.

STOLLER, P. (1986), 'The Reconstruction of Ethnography'. In *Discourse and the Social Life of Meaning,* ed. P. P. Chock and J. R. Wyman, pp. 51–74. Washington, D.C.: Smithsonian Institution Press.

——— (1989), *Fusion of Worlds: An Ethnography of Possession among the Songhay of Niger.* Chicago: University of Chicago Press.

STOLLER, P. and OLKES, C. (1987), In *Sorcery's Shadow: A Memoir of Apprenticeship among the Songhay of Niger.* Chicago: University of Chicago Press.

STRACHEY, J. (1962), 'Editor's note to "Further remarks on the neuro-psychoses of defence", by S. Freud'. In *Standard Edition,* 3: 159–61.

SUKUMARAN NAIR, K. (1976), *Rural Politics and Government in Kerala.* Trivandrum: Kerala Academy of Political Science.

SUTHERLAND, G. H. (1991), *The Disguises of the Demon: The Development of the Yaksa in Hinduism and Buddhism.* Albany: State University of New York Press.

TAMBIAH, S. J. (1979), 'A Performative Approach to Ritual'. *Proceedings of the British Academy,* 65: 124–51.

TAPPER, B. E. (1979), 'Widows and Goddesses: Female Roles in Deity Symbolism in a south Indian Village'. *Contributions to Indian Sociology,* n.s. 13(1): 1–31.

TARABOUT, G. (1986), *Sacrifier et donner a voir en pays malabar: les fêtes de temple au Kerala (inde du Sud): étude anthropologique.* Paris: École Française d'extreme-orient.

TAUSSIG, M. (1987), *Shamanism, Colonialism, and the Wild Man: A Study in Terror and Healing*. Chicago: University of Chicago Press.

THAMPURAN, H. H. K. (1936), 'Kali Cult in Kerala'. *Rama Varma Research Bulletin*, 4: 77–97.

THANKAPPAN NAIR, P. (1969), 'Nair Women in Malayalam Proverbs'. *Journal of the Anthropological Society of Bombay*, n.s. 14(1): 1–14.

THIMMAIAH, G. and J. V. M. SHARMA, (1978), *Socio-economic Impact of Drinking in Karnataka*. Calcutta: Institute of Social Studies.

THOMPSON, C. (1983), 'Women, Fertility and the Worship of Gods in a Hindu Village'. In *Women's Religious Experience*, ed. P. Holden, pp. 113–31. London: Croom Helm.

TIRUMUMP, T. S. (1975), *Sri Bhadrakaaleemahatmya* (*Darukavadha*). Trichur: Geeta Press.

TRAUTMANN, T. R. (1982), *Dravidian Kinship*. Cambridge: Cambridge University Press.

TRAWICK, M. (1990a), 'The Ideology of Love in a Tamil Family'. In *Divine Passions: The Social Construction of Emotion in India*, ed. O. M. Lynch, pp. 37–63. Berkeley: University of California Press.

——— (1990b), *Notes on Love in a Tamil Family*. Berkeley: University of California Press.

TSING, A. L. (1993), *In the Realm of the Diamond Queen: Marginality in an Out-of-the-way Place*, Princeton, NJ: Princeton University Press.

TURNBULL, C. (1990), 'Liminality: A Synthesis of Subjective and Objective Experience'. In *By Means of Performance: Intercultural Studies of Theatre and Ritual*, ed. R. Schechner and W. Appel, pp. 50–81. Cambridge: Cambridge University Press.

TURNER, V. W. (1969), *The Ritual Process: Structure and Anti-structure*. Harmondsworth: Penguin.

——— (1974), *Dramas, Fields and Metaphors: Symbolic Action in Human Society*. Ithaca: Cornell University Press.

TYLER, S. A. (1986), 'Post-modern Anthropology'. In *Discourse and the Social Life of Meaning*, ed. P. P. Chock and J. R. Wyman, pp. 23–50. Washington, D. C.: Smithsonian Institution Press.

UCIDA, N. (1977), 'Folk Songs and the Observance of Puberty Ceremony in south India'. *Journal of Intercultural Studies*, 4: 51–4.

——— (1979), *Oral Literature of the Saurashtrans*. Calcutta: Simant.

UNNITHAN, T. K. N. (1974), 'Contemporary Nayar Family in Kerala'. In *The Family in India*, ed. G. Kurian, pp. 191–203. The Hague: Mouton.

UPADHYAYA, U. P. and S. P. UPADHYAYA (1984), *Bhuta Worship: Aspects of a Ritualistic Theatre*. Udupi: Regional Resources Centre for Folk Performing Arts.

VAIDYANATHAN, K. R. (1988), *Temples and Legends of Kerala*. Bombay: Bharatiya Vidya Bhavan.

VAN KLEY, P. A. (1992), 'Women Incest Survivors and How They Experience Their Own Anger'. Ph.D. dissertation, University of Toledo, Toledo, Ohio.

VATSYAYAN, K. M. (1989), *The Arts of Kerala Kshetram.* Tripunithura: Sree Rama Varma Govt. Sanskrit College.

VATUK, V. P. and S. VATUK (1975), 'The Lustful Stepmother in the Folklore of Northwestern India'. *Journal of South Asian Literature*, 11(1/2): 19–43.

VENU, G. (1984), 'Mudiyettu: Ritual Dance-drama of Kerala'. *Quarterly Journal of the National Centre for the Performing Arts*, 13(4): 5–12.

VIDYARTHI, G. (1976), 'Mudiyettu: Rare Ritual Theatre of Kerala'. *Sangeet Natak*, 42: 41–63.

VISWESWARAN, K. (1994), *Fictions of Feminist Ethnography.* Minneapolis: University of Minnesota Press.

WADLEY, S. S. (1975), *Shakti: Power in the Conceptual Structure of Karimpur Religion. University of Chicago Studies in Anthropology, Series in Social, Cultural, and Linguistic Anthropology,* 2. Chicago: University of Chicago, Department of Anthropology.

——— (1976), 'The Spirit Rides or the Spirit Comes: Possession in a North Indian Village'. In *The realm of the Extra-human: Agents and Audiences*, ed. S. Agehananda Bharati, pp. 233–51. The Hague: Mouton.

——— (1977), 'Women and the Hindu Tradition'. *Signs*, 3(1): 113–25.

——— ed. (1980), *The Powers of Tamil Women.* New York: Maxwell School of Citizenship and Public Affairs, Syracuse University.

——— (1992) [1977], 'Women and the Hindu Tradition'. In *Women in India: Two Perspectives*, ed. D. Jacobson and S. S. Wadley. New Delhi: Manohar.

WOOD, A. E. (1985), *Knowledge Before Printing and After: The Indian Tradition in Changing Kerala.* Delhi: Oxford University Press.

WULFF, D. M. (1982), 'Prolegomenon to a Psychology of the Goddess'. In *The Divine Consort: Radha and the Goddesses of India*, ed. J. S. Hawley and D. M. Wulff, pp. 283–97. Boston: Beacon Press.

YALMAN, N. (1963), 'On the Purity of Women in the Castes of Ceylon and Malabar'. *Journal of the Royal Anthropological Institute*, 93(1): 25–58.

YESUDAS, R. N. (1975), *A People's Revolt in Travancore: A Backward Class Movement for Social Freedom.* Trivandrum: Kerala Historical Society.

YOUNG, K. K. (1991), 'Goddesses, Feminists, and Scholars'. In *The Annual Review of Women in World Religions*, ed. A. Sharma and K. K. Young. 1: 105–79. Albany: State University of New York Press.

ZARRILLI, P. (1979), 'Kalarippayatt: Martial art of Kerala'. *Drama Review*, 23(2): 113–24.

——— (1984), '"Doing the Exercise": the In-body Transmission of Performance Knowledge in a Traditional Martial Art'. *Asian Theatre Journal*, 1(2): 191–206.

ZIMMERMAN, F. (1987), *The Jungle and the Aroma of Meats: An Ecological Theme in Hindu Medicine.* Berkeley: University of California Press.

INDEX

abuse 6, 8, 24, 182, 187, 221–42, 250, 263, 265, 277 (see also trauma)
acting 18, 47
agriculture 106–15, 134, 157
alari 82, 91, 286
alcohol 27, 43, 52, 64,110, 192 (see also liquor, toddy)
alcoholism 235
Alter, J. 175–80, 192
Ambalavāsi 17, 33, 139, 286
Americans 42–56, 71, 159, 208, 226–7, 256, 264–6, 277
Ammachi 242, 262
anaṅku 16, 30, 118, 129
anger 21, 30, 41, 46, 87, 119, 122, 128–9, 131, 134, 144–5, 150, 152, 156–64, 167–75, 183, 187, 189–90, 200–1, 203–4, 208, 216–17, 220, 227, 236, 238, 240, 244, 257, 262–5, 270
anthropology vi, 1–9, 155, 265, 269–71, 278 (see also ethnography, fieldwork)
aṟa 47, 117, 286
architecture 16, 60, 139
Arya Samaj 55
Aryan 15, 21, 25, 27, 60, 104
āśān 42–3, 47, 79, 286
astrology 27, 41, 46, 69, 134, 215 (see also praśnam, divination, calendar, seasons)
asura 19–21, 30, 83, 86, 136, 178, 286
Ayyappa(n) 107, 130, 135–7, 143, 153, 154, 180–1

Babb, L. 152
bādhā 213–17, 220, 228–31, 233, 236, 262, 286
bījam 110, 113, 116, 142, 171, 176, 179 (see also Raktabījāsura, semen)
Baker-Reynolds, H. 16
banana 71, 73, 75–7, 106, 144, 146, 214, 252
battle 15, 21, 23, 29–31, 48, 64–7, 89, 91, 103n, 112–13, 117, 121–2, 132, 136, 138, 143, 146, 158, 164, 169, 178 (see also war)
beating 99, 159, 161, 217–18, 251, 281 (see also abuse)
Beck, B. E. F. 121
Behar, R. 9, 273
Bennett, L. 138, 152
Berreman, G. D. 2, 63, 187, 247, 251
bestiality 165, 192, 250
Bhadrakāḷi 12, 15, 18, 33, 59, 64–7, 71–2, 77–8, 81–3, 88, 107, 109–12, 118–19, 121–2, 126, 129, 131–5, 137–8, 141,

144, 147–8, 150, 153, 158, 161, 163, 167, 170, 174, 176–8, 182–3, 189, 200, 202, 212, 214–16, 219, 221, 242, 251, 262–3, 275, 277, 285, 286
kaḷam of 75–6
mythology 19–21
origins of 24–7
offerings to 44, 46, 210
relation to kaḷari 29–31
(see also Dēvi, Bhagavati, Kāḷi)
Bhadrakāḷi Māhātmyam 19
Bhadrōḷpatti 19, 60
Bhagavati 1, 5–7, 10–12, 14–17, 25, 27, 31, 32, 34, 37, 43–6, 48, 58–9, 67, 69, 82, 89, 92, 95, 105–7, 122, 124, 131, 134–5, 144–8, 150, 151, 152, 153, 155, 163, 167, 170, 178, 183, 188–9, 190, 200, 209, 212–14, 230, 236, 245, 258, 264, 274–5, 277–9, 285
agriculture and 108–15, 131–2
anger of 145, 156, 158, 162
as mother 138, 158, 161–2, 174
kaḷam 64, 73, 75, 107, 140, 274
menstruation and 115–19, 141
mental illness and 214–15, 229, 231, 233
mythology 19–21, 148, 162, 167–8
North direction and 140–1
offerings to 140, 142
sexuality and 164–6, 170–1, 183, 219
snakes and 144–5
virgin girls and 118, 121, 167
women and 203, 205–6, 208, 210–12, 218–19, 262
(see also Bhadrakāḷi, Kāḷi, Dēvi)
Bhairavi 34, 99
Bharaṇi 25, 95, 128–9, 165–7, 183, 212, 266, 279, 285
Bharati A. 27, 61, 104, 151, 238
bhūta 89, 103, 141, 154, 185, 286
bījam 110, 113, 116, 142, 164, 171, 176, 179, 286
birth 20, 41, 113, 115, 119, 122, 137, 140–2, 150, 154, 178, 193, 202, 205, 221, 263
of Bhagavati/Bhadrakāḷi 18, 20, 64, 67, 69, 89, 111, 147, 168
BJP (Bharata Janata Party) 191, 244
blood v, 16, 20–30 passim, 35, 59, 64–6, 73, 75–7, 80, 82, 92, 96, 99–101, 103, 110, 112–23, 126, 128, 130–7 passim, 141–2, 145–50, 151, 152, 163–4, 166–8, 171, 177–9, 187, 195, 200, 202, 205–6, 211, 213, 215, 238, 251, 263, 266, 269, 274, 284
sacrifice 17–18, 27, 66, 131, 211, 253 (see also guruti)
Boddy, J. 249
Brahma 20, 61
brahman 253
Brahmin 11, 13, 15, 17, 25, 27–8, 30–3, 35, 45, 56, 59, 60, 61, 62, 64, 94–5, 102, 103, 116, 139, 143, 159, 163, 165–6, 186, 197, 205, 209–10, 215, 244, 246, 247,
Brahmaṇi pāṭṭu 130
breasts 16, 18, 28–30, 58, 61, 64, 73, 75, 99, 105, 108, 129–30, 138, 148, 150–1, 152, 166, 169–74, 177, 179–83, 185, 189–90, 192, 193, 202–3, 208, 220, 250, 263, 269
agricultural symbolism 108–9, 111, 114, 150
covering of 173–4, 197–8
in costume 18, 77–9, 90–1, 96, 109, 144, 173–4, 215
of goddess 73, 75–6, 81, 108, 128, 130, 174, 213

breastfeeding 40, 122, 124, 128, 131, 138, 170–4, 177, 179–83, 191
Kūḷi's 96–8, 185–7
Briere and Runtz 227–9
Books, D. R. 61, 151
Brubaker, R. L. 24, 152, 237–43, 251, 257, 260
Buddhism 13, 16–17, 60, 143

caitanyam 43, 286
calendar 132, 153 (see also seasons, months)
candāṭṭam 126
Cantlie, A. 151, 176–7, 179, 191
Carstairs, G. M. 137, 151, 152, 171, 191, 249
caste 11–12, 14–18, 24–8, 31–6, 39, 42, 44–5, 55–6, 60, 61, 78, 95, 103, 111, 115–18, 124, 139, 144, 161, 166, 173, 184, 187–8, 193, 195–8, 204, 206–7, 209–11, 213, 218, 221, 223, 243–4, 247, 248, 253, 262, 274, 277 (see also Ambalavāsi, Brahmin, Ezhava, Kṣatriya, Kuṟup, Mārār, Nāyar, Parayan, Pulluvan, Pulaya, Śudra)
Castillo, R. J. 221, 228–9, 249
castration 171–2, 190, 240, 251
cat(s) 99, 178, 192n, 250n (*see also* bestiality)
ceṇṭa 21, 83, 102, 286 (see also drum)
celibacy 31, 135, 137, 154, 180–1, 200, 265
cetti 29, 79, 82, 147, 264, 286
Chakyar Kuttu 18
Chavakkad Kaḷari Sangham 28–31, 61
Chengannur Bhagvati 116, 210
chicken pox 46, 119, 133–34, 152
child abuse, See abuse
childbirth 39–40, 118, 142, 158, 205–6, 208
Chingam (month of) 124–6, 137, 139, 153
Chodorow, N. 249
Choondal, C. 17, 19, 21, 34, 59, 60, 62, 102, 185, 235, 256
choṭṭa 108, 110, 133, 214, 286
Chottanikkara Bhagavati 122, 129–31, 148, 214–16
Christian 13, 107, 153, 174, 191, 247
Cilappatikāram 61, 128, 129, 132,
Claus, P. J. 154, 244
clown 67, 181 (see also Kūḷi)
Coburn T. 152
Cochin 12, 34, 51, 209
cock 131, 142, 164, 166, 171, 181
coconut v, 10, 14, 58, 64, 70, 73, 75–9, 81, 86–94, 105–10, 119, 125, 131, 133, 137, 150, 151, 157, 236, 262, 264
comic 67, 93, 95–8, 103, 169, 184–6, 255, 260–1, 272
communism 45, 50, 54–5, 58
conversion 55, 102
costume 10, 18, 29, 34, 44, 66, 67, 71–2, 76–9, 85, 91, 93, 96, 102, 109, 117, 144, 173, 184, 191, 215, 255, 256
countertransference 7–8, 268, 270
Crapanzano,V. 3, 189, 192, 236, 273
culture, ix, x, 2–9, 12–13, 15, 17–18, 21, 24–5, 27, 32, 36, 52, 58, 60, 89, 96–7, 105, 115, 148, 151, 157, 163, 168, 170, 184, 187, 193, 205, 219, 223, 226, 233–5, 254, 265–6, 269–71, 272, 276–9
cunnilingus 168, 192

Dānavēndra 49, 67, 78, 96, 98, 186
dance 10–12, 18, 23, 34, 36, 47–8, 52, 59, 65, 67, 77, 82, 84, 86–92, 97, 99, 113, 129–30,

168–9, 186, 199, 201, 214–16, 262–4, 263–4, 283, 285
Daniel, E. V. 119, 137, 151, 153, 248
Dārika(n) 12, 15, 19–20, 48–9, 61, 64–7, 72–3, 76–8, 80, 82, 84–92, 96–100, 103, 112–13, 116, 126, 131–3, 146, 150, 158, 161, 164, 167–9, 178, 186–7, 205, 219, 231, 236, 239–40, 251, 256, 258, 266, 275, 286
Dārikavadham 18–21, 158, 159, 164, 167, 169, 176–7, 191, 240–1, 251, 286
darśan 39, 142, 286
Dāruka 19, 60–1, 154, 170 (see also Dārika)
Dārukavadham, See Dārikavadham
death 7, 13, 18, 20, 34, 41, 61, 66, 103, 112–13, 118–19, 121, 129, 131–5, 137, 140–4, 146, 150, 151, 154, 158–9, 164, 174, 200–1, 204, 218, 228, 237–8, 241–2, 248, 252, 257, 281
decapitation 67, 98, 100, 142, 166, 189, 242, 275
Debonair (magazine) 248, 250
dēva 21, 83, 86, 103, 167, 213, 233, 249, 286
Devereux, G. 268–70
Dēvi 20, 27, 29–30, 46, 59, 72, 76, 81, 101, 108, 126, 134, 151, 160, 178, 205, 210–13, 242–3
Devī Bhāgavāta Purāṇa 19
Devī Māhātmya 19, 122, 191
dēvikōpam 41, 64
Dhanu 107, 114, 117, 135, 137, 140, 181
directions (cardinal) 86, 138–9, 282 (see also East, North, Northeast, Northwest, South, Southwest, West)
discipline ix, 2, 40, 159, 161, 270
dissociation 6, 227–9, 262
divination 2, 24, 27–8, 33, 108, 116 (see also praśnam)
dowry 38, 200
drama ix, 6, 11–12, 15, 18–19, 34, 48, 52, 56, 65, 69, 75–7, 80, 83–4, 91–2, 97, 103, 105, 113, 117, 134, 150, 155–6, 170, 183, 186–8, 234, 241, 252–5, 258–61, 266, 275, 278 (see also theatre)
Dravidian 15–17, 30, 35, 60, 62, 86, 89, 103, 112–13, 128, 141, 147, 153, 188
dress x, 42, 53–5, 76–8, 121, 156, 165, 183, 185, 197–8, 202, 212, 215, 238, 246–7, 266
drum(ming) 21, 23–5, 36, 47–9, 58, 64–5, 68, 70, 72, 76, 79, 82–99, 102, 103, 111, 118, 150, 156, 214, 255, 272, 279, 285 (see also rhythm, tāḷam)
Durga 20, 61, 122, 136
Dundes, A. 192

earring 53, 70, 80, 83–4, 147–8
East 14, 37, 62, 139–40, 210
education 29, 36, 45, 47, 196–7, 216, 233, 246, 248
elephant 15, 23, 58, 64, 70, 83–4, 86, 102, 112, 116–7, 125, 133, 146–7, 154, 210, 214, 280
Ellamma 240–41
Ellenson, G. S. 228
Elwin, V. 61, 251, 268
empathy ix, 231, 242, 268
Ernakulam 12, 28, 34, 49, 51, 122, 129, 198, 214, 218
Erndi, K. M. 138, 152, 204, 244
erotic 23, 30, 39, 135, 137, 145–8, 152, 153, 170–3, 175–9, 182–3, 188–90, 241, 248–50, 269–70, 279
ethnography x, 1–8, 268–71

Ezhava 28, 34, 61, 62, 139, 210–11, 247
exorcism 249
eye 108, 174–7, 218, 240, 267
  evil 177
  third (of Śiva) 20, 64, 85, 133, 156, 167, 168, 176–7, 190, 205

fellatio 170, 179–183, 190, 192–3, 208, 230
feminism 6, 9, 187, 189, 230, 244, 275, 277
fertility 12, 16, 23, 32, 59, 107–18, 121, 124–6, 128, 131–2, 135, 137, 141, 145–6, 155, 157, 164, 177, 184, 189, 208, 211, 257, 274
festival 4, 10, 13, 23–4, 28, 33, 39, 45, 59, 64, 66, 68, 69–70, 72, 76, 95, 101, 102, 103, 108, 111, 114–15, 122, 125, 128–9, 134–5, 153, 164–6, 191, 201, 212, 214, 223, 230, 245, 257, 266, 279, 285
fever 10, 44, 65, 114, 119, 157–8, 216
field assistant x, 52, 55, 69, 270
fieldwork 4, 51–9
fire 16, 20, 27, 37, 55, 66, 75, 78, 87, 90–1, 98, 135, 137, 140, 150, 155–8, 176, 178, 252, 256, 264, 269, 280
firecrackers 64, 70, 76, 84, 90
flower 29, 44, 64–5, 70, 73, 75–6, 78–9, 82, 85–7, 90–3, 100, 109–10, 115–17, 147, 185, 201, 213, 251, 264, 280, 282
folk 12, 18, 41, 52, 57, 81, 97, 108, 110, 119, 143, 147, 162–4, 176, 200, 204, 220–3, 226, 236, 238, 252–3, 260, 277
forest 14, 20, 24–5, 46, 59, 61, 67, 93, 96–7, 101, 102, 103, 119, 124–6, 130–1, 136, 141, 143,
  147–8, 154, 164, 184–5, 252, 256, 263, 280, 283
Freeman, J. R. xiv, 14, 102, 151, 152, 187, 193, 251, 255, 272
Freud, S. 171, 219–20, 222, 232–3, 250, 278
Friday 46, 65, 107, 110, 129, 133–4, 153, 214
Fuller, C. J. 135, 138, 246
Fuller, E. F. 192

Ganesh 67, 83, 147, 153, 169
Garuḍan 21, 148, 286
Garuḍan tūkkam 148
gender x, 2, 12, 31, 55, 104–5, 145, 170, 187–8, 203, 211, 230, 261, 269–70, 274
genitals 16, 110, 116, 145, 148, 150, 183, 221
Gentes, M. J. 60, 95, 166, 212, 266
Ghaṇṭākarṇa(n) 20, 60, 167–8, 239, 286
Ghats, Western 13, 24, 96, 118
ghost 20, 23–4, 89, 103, 133, 164, 184–5, 238
goddess 59, 61, 62, 103, 151, 152, 154, 191, 248, 251 (see also Bhadrakāḷi, Bhagavati, Bhairavi, Durga, Kāḷi, Kannaki, Koṯṯavai, Lakṣmi, Oṯṯamulacci, Pārvati)
Gold, A. 217, 243, 249
Gough, K. x, 62, 151, 168, 191, 219–22, 246
guruti 29, 66, 100–2, 103, 114–15, 130, 141, 171, 210–11, 215

hair 1, 64, 66, 70, 76, 78, 81, 88–91, 94, 96–8, 100, 103, 105–8, 119, 121, 130, 167, 175, 185–6, 201, 208, 212, 214–15, 218, 221, 229, 236, 269, 279

Hardy, F. 18, 21, 24, 152, 253
Harman, W. P. 124
Hart, G. 16, 17, 103, 113, 129, 141, 153, 193, 255
Hawley and Wulff 138, 152
heat 12, 51, 85, 92, 104, 106, 110, 119, 121, 129, 135, 137, 150, 156–8, 161–4, 168, 175–7, 189, 202, 239, 249, 251, 257, 279, 280–1
Hemambika 27, 61
Herdt, G. 180, 192, 193
Herdt and Stoller 7, 273
Hess, L. 273
Hiltebeitel, A. 60, 103
Hindu, ix, 10–11, 16–17, 27, 37, 55–6, 58, 60, 62, 80, 102, 104, 111, 121–3, 132, 139, 142–3, 153, 165, 191, 193, 219, 221, 236–7, 246, 253, 262, 264–5
history ix, 8, 12–13, 15, 21, 27, 33, 56, 59, 60, 61, 103, 141, 150, 228, 235, 237, 245, 259, 265, 270, 277, 278
homosexuality 136, 180–3, 187–90, 192, 193, 199, 231, 233, 235, 250
house x, 13–14, 18, 20, 32, 34–41, 43, 47, 51–2, 55, 79, 81, 94–5, 105–7, 109, 117–18, 132, 139–40, 143, 145, 159–62, 174, 182, 196–8, 201–3, 205–7, 209–10, 213–14, 217, 225, 234, 236, 245, 246, 264, 266, 274, 284
hysteria 213, 222, 228–9, 231–3, 249

iconography 10, 17, 21, 32, 112, 144, 148, 179, 277
Idavam 135 (see also months, calendar)
incest 138, 167–70, 190, 219–30, 239–41, 250–1
Induchoodan, V. T. 115, 128
Irula 184

jackwood 77, 81, 83, 101, 102, 126, 150 (see also plāvu)
Jain 13, 16, 60, 143, 154
Jeffrey, R. 59, 62, 196–7, 246

Kailāsam 20, 67, 85, 92, 169–70, 187, 239, 286
Kakar, S. 9, 152, 171–2, 174, 191, 249
kaḷam xvii, 28, 33, 48, 65–6, 71–7, 82, 85, 95, 107, 109, 112, 114, 116–17, 120, 124, 138, 140, 143, 150, 153, 169, 255, 274, 286
kaḷam pāṭṭu 33, 65, 73, 102, 124, 286
Kalambukavu Bhagavati 46
kaḷari 6, 27–31, 286
kaḷarippayaṯṯ 28–9, 31, 48, 286
Kāḷi (Skt. Kālī) xv, 15, 18, 20–2, 27, 29–30, 43–4, 48–9, 59, 65–8, 72, 77–93, 95–100, 103, 108–9, 112, 115–16, 118–19, 122, 131, 137, 144, 146, 148, 150, 156–8, 160–1, 164, 167–71, 178–9, 183–90, 202, 204–5, 208, 215, 231, 233–5, 238–40, 242–64, 266–7, 276–8, 286
Kannaki 61, 128–9
Kanni (month of) 138–9, 145
Kanniyākumāri 27, 61, 104
Kapadia, K. 194
kārṇavar 35, 47, 50, 286
Karnataka 24, 28, 61, 130, 141, 148, 178, 243–4, 251
Kathakaḷi 11, 17, 72, 77, 102, 252, 286
kēḷi 5, 83
Kersenboom, S. C. 23, 60
kinship 35, 62, 249, 251

Kinsley, D. R. 60, 151, 152, 153, 191, 237
Kishwar, M. 203
Klein, M. 6, 171, 180
Kodungallur Bhagavati 13, 16, 25, 27, 95, 126–31, 134, 140, 142, 151, 164–6, 171, 183, 191, 205, 212, 266, 279, 285
Koratty 49–50, 209, 246
Koṯṯavai 23–4, 148, 286
Kōyimbaṭa Nāyar 67, 78, 93–5, 97, 103, 186, 255, 260, 272
Kripal, J. J. 137, 178, 191, 259, 277
Krishna 107, 125, 130, 137, 157, 204, 263
Kṣatriya 31, 45, 287
Kūḷi 49, 67, 78, 83, 93, 95–9, 101, 103, 181, 183–7, 193, 239–40, 242, 255, 260–1, 272, 287
Kūḷiāṭṭam 184
kumkum 29
Kurava 21, 117, 152, 247, 256, 287
kurinji 111, 146, 148, 150
Kurtz, S. M. 123, 152
Kurumba 84, 248
Kurumbakāvu Bhagavati 151
Kuṟup 12, 33–6, 39, 41–2, 48, 50, 62, 128, 221, 239, 287
Kūṭiyāṭṭam 11, 18, 86, 102, 252

LaBarre, W. 192
Lakṣmi 122, 130, 138, 212, 280
landscape 10, 12, 15–16, 51, 104–6, 111, 114, 121, 125, 131–2, 135, 143, 146–50, 155, 276
Liṅga Purāṇa 19, 170
liquor 24, 28, 110, 160, 236 (see also alcohol, toddy)
Long-Tongue 178
love x, 37–8, 47, 51, 53–4, 56, 59, 92, 105–6, 112, 121, 124, 134, 147, 159–62, 170, 172, 175, 180, 182, 190, 196, 213, 224, 238–9, 245, 263–4, 267–72, 275, 279
lovemaking 132, 147
lust 65, 119, 135, 146, 158, 165, 176, 183, 191, 261

Mahiṣāsuramārdinī 136
makeup 18, 44, 49, 67, 77–81, 96, 101, 131, 152, 156, 168, 184, 201–2, 234, 256
Malabar 18, 219
Malayalam xv, 4, 17, 54, 59, 66, 93, 103, 107, 113, 134, 138–9, 147, 153, 164, 177, 196, 216, 245, 255, 257, 263, 272
Malinowski, B. 3, 270
Manōdari 20, 167, 287
mango 76, 79, 90, 94
leaves 17
Maṇipravāḷam 17, 255
Mannarsala 145
mantra 20, 28, 73, 80, 95, 110, 168, 213
mantravādam 15, 27–8 (see also sorcery)
Mārār 12, 34–42, 50, 62, 80, 158, 221, 239, 287
Marglin, F. A. 124, 151, 152, 169
Māriyammaṉ 212–13
marriage 13–14, 33–8, 42, 58, 62, 117, 119, 124–5, 135, 152, 181–2, 184, 191, 196, 198–201, 208, 217, 219, 221–3, 233, 235, 239, 245, 248, 251, 263, 265, 270
marumakkattayam 35
Marutam 105, 107, 112, 121, 148, 150
masochism 171–2, 190, 194, 230, 251
Masson, J. M. 182, 222, 249, 265
masturbation 191, 246, 248

Matangi 24, 32, 243
matriachy 195
matrilineal 13–14, 18, 29, 31, 34–8, 42, 56, 124, 161, 188, 195–7, 209, 219, 221, 246, 262, 277
McGilvray, D. B. 121, 247
Medam (month of) 114, 153
Mencher, J. P. 161, 173, 236, 243, 246
Menon, C. A. 61, 152, 193
menstruation 46, 115–22, 128–9, 131, 137, 140–2, 146, 152, 167, 171, 179, 202, 204–8, 215–17, 231, 249
milk 44, 106, 146, 150, 176–7
  breast 124, 169–70, 179–80
  coconut 109
  offering 144, 146, 174–5
Miller, A. 230
Minam (month of) 111, 114, 128, 131, 138, 145, 266
mirror 70, 78, 80–1, 102, 117, 136, 148, 152, 201, 283
Mohini 136
month(s) 42, 43, 64, 107, 117, 124–5, 130, 132, 135, 145, 153, 181, 185, 207, 245, 266–7 (see also individual months of Malayalam calendar)
  symbolic values of 137–40
Moore, M. A. 62, 139–40, 145, 246
mother x, 35–7, 40–1, 98, 101, 103, 106, 108–9, 123–4, 131, 152, 154, 168, 170–3, 180, 186–7, 189–92, 196, 202, 204, 207–9, 211, 217, 239, 244, 246, 263–4, 269, 274, 276
  anger of 155, 158–62, 170, 172, 182, 231
  breastfeeding 124, 128, 138, 172–3, 183
  breast of 171, 173–4
  earth 113, 115, 122, 150
  eroticism of 171–2, 179, 189–90, 220, 225, 233, 240
  goddess, x, 10, 29, 59, 84, 96, 122, 126, 173, 242
  idealization of 161
  love 128, 170, 213
  milk of 177, 179
  'phallic' 171
Mūkāmbika Bhagavati xvii, 27, 61, 148–9, 178
Murugan 147, 194
music ix, 11–12, 18, 23, 34, 36, 47, 52, 59, 66, 68, 73, 75, 82–4, 90, 93, 146, 216, 253–5, 272, 282, 283 (see also drum, rhythm, tāḷam)
musician(s) 21, 70, 76, 79, 128, 226, 234
Muslim 13, 18, 153, 247
muṭi 11, 33–4, 43, 46–7, 67, 71, 72, 78–81, 88–93, 95, 97–102, 173, 185, 202, 256, 264, 287
  agricultural symbolism 107
  and jackwood 111
  as hair 108
  meanings of word 107
  sacred power of 46–7, 67, 72, 78, 81
  snakes adorning 144
Muṭiyēṯṯu ix–x, 1, 4–6, 16–18, 106, 152, 248, 287
  agricultural symbolism 106–14, 132, 150–1
  characters 67, 93
  comedy in 93–8, 184–7, 260–1
  costumes 77–8, 102, 103
  description of 11–12, 64–101
  directional symbolism 140–2
  economic aspects 49–51, 62, 63
  heat and 155–7
  makeup 76, 78–80
  music 82–3, 86, 88, 124
  performers 33–45, 49, 57
  preliminary rituals 65, 72–5, 77
  previous studies 59

relation to martial arts 28–30, 48
relation to smallpox 45–6
sacred power of 188, 258
scenes 67–8
styles 49
texts 18–19, 83–4, 86, 272
time of performance 114, 132–4, 153
training 47–8
women and 202–6, 261–2
Muvattupuzha 49, 50, 57, 82, 97

nāga 17, 143–4, 174, 287
nāgayakṣi 174, 287
nalukeṭṭu 37
Nambūtiri See Brahmin
Nambiar (caste), 34, 62
Nambiar, A. K. 102
naming 35–6, 41
Nārada 20, 67, 78, 84, 85
Nātya Śāstra 1, 12, 253
Navarātri 28, 122
Nāyar 11, 13, 14, 17, 24, 28, 29, 31–4, 36, 44–5, 56, 61, 62, 85, 139, 195–7, 206–7, 219, 246, 247, 248, 262, 287
Ethnic stereotypes 31–2
Nāyar, S. K. 102, 103, 153
Neff, D. 33, 154, 192
newspaper articles 56, 236
neytal 143, 146, 148, 150
nipple 29, 91, 97–8, 177, 263
nityasumaṅgalī 23
North 29, 101, 125, 138–42, 154, 205, 206
Northeast 138, 145, 269
Northwest 28, 139
noyimbu 43

O' Flaherty, W. D. 151, 152, 164, 176–8, 180, 191, 192
Obeyesekere, G. 6–7, 32, 59, 60, 61, 128, 170–1, 175, 191, 192, 217, 220, 229, 234, 241, 243–4, 247, 248, 249, 251, 259–61, 264, 272, 276–7
objectivity 2, 8, 266, 268–9
obscenity 24, 71, 95, 97, 128, 135, 164–6, 185, 191–2, 229, 260, 272
in folklore, 192, 250, 272
Oedipal 171, 190, 192, 194, 217, 220, 230, 239–40, 251
oracle 11, 25, 29, 33, 89, 165, 204, 210, 216, 239, 252, 287 (see also veḷiccappāṭu)
Orissa 60, 113, 151, 169
Oṯṯamulacci 28, 61
paddy 10, 14, 50, 64–6, 69, 75, 77, 82, 99, 101,105–7, 109–11, 114–15, 119, 124–5, 131, 150, 151, 213, 236, 253, 264, 281, 287
Pakkattil 61, 203–4, 209–10, 246
Palghat 25, 61, 165, 212, 248
pāḷum nūṟum 144
pāna 153
Panayannarkava Bhagavati 210–11
pancavādyam 79
pantal 117, 287
Parayan 118, 206
Parpola, A. 60
participant observer 52 (see also fieldwork)
Pārvati 59, 61, 122, 130–1, 135, 147, 153, 167–8, 204, 239, 242, 287
pātāḷam 98, 143, 146 (see also underworld)
paṭayaṇi 177, 191, 287
patriliny 13, 31–2, 35–6, 39, 62, 194, 197
Pazhur 49, 173
peeping 213, 248, 250
penis (or phallus) 110, 154, 165, 169–71, 178, 180, 183, 186, 191, 251
performance x, xi, 1, 4–6, 12, 16, 18, 25, 34, 43–7, 59, 62, 65–6,

68–9, 73, 75–6, 78–83, 86–7, 91, 96–7, 103, 107–8, 112, 114–15, 131–2, 141, 144–5, 150, 152, 153, 156, 165, 173, 184–5, 188–9, 203–4, 206, 208, 216–17, 226, 231, 233–4, 236, 242, 244–5, 248, 252–61, 265–7, 272, 273, 274–6
Peterson, I. V. 60, 151
pey 24
Phoolan Devi 251
pilgrim(age) 28, 98, 136–7, 153, 154, 165, 180–1
Pintchman, T. 152, 245
Piravom 49, 50
plantain, See banana
plāvu 83, 111, 151 (see also jackwood)
pollution 17, 25, 32, 42, 118, 140, 142, 206–9, 231, 238
possession (spirit) ix, x 4, 6, 10–12, 16–18, 24–5, 27–8, 62, 66–7, 73, 83, 86, 89–90, 92–3, 97–8, 103, 117, 128–9, 141, 147, 156–8, 175–6, 184–6, 189, 192, 204, 208, 213, 215–17, 219–20, 222, 228–31, 233, 235–6, 238, 242–5, 249, 250–9, 262, 272, 274–5, 277, 279, 285, 286, 287 (see also bādhā darśan, tuḷḷal)
postmodern ix, 1, 7, 9, 268, 270, 278
power 2, 5–8, 10–14, 16–18, 20, 23–5, 30–3, 42–4, 46, 57, 59, 62, 65–7, 73, 84, 89, 97, 100, 104, 108, 111–13, 115, 118, 126–33, 135–7, 143, 145, 147–8, 155–6, 158–9, 170, 174, 177, 183, 187–90, 195, 200, 202, 205, 209, 215, 221–2, 238, 240, 242–4, 254–9, 263–4, 268, 270, 274–5, 278–9
  ascetic males 177, 180
  as factor in anthropology/ ethnography 2, 5, 8, 57, 268, 270, 278
  breasts 30, 129, 131, 174, 263
  drums sacred power of 83, 102, 255
  female/feminine 6, 16, 18, 23–5, 30–3, 57, 89, 97, 104, 108, 118, 126–9, 137, 145, 155, 159, 183, 188–90, 195, 200, 215, 219, 238, 240, 244, 257, 274, 279
  hair, sacred power of 89, 108
  natural world 16, 104, 111, 115, 147–8
  ritual performance, power of 44, 46, 242, 254–9, 264
praśnam 27, 41, 287 (see also divination)
prasādam 75, 77, 108, 287
pregnancy 39, 42, 52, 96–7, 119, 154, 177, 184–7, 193, 205, 210–11, 217, 238
prostitute 94–5, 97, 147, 182, 199, 245
psychoanalysis 222
PTSD 227, 231
puberty 40–2, 108, 110, 116–9, 152, 166–7, 198, 207, 218–22, 240, 249
  rituals 42, 62, 110, 117–18, 219
  songs 166–7
pūjā 11, 28, 47, 73, 75, 77, 79, 80, 89, 91, 117, 122, 125, 201, 267, 287
Pulaya 25
pulluvan 14, 144
purāṇas 18–19, 139, 143, 170
puṟappāṭu 85, 287
purification 42, 44, 67, 89, 91, 103, 186, 193
purity 17, 31–2, 43, 97, 186, 207

Raheja and gold 152, 203

Rajagopalan, L. S. vii, 60, 102, 103
raktabitasura 164, 191
Rakteswari 29
Ram, K. 15–16, 187, 189, 194, 217, 244, 246
Ramakrishnan, K. 121, 279–85
Ramakrishnan, M. 191
Ramanujan, A. K. 105, 112–13, 146, 151, 152, 194, 220, 276
Ramaswamy, S. 60
rape 96, 186–7, 219–20, 222, 231, 237–9, 241–2, 244, 251, 270, 283
red 18, 28–30, 59, 70, 72–3, 75–82, 85, 87–8, 90–2, 96–7, 99–101, 102, 105–6, 108–9, 113–22, 131–2, 141, 144, 146–7, 150, 151, 156, 163, 181, 184–5, 201–3, 205, 213, 215, 263–4, 269, 286
reflexivity 7
rhythm 48, 75, 85–6, 88, 207, 255, 276
rhythmic 18, 47, 68, 83, 86, 88, 216
rice 34, 41, 44, 47, 50, 66, 73, 75–80, 94, 106–17, 124–5, 150, 157
Richmond, Swann, and Zarrilli 59, 102, 253
ritual ix, 1, 5, 10–12, 14, 16–19, 23–7, 30–2, 34, 42–9, 58–9, 65–6, 72–3, 75–6, 78–80, 83, 89, 93, 95, 101, 102, 107–18, 121–5, 128–34, 140–2, 145, 148, 150–3, 155, 157–8, 162, 164, 166, 171–4, 178, 184–90, 194, 202, 204–8, 211–13, 215–16, 219, 222–3, 226, 230–1, 233–6, 238, 241–3, 249, 252–5, 257–62, 264, 274–7, 279, 286–7
Roland, A. 177
Ryan-Blaney, B. 227–8, 250

Śabarimala 98, 130, 136–7, 143, 153–4
sacrifice 17–18, 27, 50, 55, 66, 100, 102, 103, 110, 113–15, 121, 128, 131, 133, 135, 141–2, 145, 150, 164–7, 171, 187, 191, 210–11, 238, 246, 253–5, 266, 269, 276
Śākta 27–8, 30–1, 48, 116, 188–9, 287
śakti 16, 29–30, 88, 92, 100, 104, 117–18, 132, 174, 188–9, 287
sambandham 196
sanctum 11, 33, 64–5, 71, 115–17, 126, 128, 141, 150, 201
Sangam 15–18, 21, 24, 28–9, 32, 105, 111–12, 132, 153, 253, 274, 287
Sanghakkaḷi 103
Sanskrit xv, 1, 10–12, 15, 17–19, 25, 27, 30, 32, 36, 75, 83, 86, 93, 100, 103, 116, 138, 143–4, 148, 152, 153, 184, 192, 253–5
Sanskritization 247
śānta bhāva 124, 126
saptamātrakkaḷ 29, 126, 287
Sarasvatī 122, 130, 138, 173, 287
sarppa kōpam 174–6
sarppakāvu 143–4, 287
sarppam tuḷḷal 145, 174, 192, 213
Schechner, R. 6, 9, 254, 258
scythe 25, 151
season 4, 39, 43, 45, 47, 59, 103, 104, 107, 111, 114–15, 122, 129, 131–2, 134–5, 137–8, 145–6, 150, 157, 208, 245, 274, 276
Sedgewick, E. 192
seed 110–11, 113–14, 116, 132–5, 142, 151, 164, 263, 279, 286
semen 110, 113, 136, 146, 151, 163, 164, 171, 175, 177, 179–80, 182–3, 286
Sered, S. S. 175, 220, 249
serpent 14, 17, 33, 143–6, 180, 222, 287 (See also nāga)

sex 39, 43, 54, 110, 133, 151, 163, 165, 167, 175, 177, 179, 182, 186, 191, 192, 198–9, 216, 220–1, 224–5, 227, 240, 250
sex (gender), 55, 198, 232, 236
sexual 3, 16, 27, 31–2, 37, 39, 43, 54, 56, 90, 97–8, 102, 112–13, 118–19, 124, 128–9, 132, 136–8, 145, 147, 151, 158, 162–4, 166–72, 174–6, 180, 182–3, 187, 189–91, 196–200, 202–3, 209, 216–20, 222–35, 237–41, 247, 250–57, 262, 265, 267–9, 275, 277, 286
sexuality x, 4, 16, 32, 89, 110, 112, 119, 128–9, 132–3, 136–7, 145, 147–8, 150, 153–5, 157, 162, 167–8, 170, 172, 175, 177–80, 183, 186, 189–90, 192, 200, 208, 215–16, 218–22, 231, 236, 238, 240–1, 257, 274
shaman 2, 7, 11, 24–5, 147, 211, 213, 261, 277
shield 29–30, 78, 112, 263
shrine 11, 16, 26, 27–9, 33, 64–6, 70–2, 76, 85, 88, 90, 96, 101, 104, 107–8, 110, 112, 116, 118, 122, 125, 128–31, 135–7, 141–3, 145, 150, 166, 180, 185, 202, 210, 212–15, 248, 252, 264, 279, 285
Shulman, D. 60, 124, 136, 152, 164, 191, 240
sickle 41, 65, 111–12, 115–16, 118, 236, 251
Śiva 4, 20–1, 30, 64, 67, 78, 85–6, 89, 93, 107, 122, 125, 128, 130–1, 135, 137–8, 141–2, 144, 147, 154, 156, 167–70, 176, 180, 190, 204–5, 214, 239–40, 269, 287
Śiva lingam 125, 141
Śiva Purāṇa 19
Slater, P. E. 220–1, 236
sleep 6, 40, 43, 51, 53, 65, 78, 85, 88, 92, 99, 100–1, 132, 143, 146, 162, 169, 176, 182, 199, 214, 224–5, 227, 259, 281
smallpox 20, 44–6, 59, 65, 77, 79–80, 103, 119, 134, 167–8, 190, 213, 239, 248, 282–3, 286
snake 17, 70, 75, 77, 81–2, 106, 109, 131, 142–5, 154, 174–7, 179–80, 183, 190, 192, 201, 207, 219, 256, 285–7 (See also nāga, sarpa kōpam, sarppakāvu, sarppam tuḷḷal, serpent)
sōpāna sangītam 33, 48, 83
sorcery 15, 27 (See also mantravādam)
Southwest 28, 145
spirit possession. See possession
spirits 17, 23, 32, 65, 66, 99, 100–1, 107, 110–11, 114–15, 118, 132–3, 140–1, 145, 150, 163, 175–6, 213, 215, 220
Spiro, M. 190
sponsor 45, 46, 50, 73–6, 125, 205, 245, 257, 264
Sri Lanka 16, 86, 170, 175, 192, 244, 248, 260, 272, 277
Śrī Yantra 48, 274
Śrī Vidyā 27, 48
Srinivas, M. N. 153, 247
Srinivasan, A. 278
stone 25, 29, 51, 58, 64, 70, 78–9, 114–16, 139, 141, 143, 150, 201, 205, 213, 269, 283, 285
subtext 3–4, 6, 8, 278
Śudra 33, 61
suffering 7, 20, 41, 88, 156, 158, 162, 167, 172, 190, 200, 210, 213–15, 217–18, 223, 226, 228–9, 232–3, 236–7, 241, 244, 257–8, 264, 266–7, 275–8
suicide 37, 41, 141, 227, 238
sumaṅgalī 124

sweat 64, 70, 92, 156, 158, 167–78, 191, 212–13, 218, 227, 239, 280, 282, 284–5
sword 11, 20, 23, 29–30, 48, 65, 75, 78, 84, 86, 88–92, 97–9, 111–12, 118, 137, 150, 151, 167, 170–1, 183, 186–7, 205–7, 236, 241, 243, 262, 277, 287

tāḷam 83, 86
    triputa 83, 255
tāli 38, 41–2, 103, 152, 194, 218–19, 221, 249, 272, 287
Tamil, xv 12–15, 23, 60, 104–5, 108, 121, 124, 143, 146–7, 166, 172, 288
Tamil Nadu 11, 17, 23, 61, 124, 138, 161, 167, 172, 217, 248
tantra 27–8, 48, 61, 73, 116, 135, 152, 169, 191, 263
tantri 27, 81, 287
taṟavāḍu 13, 45, 287
Tapper, B. E. 129, 152, 220, 222
Tarabout, G. 59, 193
teḷḷi 65, 86–7, 102, 103, 156, 256, 287
temple 1, 10–14, 16–18, 23–8, 33–5, 37–9, 41, 43–6, 48–50, 55–6, 58, 59–61, 62, 64–5, 69–72, 75–6, 78–9, 81–3, 85, 87–90, 92, 95, 97–8, 100–1, 102, 104, 106–7, 111–12, 114–18, 121–2, 124–31, 134–44, 147, 151, 153, 154, 163–5, 170, 173–4, 183, 185, 191, 200, 204–6, 208–16, 226, 244–6, 248, 255–6, 262, 264, 267, 269, 279, 285–7
text 1–3, 5, 8–9, 17–19, 49, 60, 69, 73, 75, 147, 165–6, 170, 272, 275
teyyam 16–17, 102, 152, 206–7, 243–4, 252, 272
Thampuran, H. H. K. 24, 59, 215
theater iv, vi 5, 10–12, 85–6, 93, 252–4, 257, 286 (see also drama)
third eye 20, 64, 85, 135, 156, 167–8, 170, 176, 190, 206, 240, 251
tiger 21, 100, 102, 133, 146–8, 154, 178, 263
tiṟayāṭṭam 167, 252
tiriyuḻichaḷ 75
Tirumāndāmkunnu Bhagavati xvii, 124–8, 130–1, 151, 170, 174
Tiruvātira 153
toddy 10, 23–4, 110, 133, 151
tongue 20–1, 70, 89, 92, 94, 99, 144, 148, 161, 164, 169–71, 177–9, 183, 187, 190, 203, 214–15, 263, 282
tōṭṭam pāṭṭu 31
training 19, 28–9, 42, 47–8, 50, 172, 270
transformation 6, 44, 60, 117, 119, 150, 179, 206, 208, 252, 257–62, 264, 271, 275, 277
trauma 171, 221, 227–36, 259, 261–2, 275, 277
Travancore 12, 34, 61, 148, 209
Trawick, M. 35, 62, 161, 172–3, 239, 249
tree 15, 17, 58–9, 65, 70, 75, 81–2, 84, 90–1, 93, 97, 102, 104–6, 108–11, 114, 126, 130–3, 142–4, 150, 163, 213, 215, 229, 238, 251, 264, 272, 281, 284–5, 287–8
tribal 18, 21, 24–5, 27, 78, 96, 102, 104, 111, 118–19, 130, 148, 152, 184–5, 187, 193, 212–13, 268
    priestess 61
Trichur 28, 34, 49, 51–2, 56, 58, 72, 76, 128, 141, 151, 181–2, 245
troupe 19, 34, 42–3, 49–50, 57, 63, 67, 69, 76–80, 82, 86, 89,

93, 95, 97–8, 115, 132, 141, 146, 167, 172–3, 184, 205, 215, 234–5, 252, 259–61, 264, 272, 286
Tuesday 46, 107, 110, 129, 133–4, 153
tūkkam, See Garuḍan tūkkam
tuḷḷal 129, 145, 165, 174, 210, 213–14, 216, 285, 287
Tulunad 141
underworld 19–20, 98, 142–4, 146, 287 (See also pātāḷam)

vagina 115, 148, 154, 164, 170, 175, 177–9, 183, 189–91, 193, 205, 208, 214, 251
Vaidyanathan, K. R. 25, 116, 163
vāḷ 88, 111–13, 116, 118, 151, 287
veḷiccappāṭu 11, 23–6, 33–4, 89, 153, 171–2, 175–6, 183, 210, 212, 215, 229–31, 243, 252, 287
vengeance 236–8, 240–1, 275
Vētāḷam 20–1, 27, 83, 92, 96, 100, 103, 118–19, 147–8, 164, 171, 177–9, 183, 185, 189–90, 288
viḷakku 40, 65, 288
violence 4, 6, 115, 122, 132, 135, 138, 147–8, 157, 187–8, 214, 221, 228, 236–8, 240, 244, 267
viṟali 23, 152, 288
vīrali 117
virgin 10, 19–20, 23, 59, 64, 108, 118–24, 128–31, 136, 145, 162–5, 167–8, 174–7, 183–4, 186–7, 198, 205, 210–11, 218–22, 239, 242, 265, 276
Viṣṇu 4, 19–21, 130, 136–8, 180, 286, 288
Vrischikam (month of) 135

Wadley, S. S. 119, 124, 152
war 16, 18–19, 21, 23–4, 29–30, 48, 67, 82, 86, 89, 92–3, 96, 98, 101, 103, 112–13, 119, 126, 132–3, 147, 152, 158, 178, 185–6, 219, 239, 256–8, 266, 286–7
West 13, 39–40, 46, 62, 125, 140, 154, 212
Asia 212
West/Western (countries/culture) 2, 5, 19, 52–5, 167, 197, 226, 228, 230, 232, 243, 253
widow 51, 123–4, 129, 131, 164, 219, 221, 262, 284
women, seclusion of 31, 115–19, 206, 208, 213, 247
worldview ix, 30–2, 113, 188
Wulff, D. M. 138, 152, 171

yakśa 60, 144
yakṣi 17, 58, 143–5, 148, 162–4, 171, 174–5, 187, 200, 206, 208, 215, 218–19, 222, 224, 238, 241, 251, 285, 288
Yalman, N. 61, 151, 197, 218, 221, 247
yantra 1, 152
Yatrakali 103
Yesudas, R. N. 25, 62
yoni 116, 214

Zarrilli, P. 61, 253
Zimmerman, F. 134